Praise for *A Rope and a P*

"Smart, deep thoughts, won at very high cost."

"Vivid . . . Packed with suspense and betrayal . . survival and escape."
　　　　　　　　　　　　　　　　　　　　　—Time

"The dual story is the gem of this work."　*—The Christian Science Monitor*

"Equal parts love story and international intelligence thriller, this memoir delivers a crash course in resilience and loyalty."　*—Allure*

"A gripping, true-life romance."　　*—The Observer's Very Short List*

"Some of the best moments in the book are Mulvihill's discussions of juxtaposing her day job coordinating celebrity photo shoots and her phones with . . . the kidnappers or their envoys."　*—Milwaukee Journal Sentinel*

"The most informative segments of the book are the masterly observations of life with the jihadists . . . smart and edgy commentary on terrorism, hostage negotiation, political agendas, and the human heart."
　　　　　　　　　　　　　　　　　　　　—Publishers Weekly

"The touching tale of two latecomers to marriage who rely on love, prayer, and quotidian memories to survive their separation. . . . An absorbing read filled with wonderful details and high irony."
　　　　　　　　　　　　　　　　　—Columbia Journalism Review

"Truly remarkable and bold . . . A painstakingly reconstructed, harrowing account."　　　　　　　　　　　　　　　　*—Kirkus Reviews*

"Part love story, part thriller, part war story—and a mesmerizing read."
　　　　　　　　　　　　　　　　　　　　—Town & Country

"Valuable . . . impressive."　　　　　*—The New York Review of Books*

"A propulsive and harrowing read, packed with hard-won lessons about the Taliban, journalism, and bravery."
　　　　　　　　　　　　　　　　　　　　—Foreign Policy

PENGUIN BOOKS

A ROPE AND A PRAYER

David Rohde, winner of two Pulitzer Prizes in journalism, is a foreign affairs columnist for Reuters. Previously, he worked as a reporter for *The New York Times* for fifteen years. He won his first Pulitzer Prize in 1996 for uncovering the Srebrenica massacre in Bosnia for *The Christian Science Monitor* and his second in 2009 as part of a team of *New York Times* reporters covering Afghanistan and Pakistan. He is also the author of *Endgame: The Betrayal and Fall of Srebrenica*.

Kristen Mulvihill has been a fashion and photography editor at various women's magazines, including *Marie Claire* and *Self*. Most recently, she was the photography director of *Cosmopolitan* magazine. She is also a painter and illustrator.

They both grew up in New England, graduated from Brown University, and live in New York.

A ROPE and
A PRAYER

THE STORY OF A KIDNAPPING

DAVID ROHDE and
KRISTEN MULVIHILL

PENGUIN BOOKS

PENGUIN BOOKS

Published by the Penguin Group

Penguin Group (USA) Inc., 375 Hudson Street, New York, New York 10014, U.S.A.

Penguin Group (Canada), 90 Eglinton Avenue East, Suite 700, Toronto, Ontario, Canada M4P 2Y3
(a division of Pearson Penguin Canada Inc.)

Penguin Books Ltd, 80 Strand, London WC2R 0RL, England

Penguin Ireland, 25 St. Stephen's Green, Dublin 2, Ireland (a division of Penguin Books Ltd)

Penguin Books Australia Ltd, 250 Camberwell Road, Camberwell, Victoria 3124, Australia
(a division of Pearson Australia Group Pty Ltd)

Penguin Books India Pvt Ltd, 11 Community Centre, Panchsheel Park, New Delhi – 110 017, India

Penguin Group (NZ), 67 Apollo Drive, Rosedale, Auckland 0632, New Zealand
(a division of Pearson New Zealand Ltd)

Penguin Books (South Africa) (Pty) Ltd, 24 Sturdee Avenue,
Rosebank, Johannesburg 2196, South Africa

Penguin Books Ltd, Registered Offices: 80 Strand, London WC2R 0RL, England

First published in the United States of America by Viking Penguin,
a member of Penguin Group (USA) Inc. 2010
Published in Penguin Books 2011

10 9 8 7 6 5 4 3 2 1

Portions of this book appeared in different form in *The New York Times*.

THE LIBRARY OF CONGRESS HAS CATALOGED THE HARDCOVER EDITION AS FOLLOWS:
Rohde, David.
    A rope and a prayer : a kidnapping from two sides / David Rohde & Kristen Mulvihill.
        p.   cm.
    ISBN 978-0-670-02223-6 (hc.)
    ISBN 978-0-14-312005-6 (pbk.)
    1. Rohde, David—Captivity, 2008–2009.   2. Hostages—Afghanistan—Biography.
3. Journalists—United States—Biography.   4. Afghan War, 2001—Personal narratives,
American.   5. Taliban.   6. Mulvihill, Kristen.   I. Mulvihill, Kristen.   II. Title.
    DS371.43.R64A3 2010
    958.104'7—dc22
    [B]   2010024534

Printed in the United States of America
Designed by Nancy Resnick
Chronology and map by Jeffrey L. Ward

Penguin is committed to publishing works of quality and integrity. In that spirit, we are proud to offer this book to our readers; however, the story, the experiences, and the words are the authors' alone.

To Faith

Every man's hand is against the other, and all against the stranger.

—Winston S. Churchill

The fruit of patience is sweet.

—Pashto proverb

ACKNOWLEDGMENTS

For Pashtunwali: Tahir Luddin and Captain Nadeem.

For countless hours: Mary Jane Mulvihill, Lee Rohde, David McCraw.

For never giving up: Arthur Sulzberger, Jr.

For steadfast support and encouragement: Bill Keller, Jill Abramson, John Geddes, William Schmidt, Craig Whitney, Susan Chira, Matt Purdy, Christine Kay, and so many other longtime friends at *The New York Times*.

For friendship, insight, and bravery in Afghanistan: Afghan colleagues and friends, Carlotta Gall, Chris Chivers, Tyler Hicks, Dexter Filkins, Rich Oppel, and many others.

For friendship, insight, and bravery in Pakistan: Ismail Khan, Salman Masood, Beena Sarwar, Pir Zubair Shah, Jane Perlez, and many others.

For pointing Kristen in the right direction: Richard Holbrooke, Karl and Ching Eikenberry, Marin Strmecki, Tim Golden, Kay McGowan, Samantha Power.

For consistency, clarity, eloquence, and humor: Michael Semple.

For working on the case: "John," Mike Taylor, Duane Clarridge, Jack Holly, Dwight, Mark, Chris, Wayne, and all the incarnations of Team Kabul.

Thank you to the government officials who tried to help us, especially Jim, Tom, Joe, John, Cathy, Phil, Leanne, Ken, Tenzen, Mike, Eric.

For help in Washington: Mark Mazzetti, Eric Schmitt, Douglas Frantz, Milt Bearden.

For expertise: Ahmed Rashid, Rina Amiri, Barnett Rubin, James Alvarez, Nancy Dupree, John Dixon, Tom Gregg, Patricia Ferrari, Kelly Moore, Ed Rosenthal.

For support and understanding at *Cosmopolitan,* especially: Kate White, Abby Greene, Ann Kwong, John Lanuza, Micah Rubin, Heather Pfaff, Miriam Friedman, Micaela Walker, Maggie Hong, Rebecca Hessel.

For maintaining privacy: Catherine Mathis, Diane McNulty, and Vanessa Palo.

For friendship, empathy, and holidays: Eric and Sylvan Wold.

For support, guidance, confidence: Jonathan and Katie Moore, Chloe Breyer, Marcello Picone.

For happy memories: Vincent Manoriti, Denise Morgan, Julian Borger, Kathleen Reen, Ivan Obregon, Greg Scholl, Lisa Ferrari, Kannan Sundaram, Jay Solomon, Don Nay, Dan Morrison, Paul Haven, Victoria Burnett, Tomas Munita, Bob Nickelsberg, Celia Dugger, Barry Bearak, Shelley Thakral, Anthony Loyd, Gary Bass, Stacy Sullivan, Emma Daly, Laura Pitter, Kit Roane, Katya Jestin, Joel Brand, Mike O'Connor, Tracy Wilkinson, John Pomfret, Roger Cohen, Ben Ward, Mark Dennis, Fred Abrahams, Leigh Cheng, John Bastian, Pete Brandt, Al Erickson, Matt Borger, Rod Peterson, Damon Struyk, Jim Williamson, Bob Perkins, Eric Mabley, Ian Marsh, Steve Cote, Jim Webb, Chris Charters, Peter Boisvert, Jay, Joe, and Doris Brenchick, Rocky and Martha Manoriti, John Atwood, Ed Quinn, and many others in Fryeburg.

For sustenance and support from friends, including: the Moss family, the Chivers family, the Bissell family, Andrea Elliott, Salman Ahmed, Chuck Sudetic, Cindy Searight, Renannah Weinstein, Josh Brown, Claire Mysko, Judson Wright, Madeleine Arthurs, Adivije Sheji, Arthur Belebeau, Juliette Merck, Natalie Hawwa, John Lin, Tamara Schlesinger, Jamal Rayyis, Neal Lesh, Erinn Bucklan, Jim Ledbetter, Erik Swain, Noah Green, Frances Northcutt, Amy Waldman, Megan Re, Sarah Smith, Elliot Thomson, Mariane Pearl, Kati Marton, Nic Robertson, George Packer, Leon Wieseltier, Peter Bergen, Somini Sengupta, Elizabeth Rubin, Jonathan Landay, Faye Bowers, Mary Anne Schwalbe, Sandra Cook, P. J. Anthony, Hari Kumar, Chuni Lal, Pan Singh.

For prayers: Marie Chisholm, Maryann Zocco, Fabienne LeRoux,

Father Renald Labarre, Monika Stedul, Ben Borger, Helen D'Elia, and many others.

For listening: Barbara, Roberta, Jan, Lynne.

For supporting David's research: Aryeh Neier, Patricia L. Rosenfield, and Laura Silber. This book was made possible in part by grants from the Open Society Foundations and the Carnegie Corporation of New York. The statements made and views expressed are solely the responsibility of the authors.

For making this book a reality: Sarah Chalfant, Clare Ferraro, Wendy Wolf, Carolyn Coleburn, Linda Cowen, Sonya Cheuse, Risa Chubinsky, Nancy Resnick, Jeffrey Ward, Emily Votruba, Margaret Riggs, Meredith Burks, Carolyn Freeman, Tracy Breton, Kate Toth.

For courage and bravery: Sultan Munadi, Daniel Pearl, Piotr Stanczak, Asad Mangal, Jere Van Dyk, Sean Langan, Stephen Farrell, John Solecki, Alan Johnston, Roxana Saberi, Maziar Bahari, Amanda Lindhout, Nigel Brennan, Laura Ling, Euna Lee, and all journalists who remain in captivity.

For everything: our parents Carol, Harvey, Mary Jane, James, Andrea, and George; our siblings Lee, Laura, Erik, Karen, Jason, Joel, Daniel, Christie, Chris, Howard, Christina, and all of our family.

CONTENTS

xiv   Contents

PRINCIPAL CHARACTERS, ORGANIZATIONS, AND PLACES—AFGHANISTAN AND PAKISTAN

Abu Tayyeb: Taliban commander who invites David to interview and kidnaps him

Akbar: Guard who allows access to newspapers and radio; nephew of Akhundzada

Akhundzada: Taliban commander who serves as Abu Tayyeb's "intelligence chief"

Asad Mangal: Afghan driver kidnapped with David

Badruddin Haqqani: Son of Jalaluddin Haqqani who provides houses and cash during kidnapping

Chunky: Heavyset guard who leads prayers

Jalaluddin Haqqani: Patriarch of the Haqqani family and famed anti-Soviet fighter who is supported by the CIA in the 1980s and who joins the Taliban in the 1990s

Mansoor: Guard who speaks broken English; son of Akhundzada

Mullah Omar: Leader of Taliban movement. Since 2001, he is believed to have been based in the Pakistani city of Quetta. Said to now lead a more moderate Taliban faction known as the Quetta Shura.

Qari: Taliban fighter who carries out kidnapping and later serves as guard

Sharif: Taliban commander whose house serves as a prison

Sirajuddin Haqqani: Son of Jalaluddin Haqqani who succeeded his elderly father as commander of the Haqqani network

Timor Shah: Chief guard, younger brother of Abu Tayyeb

Tahir Luddin: Afghan journalist kidnapped with David

Federally Administered Tribal Areas: Mountainous region in northwestern Pakistan—also known as the tribal areas—that is a Taliban and Al Qaeda stronghold

Helmand: Province in southern Afghanistan—also known as "Little America"—that was the focus of the author's original book project

North and South Waziristan: Regions inside the tribal areas where the author was held captive

Frontier Corps: Pakistani-government–funded tribal militia charged with policing the tribal areas

ISI: Directorate for Inter-Services Intelligence, the Pakistani military's top intelligence agency.

PRINCIPAL CHARACTERS AND ORGANIZATIONS—NEW YORK

David McCraw: Assistant general counsel for *The New York Times*

Mary Jane Mulvihill: Kristen's mother

Lee Rohde: David's older brother

Carol Ruffo: David's mother

Michael Semple: Expert on the region who works on case

AISC: American International Security Corporation. Security consultants hired to work on case

Clayton Consultants: *The New York Times'* crisis management firm

AUTHORS' NOTE

We wrote this book in the hope of helping readers learn more about Afghanistan, Pakistan, and the American effort there. The book's central narrative is the seven months when David, Tahir, and Asad were held captive in the tribal areas of Pakistan and Kristen's effort to bring them home. Woven throughout the story are sections of history and analysis that are based on David's seven years of reporting in Afghanistan and Pakistan since 2001. We also explore militancy, faith, and religion's role as both a positive and negative force.

The second reason we wrote this book is in the hope of helping other kidnap victims and their families. Around the world, the number of kidnappings is steadily rising, but governments have failed to develop a coordinated international response. Most hostages survive, but their panicked families often empty bank accounts, sell homes, or go into staggering debt to save the lives of their loved ones. We urge governments to develop a more unified response to kidnapping.

Lastly, we believe that our story resonates beyond kidnapping. We hope it helps anyone dealing with separation from a loved one, confronted with making life and death decisions for a partner when they are unable to do so for themselves or simply blindsided by a situation beyond their control.

A portion of our earnings from this book was donated to the FATA

Education Foundation, a Pakistani government organization that provides educational opportunities to the people of Pakistan's tribal areas, and to Kiva.org, a nonprofit group that allows people to lend money to microfinance institutions in developing countries and the United States. We also work with the Committee to Protect Journalists, a nonprofit press advocacy group, to support and assist the families of kidnapped journalists.

For seven months our family negotiated with the kidnappers—directly and through contractors—regarding a potential ransom. No ransom was paid. We believed the only way to keep David and his Afghan colleagues alive and encourage the kidnappers to remain in contact was to appear to be willing to pay for their release. In this book, we discuss Kristen's calls with the kidnappers and the negotiations because they bring home the reality and pressures placed on a kidnap victim's family. Yet we are not divulging details of our negotiation or the amounts of money discussed. We believe such disclosures could encourage or complicate future kidnappings. For safety reasons, certain details, information, and names have also been withheld.

What follows is a good-faith effort to reconstruct the period in our lives surrounding David's kidnapping and eventual escape. David was not able to take notes for the seven months he was in captivity. All descriptions of his experience stem from his memory, supplemented, where possible, by records kept by Kristen, other family members, and colleagues. Direct quotations from his captors are his recollections of what they said and are based on translations from Pashto, the language they spoke. Kristen's descriptions stem from memory and, where possible, journal entries, e-mails, and recordings. Undoubtedly, our recollections are incomplete, altered by the passage of time and flawed in places. All of the views expressed in this book are solely those of the authors. Any mistakes in the pages that follow are wholly our own.

Chronology

∎

1. Flew from Laskhar Gah, Helmand, to Kabul, Afghanistan: *November 9, 2008.*

2. Kidnapped outside Pul-e-Alam, Logar: *November 10, 2008.*

3. Held in four different locations in eastern Afghanistan: *November 10–17, 2008. Moved by car through Logar, Wardak, Ghazni, and Paktika provinces.*

4. Walked over mountains from Paktika, Afghanistan, into South Waziristan, Pakistan: *Night of November 17–18, 2008.*

5. Drove through Wana, South Waziristan, to Miran Shah, North Waziristan: *November 18, 2008. Held prisoner in five different houses in Miran Shah, North Waziristan: November 18, 2008 to mid-March 2009.*

6. Moved from Miran Shah, North Waziristan, to Makeen, South Waziristan: *Mid-March. Held in one house in Makeen until late April 2009.*

7. Moved from Makeen, South Waziristan, to Dosali, North Waziristan: *Late April 2009. Held in one house in Dosali until late May 2009.*

8. Moved from Dosali to Miran Shah, North Waziristan: *Late May 2009–June 19, 2009. Held in two different houses in Miran Shah from late May 2009–June 19, 2009. Escaped night of June 19–20, 2009.*

9. Flown by Pakistani army helicopter from Miran Shah, North Waziristan, to Islamabad, Pakistan: *June 20, 2009.*

10. Flown by American military plane from Islamabad, Pakistan, to Bagram Air Base, Afghanistan: *June 20, 2009. Flown by private plane from Bagram to Dubai, U.A.E., June 21, 2009.*

∎

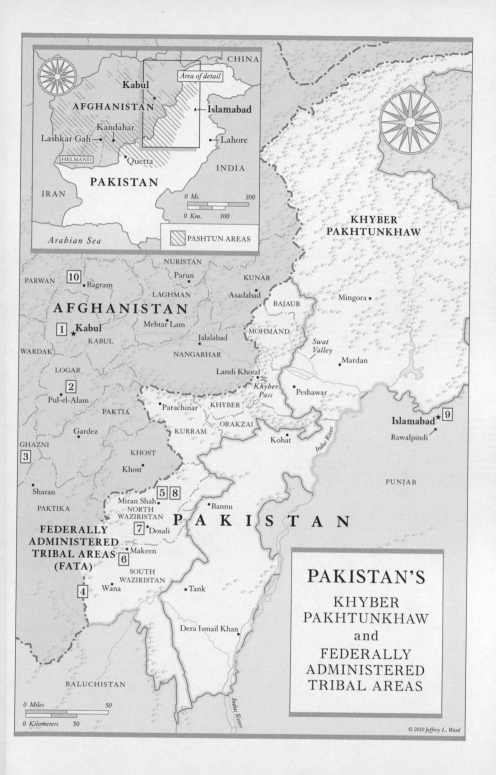

PAKISTAN'S

KHYBER
PAKHTUNKHAW
and
FEDERALLY
ADMINISTERED
TRIBAL AREAS

© 2010 Jeffrey L. Ward

A BLOOD MESSAGE TO OBAMA

David, November 9–10, 2008

On a Sunday afternoon, the Kabul Coffee House and Café is an island of Western culture in Afghanistan's capital. American and European contractors, aid workers, and consultants sip four-dollar café lattes and cappuccinos. Young, English-speaking Afghan waiters dressed in Western clothes serve chicken quesadillas, fried-egg sandwiches, and cheeseburgers.

I marvel at—and dread—how much Kabul has changed since I first came to the country to cover the fall of the Taliban seven years earlier. A city I grew to know well has become more and more unfamiliar. Kabul has boomed economically and modernized to an extent I never dreamed when joyous Afghans gouged out the eyes of dead Taliban militants in 2001. At the time, Afghans yearned for a moderate and modern nation and an end to decades of meddling from neighboring countries.

Now, the gulf between the wealthy, westernized pockets of the Afghan capital and the grinding insecurity and endemic corruption that dominate most Afghans' daily lives alarms me. Rivalries between the country's ethnic groups that ebbed after the fall of the Taliban simmer again. Growing mistrust between Afghans and foreigners worries me as well. The American journalists, diplomats, and aid workers who were welcomed here in 2001 are seen by growing numbers of Afghans as war profiteers who do little to aid their country.

I am in the final stretch of conducting research for a book I am writing about the failing American attempt to bring stability to the region since 2001. I hope the book will be the culmination of seven years of reporting in Afghanistan and Pakistan for *The New York Times*. Yet I have become increasingly concerned that I am losing touch with the rapidly deteriorating situation on the ground. After serving as the newspaper's South Asia bureau co-chief and living in the region from 2002 to 2005, I moved back to New York and joined the newspaper's investigations unit. Over the last three years, reporting trips sent me back to Afghanistan and Pakistan roughly every six months, but that is a fraction of the time I spent on the ground when based here. During that period, the Taliban have reasserted control over vast swaths of both Afghanistan and Pakistan.

After privately wrestling with the decision for weeks, I have decided I need to interview a Taliban commander for the book to be as rigorous and thorough as possible. The majority of the population in Helmand— the southern Afghan province that is the focus of my book—appears to now support them. But it's a fraught proposition, one that comes with the kind of extreme risk that I have tried to avoid for years.

Across the table from me at the Kabul Coffee House is Tahir Luddin, an Afghan journalist I met two years ago who works for *The Times* of London. Burly, boisterous, and confident, Tahir has short brown hair, hazel eyes, a round face, and a thin brown beard. He is a proud Afghan and prefers wearing local clothes to Western ones. We had met in 2006 but never worked together before. Recommended to me by two correspondents from *The Times* of London, Tahir is known for having good Taliban contacts and the ability to arrange interviews with them.

Tahir explains that his most trusted contact is a Taliban commander who uses the nom de guerre Abu Tayyeb, or "son of Tayyeb." Abu Tayyeb commands several hundred Taliban fighters in three provinces around Kabul, and has fought against NATO and American troops in Helmand as well. Tahir says he has met him a half dozen times and that Abu Tayyeb has done face-to-face television interviews with two different European journalists without incident. He is aligned with a moderate Taliban faction based in the Pakistani city of Quetta.

"Would you be willing to go to Ghazni?" Tahir asks, referring to a dangerous province that is roughly three hours south of Kabul by car.

Tahir says I could interview Abu Tayyeb there. He could be the final character in the book, I think to myself, a Taliban commander who is the vehicle for describing the hard-line movement's reemergence. I had tried for the last two weeks to set up an interview with a Taliban fighter in Helmand but had failed. I was not willing to leave the heavily guarded center of the provincial capital. No Taliban were willing to meet me there. Dozens of other journalists and I have been doing phone interviews with Taliban spokesmen for years. Yet it was impossible to verify whom, in fact, you were speaking to over the phone or their claims, which were often blatantly false propaganda screeds. I could briefly meet Abu Tayyeb in person, verify that he was, in fact, a Taliban commander, and then do follow-up interviews by phone.

From New York, it seemed as if a growing number of foreign journalists were safely interviewing the Taliban face-to-face. Over the last two months, interviews with Taliban had appeared in my old newspaper, *The Christian Science Monitor,* a French magazine, and one of my colleagues had safely interviewed them for my current newspaper's Sunday magazine. I increasingly worried I was becoming a New York-based journalistic fraud whose book would be superficial and out of date. I felt I had fallen behind reporters based in the region.

At the same time, I knew meeting with the Taliban was perilous. Getting both sides of a story is vital in journalism but hugely dangerous in an armed conflict. In the end, each interview is a judgment call. As we sit in the café, Tahir warns of the danger involved. That spring, an American journalist and a British journalist who ventured into Pakistan's tribal areas to interview militants were kidnapped in separate incidents, Tahir explains. He says the British journalist's family sold their home to pay a ransom for his release. The concept of putting my own family through such an ordeal horrifies me. I had also recently read a story in *Rolling Stone* by an American journalist who was nearly kidnapped by a rival Taliban faction when he drove to Ghazni to interview a Taliban commander.

"Ghazni is too far," I tell Tahir. "I only want to do a Taliban interview in Kabul."

We part ways and Tahir tells me he will contact another Taliban commander who he believes is in Kabul. He promises to call me later that night. I leave with a sense of dread. I have long viewed journalists who interview the Taliban as reckless. Yet I find myself contemplating doing something I have resisted for years.

I was imprisoned for ten days in 1995 while covering the war in Bosnia for *The Christian Science Monitor.* Serb officials arrested me after I discovered the mass graves of Muslim men executed in the Serb-controlled part of Bosnia around the town of Srebrenica. I was freed after my family, friends, and editors put intense pressure on American officials to force the Serbs to release me. War crimes investigators later found that more than 8,000 Muslim men had been executed around the town. My detention in Bosnia was excruciating for my family, and I promised them I would never put them through such an ordeal again. And two months ago, before I left for Afghanistan, I took a momentous step. I married my girlfriend, Kristen Mulvihill.

Kristen is a photo editor at a women's magazine as well as a painter. Her sunny disposition, determination to see the positive side of everything, and fierce love have created a tranquility in my life. My two years with her in New York left me feeling gradually more at peace and at home. At thirty-nine and forty-one, respectively, Kristen and I are eager to focus more on our personal lives and start a family. To the delight of my ever-patient mother, we married in a small wooden chapel in Maine, a state both of us adore and where we each spent time while growing up. I see our marriage and the book as long-delayed positive steps that will take me away from reporting in war zones and allow me to move into a more stable form of journalism and life.

I am also extremely close to my family. My mother is the most iron willed and loving person I know. She successfully raised four children while having a career as a fashion industry executive. She and my father are divorced but he is dogged, successful, and determined as well. He has built an independent insurance practice and a rich life for himself in Maine, where he loves hiking in the woods, running marathons, and exploring spirituality. My stepparents, Andrea and George, have brought joy to my parents and me for more than two decades.

My older brother, Lee, is president of a small aviation consulting firm and the rock of our family who hides his emotions beneath a calm exterior. My younger sister, Laura, has soared in recent years, thriving professionally in the human resources field, marrying, and becoming the mother of two children. And my younger brother, Erik, has happily shifted from being a police officer and paramedic to a business operations manager for a helicopter ambulance company. He has also become one of my closest friends. After driving across the country together three years ago, we talk by phone once or twice a week. My stepbrothers, Joel and Dan, have become dear friends with whom I share an avid love for Boston sports teams. I have a tremendous amount to return to.

My cell phone rings at dusk as I am about to begin an interview. Tahir says the Taliban commander he knows in Kabul despises Americans and refuses to meet me, but Abu Tayyeb is willing to be interviewed tomorrow morning in neighboring Logar Province. We can meet him after a one-hour drive on paved roads in a village near an American military base, he says. Abu Tayyeb needs an immediate answer, he adds. The Taliban have ordered local cell phone companies to shut off service after dark to prevent people from reporting their movements to Afghan and American forces. I ask Tahir if he thinks it is safe. The danger, Tahir says, will be thieves abducting us during the drive itself.

"Nothing is 100 percent," he tells me. "You only die once."

I feel my stomach churn. My mind races. My trips to Afghanistan and Pakistan have become an increasing source of tension with Kristen, who has asked me to be gone no longer than three weeks. A few days ago, I extended the trip to four weeks after landing an interview with Afghanistan's president, Hamid Karzai. I called my father and stepmother and canceled a weekend trip Kristen and I had planned to make with them to his college.

Going to Logar seems safer than Ghazni. If I do the Taliban interview, I can return home with a sense that I have done everything I can to understand the country, get the story, and write the best book possible. The interview is just outside Kabul, I tell myself. I would not be going into the tribal areas of Pakistan, as the kidnapped American and British journalists did. This is safer.

"Yes," I say to Tahir. "Tell him yes."

Tahir tells me he will call me later to set a departure time. As a precaution, I ask him for the number of a European journalist who has already interviewed Abu Tayyeb twice with Tahir. In the fall of 2007, the reporter spent two days filming Abu Tayyeb and his men as they trained. In the summer of 2008, the journalist spent an evening with them and filmed an attack on a police post. I call the reporter and they say we should talk in person. We agree to meet at a restaurant later that night.

Privately, I am still not sure I will go. I am having dinner with two close friends, an experienced journalist and a veteran aid worker who have both worked in Afghanistan for years. I plan to ask them if the interview is a crazy idea. I hurriedly finish the interview and meet the journalist and aid worker at a new Italian restaurant frequented by foreigners. Concrete blast walls separate it from the rest of Kabul. When I describe the opportunity to interview a Taliban commander, the aid worker immediately opposes it.

"You just got married," she says.

"But this is what we do," the reporter interjects.

Then the reporter expresses their own reservations. The journalist says she has never felt the need to interview the Taliban in person and prefers phone conversations. She recommends that Tahir and I hire a driver to serve as a lookout and end the meeting after no more than an hour.

"I know how you drag out interviews," the reporter says, teasing me.

I leave dinner early to meet the European journalist at L'Atmosphère, a well-known French restaurant in Kabul that caters to Westerners. As I enter I notice that it recently installed a reinforced door to stop suicide bombers. The reporter, who I have never met before, says deciding to go to the interview is my responsibility. I agree and say I know the risk. They point out that as an American I am more vulnerable than a European. But they also believe that Abu Tayyeb will not kidnap us, and that his objective is to use the media to get across the Taliban's message.

"I think it is a good chance," they say.

I drive home with an Afghan journalist I regularly work with in Kabul.

I ask him about the interview. He tells me not to make the trip. There are many criminals, he says, on the road to Logar.

Back at the *Times* bureau, the power is out, a daily occurrence in Kabul seven years after the American invasion. I had planned to look up other recent interviews with the Taliban but now have no Internet access. I had also wanted to study maps of Logar. All of my colleagues are asleep.

I go up to my bedroom and wrestle with the decision. I put my video camera, a blank notebook, and my passport on the desk. The European journalist has recommended I bring identification to prove who I am. Otherwise, the Taliban will think I am a spy. They said a passport was best. The Taliban see press accreditations from the American government, U.S. military, or NATO as proof of spying.

I tell myself not to be a coward, that the interview is a risk worth taking. Many other journalists have done the same thing. In 2007, at the last minute I had canceled a drive to Kandahar for safety reasons and been embarrassed by it. If we can make it to Abu Tayyeb, I think, we will be safe.

I text Tahir and tell him to pick me up at 7 A.M. tomorrow morning.

As I lie in bed, I call Kristen, as I do every night. I am convinced that if I tell her about the interview she will demand that I not go and I will silently resent her for curtailing my professional life. I also know that if my new wife asks me to cancel the interview, I will abide by her wishes.

I decide not to mention my plans. I am sparing her worry, I tell myself, and sparing the relationship from conflict. I decide I will tell her about the interview after I return to New York.

I have trouble sleeping. My mind drifts to my captivity in Bosnia. I know this is an enormous risk. If anything goes wrong, the results will be catastrophic.

The next morning, November 10, Tahir arrives fifteen minutes early. The earlier we are on the road, he says, the better our chances of safety. I again tell myself not to be a coward and that other journalists have taken this same risk. I hurriedly put on a pair of boxer shorts my wife gave me on

Valentine's Day followed by running shorts my sister gave me for my birthday. I dress in Afghan clothes so I will not be spotted as a foreigner during the drive. The boxers are emblazoned with dozens of "I love you" logos. I hope they will bring us good luck.

I leave two notes behind. The first is for one of my colleagues in the bureau. It lists Abu Tayyeb's name, describes the location of the meeting, and instructs them to call the American Embassy if we do not return by midafternoon. The other is to Kristen if something goes wrong. The note is rushed but I hope that Kristen will never see it.

I walk outside and meet Tahir and Asad Mangal, a friend who Tahir has hired to work as a driver and lookout for the day. Asad is friendly and appears to be in his late twenties. It is a gray, cloudy morning. As we drive away, Tahir suggests that we pray for a safe journey. We do.

I call Kristen. It is roughly 11 P.M. in New York. I am nervous and she can sense it. When she asks me what I'm doing, I panic and respond that I am going to an interview at a ministry in Kabul. I am saving her from worrying, I again tell myself, and allowing her to sleep. I do, in fact, have an interview at a ministry, but it is scheduled for later that day—after the one-hour Taliban interview. Then I will fly to Islamabad in the late afternoon for a week of reporting there. I tell her I will call her after I arrive in Pakistan.

"I love you," I say.

"I love you too," she replies.

Clad in Afghan clothes and seated in the back of the car, I cover my face with a scarf to prevent thieves from recognizing me as a foreigner. In the car, I get Abu Tayyeb's cell phone number from Tahir and send it to my colleague in the bureau in a text message. I tell them to call him if they do not hear from me by early afternoon. If something goes wrong during the drive, Abu Tayyeb and his men will rescue us. Under Afghan tradition, guests are treated with extraordinary honor. If a guest is threatened, it is the host's duty to shelter and protect him.

During the hour-long drive, I delete all the military, intelligence, and government numbers from my cell phone as a precaution. I worry that the Taliban may check the phone and grow suspicious. I fantasize about the relief I will feel as we drive back to Kabul. After the interview, I will have completed the most dangerous portion of the reporting needed for the book. I will have done everything I could. I will be able to start a new life with Kristen.

We arrive at the meeting point in a town where farmers and donkeys meander down the road. But none of Abu Tayyeb's men are here. Tahir calls Abu Tayyeb, who says an American military operation is going on that morning and he had to change the meeting point. He asks what kind of car we are driving, instructs us to drive down the road another mile, and meet his men there. Asad accelerates down the road. About thirty seconds later, our car swerves to the right and abruptly comes to a halt.

I look up. Two bearded Afghan men carrying Kalashnikov assault rifles run toward us shouting commands in Pashto, the local language. Behind them, a car is blocking the road. The gunmen open the front doors of our car, point their rifles at Tahir and Asad, and order them to get in the backseat with me.

One of the gunmen gets behind the wheel of our car and drives down the road. The other sits in the front passenger seat and trains his rifle on us. Tahir shouts at the men in Pashto. I recognize the words "journalists" and "Abu Tayyeb" and nothing else. The man in the front passenger seat shouts something back and waves his gun menacingly. He is small, with dark hair and a short beard. He seems nervous and belligerent.

I hope there has been some kind of mistake. I hope the gunmen will call Abu Tayyeb. He will vouch for us and quickly order our release, a scenario that played out with the American journalist who ventured to Ghazni.

Instead, our car hurtles down the road, following a yellow station wagon with more armed men in it. The gunman in the passenger seat shouts more commands. Tahir tells me they want our cell phones and other possessions. "If they find we have a hidden phone," Tahir says, "they'll kill us."

"Tell them we're journalists," I say. "Tell them we're here to interview Abu Tayyeb."

Tahir translates what I say, and the driver—a bearish, bearded figure—starts laughing. "Who is Abu Tayyeb? I don't know any Abu Tayyeb," he says. "I am the commander here."

The first hints of panic creep into my mind, but I try to rationalize what is happening. The gunmen could be thieves or members of another Taliban faction. I know that what Americans call the Taliban is really a loose alliance of local commanders who often operate independently of one another. "Taliban"—Pashto for "students" —is a label of convenience that disenfranchised villagers, hardened Islamists, and criminals all use.

In an ominous sign, we turn left off the main asphalt road onto a dirt track. If we somehow overpower the gunmen in our car, the men in the station wagon will shoot us. I don't want to get Asad and Tahir killed. My imprisonment in Bosnia ended safely after ten days. I am hoping our luck is as good here. One of the gunmen says something and Tahir turns to me. "They want to know your nationality," Tahir says. I hesitate and wonder whether I should say I am Canadian. Being an American is disastrous, but lying is worse. If the gunmen search me, they will discover my passport. If I say I'm Canadian and they later find out I'm American, I will instantly be declared a spy.

"Tell them the truth," I say to Tahir. "Tell them I'm American."

Tahir relays my answer and the burly driver beams, raises his fist, and shouts a response in Pashto. Tahir translates it for me: "They say they are going to send a blood message to Obama."

The driver punches the accelerator and we cross into the open desert. The gunman still aims his Kalashnikov at us. No one speaks. I glance at the bleak landscape outside—reddish soil and black boulders as far as the eye can see. I fear we will be dead within minutes. The longer I look at the gunman in the passenger seat, the more nervous I become. His face shows little emotion. His eyes are dark, flat, and lifeless.

I think of my wife and family and am overcome with shame. An interview that seemed crucial hours ago now seems absurd and reckless. I have needlessly risked the lives of Tahir, Asad, and me. We reach a dry riverbed and the station wagon we are following stops. Our car does the same. "They're going to kill us," Tahir whispers. "They're going to kill us."

Tahir and Asad are ordered out of the car. Gunmen from the station wagon beat them with their rifle butts and lead them away. A gunman from our car motions for me to get out of the vehicle and take a few steps up a sand-covered hillside. While one guard points his Kalashnikov at me, the other takes my glasses, notebook, pen, and camera. I am blindfolded, my hands tied behind my back. My heart races. Sweat pours from my skin.

"*Habarnigar,*" I say, using the word for journalist in Dari, another local language. "*Salaam,*" I say, using an Arabic expression for peace. The few words I know in Pashto, which is spoken by most Taliban, escape me. I wait for the sound of gunfire. I know I might die but remain oddly calm.

A hand pushes me back toward the car. I am forced to lie down on the backseat. Two gunmen get in and slam the doors shut. The car lurches forward. Tahir and Asad are gone and, I think, probably dead.

As we drive away, Taliban prayers blare out from the radio and my captors laugh with glee. They are clearly elated to have an American captive. I try again. "*Habarnigar, salaam.*" In response, the guard sitting in the backseat beside me pats me on the shoulder and says a phrase in Pashto that includes the word for American. I can't tell whether he is gloating over his prize or trying to comfort me.

We drive down what seem dirt roads. Waves of regret, remorse, and humiliation wash over me. I have gotten two Afghans killed in my foolish pursuit of a better book. I have betrayed my wife and family. Even if Tahir and Asad stay alive and we all survive, I will be mocked by my peers as a two-time kidnap victim with a judgment problem.

The car comes to a halt after what seems like a two-hour drive. Guards untie my hands, take off my blindfold, and guide me through the front door of a crude mud-brick home hidden in a ravine. I am put in some type of washroom the size of a closet. After a few minutes, the guards open the door and push Tahir and Asad inside. We stare at one another in relief. About twenty minutes later, a guard opens the door and motions for us to walk into the hallway.

"No shoot," he says, "no shoot."

For the first time, I think our lives might be spared. The guard leads us into a living room decorated with maroon carpets and red pillows. A half dozen men sit along two walls of the room, Kalashnikov rifles at their sides. I sob, bow my head, and try to look like a frightened reporter.

The guard motions for me to sit down across from a heavyset man with a *patu*—a traditional Afghan scarf—wrapped around his face. Sunglasses cover his eyes, and he wears a cheap black knit winter cap. Embroidered across the front of it is the word "Rock" in English.

"I'm a Taliban commander," he announces. "My name is Mullah Atiqullah."

In the months ahead, I will learn that his name means "gift from God."

Seven years earlier, in September 2001, I had arrived in Afghanistan with a consuming desire to cover what I thought would be the defining conflict of my generation. On September 11, I had heard a distant explosion, looked out the window of my Brooklyn apartment, and seen a cloud of smoke rise up the side of the World Trade Center's north tower. After hearing on the radio that both towers had been struck in a terrorist attack, I jumped on the subway to the trade center.

Ten minutes later, I walked out of a deserted subway exit and found myself standing four blocks from the two burning towers. Ten full stories appeared to be ablaze. I scribbled a few words in my notebook: "smoke from something on the ground. Debris all over the ground." I walked closer and ran into Sherry Day, another reporter from the paper, and scribbled more notes: "Debris cascading. People snapping pictures. Smoke rising."

I heard a sharp crack and what sounded, oddly, like a waterfall. Somewhere above us, thousands of panes of glass shattered as the south tower buckled. Looking up, I saw the top half of the skyscraper begin slowly plummeting toward the ground. I grabbed Sherry's hand and we sprinted away from the tower as a roar filled our ears. I felt her hand pull away and turned back to see what had happened. She was gone and a thick cloud of dust—like a giant wall—surged up the street.

I ran around a corner and down a flight of stairs into a subway station, the dust engulfed me and the world turned white. A few feet away, a woman began screaming. After several moments, we took each other's hand, walked upstairs, and emerged into what we thought was the street. We could see nothing in front of us. Finally, a gust of wind revealed a speck of blue in the sky to our right. I told her to walk in that direction and she disappeared.

I tried to find Sherry. White dust covered cars, buildings, and streets. Car alarms wailed. Pieces of office paper cascaded to the ground like oversize snowflakes. Filled with a vague idea of somehow helping survivors, I walked toward the towers. The story—any story—no longer mattered. I simply wanted to help. As I walked, I realized I had no medical or rescue skills to offer. I felt like a vulture with a notebook. A man appeared on the street covered head to toe in dust. I asked him, "Is there anything I can do?" He replied, "There's nothing anybody can do."

Over the next two weeks, the heroism of thousands of volunteers from New York and across the country amazed me. I found Sherry and learned she was unhurt and had run into a store. Still nagged by my sense of helplessness that morning, I considered joining the military or becoming a paramedic. Two weeks after the attack, editors asked me to go to Afghanistan and I leapt at the chance. I had covered religious extremism in the Balkans and thought my stories could investigate, examine, and expose militant Islam. With thousands dead in my home city, I also hoped my journalism might somehow help prevent future attacks.

On September 25, 2001, a rickety, Soviet-built helicopter operated by the Northern Alliance—the ragtag Afghan anti-Taliban group—dropped me and several other journalists in the Panjshir Valley, one of the few areas in the country the alliance controlled.

On the ground, the epic scale of what the United States faced in Afghanistan was humbling. Dozens of burnt-out Soviet tanks lined the valley, a maze of mountains and ravines that seemed to epitomize Afghanistan's reputation as a geographic and cultural fortress. With billions in aid from the United States in the 1980s, the Afghan "mujahideen"—an Arabic term that means "strugglers" or "fighters for justice"—had defeated the Soviets and fulfilled the mountainous country's reputation for repelling foreign armies and humbling empires.

In the 1990s, civil war had erupted with India, Pakistan, and Iran backing the Northern Alliance and Pakistan backing Taliban fighters from the south. When I arrived in 2001, the Taliban and their foreign militant allies controlled roughly 90 percent of the country. The depth of the country's poverty was staggering. Most towns had no paved roads or electricity. Farmers used oxen and wooden plows to till their fields. Twenty years of conflict had shattered government and social structures. Afghanistan was the world's fifth poorest nation. Fifty-five percent of men and 85 percent of women were illiterate. The average life expectancy was forty-three.

When the Taliban front lines collapsed under heavy American bombing in early November, exuberant young Afghans thronged Kabul's streets and hailed the fall of the Taliban. They devoured cellular phones, computers, and any other means of access to the outside world. Girls flocked to school and women relished basic freedoms. After twenty-four years of Soviet occupation, civil war, and brutal Taliban rule, Afghans welcomed stability, moderation, and foreigners. On December 22, 2001, I watched Afghan men weep with joy as Hamid Karzai was sworn in as the country's interim leader. Hope filled the hall and the city. The Taliban appeared vanquished.

Like other foreigners, I was beguiled by Afghans, their bravery and sense of honor. I wanted to follow what unfolded in the country over the long term and answer a central question: how can religious extremism be countered?

I had been intermittently covering religious and ethnic conflict for the past fourteen years. I covered the war in Bosnia for *The Christian Science Monitor* in the mid-1990s and after joining *The New York Times* in 1996 reported on religious conflict in Israel–Palestine, Kosovo, Indonesia, and Nigeria. After covering the fall of the Taliban in 2001, I served as the newspaper's South Asia bureau chief from 2002 to 2005, reporting on sectarian tensions in India, Sri Lanka, and Bangladesh as well. The vast majority of my time, though, was spent reporting in Pakistan and Afghanistan.

I visited Helmand Province in southern Afghanistan for the first time in 2004 while reporting a story on Charles Grader, the last American to head the U.S. Agency for International Development, or USAID, mission in Kabul before the 1979 Soviet invasion. A quarter century later, Grader had returned to Kabul at the age of seventy-two to manage an agricultural development program. We drove into Lashkar Gah, Helmand's provincial capital, and he raved about how the town had changed since the 1970s. Stores brimmed with food, household goods, and televisions.

"Look at that construction!" Grader shouted as we drove down through the city trailed by a half dozen Afghan security guards. "Look at the tractors!"

Lashkar Gah had fascinated me ever since. The town was built by American engineers as part of one of the largest foreign development projects in United States history. For thirty-three years, from 1946 to 1979, a massive American Cold War program tried to wean Afghans from Soviet influence.

In a bleak stretch of Afghan desert that resembled the surface of Mars, several dozen families from states like Montana and Wisconsin lived in suburban tract homes with one-car garages, green lawns and backyard barbecues. The Americans constructed a new provincial capital, two earthen dams, 1,200 miles of gravel roads, and 300 miles of irrigation canals. They promised to make 350,000 acres of desert bloom and create an Afghan version of the Tennessee Valley Authority, the Depression-era hydroelectric system that spans five American states.

In 1960, the British historian Arnold J. Toynbee visited Lashkar Gah and declared it "a piece of America inserted into the Afghan landscape." The American-designed town was an "ultramodern world of workshops and offices," Toynbee wrote in a memoir of his journey. Afghans called it "Little America."

Laid out in a neat square grid, Lashkar Gah during the Cold War was a sweltering, dust-covered settlement of 15,000 residents perched above the swirling brown waters of the Helmand River, according to books and reports from the time. It had a four-lane, pine-tree-lined Main Street, a new hotel with a swimming pool and tennis court, and southern Afghanistan's only coeducational high school. Downtown, a movie theater played the latest Indian films. The province and its massive development project was even a setting of a James Michener novel. After traveling through Afghanistan in the 1950s, Michener wrote *Caravans,* a 1963 novel that described local Afghan disappointment with an expensive foreign aid project that failed to meet their high expectations.

Toynbee, Michener, and other foreign visitors were enthralled by the Pashtuns, a fiercely independent ethnic group of 40 million people that predominate in Helmand, southern Afghanistan, and northwestern Pakistan. Their ancient system of governance is Pashtunwali, a 5,000-year-old tribal code of honor that governs all aspects of a Pashtun's life. Under Pashtunwali, all Pashtuns must display hospitality toward guests, give asylum to anyone in distress, exact revenge on those who injure or insult them, protect the honor of women, and always display unflinching bravery, loyalty, and trust in God.

In rural villages, conservative Pashtun tribal elders tended to be devoutly religious, opposed to central government rule, and suspicious of foreigners. In the large cities and towns, an educated Pashtun elite generally supported modernization of the country.

In "Little America" of the 1960s and 1970s, educated Pashtun moderates dominated. During Christmas and Ramadan in Lashkar Gah, Pashtuns and Americans invited one another to each other's homes to celebrate their respective religious holidays. Americans who worked in Lashkar Gah at the time told me Pashtuns were shockingly poor and isolated, yet dignified, generous, and welcoming.

David Champagne, a Peace Corps volunteer from Chicago, taught English at the high school in Lashkar Gah from 1968 to 1971. He recalled an experimental school where Afghan and American teachers worked together to train a new generation of Afghan leaders and technocrats. Champagne tried to infuse his students—particularly girls—with a sense that they could achieve anything through hard work. The school's goal was to instill an ethos that Afghanistan could develop into a prosperous country through slow, painstaking education and government reform efforts over many years. "There was a certain amount of realism and optimism," Champagne told me. "People thought they could help people with technology. Make the deserts bloom."

The grand American project, though, never achieved the agricultural production promised. It consumed vast amounts of American and Afghan finances and took three times longer to complete than planned. Arriving with Grader in 2004, I found that the American-built suburban tract homes still stood, but their Afghan occupants had built walls around them, a sign of the gulf between American and Afghan notions of privacy.

I learned that "Little America" was one chapter in a century-long effort by the Pashtun elite to modernize the country, all with mixed results. In many ways, Afghan history followed a cycle of Kabul-based, elite-backed reform movements provoking violent opposition from the country's conservative rural tribes.

Yet whenever I began to write off the American Cold War project, other experiences gave me pause. Pashtun farmer after farmer told me "Americans built Helmand." I met scores of Pashtuns who had attended the experimental American-funded high school in Lashkar Gah in the 1960s and 1970s. Thirty years later, they warmly recalled the names of David Champagne and their American teachers, often with tears in their eyes. Dozens had become senior government officials or doctors, engineers, and teachers.

In particular, the sophistication and bravery of one man and one woman from the classes of 1972 and 1974 intrigued me. After the fall of the Taliban, Muhammad Hussein Andiwal became the provincial police chief and Fowzea Olomi became the head of women's affairs in Helmand. They insisted that "Little America" was ripe for another American-backed renaissance.

For my book, I planned to chronicle Fowzea's and Andiwal's efforts to modernize Helmand after 2001. On the day before we drove to our ill-fated Taliban interview, I had met in Kabul with Andiwal, who had been recently fired from his job as Helmand's police chief. Despite the presence of 8,000 British and American troops, the Taliban had gained control of most of the province. Andiwal blamed the British and the British blamed the Afghans. I began to wonder who was telling the truth and if there were any heroes in Helmand.

Twelve hours after interviewing Andiwal, I lay in the back of the car bound and blindfolded. A dynamic that has always existed in journalism had escalated in Iraq and Afghanistan. In an intensifying race to the bottom, the reporter who took the greatest risk often received the highest acclaim. In Bosnia, a desire to expose injustice had primarily driven me, followed by competitiveness and ambition. In Afghanistan, competitiveness and ambition had gotten the best of me. I had lost my way.

As my Taliban captors blared prayers over the car radio and celebrated the capture of their quarry, a new meaning enveloped the sweeping question I had grandly posed to myself in 2001: how can religious extremism be curbed? My life and the lives of Tahir and Asad now hinged on whether we could find a way to placate our captors, gain their sympathy, and stop them from killing us. As I lay powerless in the backseat, the question was simple: how do we survive?

Our kidnapper, Atiqullah, eyes me suspiciously in the living room of the house where Tahir, Asad, and I have been taken. Roughly two hours have passed since we were kidnapped. I still do not know which Taliban faction has abducted us or who Atiqullah is.

A large man with short dark hair protruding from the sides of his cap, Atiqullah appears self-assured. He speaks calmly and confidently, and is in clear command of his men. He offers me back the eyeglasses his gunmen had taken from me and tells me to stop sobbing, a tactic that had eased the suspicions of my captors in Bosnia. Weeping is a great shame, he explains, and it upsets him and his men to see it. Later, I will learn that the Taliban consider crying to be a sign of guilt. If a person is innocent, he does not fear death, because he knows God will save him.

"You will be treated well," he assures me, citing Islam's mandate that prisoners not be harmed. "I understand foreigners get sick. You will be given bottled water. If you need to see a doctor, you will see a doctor."

"Whatever we eat," he adds, "you will eat."

His beliefs appear to be a combination of Pashtunwali and fundamentalist Islam. Gracious treatment of guests is a Pashtun hallmark. Deep suspicion of nonbelievers is an excess of radical Islam. Since the Taliban emerged in the early 1990s, religiously conservative rural Pashtuns have been their base of support.

With Tahir translating, I try to convince him to release us. I tell him that we were invited to Logar Province to interview Abu Tayyeb and hear the Taliban's side of the story. We are journalists, I say, and I served as *The New York Times*' South Asia bureau co-chief from 2002 to 2005. I describe the articles I wrote in Bosnia exposing the mass executions of 8,000 Muslims. I tell him Christians there imprisoned me when they caught me at a mass gravesite and accused me of being pro-Muslim. I tell him I had won the Pulitzer Prize and a half dozen other journalism awards for helping expose the massacres.

I hope I am convincing him that I am an independent journalist. I hope I am convincing him that the United States is not a monolith and some Americans defend Muslims and are rewarded for it. For years, I have thought that if the Taliban ever kidnap me, my work in Bosnia would protect me. I would be investigated online, declared a friend of Islam, and, I hoped, released.

Finally, I take off my wedding ring, show him the engraving of my wife's name on the inner band, and explain that we were married only two months ago. Tears roll down my cheeks again and I beg him to free us. The melodrama is intentional. I have read that a captive's best chance of survival is getting their captor to see them as a human being. I hope my display of emotion will help us.

Atiqullah grows angry, orders me to stop crying, and tells me I will see my wife again. But he denies our requests to call Abu Tayyeb or a Taliban spokesman Tahir knows. He says he controls our fate now.

He hands me back my notebook and pen and orders me to start writing. American soldiers routinely disgrace Afghan women and men, he says. They force women to stand before them without their burqas, the head-to-toe veils that conservative Pashtun villagers believe protect a woman's honor. They search homes without permission and force Afghan men to lie on the ground, placing boots on their heads and pushing their faces into the dirt. He views the United States as a malevolent occupier.

Atiqullah produces one of our cell phones and announces that he wants to call the *Times* bureau in Kabul. I give him the number and he briefly speaks with one of the newspaper's Afghan reporters. He hands me the phone. One of my colleagues from the paper's Kabul bureau is on the line. I say that we have been taken prisoner by the Taliban.

"What can we do?" my colleague asks. "What can we do?"

Atiqullah demands the phone back before I can answer. My colleague—one of the bravest reporters I know—sounds unnerved.

Atiqullah turns off the phone, removes the battery, and announces that we will move that night for security reasons. My heart sinks. I hoped that we would somehow be allowed to contact Abu Tayyeb, the commander we had arranged to interview, and be freed before nightfall. Now, as we wait in the house, I know that my colleague will be calling my family and editors at any minute to inform them that I have been kidnapped.

After praying, our captors serve us a traditional Afghan dinner of rice and flatbread. After sunset, they blindfold us, load us into cars, and drive us into the darkness.

Atiqullah is at the wheel. A man who has been introduced to us as "Akhundzada," Atiqullah's "intelligence chief," sits in the passenger seat with a scarf over his face as well. I am seated in the backseat between Tahir and Asad. Roughly thirty minutes into a jarring drive down dirt roads, Atiqullah allows me to take off my blindfold. We traverse a barren, moonlit desert landscape of dust-covered plains and treeless hills. I recognize nothing. We could be anywhere in Afghanistan.

With Tahir again translating, I ask for permission to speak and offer to answer any questions Atiqullah might have. He assails Israel and accuses the United States of being a greedy colonial power bent on stealing the Muslim world's resources. He is doctrinaire, but we are not being beaten or abused.

After a roughly two-hour drive, we arrive in a remote village where Atiqullah says we will spend the night with his guards. He is leaving and will return the following day. His men lead us into a small, one-room dirt house. A half dozen of us—three guards and three prisoners—lie down on the floor under musty-smelling blankets. I think of my wife and family. By now, they must know.

"FUN FEARLESS FEMALE"

Kristen, November 10–11, 2008

I am sitting atop Times Square. From the thirty-eighth floor, I can see all way to the mouth of the Hudson River. I have just assigned a photographer to shoot a portrait to accompany a first-person magazine account titled "My Bra Saved My Life." We will photograph the once injured hiker who hung her bra out as a beacon to alert passersby. Nothing attracts attention like a bright red sports bra with size D cups, apparently. In a pinch, it's a real lifesaver. I smile to myself. This is a far cry from my husband's line of work.

I am about two weeks into my new job as photography director at *Cosmopolitan* magazine. My train of thought—the combination of humor, absurdity, and mass-market appeal my new job straddles—is interrupted. It's 4:30 P.M. I wonder why I have not yet heard from David, even though I know that power outages are common in Pakistan, as are travel delays. Perhaps he has not yet figured out how to access the Internet from his guesthouse. He's there on assignment and is researching a book on the history of American involvement in Afghanistan and Pakistan since 2001—what went wrong and what should be done to remedy the situation. This is David's final reporting trip to the region. He was scheduled to depart Kabul for Islamabad this morning.

The phone rings. It's my brother-in-law Lee. Not a good sign. "Hello," I say. "Nice to hear your voice, but I am not so sure I want to be hearing from you. What's wrong?"

Lee is the person my husband has designated as a first point of contact for all "worst case scenarios." In the event of a mishap during a reporting trip, the plan is that Lee will be alerted and will in turn contact me. A former member of the Air Force and a pilot, Lee has nerves of steel, but is also a sensitive guy. Three years older than my husband, he has gotten David out of several tight situations. He is the consummate big brother, responsible and protective.

He laughs, understanding my predicament. "Well, it's not good. But it could be worse."

He tells me that David never returned from his last interview in Kabul, a meeting he had arranged with a Taliban commander. This is news to me. David left a note at the bureau with instructions on what to do should he fail to return in three hours. Lee tells me that David wanted him to wait twelve hours before reaching out to me. "Screw that," he says. "I figured you would want to know. And I do not want to deal with this alone."

Right away, my brother-in-law gains a spot near and dear to my heart. He is right. I would have been absolutely livid had he waited to inform me. David's need to "protect" me sometimes infuriates me.

"Christie and I are in Florida on vacation," Lee says, referring to his wife. "Stay calm. Take a moment to take this in." My mind reels as I try to process what he is telling me. Then he continues, "You should jump on the next shuttle to Boston. We'll meet you at Logan." From there, we will drive back to his house in southern New Hampshire for the night. Apparently a meeting has been scheduled with the local FBI bureau there for early tomorrow morning. The FBI agents contacted Lee after David was reported missing to the United States Embassy in Kabul.

Shuttle to Boston? I am new on the job and a little busy at the moment arranging the photo shoot. I am trying to locate a reasonable facsimile of the sports bra worn by the hiker, to run as a still along with her portrait. My rational mind grapples for control. Of course, I quickly realize this is absurd. I need to get to the airport as fast as possible. David is my number one priority. I fight a wave of overwhelming terror, fear, and uncertainty. I am momentarily immobilized, numb, as I glance out the window.

It's a crisp afternoon. The sky is clear, the river calm. Despite the tidiness of my new, modern surroundings, I feel as if my life has plunged into disarray. I thought I was prepared for this kind of call. Before we married, David and I discussed the inherent risks in his work as a foreign correspondent. We talked about several worst case scenarios, including injury and even death. These tragedies are concrete and would follow a prescribed protocol. But I never anticipated what to do in the uncertain face of David going missing. Here it is, I think, my worst fear come true.

I call the managing editor at *Cosmopolitan* and say something vague about a "family health emergency" and that I need to head to New England. She is gracious and does not ask questions. I tell her I will probably be out the next day or so. "Do what you need to do," she says. She knows that my parents live in Maine. I secretly hope the magazine thinks I am running off to comfort an ailing elderly relative. The real explanation is too absurd to believe.

By the time I leave my office and head home to collect my things, I am composed and steady. I have prided myself on being able to stay calm in tense situations. And this is not my first brush with terror. I live a few blocks from Ground Zero. I recall the shock of being displaced for three months following the 9/11 terrorist attacks, the exhaustion, uncertainty. And all my adrenaline-fueled mistakes: forgetting to eat, sleep, and rest. What I learned then protects me now. On my way to Boston, I resolve to take better care of myself this time around, and to call on family and friends for support when necessary.

It's 9:30 p.m. when I arrive at Logan Airport. I wait in the sterile baggage terminal. It's Monday night. A bit deserted. No one else in David's family has been alerted aside from his brother Lee. By chance I hear from my own brother, Jason. He is calling to check in and catch up. All he knows is that I returned from my honeymoon three weeks ago and started a new job. I try to keep my voice calm and upbeat. Jason is exuberant chatting about what a great time he had at our wedding at our family's home in Maine. My sister-in-law chimes in on speakerphone. They are both so happy for us.

When he takes me off speakerphone, I ask if I can tell him a secret. "This is going to sound so far-fetched," I say. "I am sitting at Logan.

David went into an interview and never returned. We think he's alive, but do not know where he is." My brother is a rock. I know he feels terrible for me, but I also know he will not share this information with anyone.

I meet Lee and his wife, Christie. Their two-year-old is asleep in her stroller. We drive to their home in coastal New Hampshire. The last time I was here was five months ago, during a visit with David. It's about eleven o'clock, an exhausting seven hours after I first heard the news. Tonight, none of us will get any sleep.

At eight the next morning, Lee and I go over to the local FBI office, which is nestled discreetly in a bland suburban 1980s-style office park. We are greeted by several agents. This, I will learn, is typical. They travel in packs. They sport clean haircuts and monosyllabic names: Jim, Tom, John, Joe. One would be hard-pressed to pick any of them out of a police lineup. They are nondescript and practically identical in their uniformity.

The FBI is the lead agency in all kidnappings of American citizens, whether at home or abroad. We are a bit baffled, though, as to why we were instructed to meet them in New Hampshire, given that David and I live in New York. It turns out to be agency protocol, which was set in motion when the newspaper's Kabul bureau notified the U.S. Embassy that David did not return from the interview. The case was immediately reported to the FBI, then to David's employer. The newspaper then called Lee, who is still listed as David's emergency contact. I make a note to update this information when David returns. Because Lee's phone number bears a New Hampshire area code, local field agents there were assigned to get in touch with our family. If I was the contact, we'd be having this meeting in New York City.

The local case agent informs us that David was abducted along with his driver and translator as they headed to interview a Taliban commander outside Kabul. I proceed to reel off the name of everyone David has mentioned to me in the past two and a half years who is affiliated with Afghanistan, Pakistan, and the United States government. It's a long list. The interview is largely a one-way flow of information. As we talk about the situation, I begin to feel like I am better versed in the tribal areas of Pakistan and the nuances of Afghan culture than the local agents. This is a little disturbing, since most of what I know is limited to what I have absorbed from David—and from visiting his colleagues, briefly traveling with him to Pakistan, and reading popular books like *Three Cups of Tea* and *The Kite Runner.*

Lee is asked to provide a DNA sample, a cheek swab. This is to help identify David in a worst case scenario, or if any evidence is found in Afghanistan that could indicate the location where he is being held captive.

The agents ask whether David is a friend of the Taliban, and whether the book is about them. I explain that he is writing about the struggling American effort in the region. I edit my words carefully before speaking, fearful of saying anything that could mislead them into thinking that David is somehow in cahoots with the Taliban.

Lee and I leave the interview several hours later with the understanding that another set of agents will be assigned to our case in New York City. We are to update the agents if we receive any new information about David from his colleagues. In turn, the agents will keep us posted on any new developments on their end.

Calls begin to flood in: David's literary agent, the editor of *The New York Times.* The newspaper alerted David's book publisher about the kidnapping. David's agent, in turn, was contacted by his publisher. Despite the fact that Lee and I have made no public announcement of David's predicament, word has traveled like wildfire among the journalism community.

I am relieved to hear from a colleague of David's in Kabul. Upset but calm, this reporter informs me that David left behind a note addressed to me. I ask the reporter to read it over the phone. I sense a hesitation. "He has rather unfortunate handwriting," the reporter jokes between tears. "I will scan and e-mail it to you and send the original in the mail."

A few hours later, the infamous note appears in my BlackBerry inbox. I smile: David's colleague is right about the handwriting. The letter has been scribbled on a page from a notebook. The whole thing feels rushed, like an afterthought. Knowing David, though, he probably agonized over its content.

Kristen—

I believed I had to do this to make this a credible book. Most people in Helmand support them now and I need to tell that part of the story. I honestly believe this is a calculated risk that will be ok.

Scribbled in the margin is a phrase that makes my heart sink: *This is my passion and I must do what I love.*

The letter continues:

If I get kidnapped, use money from my book advance. Do not involve money from your family or mine. This is my responsibility.

I love you so much and am sure this will be ok. Please go and be happy and move forward if things go very wrong.

I love you so very much and thank you for giving me more joy and love than I've ever known.

I love you,

David

Afghanistan has been David's preoccupation for the past seven years, since 9/11. For me, it has been a source of intrigue, sadness, and anxiety— a needy child or mistress that requires his attention, often with the cost of long separations. The events on the ground in Afghanistan have a direct impact on David's moods and motivations. It has been a challenge for me to support such an all-consuming interest.

I was introduced to David by a mutual friend two and a half years ago. We were both in our late thirties at the time and ready to move on to a new phase of life, one that we each hoped would include family and children. Our relationship progressed steadily, despite several month-long periods of separation to accommodate David's overseas reporting trips. These separations were often a strain on my nerves as we both struggled with the tensions inherent in straddling two very different worlds together.

The note does not comfort me. Part of me immediately recognizes that he's thrown us under the bus at month two of marriage. I know that David is writing the book in part to distance himself from his dangerous work as a war correspondent. But pursuing an interview with a Taliban commander was a bachelor's decision. I have just committed the rest of my life to David. I haven't even unpacked from our honeymoon. But if I—we—are going to get through this, I'm going to have to forgive him and set aside my anger. At some point, I am also going to have to deal with the fact that I *am* angry. I realize he took a risk imagining a positive outcome. David does not think that lightning can strike twice. But it has. This is his second detainment. He was jailed in Bosnia for ten days in 1995 while reporting on the mass execution of Muslims in Srebrenica.

I feel like I've been hit by a thunderbolt. I recall our engagement. David proposed to me on a sailboat in the middle of New York Harbor. "Let's lead a big life," he said. I agreed. This is not exactly what I had in mind. I glance at my engagement ring, a pear-shape diamond set on its side. I remember thinking it looked like a teardrop on first viewing. I somehow worried this was a premonition of things to come, but later convinced myself it was a raindrop, which was a more refreshing and fitting thought. Rain is a recurrent theme for us. There was a torrential downpour just before we set sail in New York that day. Hurricane Hannah struck on our wedding day. I often liken the extreme, unpredictable shifts in our circumstances to weather patterns.

Lee offers to drive me to my parents' home in Maine for the night. I will meet up with him tomorrow before I leave for New York. I call my mother from the road. Unaware of what has been going on, she is excited to hear from me. I tell her I have brought a guest along. I know she immediately assumes it's David—perhaps he's come to his senses and returned from Afghanistan early.

I haven't been to the house since we were married in September. David and I decided to marry there, as we each have fond memories of summer childhoods spent in Maine. We wanted to celebrate with our families at a place that had special meaning for us.

The house sits on a sandy tidal beach. The scenery and light shift as the water advances and recedes twice each day. I have always loved the sense of motion, possibility, and renewal these natural changes provoke daily.

I walk into a perfectly preserved moment. The room is still full of an almost palpable sense of love and hope from our celebration. We are greeted by my mother, Mary Jane, a petite, upbeat brunette with a welcoming smile. Despite her five-foot frame, my mother is a powerhouse of strength, tenacity, and positivity. She is a healthy dose of Sally Field, tempered with a shot of Anne Bancroft. She has been drying the wedding flowers. Full bridal bouquets sit in their original places, vibrant, slightly shrunken, preserved. Two months ago we were rolling up the carpets, dancing in the living room, mingling with friends and family. It's odd to be in this space alone, an observer. As I glance out the sliding doors, the ocean is calm, glasslike. I am comforted by memory and surroundings, yet pained to be here without David.

I remember that David looked nervous as we exchanged our vows. To lighten his mood, when I declared "For better or worse," I winked at him on "worse." This definitely qualifies as worse. I now regret my well-intentioned and whimsical act. Perhaps I should not have tempted fate. I promise myself that when David returns, I will restate this promise sans blink.

My mother has prepared a lobster dinner in anticipation of my arrival. I tell her there is no cause for celebration and bring her up to speed while Lee phones his wife from the other room. Mom is quiet, recognizing that this was always within the realm of possibility, given the nature of David's work. When I tell her I am shocked and upset by David's letter—that he was willing to risk everything for the sake of the story, without consulting me—she does not finger point.

"Okay, he made a mistake," she says. "But you need to move forward from there and think positive if you are going to get through this. Don't let your mind be clouded by anger. It's not going to do you any good now. Focus on bringing him home."

"We just took a wedding vow," I say.

"And now it's your chance to live up to it," she responds.

This is a calm but tough pep talk. Confronted by my worst fear, Mom figures the last thing I need is for someone else to stir the pot. She tells me to remain open-minded and offers to accompany me back to New York. I am slightly surprised but thankful for her reaction. Her outward composure keeps me centered. I recognize that while David took a risk in going to the interview, the kidnapping is not his fault. Blaming him for it provides a momentary sense that he has some control over his circumstances. Our reality is much worse—David and the rest of us are helpless in this situation.

I begin to receive calls from friends offering condolences. Each of them has learned about David's situation from a "friend at the *Times*." I have my first brush with what will be an ongoing battle: keeping David's case quiet. Throughout the first days of David's kidnapping, we are able to draw on the camaraderie of the press and the gravitas of *The New York Times* to keep his story out of the public eye. But any bit of information I relay to David's colleagues is quickly common knowledge inside the media bubble. I have to fight repeatedly during these early days to protect our privacy as a couple. I begin my battle at the top, with a heated call to Bill Keller, the paper's executive editor, from my parents' living room. I tell him that his reporters are spreading the word and ask him to put a lid on it. As the wife of a kidnap victim, I have tremendous leeway. Bill is extremely gracious and apologetic. He promises to limit communications within the office.

A call arrives from the FBI on behalf of the Department of Defense. David's brother Lee and I face our first big decision: will we give advance approval for a military raid if it could secure David's release? We are both stunned. "Do you know where he is?" we ask. They cannot say. "How much time do we have to decide?" A few hours.

The Department of Defense ensures us they will not undertake a raid unless they are very confident they will be able to get David and his colleagues out alive. But they give no indication as to how they will assess this risk.

This is the first of many decisions we will agonize over—and revisit during the subsequent months. For now, Lee and I decide against a military raid, unless David or one of his co-captives is severely sick or injured, or if their lives are in immediate danger. We still do not have any information on who is holding him and what it is they are after.

We decide to wait a few days to make a final decision, until we have more information and a sense of David's physical location. We also want to run this by David's parents and other siblings. We do not want to make this decision alone. It is shocking to be confronted with this reality and the grim nature of our choices. We want David to return as quickly as possible. But Lee and I agree that David would never forgive himself if anyone was killed or injured during an attempt to free him by force. Still, we wonder whether our delayed response will work against us, whether this lapse in decision making will mean the difference between his returning home or not.

A short time later, we hear back from the FBI. There is no rush on deciding whether to use military intervention. We are advised that while the kidnappers may move David, there is no imminent threat of harm. In the frustrating days and months to come, we will discover that most of the information and advice we are given is pure speculation.

Night arrives—finally. Unable to sleep in the room I last shared with David at my parents' house, I collapse in my younger brother Jason's vacant room.

My mind races and my body is completely restless, on full alert. I drag my laptop into bed and scan my e-mail for updates from the Kabul bureau and messages from David's family. Lee has told his family the news. I talk to my mother-in-law, Carol, David's sister, Laura, and his younger brother, Erik. Erik and I share our fears. While the situation remains uncertain, we are hopeful. Our collective gut check is that David will return, yet we have no idea how or when. We assume it will be a matter of one to three months, based on what I have learned from the FBI about recent kidnappings in Afghanistan.

I already miss my husband's voice. We routinely speak each night when he is away. Despite the uncertainty of his whereabouts I'm determined to maintain our nightly ritual. I send an e-mail to my husband. I type three simple words into the subject line in the hope that he will one day read them: I love you.

MILLIONS

David, November 11–17, 2008

I awake to the sound of the guards performing a predawn prayer with Tahir and Asad. I sit silently as they press their foreheads to the ground and supplicate to God. We are crammed with three guards in a small, claustrophobic room in a dirt house. Measuring roughly twenty feet by twenty feet, its only furnishings are the carpet on the floor and a dozen blankets.

The gunman with the flat, expressionless eyes who kidnapped us the day before introduces himself as "Qari," an Arabic expression for someone who has been trained to properly recite the Koran. He is shorter and skinnier than he seemed when he glared at me from the front seat of the car the previous day. His mentality proves more disturbing than his appearance. He proudly announces that he is a "fedayeen," an Arabic term the Taliban use for suicide bombers.

Bread arrives for breakfast, and the guards are polite and courteous. No one has beaten us since Tahir and Asad were pummeled with rifle butts during the first minutes of the kidnapping. As the day progresses, though, I grow more worried. Atiqullah has not reappeared. There is no talk of our release.

Confined to the small, crowded room as the morning slowly passes, I find it more and more suffocating. Allowed outside only to go to the bathroom, I am accompanied by an armed guard at all times. As the day crawls by, our guards pray methodically and Qari speaks of his eagerness to die. They act as if I am the first American they have ever seen. They stare at me as if I were a zoo animal, a strange, exotic creature they have long heard about but never beheld.

All this makes me increasingly worried about who is holding us. Thieves might release us if Abu Tayyeb comes to our rescue, or they might settle for a quick deal. Instead, our captors appear to be hard-line Taliban.

Several hours after sunset, we are hustled outside and ordered to get into a small Toyota station wagon.

"We have to move you for security reasons," announces Atiqullah, who is sitting in the driver's seat, his face still concealed behind a scarf. Arab militants and a film crew from Al Jazeera are on their way, he says. "They're going to chop off your heads," he announces. "I've got to get you out of this area."

As we drive away, I ask for permission to speak. Atiqullah agrees. I tell him we are worth more alive than dead. He asks me what I think he can get for us. I hesitate, unsure of what to say. I am desperate to keep us alive.

I have a vague memory of a one-week hazardous environment survival training class that I took in 2002 before being posted abroad. I remember being told by instructors to prolong captivity for as long as possible. The most dangerous period of an abduction is the initial hours. The longer a kidnapping lasts, the higher the chance of survival.

I know that in March 2007, the Afghan government exchanged five Taliban prisoners for an Italian journalist after the Taliban executed his driver. Later, they killed his translator as well. My memory of the exchange was vague, but I thought money was included. In September 2007, the Taliban claimed the South Korean government paid $20 million for the release of twenty-one Korean missionaries after the Taliban killed two members of the group.

"Money and prisoners," I say.

"How much money?" Atiqullah asks.

I hesitate again.

"Millions," I say, immediately thinking I will regret the statement.

Atiqullah and his intelligence chief look at each other. Over the next hour, the conversation continues. Atiqullah repeatedly promises to do his best to protect us. I repeatedly promise him money and prisoners.

As we wind our way through steep mountain passes, an American drone follows us. Remotely piloted propeller-driven airplanes, the drones can easily be heard as they circle overhead for hours. To the naked eye, they are small dots in the sky. But their missiles have a range of several miles. We know we can be immolated without warning. Atiqullah glances warily out the window and tries to locate the drone in the night sky. I silently hope that we miraculously might be found. After a few minutes, the drone disappears.

Atiqullah asks for the names and professions of my father and brothers. I tell him the truth. Given the unusual spelling of my last name, I think he can easily find my relatives online. From past reporting I know that the Taliban are not primitive men who live in caves. They operate in cities across Afghanistan and Pakistan that teem with Internet cafés.

My father, Harvey, is a retired insurance salesman, I say. My two brothers, Lee and Erik, work for an aviation company and an ambulance company. My two stepbrothers, Joel and Dan, work for a bank and a restaurant. I hope being forthright is helping convince him I am a journalist, not a spy. More than ever, I am convinced that being caught in a lie will prove fatal.

In the darkness, I can see little outside the car windows. I don't know if we are passing through clusters of villages or remote areas. After several hours of driving down jarring dirt tracks, we arrive at another small house. Guards cover my face with a scarf and lead us inside in the dark. Atiqullah politely asks me to repeat my earlier statements in the car as a guard records a video of me on his mobile phone. I promise him money and prisoners, recite the names of my male relatives, and list the awards I won for my reporting in Bosnia.

Atiqullah has us answer a series of questions that our families have apparently already relayed to our captors. If our answers are correct, it will prove we are alive. Tahir and Asad are asked to name the first schools they attended. I am asked my wife's name and birth date and what kind of car I have in New York. When I say I do not have a car, Atiqullah is suspicious that I am somehow giving a secret message.

Finally, Atiqullah asks me if I want to convey anything to my wife. "Tell her that the place where I'm staying is better than the farm in India." I'm making a reference to a friend's rustic farm in northern India where we spent a week of our honeymoon. After arriving and discovering it was far hotter than expected, we departed early. I hope the message will prove I am alive, being held in decent conditions, and that it will somehow comfort Kristen.

Then Atiqullah and his intelligence chief disappear. For the next four days, we live in the small house with Qari, the gunman who kidnapped us and hopes to become a suicide bomber. On most days, we hear a motorcycle circle in the distance. More guards have created a perimeter around us.

On the first day, no food or water arrives. For eight hours, we lie on the floor and fitfully try to sleep. My stomach aches. I wonder if the lack of food means they plan to kill us. Qari tells us that an Afghan policeman who secretly supports the Taliban spotted me at a checkpoint. He then warned the Taliban we were coming. I curse myself for not covering my face better.

In brief exchanges, I learn more about Tahir and Asad. In truth, we are strangers. The three of us have never worked together before. Tahir has been working with foreign journalists since 2001 and adores the profession. He brightens when he speaks about other foreign and Afghan journalists we both know. Thirty-four years old, he is a university-educated and religious Afghan who hails from the southern province of Zabul. He has two wives and is the father of seven children, all of whom he moved to Kabul three years ago. He opposed the 2001 invasion of Afghanistan and like many Afghans now views the American and NATO troop presence as a foreign occupation. He is deeply disappointed with the United States' failure to deliver on its promises of stability and reconstruction. A proud Afghan nationalist, he is tired of meddling by foreign countries in his country and wants Afghans to be allowed to decide their own fate.

Asad is twenty-four years old and a scrappy Afghan survivor. He is rail thin, has jet-black hair and beard and dark eyes. Pashtun as well, his family originally hails from Khost province, but Asad was born and raised in Kabul. Married with two young sons, he has worked as a taxi driver in the city and a driver for Tahir and foreign journalists. He and Tahir have become close friends while working together for the past six years.

After dark, someone knocks on the wall of the house and Qari ventures outside. I wonder if our Arab executioners have arrived. Qari and another guard walk in with freshly cooked rice, bread, and meat, as well as bottled water. The guard, whose name is Akbar, profusely apologizes for his lateness. He says Atiqullah has ordered him to see to all our needs. I believe Akbar is the same guard who whispered "no shoot, no shoot" to me on the first day of the kidnapping. The kind treatment surprises and encourages me.

On the second day, Akbar brings us new clothes and warm blankets. I appreciate the good treatment but I am becoming more concerned. There is no word on negotiations. I still hope Abu Tayyeb will hear what has happened and somehow rescue us. Atiqullah is nowhere to be seen and Tahir is barred from calling any of his Taliban contacts.

That afternoon, I decide to pretend I'm sick in the hope it will pressure our captors into resolving our case. After forty-eight hours in one room, Tahir and Asad are increasingly frustrated. I am furious that Kristen and my family are suffering. I go to the bathroom, put my finger in my mouth, and make myself loudly vomit. I return to the room, tell the guards that the food is making me sick, and curl up under a blanket. The guards appear alarmed and I think they call Atiqullah. I make myself vomit once more that evening.

The following day, our third in the house, I make myself vomit several times and spend the day lying on the floor playing sick. The guards appear anxious. After dinner, there is a knock on the exterior wall. I expect a concerned Atiqullah to stride through the door. Instead, a young Taliban doctor does.

To my amazement, he speaks English and carries a fully equipped medical bag, replete with a blood pressure gauge, antibiotics, and an intravenous drip. The doctor takes my blood pressure and gives me an injection that he says will make me feel better. I am afraid the needle is dirty but notice it is wrapped in new plastic. I have no choice but to acquiesce to treatment. I am surprised—and depressed—by the Taliban's infrastructure in Afghanistan. They appear to be well supplied and feel that they are firmly in control of the area where we are being held.

The fourth day, Qari allows us to sit outside in the small walled courtyard. A few hours later, he lets Tahir play a game on his cell phone. I suggest that Tahir try to text "track this phone" or a similar message to the Kabul bureau from Qari's mobile when he is not paying attention. Tahir agrees. When he asks for the phone a second time, Qari is suspicious. He notices that Tahir and I have been talking quietly beforehand. He starts shouting in Pashto. Tahir says he accuses us of trying to send a text message. We deny it. Qari denounces us as liars. Enraged, and irrational, he picks up his Kalashnikov, points it at Tahir's chest, and threatens to shoot him.

Tahir stares back, unmoved. The Pashtun code of honor prevents each man from showing fear or losing face. Asad and I step in front of Tahir. Qari will have to shoot us first before hitting Tahir.

We beg him to put down his gun.

"*Lutfan, lutfan,*" I say, using an expression Tahir has told me means "please."

Slowly, Qari lowers his weapon. Then he motions for Tahir to step into an outer room.

I stare at Asad's face to try to gauge what is happening. My limited knowledge of Pashto prevents me from understanding what is being said.

Through the wall, I hear Tahir praying in Arabic. Then I hear a thump and Tahir cry out, "Allah!" A second thump and "Allah!" More thumps follow. Several minutes later, Tahir walks back into the room, crawls under a blanket, and begins moaning. Qari has beaten him with the butt of his rifle. Blow after blow was delivered to his lower back.

Qari unnerves me. In brief and depressing conversations over the last several days, he has earnestly recited hugely inaccurate propaganda about the West's trying to enslave all Muslims. It matches the conspiracy theories I have seen on jihadi Web sites. Qari seems utterly detached from reality. Our other guard, Akbar, jokes that Qari has mental problems.

In my mind, Qari and Atiqullah personify polar ends of the Taliban. Qari represents a paranoid, intractable force. Atiqullah embodies the more reasonable faction: people who could compromise on our release and, perhaps, even on peace in Afghanistan.

I do not know which one represents the majority. I want to believe that Atiqullah does. Yet each day I grow more fearful that Qari is the true Taliban.

Like many other American journalists, I rushed to Afghanistan after the September 2001 attacks with a limited understanding of the Taliban and a cursory knowledge of the country's history. I knew Afghanistan as the "graveyard of empires," a reference to its reputation as a land of indomitable mountain warriors who vanquish invading armies.

Over the next seven years, I gradually developed a more nuanced understanding. Afghanistan was not unconquerable. Foreign armies had taken control of Kabul and other large cities in the strategically located swathe of Central Asia dozens of times. First the Persians, then Alexander the Great, then the Safavids, and finally the Muslim Arabs; Ghengis Khan's Moguls, British, and Soviets did the same.

As a means of self-defense, Afghans deftly cultivated an image of their country as "Yaghestan"—a term used by Persians to describe the lawless areas to their east, a place both chaotic and criminal. In truth, Afghanistan was an impoverished band of high mountains and barren deserts with few natural resources, wholly dependent on outsiders for trade, arms, and wealth. Fractious Afghans also fought among themselves, created divisions outsiders exploited.

Centuries of conquest created a clear pattern. Afghans initially put up little resistance to invading armies and then extracted what lucre they could from their new rulers. Quickly shifting their loyalties, Afghans rebelled when they sensed an end to subsidy, the approach of a wealthier suitor, or flagrant disrespect. Foreigners found that the country was extraordinarily difficult to govern over the long term. The pattern led to a clichéd adage about the country: you can rent an Afghan, but you cannot own one.

Afghanistan did not become an independent nation until 1747, when a tribal council, or "jirga," chose a young Pashtun tribesman from Kandahar, Ahmad Shah Durrani, to serve as its king. For the next 225 years, Durrani's descendants ruled the country.

The new nation was a dizzying ethnic, tribal, and religious mix, "a purely accidental geographic unit," in the words of Lord George N. Curzon, the nineteenth-century British colonialist.

Ethnic Pashtuns spoke Pashto, dominated the south and east, and made up the vast majority of the population. Ethnic Tajiks of Persian descent dominated the north and west, spoke Persian, and were the country's second largest group. Ethnic Hazaras, descendants of the Mongols and minority Shia Muslims, were the country's third largest group. Uzbeks, Turkmen, and other ethnic groups from neighboring countries made up the remainder.

In the mid-1800s, Afghanistan became the coveted prize in the "Great Game," the celebrated British and Russian competition for control of Central Asia. The same pattern of conquest and rebellion emerged. In 1838, a British army seized control of Kabul. Three years later, Afghans revolted, hacking to death two British envoys in Kabul's main bazaar. When the British withdrew from Kabul several months later, Afghan marksmen firing from surrounding hills decimated the column. Out of a force of 15,000, only one man survived, purportedly spared so that he could describe the horrors that awaited future invaders.

In 1878, a larger British force of 40,000 soldiers bent on reasserting the empire's supremacy seized Kabul and other large cities. Three years of relative calm followed, until a rebellion erupted and 1,000 British were killed in the Battle of Maiwand, a few dozen miles from where "Little America" would be built decades later. Two months later, a larger British force decisively defeated the Afghans in Kandahar.

Aware that a long-term British presence would spark another uprising, the British installed an Afghan regent named Abdur Rahman. He agreed to British protection, subsidy, and control of Afghanistan's foreign affairs, moves all designed to block Russian expansionism toward British-controlled India.

In 1893, the British imposed a 1,600-mile border between Afghanistan and British-controlled India that annexed vast parts of Afghanistan and divided the Pashtuns, placing roughly 25 million of them in British-controlled India and 10 million in Afghanistan. The division would rankle Afghan Pashtuns for decades and lead to repeated calls for the establishment of a new nation called Pashtunistan. With the stroke of a British pen, the Afghan Pashtuns lost two-thirds of their population and dropped from being Afghanistan's overwhelming majority to a plurality of its people. Ethnic Tajiks, who dominate Afghanistan's north, had their hand strengthened.

In 1919, a bold young Afghan king named Amanullah Khan attacked the British and tried to retake the Pashtun areas the British had seized. In a three-month war he failed to do so, but regained control of Afghanistan's foreign affairs. For the next decade, American diplomats considered Afghanistan within Britain's "sphere of influence," though, and declined to recognize it as an independent nation.

Leon B. Poullada, an American diplomat who served in Afghanistan in the late 1950s and wrote a history of relations between Washington and Kabul, referred to the American view as the "Afghan blind-spot." Poullada argued that American policy makers dismissed the country as hostile and hapless, and repeatedly failed to see its strategic importance. "This feeling of unreality, of an inability to focus or define American interests in this 'far-off' land will appear as a recurring theme," Poullada wrote, "and will help to explain the many inconsistencies of American diplomacy in Afghanistan."

Poullada blamed the misperceptions on early American writing about Afghanistan. It began in 1838 when Josiah Harlan, a quixotic mercenary from Pennsylvania, became the first American to enter Afghanistan. Over the course of a decade, Harlan carried out an astonishing run of opportunism and skullduggery across South Asia, posing as a surgeon at one point and culminating in his 1838 position as a military adviser to Dost Muhammad, Afghanistan's ruler.

Harlan claimed he led an entire division of Afghan troops—and a heavy artillery train—over the Hindu Kush range, the forbidding mountains that separate northern and southern Afghanistan. Standing astride a 12,500-foot mountain pass, Harlan said he ordered his men to fire a twenty-six-gun salute as he unfurled an American flag. "I unfurled my country's banner to the breeze, under a salute of twenty-six guns, and the star-spangled banner gracefully waved amidst the icy peaks, seemingly sacred to the solitude of an undisturbed eternity," he wrote grandiloquently.

Months later, the British deposed Dost Muhammad and ousted the upstart American, who fancied himself heir to Alexander the Great. Harlan returned to the United States and published a memoir of his exploits, which years later became the basis for Rudyard Kipling's *The Man Who Would Be King*.

Poullada questioned the accuracy of Harlan's memoirs and maintained that Harlan was the first in a long line of American writers who unfairly portrayed Afghans as savages. After driving from British-controlled India to Kabul in 1922, Lowell Thomas, the famed American journalist, wrote a travelogue called *Beyond Khyber Pass: Into Forbidden Afghanistan*. Thomas assailed the Pashtuns, who he said were "more elusive than the robber bands of Albania, more daring than the Moros of Mindanao, more cunning than the Yaquis of Sonora, even more savage than the Mongol bandits of Chinese Tibet."

In truth, Afghanistan's ruling family, which was Pashtun, was desperate for help modernizing the country. Dismissed by British and American officials, Afghanistan's royal family eventually turned to continental Europe for help. In 1929, King Nadir Shah had French and German advisers train a 40,000-soldier army. Palace guards sporting incongruous Prussian-style helmets patrolled Kabul's streets. German-made aircraft supported military expeditions that punished rebellious tribes.

In 1933, Nadir Shah was assassinated and his nineteen-year-old son, Zahir Shah, took the throne. For the next forty years, he and his uncles would rule Afghanistan. Zahir Shah, who inherited a kingdom with only six miles of railway, all of them in Kabul, and few telegraph and phone lines, redoubled his father's modernization efforts. He recruited Italian, Japanese, and German advisers to develop a new road and communications system. Japanese built Helmand's first canals.

The outbreak of World War II finally ignited serious American interest in Afghanistan. American officials saw that the country offered a land route Allied forces could use to supply Soviet troops. Following the war, the United States vied with the Soviet Union for influence in Afghanistan. While Soviet engineers built roads and factories in the country's north, Americans built a highway linking Kabul and Kandahar, a sprawling new airport in Kandahar, and the massive Helmand project. Professors from the University of Nebraska taught agriculture at Kabul University and Pan American World Airways stewards trained employees of Afghanistan's new national airline.

The massive 1979 Soviet invasion followed the same pattern as past conquests. Soviet forces took control of major cities and faced primarily rural resistance. Thousands of Soviet advisers introduced atheism, a state-controlled economy, and a massive secret police system. Over time, brutal repression by Soviet forces and their Afghan allies—as well as billions in American aid—fueled a broad-based uprising led by religious conservatives.

In 2001, the ease of the American victory should have come as no surprise, given the country's history. A simple lesson should have been apparent to American policymakers: Afghans would welcome Americans, but only temporarily. At most, Washington had three to five years to demonstrate to Afghans that allying with the United States was to their benefit. Otherwise, Washington's newfound allies would desert them.

As our captivity enters its fifth day, Tahir, Asad, and I talk about trying to escape. Asad believes our captors will either kill us or hold us indefinitely. That afternoon, when Qari steps outside and leaves his Kalashnikov rifle behind, Asad grabs the weapon, loads it, and announces he wants to shoot his way out.

We urge Asad to wait. He will kill one or two guards, we tell him, and then be killed by others who hear the gunfire. Asad says he does not care, then reluctantly relents and places the rifle back on the floor.

We agree that Asad should try to escape that night after the guards fall asleep. If he makes it to Kabul, Asad can give the newspaper our location. Tahir and I are happy to stay behind if it allows Asad to return home.

We all know that in post-9/11 Afghanistan and Pakistan all lives are not created equal. If our captors are going to kill one of us, Asad will be the first. Tahir will follow, and I will likely be last, given their view of me as the hostage who can produce the most ransom or publicity.

Our calculus is based on the 2007 kidnapping of Italian journalist Daniele Mastrogiacomo. Two weeks after their abduction in Helmand, the Taliban beheaded the group's driver, Sayed Agha, and threatened to kill Mastrogiacomo and the Afghan journalist working with him, Ajmal Naqshbandi.

After Italian officials pressured Karzai, he released five senior Taliban prisoners in exchange for Mastrogiacomo. The Taliban then demanded another Taliban prisoner in exchange for Naqshbandi. When the Afghan government refused, the Taliban decapitated the soft-spoken twenty-four-year-old Afghan. Tahir and hundreds of Afghans attended Naqshbandi's funeral in Kabul. They bitterly accused the Karzai government of caring more about the life of a foreigner than the life of an Afghan.

While many foreigners are shuttled around Afghanistan in armored cars, Afghan civilians are forced to negotiate Taliban checkpoints largely on their own. The Taliban stop cars, trucks, and buses and arrest or execute Afghans who work with foreigners or the Afghan government. A month before our abduction, the Taliban had killed twenty-seven bus passengers who they believed were Afghan army soldiers in civilian clothes, decapitating six of them. The Afghan government, in fact, does not allow soldiers to travel by civilian bus. The Taliban-executed passengers were innocent men journeying to Iran for work.

That night, Atiqullah arrives with no warning and scuttles Asad's escape plans. "We're going to move you to a place where David can have bottled water," he says. "A place to walk. There will be doctors."

Guards load us into what looks like the same four-door Toyota station wagon. They put blankets in the hatchback and tell me to lie on top of them. Just before we depart, the Taliban doctor returns and gives me a final needle injection for my stomach.

In the car, Atiqullah tells me to cover my face with a scarf whenever we pass through a village or town. Arab militants and hard-line Taliban will try to kidnap and kill me, he says, if they recognize me as an American. He is probably lying, but I feel I have no choice but to obey him.

The four-door Toyota sedan we drove to our ill-fated interview follows behind our station wagon. At times, Asad is ordered to drive it so guards can rest. Qari rides a motorcycle to scout the way ahead. For four to five hours at a time, he rides through billowing dust clouds. He seems inhuman. Altogether we are a small group—two cars and a motorcycle—a modest, seemingly innocuous convoy moving across the Afghan countryside. Tracking us is next to impossible.

For the next three days, we live in the car and endure a bewildering and grueling journey. We traverse mountains and vast stretches of open desert where no roads exist. We cut across paved roads but never drive down them. And we pass through villages where local children bring the Taliban bread and tea. I don't know if they do so out of support or fear. I spend twelve hours a day lying in the back of the station wagon, forbidden from looking out the windows. Meals consist of pieces of flatbread handed to me by guards and sips from bottles of water. Bathroom breaks every few hours occur on deserted stretches where only our captors see me. The entire enterprise is designed to move us while arousing the least possible suspicion.

Throughout the journey, I try to talk with Atiqullah, still blindly hoping he will see us as human beings and quickly agree to a deal. During the first night of the drive, Atiqullah asks us if his guards are treating us well. We lie and say yes, fearing retaliation from Qari if we report his beating of Tahir. Long bouts of silence are interrupted by brief exchanges between Atiqullah and me. Attempting to be cautious, I try not to be cavalier in what I say and offend him.

After journeying all night, the sun rises and we continue driving. Atiqullah and I engage in a seemingly friendly conversation about our families, politics, and religion. We joke, laugh, and discuss life. He tells me the names of his children. I do my best to appease him. When we speak about politics, I say that the United States' dependence on Middle

Eastern oil has warped its foreign policy. When we speak about religion, I try to emphasize the commonalities between Islam and Christianity. I offer to read an English-language Koran if he can find one.

After I describe the book I am writing in an effort to prove I'm a journalist, Atiqullah announces he is taking us to Helmand, where he said we will be released in a few days.

"You will fly home from the British base," he tells me. I do not tell him that I had been on the base three weeks earlier. While researching my book, I had embedded with an American marine unit in northern Helmand Province. The unit arrived for what it thought was a police training mission. Instead, it took far more casualties in Afghanistan than it did in a tour of similar length in Iraq.

As we drive south, I fantasize about seeing the massive American-built hydroelectric dam and irrigation canals of Helmand. I'm getting desperate. I don't want to be the latest in a long line of Americans dating back to Josiah Harlan who experience initial success in Afghanistan, followed by spectacular failure. I tell him I plan to quit journalism if I survive. He encourages me to stay in the profession.

Knowing that Atiqullah is likely to disappear again with little warning, I try to extract promises from him. Under the Pashtunwali code of honor, a promise of protection should be ironclad. I begin by asking him to promise to protect the three of us. Atiqullah responds that he will protect only me.

"I will not kill you," he says. "You will survive."

I insist that he promise to save Tahir and Asad as well. "You will not kill the three of us," I say. "It has to be the three of us."

Atiqullah refuses, and I raise the issue over and over as the drive drags on. At one point, I suggest that he cut off my finger instead of harming Tahir and Asad. He replies that the Taliban are not criminals.

Later that day, he finally promises to protect all three of us. "I give you my promise," he says, as I lie in the back of the station wagon. "I will not kill any of the three of you."

Then he says, "Let's kill Asad first," and laughs. I have no idea what to believe.

On the second night of our drive across rural Afghanistan, we arrive in a darkened village. Its dirt streets are deserted and the cold air suggests we are at high altitude. A spectacular array of stars that is the brightest I have ever seen blazes overhead.

Atiqullah, Tahir, Asad, and the other Taliban get out of the car and go to sleep in a mosque. Under the Taliban's strict interpretation of Islam, I am not allowed in a mosque because I am a *kafir,* or nonbeliever. In the past, moderate Muslims have welcomed me in mosques.

I stay in the car with Akbar, the guard who speaks broken English and brought us food and clothes. Akbar whispers that Atiqullah has told him we will be exchanged within ten to fifteen days. I feel enormous relief. My patience, faith in Atiqullah, and statements about our worth appear to have paid off. Later that night, in another positive sign, I am brought into the mosque. Tahir has convinced the Taliban that it is wrong under Pashtunwali to make a guest sleep in the cold. After spending nearly twenty-four hours straight lying in the back of the car, I am exhausted.

On the third morning of our drive, Tahir's car breaks down. Atiqullah sells it and buys a second station wagon. Tahir is furious but powerless to stop him. During the wait for the new vehicle, Akbar and the guards hold an impromptu machine gun marksmanship competition. Akbar wins.

At dusk, we drive through a barren mountainous area and are met by another Taliban commander. A bone-thin man with a long beard and one arm, he gets into the driver's seat and guides us through barren, rock-strewn territory, steering the car and shifting gears with lightning-quick movements of his one hand.

I will later realize that we are making our way across rural Afghanistan with the help of a network of local Taliban fighters. They escort us from remote district to remote district. As we cross a particularly deserted area with no villages in sight, Atiqullah is so confident of the security vacuum that he allows me to walk outside at dusk. I stretch my legs as he and his men pray. Deserted, dirt-covered mountains surround us in every direction. We have crossed dozens of miles of Afghan government territory. I have not seen any signs of Afghan government or American forces in days.

I knew the vast security vacuum Atiqullah took advantage of was the product of years of American and Afghan government missteps. In 2002 and 2003, early decisions made by officials in Washington severely handicapped the effort to create a strong new Afghan government and national army. And then as Iraq unraveled in 2004 and 2005, Afghanistan was relegated to an afterthought.

A saying I first heard in postwar Bosnia—"Law and order first"—proved true in Afghanistan. Without a basic degree of security, political and economic reforms will all be handicapped. Local corruption as well will stymie reform.

For months in the spring of 2002, Defense Secretary Donald Rumsfeld clashed with Secretary of State Colin Powell over what role American troops should play in Afghanistan. The outcome of the debate was critical. The number of American troops initially deployed—and their marching orders—would set the tone for the international effort for years to come.

In a February 2002 White House meeting, Powell called for American troops to participate in the expansion of a 4,000-soldier international peacekeeping force then patrolling Kabul. In addition to hunting Taliban and Al Qaeda members, the expanded force would patrol Afghanistan's other major cities and enforce the decisions of Karzai's fledgling government.

Powell told me in a 2008 interview that he believed that all other reform efforts would fail in Afghanistan if adequate security was not established. "This would be the number one thing," he said, "You've got to have order in society."

Richard N. Haass, the former director of policy planning at the State Department, told me that informal conversations with European officials led him to believe the United States could recruit a force of 30,000 peacekeepers, half European, half American.

Rumsfeld and his aides were skeptical. Douglas J. Feith, then the Pentagon's undersecretary for policy, told me they feared European countries would not provide enough troops. They also wanted to avoid the

Clinton administration approach of having United Nations officials administer a postconflict country, arguing it would breed passivity and anger in the local population.

"There is a way to do nation building where the UN or someone else takes responsibility out of the hands of the local people and runs the place as a colony," Mr. Feith told me. "We were going against that model."

Feith said Pentagon officials hoped to train Afghan security forces, but not create such a large American troop presence in the country that it stoked what they saw as Afghans' historic resentment of foreigners.

Ali Ahmed Jalali, the country's interior minister from 2002 to 2005, told me in an interview that Afghan resentment of American troops was "a myth." After ten years of internecine civil war fueled by neighboring counties that funneled cash and weapons to each warring faction, he said, Afghans yearned in 2002 for the United States to step in. He said Afghans saw Americans as neutral because they had not strongly backed a side in the bloody civil war as had Pakistan, India, Russia, and Iran.

"They could not help themselves," he argued, referring to Afghans. "They were at war with themselves."

The deadlock dragged on for months.

In the late spring of 2002, Powell's proposal died. "The president, the vice president, the secretary of defense, the national security staff, all of them were skeptical of an ambitious project in Afghanistan," Haass said. "I didn't see support."

Powell said the United States did not make the sweeping commitment needed in Afghanistan. "We never quite bit the bullet that it was going to take all it could," he told me.

President Bush, though, remained skeptical. During the 2000 presidential election, he had said he opposed using U.S. troops for "nation-building." Following the 9/11 attacks and postinvasion chaos in Iraq, his views gradually shifted. He slowly accepted that if the United States toppled a regime it had to help create a new government and security force to fill the ensuing vacuum. By the time the shift in Bush's thinking occurred in Afghanistan, though, it was too late. In the end, the Bush administration deployed 8,000 troops to Afghanistan in 2002, with orders to hunt Taliban and Qaeda members and not to engage in peacekeeping or reconstruction. The 4,000-member international peacekeeping force did not venture beyond Kabul.

As an alternative, the United States and its allies hatched a loosely organized plan for Afghans to secure the country themselves. The United States would train a 70,000-member army. Japan would disarm some 100,000 militia fighters. Britain would mount an antinarcotics program. Italy would carry out reforms in the judiciary. And Germany would train a 62,000-member police force.

But that left no one in overall command. On the ground, holes quickly emerged in the American and European security effort.

The training of a new Afghan army proved difficult. When Robert Finn, the U.S. ambassador, reviewed the first Afghan National Army troops trained by the Americans in the summer of 2002, he was dismayed.

"They were illiterate," Finn told me. "They were at a much lower level than people expected."

American military officials told him that local Afghan commanders sent them their worst conscripts. In 2004, three years after the fall of the Taliban, the new force had only 21,000 soldiers. By comparison the United States had trained five times as many Iraqi soldiers three years after the fall of Baghdad.

The police were even more challenging. Seventy percent of the existing 80,000 officers were illiterate. Eighty percent lacked proper equipment, and corruption was endemic. Afghan police did not patrol. They set up checkpoints and waited for residents to report crimes. Afghans said they had to bribe the police, in fact, simply to report a crime.

Yet Germany, the country responsible for police training, dispatched only forty advisers in 2002 and 2003. They reopened the Kabul police academy and began a program designed to graduate 3,500 senior officers in three years. German officials said developing a core of skilled commanders was the key to reform, frustrating American officials who backed a large, countrywide training effort. Some American and European military units conducted ad hoc, two- to six-week training sessions around the country, but no comprehensive instruction occurred outside Kabul.

James Dobbins, the administration's former special envoy for Afghanistan, said Defense Department hopes that Afghans could quickly take responsibility for their own security proved unrealistic.

"The reason we are there is that these are failed states," said Dobbins, who had also served as special envoy to Haiti, Bosnia, Kosovo, and Somalia. "The thought that this can be quickly remedied has proved unjustified in most cases."

Confusion, infighting, and a failure to grasp the depth of Afghanistan's problems hampered the American reconstruction effort as well. After privately rejecting a large American troop deployment in Afghanistan, Bush publicly announced a vast American reconstruction effort. The move surprised Dobbins, who had lost the fight for more troops. In April 2002, Dobbins received a phone call as he sat in his State Department office. Mr. Bush, he was told, was planning to proclaim America's commitment to rebuild Afghanistan.

"I got a call from the White House speech writers saying they were writing a speech and did I see any reason not to cite the Marshall Plan," Dobbins recalled, referring to the American rebuilding of post–World War II Europe. "I said, 'No, I see no objections,' so they put it in the speech."

On April 17, Bush traveled to the Virginia Military Institute, where General George C. Marshall had trained a century before. In a speech that received scant media attention in the United States but raised hopes in Afghanistan, Bush promised a sweeping reconstruction effort.

"Marshall knew that our military victory against enemies in World War II had to be followed by a moral victory that resulted in better lives for individual human beings," Bush said. He called Marshall's work "a beacon to light the path that we, too, must follow."

Aware that Afghans felt his father's administration had abandoned the country following the 1989 Soviet withdrawal, he vowed to avoid the syndrome of "initial success, followed by long years of floundering and ultimate failure."

"We're not going to repeat that mistake," he said. "We're tough, we're determined, we're relentless. We will stay until the mission is done."

Within hours of Bush's speech, Rumsfeld announced his own approach at a Pentagon news conference. Again, he called for the Afghans to help themselves.

"The last thing you're going to hear from this podium is someone thinking they know how Afghanistan ought to organize itself," Rumsfeld said. "They're going to have to figure it out. They're going to have to grab ahold of that thing and do something. And we're there to help."

At the same time, the American government had nowhere near the personnel needed to carry out such a sweeping reconstruction effort. By 2001, the agency that had spearheaded the Lashkar Gah project decades back had stopped mounting construction projects. USAID officials initially opposed road building and other large infrastructure programs. They said they feared they would consume too much of their agency's limited staff and budget.

The end of the Cold War, complaints from Congress of tax dollars being poured down "foreign rat holes," and the failure of some foreign infrastructure projects prompted massive cuts at USAID. Criticism of failed foreign projects and a drive to privatize aid work by the Reagan and Clinton administrations had shrunk the agency from 3,000 Americans posted abroad in the 1980s to 1,000.

In the fall of 2003, sixteen months after the president's Marshall Plan speech, USAID had seven full-time staffers and thirty-five full-time contract staff members in Afghanistan, most of them Afghans. Sixty-one agency positions were vacant. Slashed in size, USAID had no experts to field.

Overall, from 2001 to 2005, Afghanistan received less assistance per capita than did postconflict Bosnia and Kosovo, or even desperately poor, postcoup Haiti in the 1990s. At the same time, reports began to emerge of endemic corruption in the Karzai government.

The invasion of Iraq only intensified the shortage of troops, civilian experts, and high-level focus. As Washington turned its attention to Baghdad, a massive troop imbalance emerged. In 2003, the United States had 250,000 troops in Iraq and 20,000 in Afghanistan. At the same time, Washington spent half as much money in Afghanistan as it did in Iraq—even though the countries are roughly the same size.

Former CIA officials told me that the agency's best, most experienced officers were shifted from Afghanistan to Iraq in late 2002 and early 2003. That reduced the United States' influence over powerful Afghan warlords who were refusing to turn over to Karzai's weak central government tens of millions of dollars they had collected in border crossing customs payments. The military's elite special operations units were also diverted to Iraq, along with remotely piloted drones.

"We were economizing in Afghanistan," a former military official, who spoke on condition of anonymity, told one of my colleagues in 2007. "Anyone who tells you differently is blowing smoke."

With a growing insurgency overstretching American forces in Iraq in 2005, Bush further reduced the American commitment in Afghanistan. He asked European officials to have NATO forces take over responsibility for securing southern Afghanistan. Condoleezza Rice, then secretary of state, cut American assistance to Afghanistan by $200 million.

The president and other senior officials saw Afghanistan as a success. They cited improvements in health care, roads, education, and the economy, as well as the quality of life in the cities and the holding of parliamentary elections. President Bush saw President Karzai as a more skilled leader than critics contended and saw no Afghan leader who could replace him. Reports of corruption by Karzai's brother surfaced, but no evidence emerged of Karzai's personal involvement

The then American ambassador in Kabul, Ronald Neumann, bluntly demanded that the $200 million in funding be restored and warned of a Taliban resurgence. In a February 2006 cable to his superiors, he predicted that the cut would handicap U.S. counter-narcotics programs, slow the training of the Afghan army, and make the "Taliban's role easier."

Neumann's warnings fell on deaf ears in Washington. President Bush and his top aides left Afghanistan to European troops and reduced aid levels. Troops from Britain—the historic enemy of the Pashtuns—led the NATO takeover of security in Helmand. Rumors that the West wanted to occupy Afghanistan, not rebuild it, gained credence among Afghans.

In the spring of 2006, the Taliban carried out their largest offensive since 2001. Suicide bombings quintupled to 136, roadside bombings doubled, and Taliban fighters seized control of large parts of southern

Afghanistan. NATO forces—many of whom were barred from engaging in combat by their government—were overmatched. American and NATO casualties rose by 20 percent. For the first time it became nearly as dangerous, statistically, to serve as an American soldier in Afghanistan as in Iraq.

In southern Afghanistan, many rural Pashtuns took up arms against corrupt officials appointed by the Karzai government and joined the Taliban. In eastern Afghanistan, the Taliban mounted cross-border attacks from Pakistan, the United States' purported ally.

As the Taliban confidently ferried us across the Afghan countryside in November 2008, it confirmed what I already knew. The haphazard, eight-year American effort in Afghanistan was a failure.

At sunset, the car stops and Atiqullah announces that we will have to hike through the mountains. A large American base blocks the path in front of us, he says. We protest, but he insists that we must walk. He promises that he will carry me on his back if I am unable to complete the journey.

The Afghan sandals I have been wearing since we were kidnapped will not be strong enough for a trek. The one-armed commander gives me a pair of worn loafers with the words "Made in East Germany" printed on the insole. A guard gives me his jacket.

As we walk, I understand why Western journalists grew enamored of anti-Soviet Afghan resistance fighters in the 1980s. Under a spectacular panorama of stars, we wind our way along a steep mountain pass. Emaciated Taliban fighters carry heavy machine guns with little sign of fatigue. Their grit and resilience seem boundless. I think about making a run for it but have not been able to freely talk with Tahir and Asad. If I run without warning, all three of us could be shot.

As the hike continues, I grow skeptical of Atiqullah's boasts. The man who has promised to carry me if needed proves to be in poor shape. On one of the steepest parts of the ascent, he stops, sits on a rock, and pants for air. Until now, I have only seen him seated on the floor or behind the wheel of a car. As we hike through the mountains, I see that Atiqullah is chubby, fat even, and does not have the same strength as his men.

Nine hours after we set out, the sun rises and the hike drags on. We are walking through low hills covered by orange dirt, an Afghan version of scrub brush, and the occasional tree. The landscape is lifeless. At dawn, we silently pass through a village and our guards ready their weapons for any problems. No one emerges from the houses.

Asad approaches me when the guards lag behind, points at the way ahead and whispers "Miran Shah." Miran Shah is the capital and largest town in North Waziristan, a Taliban and Al Qaeda stronghold in Pakistan's tribal areas. North Waziristan is the home of some of the Taliban's most hard-line members. If we are headed there, we are doomed.

Inside Afghanistan, the American military and Afghan government can carry out raids and put other pressure on our captors. In Pakistan's tribal areas, the Afghan Taliban have free rein. No American combat troops are present, the Pakistani government opposes American raids, and the Pakistani army turns a blind eye to the Afghan Taliban. In Pakistan, our captors can hold us as long as they please.

After eleven hours, our hike finally ends. The guards light a fire, and we warm our hands as we wait for a vehicle to pick us up. For a brief moment, there is camaraderie. We are all bone tired and happily crouch around the warm flames.

I stand up for a moment and walk back and forth to stretch my aching legs. I notice that none of the guards have their Kalashnikov assault rifles at their sides. Instead, one lies on the ground near Asad and another lies near where I am walking. If I move fast enough, I can grab a rifle, signal to Asad to do the same and we can kill Atiqullah and the guards.

As I walk back and forth, I glance at the rifle's safety mechanism but try not to draw attention to myself. I fired rifles while hunting for deer with my father as a teenager and fired them at ranges with my uncle in Colorado as a college student. I am not sure, though, how to disable a Kalashnikov's safety and shoot rounds. The stakes are enormous. Grabbing the weapon could lead to all three of us being immediately shot.

I look at Tahir and Asad and cannot catch their eyes. At the same time, I am not sure I am ready to kill anyone—something I have never done before. I decide to wait. I don't want to risk Tahir and Asad's lives without a clear signal from them.

Roughly fifteen seconds later, Atiqullah notices the situation and angrily orders his men to pick up their rifles. Later, I see that several guards are also standing watch on a nearby hillside. For months, I will think of the moment and wonder what would have happened if I had grabbed the rifle. On many days, I will wish that I had picked up the gun.

The one-handed commander arrives in the same station wagon. Atiqullah tells us that he has pretended to be a civilian and driven past the American base. We climb into the vehicle. Exhausted and anxious, I tell myself that Asad is wrong and Atiqullah is right. I tell myself that we are heading into southern Afghanistan, not Pakistan. I tell myself we will survive.

CRASH COURSE

Kristen, November 12, 2008

My mother comes back to New York with me. For the next seven months, we become intermittent roommates, a fact that in turns disturbs and comforts me. I haven't lived with my parents since I was a teenager. Now I'm married, approaching forty, and not eager to revert to an adolescent's existence. But over the months, our relationship grows. In fact, we relate to each other on a more mature level. She becomes, in the end, my hero—and David's, by a strange twist of circumstance.

We are met at Penn Station by two FBI agents. Cathy is tall, blonde, chatty. John is a large, solid man. An unfortunate incident years earlier involving a child captive and a grenade has left him deaf in one ear. Both are middle-aged. Cathy has two children. Dressed in high-heel pumps and stylishly coiffed, she looks like the consummate Manhattan career woman. One would never suspect she is a federal law enforcement agent.

They escort me to *The New York Times* building, an imposing glass skyscraper that fills a solid block on the edges of Times Square, right in the middle of Manhattan. An impromptu meeting has been called by the newspaper's executive editor, Bill Keller. In the bright, modern lobby, hundreds of miniature screens telegraph type from the newspaper's daily stories. Trees are encased in a glass courtyard opposite the reception desk. Security guards wave us through the sleek turnstiles to the elevator bank.

On the eighteenth floor, I am greeted by Arthur Sulzberger, Jr., the paper's publisher, and escorted into a large interior conference room. Senior staff members are assembled, including David's editors in the investigations unit, the foreign editor who occasionally sends him overseas, the newsroom's administrative editor, and its assistant general counsel, David McCraw. McCraw will become a daily fixture in my life for the next seven and a half months and the point person between me, the newspaper, and security experts. David's brother Lee is on speakerphone.

Everyone in the room appears to be seasoned and serious. I feel like I've stepped into a *New Yorker* cartoon but I'm not quite sure of the punch line. David has worked at the paper for twelve years. Most of his colleagues have known him longer than I have. I am overwhelmed by the number of people already involved in his case, and by the visible display of emotion before me. Several of his colleagues have tears in their eyes. Bill Keller calmly tells me that our family has the full support of *The New York Times* staff and that the paper will work with us to secure David's release. They will honor our family's wish to keep David's case out of the press. Lee and I have agreed this is the best course of action at the moment. We think, as the FBI cautioned us, that publicity will only increase David's value as a hostage. And we know that David would not want to be the subject of a news story.

Rejecting my first impulse to crawl under the conference table, I resolve not to be visibly intimidated or upset. There is already enough to handle without the paper having the sense that they need to manage my emotions as well. I want to know as much as possible about my husband's circumstances. So I maintain a tough front. I also feel that if I fall apart, the Taliban will win this crude game of psychological warfare. Falling apart is not an option, philosophically or practically. It is not quite clear how we will work with the newspaper to resolve David's situation or how decisions will be made. I have vague concerns that our agendas could diverge at some point. But for now, I am grateful not to be in this alone.

Cathy and John start preparing me for potential contact with David's captors. Back in my apartment downtown, we begin my first training session.

It is nearly 9 P.M. and I have not been in touch with my office all day. I imagine how *Cosmopolitan* might present this situation, were they to run a dramatic first-person account: "When Danger Calls" or "What's Holding Your Husband Captive?" But this is not a situation one can dress up with a provocative cover line.

In the event that I receive a call, the objective is to keep the captor or captive on the phone as long as possible, in the hope that the call can be traced. If the government can track the call, the military has a chance of going in and rescuing my husband, or so I'm told. That is, if he is still in Afghanistan. There is now some speculation that his captors will move him over the border, into the tribal areas of Pakistan where it is easier for the Taliban to hide and the American military cannot carry out a raid.

I am slightly amused by the "high tech" recording device that is attached to my phone. It looks like the Sony Walkman I jogged with in junior high school.

I learn the key points:

Ask if there is anything the captors or their "guests" require.

Humanize David by stating that you love him, miss him, etc.

Do not make any promises, but let the captors know you will try to work to meet their demands.

Avoid setting deadlines, but try to get them to commit to a time to talk again, ideally on a regular basis.

Repeat what the captors say to indicate that you are listening and also to extend the length of the call.

Be deferential. Do not tell them to bug off or get angry with them.

Ask if the captors can put David on the phone. (It's unlikely they would call with him in tow, but it never hurts to ask.)

Keep in mind, the Taliban are religious, "holy warriors."

Mention that you are praying for your husband.

Appeal to their sense of honor.

Cathy assumes the role of the kidnapper and we rehearse potential phone interactions for about an hour. We work off several scripts, mock conversations. The dialogue has been typed in capital letters and covers many of the talking points we discussed. We spread these out on the floor in front of the sofa. A tall, fair-haired New Yorker, Cathy looks and sounds nothing like a Taliban insurgent, so I hope I will be able to keep as calm when confronted with the real deal.

Cathy forewarns me about the following: "If the captors threaten to chop off a finger or kill David on the spot, don't believe them. Stay strong. Chances are slim that they will actually do this. Remember, their goal is not to kill David, but to extort money from you. They will play on your emotions to do so. Chances are, David is worth more to them alive than dead. Under the traditional tribal honor code of Pashtunwali—and out of sheer greed—they will treat him well and keep him alive."

Over time I will come to realize that kidnapping is a global industry. It is as much a business for the consultants as it is for the kidnappers, due in part to U.S. policy on the kidnapping of American citizens. The U.S. government does not pay ransom, release prisoners, or negotiate with terrorists. Yet many of its officials, off the record, advise private citizens to do so. This creates a demand for services that is often fulfilled by contractors. I have taken my first steps into a large and complicated shadow world of public and private agencies devoted to aiding the families of kidnap victims. It can be an extremely lucrative business; whether it is also an effective one, as far as David is concerned, remains to be seen.

The FBI is the lead agency in kidnappings and proves quite helpful in facilitating my understanding of how the situation and negotiations might unfold. Yet they cannot advise on funds, carry them, directly negotiate, or disclose classified information. They cannot declassify information that has been classified by another government agency. They are not even involved in securing the victim's release. In fact, they are only gathering information in hopes of prosecuting this crime in the future.

Over time our family becomes frustrated with the one-way flow of information. We often feel we're helping the FBI a great deal more than they're helping us, and we need someone dedicated to our goal, on our side. For these reasons, the paper along with Lee and I soon decide to hire an outside security firm to conduct negotiations.

I am suddenly thrust into an atmosphere of intrigue that is both political and personal. This is a sharp contrast to my daily life at the magazine, and to my entire world before November 10. My objective is to do everything possible to keep David alive, to leave no stone unturned in this process, and to stay sane and healthy.

Lee and I meet regularly with U.S. government officials, Pakistani officials, security contractors, and private advisers. I develop love-hate relationships with all of them. I eventually form a solid camaraderie with three people: my brother-in-law, the legal counsel for *The New York Times*, and one other individual, who is operating from overseas—a well-connected Irish national who tries to help via his own network in Pakistan.

As Cathy and John depart and my training comes to an end, I reflect on the long day behind me. I have embarked on a journey through uncertainty, intrigue, and duplicity. It will challenge all my previous understanding of what faith, love, and commitment mean. I think about David. My husband is a strong-willed, patient individual. Slow and steady wins the race is a phrase he often iterates. It is a philosophy of sorts. I am also comforted by the fact that David is most likely the sharpest person in the room, possessing a rare understanding of Afghan culture as well as human nature. And he is a cat with nine lives. I know he will do all he can to keep himself and his fellow captives alive. I know he wants to come home. This is my greatest hope.

Five days have passed since I first heard about the kidnapping, and I've made it through the initial shock. I am now on a steady incline—a steep learning curve. Everything seems beyond my control. I feel the need to gather as much information as possible to have some sense of David's experience and understanding of the region.

David gave me the password to his e-mail account during a recent conversation from Afghanistan before he vanished. He does this periodically, when Internet access is limited, so I can check his account for important e-mails and relay information to him over the phone.

I log in to his e-mail account from my laptop while sitting on the couch.

My sense of boundaries, privacy, and personal space are outweighed by the need to figure out what to do. I hope to find some clue about his situation. I look through the most recent e-mails for anything pertaining to Afghanistan or Logar Province, the site of the fateful interview. I am loosely familiar with some of David's sources. I search for names of people known to be in the region at present and for whom he has expressed trust in the past.

I write to Marin Strmecki, an Afghanistan expert and former adviser to the Bush administration who also has contacts in the Afghan government. I e-mail the Pakistani journalist and Taliban expert Ahmed Rashid, whom I met with David on a trip to Pakistan in March 2008. He has written several books about Afghanistan and Pakistan, including *Taliban* and *Descent into Chaos*. He is moved by our situation and provides his personal assessment of what, perhaps, the motivation of the kidnappers might be. He advises me to keep the case out of the public eye for the moment. He does not think the Taliban will succumb to moral pressure—the argument that holding a journalist is wrong—and he warns that David could become a political pawn or bargaining chip if his case receives media attention.

David's colleagues at the paper are tremendously supportive. Michael Moss, a friend of David's and fellow reporter in the paper's investigations unit, is monitoring David's biography on Wikipedia. He edits out any reference to his recent abduction. He also adds a section about David's coverage of Guantánamo Bay prisoners and stories on injustices in the Muslim world, in the hope that it will prove to the Taliban that David is a fair and impartial journalist, motivated to tell all sides of the story. Much to our dismay, someone in cyberspace keeps trying to reedit the page to inform readers of David's kidnapping.

David's editors and I begin reaching out to international advocacy groups to get their advice on whether to take the case public or keep it quiet. People from the Committee to Protect Journalists, Reporters without Borders, and Human Rights Watch brief us on situations with other journalists who were recently detained around the world. In most cases where the journalist has been held by a government or entity that is concerned with saving face, a public campaign has expedited the process of release. This was true for Alan Johnston, the BBC correspondent who was captured by a small militant group known as the Army of Islam in Gaza in 2007. In his case, Hamas put pressure on the Army of Islam to release him. His family and the BBC waged a global campaign for his release. He was freed four months later. But it appears that in cases where captives are being held by extremists with no direct link to a specific government, remaining private has proven more successful over time. This was true in the recent case of the Canadian journalist Melissa Fung, who was kidnapped in Afghanistan earlier this year. Her employer, CBC, requested a press blackout while negotiations were being conducted for fear that media attention would complicate matters or endanger her life. She was released on November 8—two days before David's abduction—after Afghan intelligence officials detained the kidnapper's mother.

One of David's colleagues, a reporter in Kabul, expresses a strong desire to go public. We speak nightly on Skype. This, the reporter says, is what they would want if they were in David's position. I have tremendous respect for this journalist, who is well versed in the nuances of Afghan culture. The reporter feels making the case public will pressure the Taliban to release David. The reporter tells me that most Afghans trust journalists and that recently Mullah Omar has declared that the Taliban should refrain from kidnapping journalists. The reporter thinks making a public campaign would speed David's release. That said, the FBI and government officials believe it is difficult to gauge if, or how, the Taliban will react to public pressure. Even though we disagree, David's colleague and I remain in close touch over the next few weeks because the bureau remains the point of contact for any initial communication from David's captors.

The day-to-day tasks and sense of responsibility inherent in managing the kidnapping are overwhelming, and despite many opinions offered, isolating as well. I am desperate to find someone who has navigated this emotional terrain. I immediately think of Mariane Pearl, the wife of Daniel Pearl, the *Wall Street Journal* reporter who was abducted and killed by militants in Pakistan after 9/11. No one around me will actually say it, but everyone fears a repeat of the Daniel Pearl murder.

A copy of Mariane's book about her husband, *A Mighty Heart*, stares back at me from a bookshelf in my apartment. After days of resisting, I finally pick up the book and flip through the pages. The very last line is a quote from a story my husband wrote after visiting the site of Daniel Pearl's imprisonment and execution in Pakistan. It is taken from his news account of the July 4, 2003, attack on a Shiite mosque in Quetta, led by the terrorist group Lashkar-e-Jhangvi, in which forty-eight worshippers were killed or mortally wounded. "Saying nothing, looking 'very relaxed' walking 'here and there' in the words of witnesses, the three unidentified gunmen killed and killed and killed here on Friday afternoon."

I take it as a sign to contact Mariane.

We speak over the phone.

Calm and straightforward, Mariane immediately tries to console me. She's heard about David's case through the grapevine and emphasizes that it is very different from Danny's.

"There were never any demands for Danny. We always thought it would be an act of terrorism." At this point, most people assume David's captors will want money or prisoners, because the captors have not gone public.

"Everyone will tell you not to go to Kabul. This is a personal decision." With this and all other decisions to be made, she tells me to follow my gut.

The newspaper provides me with contact information for Jere Van Dyk, an American journalist who was kidnapped in Afghanistan last year and held in the tribal areas for forty-five days. He has been free for six months. I hope to learn something from his experience: how he was treated by his captors; how he stayed alive; how he was released. I want to know as much as possible, regardless of unpleasantness and disturbing details. It is better to know what is within the realm of expectation than to be surprised and horrified later.

Two days after my FBI training session, I meet with Jere at his office on a Saturday afternoon. I am a bit anxious, not knowing who or what to expect. He is waiting in front of the building when I arrive. To my surprise and relief, I recognize him immediately. I had met him at an Afghan charity's fund-raiser several months before with David. Though still shaken from his experience, he is quite lucid in his account of events.

Kind and brave, he sets aside his own discomfort in retelling his experience to help me reach a better understanding of what might be happening to David.

Jere was set up by an Afghan colleague, a friend of twenty years who arranged his interviews and served as a translator. He tells me not to rule out the possibility that one or both of David's fellow captives were complicit in the kidnapping. If they are not involved, he tells me to expect that the captors will threaten to harm or kill them to pressure our family and David. As Afghans working with a foreign journalist, they are viewed as traitors and as such are in greater danger than David. I have never met the two men being held with David. To the best of my knowledge, this is the first time David is working with them.

Jere assures me that David will be treated well. "They won't hurt him physically," he says, invoking Pashtunwali, the honor code under which the Taliban must treat prisoners as guests.

"But," he warns, "the Afghans are master actors and manipulators." He assures me they will seize every opportunity to rile us up in hopes of eliciting an emotional response. He is very forthcoming about his own experience. I ask him not to hold back.

He confides that during his captivity he was psychologically traumatized as he confronted his own mortality daily. He feared he would be beheaded. His captors joked that they would sell his body parts on the black market if his family and colleagues failed to pay for his release. He was also told that upon his release, a suicide bomber would be present to detonate, killing everyone.

"I guarantee David is thinking about you all the time," he tells me. "This will keep him going." He says he invented a wife for himself during his captivity, because the Afghans would find it strange that a middle-aged man was not married.

He tells me that David is also probably thinking about escaping—something he thought about constantly. He advises me not to go public and not to use force to get David out, because it is too dangerous.

He does not know who it was that orchestrated his own release, but tells me there is a man who worked on his case, an Irish national who lives in the region named Michael Semple. Several people involved in his own case, Jere says, have told him that Michael saved his life. I have already heard about Michael Semple from David and his colleagues at the newspaper. He is a former European Union and United Nations official who was banned from Afghanistan by the current Afghan Karzai government for trying to negotiate with the Taliban. He believes there are moderate Afghans and Taliban—and that maintaining communication is essential. Michael has been working in Pakistan and Afghanistan for twenty-five years and is fluent in several local dialects. Irish by birth, he is Muslim and now resides in Pakistan.

Michael is also someone the newspaper has used as an analyst. The Kabul bureau turned to him for advice soon after David's abduction. He has provided his assessment of how our dilemma might play out and has analyzed at great and rather eloquent length the depth of our predicament based on his experience working to resolve other kidnappings. The Kabul bureau has forwarded these written accounts to me.

Jere provides me with Michael's personal e-mail and a suggestion of what to write to make my introduction.

Soon after I write to Michael, I receive his response:

> *Dear Kristen,*
>
> *Thanks for your note. I hope that you are bearing up in this difficult time. David's experience is both depressingly and reassuringly familiar. I am sure that there was much Jere could share with you.*
>
> *Inshallah, it will pass.*
>
> *Many friends are bringing all their influence to bear to ensure that David and colleagues get home soon.*
>
> *Regards*
>
> *Michael*

While his response is ambiguous, he is prompt in his reply. I decide to try to stay in regular contact with him. I feel his counsel will prove to be beneficial.

On my walk home toward the subway, I receive a call from a colleague at *Cosmo*. There is a celebrity cover shoot tomorrow and she is
calling to make sure all the details are in place: catering, lighting equipment, car service. It is quite a shift, but a welcome one, from the conversation of the past few hours. There is always a sense of emergency and
importance around these shoots, which are orchestrated with the thought
of preventing catastrophe. A celebrity no-show, a controlling publicist, a
stubborn hairstylist, insufficient catering—these are the things that instill
panic in my other world.

David has been held captive for nearly a week.

An individual who calls himself "Atiqullah" has been contacting the
Kabul bureau of *The New York Times*. He claims to be holding David
and company. I learn that the two men taken hostage with David are
Tahir, an Afghan journalist, and Asad, their driver. Tahir is married
with two wives and seven children. Asad is married with two kids.

After spending the weekend with his family, David's brother Lee has
returned to New York.

To keep us occupied and optimistic, the Kabul office and the FBI
suggest that Lee and I compose a list of proof of life questions (POL), for
David. They think another call will be forthcoming and want to ascer-
tain whether the individual on the line does indeed have possession of
David, Tahir, and Asad and that they are still alive.

This proves to be an arduous but somewhat amusing task. The gap
between our culture and that of the captors comes into focus. Our team
suggests that we compose questions that will elicit positive feelings from
David without offending his handlers. They suggest "What is the name
of your first pet?" Lee points out that their first pet was named Scotch,
as in "Scotch and soda." This is not going to work. The Taliban have
banned alcohol. The same is true for music, so references to the first song
we danced to at our wedding is also discouraged. I am advised against
mentioning anything related to our courtship—first kiss, first date—for
fear I will seem like a loose woman.

Finally, we settle on "What is the name of your best friend's daughter who was the flower girl at your wedding?" "What is your wife's maiden name?" And "What is your wife's birthday?"

The POL questions are relayed to Chris Chivers, an intrepid reporter and longtime friend of David's who has been answering the regular calls from David's captor Atiqullah. He then sends us written transcripts of each call along with bits of information he and his colleagues discover in their local outreaches. He relays the contents of the latest phone conversation and answers to our POL questions over a conference call with me and Lee.

According to the Taliban, David claims my last name is Lohan—as in "Lindsay Lohan." There is no proper translation of the name Mulvihill, apparently. I do not know if the Taliban are joking around or if David is protecting my anonymity. Perhaps all Irish American names sound the same in Pashto.

The answer to the best friend's daughter question comes back as "David does not have a daughter." True, David does not have a daughter. But his friend does, and they have neglected to provide her name. We make note of this for the next round: names do not translate.

The birth date they provide for me is correct. This is somewhat of a relief, but not enough to assuage my fears as I worry this information could easily be found on the Internet.

Fortunately, David provides a statement that puts me at ease: "Tell my wife that life is better here than when we were on a farm in India."

I am immediately transported back to our honeymoon in Rajasthan, one month ago. The first thing I recall is the birds, their insistent chant. We lived with three pigeons that were in a perpetual state of agitation. They flew through the halls every time we moved between rooms. In the otherwise idyllic desert setting—the rolling hills of Rajasthan, the blooming roses—the wildlife was very aggressive. Atomic geckos jumped from window frames. Bugs worthy of *National Geographic* close-ups emerged at night when we donned our headlamps: walking sticks, damselflies, beetles. Some kind of creature howled—I assumed it was a wolf, but David brushed it off as a stray dog. The housekeeper clarified it for us when we inquired about the strange noise, "Ah, yes. The jackals." We joked that this was the least romantic honeymoon ever.

We neglected to gather a few details prior to our visit, namely that temperatures were unusually high that month. With temperatures soaring above 100 degrees, we relied on a generator to cool the place in the late afternoon and slept outdoors on the roof when it was impossibly hot. It was quite beautiful. We had a makeshift four-poster bed, completely encased in mosquito netting. Mornings we would awake to the sound of singing birds—and the errant pigeons, clearly annoyed by our presence. Their song was quite distinctive. It sounded like they were chanting something . . . a protest. Superstitious, I spent days trying to decode it.

"Listen to the birds," I said over breakfast one morning. "It sounds like they are saying, 'Let's all escape, let's all escape!'

"Wow, are you that miserable here?" David asked.

"No, but listen to them. They're saying 'Let's all escape'—hear it? They have British accents," I jokingly insisted.

He looked at me like I was slightly crazed—of course, due to the sweltering temperature I could claim heatstroke.

"Maybe they are a reincarnation from the colonial era," I mused, referring to the British occupation during the Raj. He smiled and laughed reluctantly. He had to admit, it did sound that way. I hoped it was not some premonition of trouble ahead.

David and I lived in a large expanse of rooms at the house, while the staff all slept in one room. The farm had an on-site groundskeeper, a cook, a sweeper, and a gardener. All this would cost a fortune elsewhere, but in India it was a matter of a few dollars a day. According to societal norms, we were supposed to ignore them and go about our business. We lacked the ability and desire to do so.

"Life is better than when we were on a farm in India." I think about the intent behind David's statement. The farm did have a generator and an in-house cook. It was quite large, with modern plumbing and a green yard, which was a stark contrast to the rugged desert terrain. I take this to mean David is being fed and taken care of and that, perhaps, he is sitting in a home with electricity. The reference to "better than India"

makes me think that he may indeed have been moved to a location beyond Afghanistan—perhaps Pakistan. I think he may be playing on the
old rivalry between India and Pakistan. Telling his captors Pakistan is
better than India would be a smart move, and I would not put it past
David to realize this. Still, I am terrified by the thought that he has been
moved into Pakistan.

David took me along for a brief trip to Lahore, Pakistan, in the spring
of 2008 just after he had finished reporting on the country's presidential
election, after Benazir Bhutto's assassination. It was my first and last visit
there. "The cultural center of Pakistan." This is how David referred to
Lahore, known for its poets, artisans, and parks.

We drove into the city on a March day to discover that a twin suicide bomb attack had killed four people at Pakistan's Navy War College
in the center of the city hours before our arrival. We stayed at the Pearl
Continental in a room in the back, away from the parking lot and car
entrance as David had requested as a security precaution. We never went
anywhere during our three-day stay without our driver close by. And we
never lingered anywhere for very long.

The air in Lahore was thick and smoky, burnt. I was never certain of
the source: coal, exhaust?

We spent a day with Ahmed Rashid and his wife and later toured a
modern, American-style university and the National College of Arts. The
students all spoke English and were inquisitive, friendly, and eager to talk
to us. On our drive to Badshahi Mosque, a main tourist attraction, women
in transit appeared curious and tried to make contact with me. Many of
them would lift their veils and smile from the backs of motorbikes. Whole
families of five rode on one bike—the babies relegated to the handlebars
or their mothers' laps. Occasionally, they would stare quizzically at my
Western uniform of jeans, a khaki jacket, and a loosely tied headscarf.

As I try to understand the circumstances around David's kidnapping, I
am thankful to have had this experience. For me, it reinforces the reality
that there are decent, moderate people in Pakistan and that they, more than
anyone, are victims of violence and unrest brought on by a few extreme
individuals who seek to limit their freedoms. I am terrified at the thought

that David has been transported into the tribal areas of Pakistan. The recent calls to the Kabul bureau have been traced to this area.

I know that unlike Lahore, it is a lawless region, one in which the United States has no jurisdiction or ground presence.

The same day as the proof of life questions are relayed, we receive word from the captors that David has told them he is worth $10 million. Lee raises an eyebrow at this. "Oh, really," he says. They also want ten prisoners released from U.S. custody in Bagram and Guantánamo Bay, Cuba, in exchange for David's freedom and that of Tahir and Asad. They claim that when David was being imprisoned in Bosnia several Serbian military officers were released from custody in the negotiations to free him. This is a complete fabrication, and these are demands we know we can never meet.

We are advised by the FBI that over time and with regular communications, the demands should drop and shift from money and prisoners to a strictly financial transaction.

There is speculation that the group holding David is part of the Haqqani network, a terrorist faction of the Taliban that have been linked to Bin Laden and Al Qaeda. They are able to operate in Afghanistan, Pakistan, and the tribal areas. In recent months, they have taken responsibility for the January 2008 bombing of the Serena Hotel in Kabul. The Kabul bureau has been trying to make contact with Abu Tayyeb, the Taliban commander that David planned to interview. They, along with members of the FBI, now think Atiqullah and Abu Tayyeb are one and the same, as their voices and accents are strikingly similar. And they also believe that David and his colleagues were set up. They think Abu Tayyeb may have handed David over to the Haqqani network, or that he is working on their behalf.

The mention of prisoners reinforces our belief that David's case should remain private. Publicity, we feel, will only increase his political value. We fear more than anything that he will become a public relations pawn or be used by the Taliban as an example of the power they hold in the region.

A day after the Taliban's demands are relayed, Lee and I are contacted by the Department of Defense through the FBI's New York office. Officials there are once again asking whether our family will give approval for a raid if the military is able to locate David, Tahir, and Asad and feels confident it can get them out alive.

At this point, Lee and I are willing to grant them permission. But we do not want to make the decision without talking to David's parents, knowing that the risk involved could be great.

From the seventeenth floor office at the *Times* that has now been assigned to us for our regular visits to the newspaper, we set up a conference call with David's parents, Harvey and Carol. We explain our current understanding of the situation. There is a pause, then Harvey speaks. "I am very confident that you are both doing everything possible to secure David's release and have his best interest at heart," David's father says. "You do not need to ask me for approval going forward. I trust you will do what is best. You have my full support in making whatever decisions you see fit."

David's mother agrees.

For the first time in days, I feel tears well up. As a new wife, having the endorsement of David's parents means a lot. I am thankful for their support and trust. And it is a relief not to bear the burden of this decision alone.

Lee and I tell the FBI and DOD that if a raid is feasible, our family supports it.

THE EMIRATE

David, November 18, 2008

A young Taliban driver with shoulder-length hair gets behind the wheel of the vehicle. Glancing at me suspiciously in the rearview mirror, he starts the engine and begins driving down the left-hand side of the road. It is some sort of prank, I hope, some jihadi version of chicken—the game where two drivers speed toward each other in the same lane until one loses his nerve. If he's not playing a game, which lane he drives down shows what country we are in. If he continues driving on the left, we have crossed into Pakistan. If he drives on the right, we are still in Afghanistan.

A mile down the road, a traffic sign appears in Urdu, the official language of Pakistan.

We're in Pakistan, I think to myself. We're dead.

Instead of taking us to Helmand as he promised, Atiqullah has brought us to Pakistan's tribal areas, an infamous belt of Taliban-controlled territory. In the months ahead, I will learn that the fundamentalist Taliban state the United States purportedly toppled in 2001 is alive and thriving. The loss of thousands of Afghan, Pakistani, and American lives and billions in American aid has merely moved the Islamic emirate a few miles east into Pakistan, not eliminated it.

During the 1980s, the American, Saudi, and Pakistani governments used the tribal areas as a base to train hard-line Islamic guerrillas and launch cross-border raids on Soviet forces in Afghanistan. Thirty years later, the area's roughly 3 million people are isolated, impoverished, and dominated by religious conservatives—and form a perfect base for the Taliban and Al Qaeda.

Through seven years of reporting in the region, I have pitied captives imprisoned here. It is arguably the worst place on earth for an American to be a hostage. The United States government has virtually no influence and is utterly despised. Since 2004, dozens of missiles fired by American drones have killed hundreds of militants and civilians. The Taliban have held Afghan, Pakistani, and foreign hostages in the area for years, seemingly immune to outside pressure.

"We're in Pakistan," I say out loud in the car, venting my anger.

Atiqullah, our kidnapper, laughs, and the driver appears surprised.

"How does he know it's Pakistan?" the driver asks.

"Because you're driving down the left-hand side of the road," I answer.

"How do you know that?" the driver asks, immediately suspicious. "When were you in Pakistan before?"

Atiqullah smiles and appears amused by the conversation. He knows from our conversations and my passport that I have been to Pakistan many times on reporting trips. For years, I have watched the Pakistani government largely stand by as the Taliban murder hundreds of tribal elders and seize control of the area. An abstract foreign policy issue is now deeply personal. When my wife and family learn that I am in the tribal areas, their distress will increase exponentially. They will not expect me to return.

The mountainous area that spans the border represents the gravest single security threat the United States faces. Seven years after being driven from Afghanistan, the Taliban and Al Qaeda have reestablished their training camps in the area. Terrorism experts I have interviewed predict that the next major terrorist attack on the United States will come from the tribal areas of Pakistan.

We arrive in a large town, and I notice a sign that says "Wana" in English. Wana is the capital of South Waziristan, the most radical of the seven administrative districts that make up the tribal areas. Its most powerful Taliban commander is Baitullah Mehsud, a widely feared Pakistani militant blamed for the assassination of Benazir Bhutto and a wave of suicide bombings that killed or wounded an estimated 5,000 Pakistanis over the last year.

We stop in the main bazaar, and I am left alone in the car with the young driver. Desperate rationalizations swirl through my mind. Our captors want a ransom and prisoners. Killing us gets them nothing. The three of us will survive. These are all delusions, of course. Simply getting us this far is an enormous victory for the Taliban. We could be held here for months or killed.

Outside the car, dozens of Pakistani tribesmen and Afghan and foreign militants mill around. Each carries a Kalashnikov assault rifle on his shoulder. Some wear thick black turbans or white prayer caps on their heads. Others wear camouflage jackets. All appear grim faced and menacing. A man with a large turban stops, peers at me in the backseat, and asks the driver a question in Pashto. The driver looks at me and says a sentence that I think includes the word for martyr. I tell myself the driver has said I am on my way to heaven.

Atiqullah gets back into the car and I feel relief for no rational reason. He has kidnapped us, but more and more I desperately view Atiqullah as my protector, the man who will continue to treat us well as other militants call for our heads.

As we drive deeper into the tribal areas, we enter a region that has been battered and neglected by the Pakistani government—and the world—for centuries. A backwater roughly the size of Massachusetts, the tribal areas are dominated by Pashtun tribes known for their independence, criminality, and fighting skills. Afghan, British, and Pakistani forces have all failed to gain firm control of the area. For centuries, bandits, smugglers, and kidnap rings have used it as a base.

The tribes that inhabit the Pakistani side of the Afghanistan-Pakistan border region are the most independent of the Pashtun belt. In Afghanistan, the Pashtun tribes have generally accepted the writ of the national government, in large part because they played a large role in choosing it. For Pashtuns, the term "Afghan" is a synonym for the word "Pashtun." Tajiks and other ethnic groups that inhabit northern and western Afghanistan, in turn, view "Afghan" as a broad term applying to all inhabitants of president-day Afghanistan.

On the Pakistani side of the border, the Pashtuns have long been alienated from the national government and neglected by it. Pashtuns complain that Punjabis, who are the country's largest group and make up 45 percent of the population, dominate Pakistan's national government. Pashtuns are Pakistan's second largest ethnic group and represent 15 percent of Pakistan's people.

The true origins of the Pashtuns are a mystery. They are one of the least studied ethnic groups in the world and follow an oral tradition in which history is passed from generation to generation in folktales and sayings. According to Pashtuns, all tribes trace their lineage back to a single man, Qais Abdur Rashid, who traveled from present-day Afghanistan to seventh-century Arabia, met the prophet Muhammad, and converted to Islam. The names of his descendants are reflected in the names of Pashtun tribes, with "Ahmedzai," for example, meaning "sons of Ahmed" and "Yusufzai" meaning "sons of Yusuf."

Researchers believe that the present-day Pashtun tribal structure goes back thousands of years. For millennia, Pashtun elders ruled tribes. Elders are expected to be well spoken, generous, and brave, and are selected on the basis of family lineage and the individual's ability to help his tribe flourish. If they protect and obtain wealth for a village, their standing soars. If they fail, they lose face. Lengthy jirgas—meetings of tribal elders—settle disputes by consensus and strive to prevent blood feuds. And wealthy tribal elders support impoverished tribesmen by hiring them as field workers. Elders also punish tribesmen who disobey their rulings or commit a crime. In its own way, the tribal system creates order.

The division that foreign visitors noticed in "Little America" between educated urban Pashtuns and conservative rural Pashtuns spans the Pashtun belt and includes those in the tribal areas of Pakistan as well. Pashtuns from a group of tribes known as the Durrani are generally more urbanized and liberal and more accepting of central government rule. Pashtuns from a group of tribes known as the Ghilzai tend to be more disenfranchised, live in rural areas, resist central government rule, and more numerous than the Durrani. Many of the Taliban leaders in Afghanistan and Pakistan are Ghilzai, while many current and past government leaders, including Karzai, are Durrani. While some western scholars highlight the division, the Taliban and many Pashtuns deny that such a rivalry exists.

The creation of the tribal areas dates back to the hated 1848 British demarcation of the 1,600-mile border between Afghanistan and Pakistan, which divided the Pashtuns. The British annexed six Ghilzai-dominated mountain districts along the border with Afghanistan and then declared them "tribal areas" as opposed to "settled areas" under firmer administrative control. Hoping to subdue the area's dozen major tribes, British colonial officials enacted an indirect system of government.

Under the system, British-appointed administrators known as political agents maintained loose control of the tribal area's inhabitants by applying a system of collective punishment. When an individual tribesman committed a crime or defied the government, political agents negotiated only with tribal elders—known as maliks—and demanded that the tribe arrest the wanted person. If that failed, the political agent used the Frontier Corps—a British-paid militia frequently made up of members of rival tribes—to punish a tribe en masse by withdrawing government funds or bulldozing homes. After a carefully calibrated punishment, the status quo resumed.

Twelve years after the creation of the new system of collective punishment, British officials complained that it was failing to stop raids and kidnappings from the tribal areas into Dera Ismail Khan and other nearby towns. "They kidnapped children from the very town of Dera Ismail Khan and demanded exorbitant sums for their release," Brigadier General Chamberlain complained in an 1860 government report. "And if the relations of the captives delayed to ransom them, they cut off their fingers and sent them to their relations to move their tender feeling."

Unbowed, the British launched a series of punitive military campaigns to try to again pacify the tribal areas. Thousands of tribesmen and hundreds of British and Indian soldiers perished in battles that achieved mixed results.

In 1897, an ambitious young British army officer named Winston S. Churchill served as a journalist in an expeditionary force dispatched to punish rebellious tribes. The result was Churchill's first nonfiction book: *The Story of the Malakand Field Force: An Episode of Frontier War.* Littered with openly racist statements, the book catapulted the future British prime minister and World War II leader to fame. It described Pashtuns as barbarians who showed a remarkable ability to embrace modern technology and brutally employ it.

"To the ferocity of the Zulu are added the craft of the Redskin and the marksmanship of the Boer," Churchill wrote. "At a thousand yards the traveler falls wounded by the well-aimed bullet of a breech-loading rifle. His assailant, approaching, hacks him to death with the ferocity of a South-Sea Islander. The weapons of the nineteenth century are in the hands of the savages of the Stone Age."

The book accurately captures a Pashtun tendency toward deeply destructive infighting. In one passage, Churchill describes the fate of a successful tribal leader, referring to him as a "Pathan," the Urdu term for Pashtun.

"His success is now his ruin," Churchill wrote. "A combination is formed against him. The surrounding chiefs and their adherents are assisted by the village populations. The ambitious Pathan, oppressed by numbers, is destroyed. The victors quarrel over the spoil, and the story closes, as it began, in bloodshed and strife."

A Pashto proverb that I had heard conveys the same sentiment: "When the one profits," it states, "the other's house is ruined."

The British struggles continued long after Churchill's departure. In one widely heralded case, a Pashtun from North Waziristan known as the Faqir of Ipi led a tribal rebellion for more than twenty years. From 1937 until his death in 1960, he successfully eluded capture by the British and Pakistani governments. At one point in the 1940s, 40,000 British and Indian troops—backed by squadrons of British airplanes—hunted him.

Despite complaints that the policy kept the area impoverished and isolated, Pakistan retained the system of collective tribal punishment after it won independence from Britain in 1947. Under the country's new constitution, Pakistani laws did not apply in the tribal areas unless specifically decreed by Pakistan's president. Its people were barred from voting in Pakistan's national elections. The 3 million people of the tribal areas had no elected representatives in Pakistan's parliament.

Over the next twenty years, many tribal elders pocketed development funds doled out to them by Pakistani-government-appointed political agents. In order to maintain power, they discouraged education and most contact with the outside world. The result was that an estimated 83 percent of the men and 97 percent of the women in the tribal areas were illiterate—vastly higher rates than in the rest of Pakistan, where roughly half the population could read.

In the 1980s, the United States and Saudi Arabia poured approximately $1 billion a year into weaponry and military aid to mujahideen fighters in the tribal areas. Pakistan's premier military intelligence service, the Directorate of Inter-Services Intelligence, or ISI, oversaw the distribution of guns and cash. Acting as kingmaker, the ISI turned young Afghan and Pakistani fighters into hugely powerful military commanders, slashing the power of Pashtun tribal elders. Pakistani intelligence officials feared that the tribal elders wanted to secede from Pakistan, join their Pashtun brethren in Afghanistan, and create "Pashtunistan."

At the same time, Pakistani intelligence officials introduced a new interpretation of Islam that further undermined the strength of the Pashtun tribal elders. With assistance from Pakistani intelligence officials, Saudi Arabia constructed religious schools that created another source of authority—fundamentalist Wahhabi Islam. When Soviet forces withdrew from Afghanistan in 1989, three sets of power brokers now existed in the tribal areas: young mujahideen commanders, radical clerics, and traditional elders.

In the 1990s, Pakistani intelligence officials used the tribal areas as one of several bases from which they funded, trained, and dispatched militants to fight Indian forces in Kashmir, the disputed region over which Pakistan and India have fought three of their four wars. Hard-line religious schools also spread across other parts of Pakistan. The schools, in turn, supported religious political parties that called for the establishment of Islamic law across Pakistan. They also indoctrinated young Afghan refugees.

In 1994, a group of young Afghans who had been educated in conservative religious schools in Pakistan founded the Taliban movement. First emerging in southern Afghanistan, the name they adopted—"Taliban"—meant "students" in Pashto. They attacked warlords in Kandahar who they accused of rampant criminality and corruption. With the backing of the ISI, the Taliban took Kabul in 1996 and established what Pakistani intelligence officials considered a friendly regime.

The next year, the Pakistani government finally granted the inhabitants of the tribal areas the right to vote in national elections. Civilian political parties, though, were barred from campaigning in the tribal areas. As a result, fundamentalist clerics aligned with Pakistan's religious parties and schools swept elections in 1997 and 2002. The clerics' dominance allowed the ISI to continue to use the tribal area as a training base.

As Atiqullah moves us farther into the tribal areas, I know we are entering an area cut off from the rest of the world where xenophobia and conspiracy theories are rife. One particularly poetic phrase that Churchill penned a century earlier has lingered in my mind for months. Since 2001, I have felt it applies to how effectively terrorist attacks sow fear, division, and mistrust.

"Every man's hand is against the other," he wrote, "and all against the stranger."

Our first home in the tribal areas is in Miran Shah, the capital of North Waziristan. We arrive at night and I see nothing of the town.

Our new quarters consist of two large sleeping rooms that look out onto a small courtyard. One even has a small washroom, separate from the toilet, for showering. Makeshift pipes have been fastened to the walls.

The next morning, I go to the bathroom and make myself vomit in the hope it will somehow pressure our captors. An amiable older man who is a local doctor visits soon after. He speaks basic English and seems puzzled by my presence in Miran Shah. I intentionally tell him I am a journalist with *The New York Times* and hope he might somehow help us. Later, I learn that he did speak with local people about me. As a result, I am banned from seeing other doctors.

All day, a parade of random Pakistani militants stops by the house to stare at us. I again feel like an animal in a zoo. Among them is a local Taliban commander who introduces himself as Badruddin. I will later learn that he is the brother of Sirajuddin Haqqani, the leader of the Haqqani network, one of the most powerful Taliban factions in the region. Miran Shah is its stronghold. Their network of commanders guided us across eastern Afghanistan. They are known for discipline, ruthlessness, and ties to foreign militants.

Badruddin, a tall, talkative man with brown hair, brown eyes, and a short beard, appears to be in his early thirties. He announces that he is preparing to make a video of us to release to the media. He smiles as he shows me a video on his camera of a French aid worker who was kidnapped a week before us as he walked to his office in Kabul. He is in chains and appears to have welts on his face. The aid worker implores his family and friends to save him.

"It's a nightmare," he says. "I really beg you to pay."

I ask if Tahir and I can speak alone with Atiqullah, who I believe is the more moderate commander. I tell Atiqullah we should not make the video. The American and Afghan governments are more likely to agree to a secret prisoner exchange, I say, than a public one. I also know that if the Taliban set a public deadline and it is not met, they will enforce it brutally. Failing to do so would be a public loss of face, something deeply shameful to Pashtuns and all Afghans.

Trying to reduce their expectations, I tell him it would be far easier to get prisoners from the main Afghan-run prison outside Kabul in the town of Pul-i-Charkhi. If the Taliban demand prisoners from the American-run detention centers at Guantánamo Bay and Bagram, they will never succeed. I am not worth that much, I tell him, and he should compromise. I do not say it but I also want to spare my family the pain of seeing me in a hostage video. I know if a video arrives they will fear it shows an execution. To my surprise, Atiqullah agrees.

"I am one of those kinds of people," he says at one point. "I am one of those people who like to meet in the middle."

In the afternoon, he announces that Tahir, Asad, and I will be allowed to call our families tonight to prove we are alive. Atiqullah tells me to emphasize during the call that he wants to reach a deal quickly. He continues to cover his face with a scarf. I hope that means he plans to release us and does not want us to be able to identify him to American or Afghan officials.

Ignoring the countless lies Atiqullah has already told me, I maintain some type of hope. This is my first brush with a dynamic that will unfold multiple times in captivity. My mind's tendency to grasp at straws despite grim evidence to the contrary.

I spend the rest of the day nervously scribbling a list of things I want to say to my wife. I add items and then cross them out. I want to ease my family's fears that I am being tortured, but I also want to do everything possible to free us. I am not sure I will have another chance to speak with Kristen.

THE TALIBAN CALL COLLECT

Kristen, November 19, 2008

T he phone rings at 6 A.M. The FBI alerts me that my husband will be calling home. Within a half hour, a group of six agents floods our small apartment in lower Manhattan: a translator, two case agents, the two-person negotiation team, and a victim's counselor. With the exception of Cathy, who led my phone training session over a week ago, all the faces are new to me.

Jim is now the lead agent and investigator on our case. A former Port Authority policeman, he lost several colleagues in the attacks on the World Trade Center on 9/11. When a national Joint Terrorism Task Force was established in the aftermath, he was eager to join the team. The lead FBI negotiation expert, Phil, is a former hostage himself. As a teenager, he and his family were held in their home for a brief but intense period of time. The ordeal ended when Phil distracted the armed hostage taker, a high school student, so his family could escape. Phil was shot in the process, but recovered. I am struck by the fact that each individual on the team has been motivated by personal loss or direct experience of kidnapping. We huddle together around the living room sofa and review the training points.

The FBI learned of the imminent call from the newspaper's Kabul bureau. Atiqullah has alerted Chris Chivers at the Kabul bureau that David will be permitted to phone home. Atiqullah says that when they call, I should look at the number that appears on caller ID and call him back at my own expense, as his phone card is running out of credits. This astounds me. In addition to being ruthless, the Taliban are also cheap! This is absurdly amusing. Finding humor in the most morbid and extreme circumstances actually keeps me from falling apart and gives me some minor sense of control.

At 8:30 A.M., the phone rings. It's David. We have been sitting by the phone for two hours and yet the call still manages to take me by surprise. It's very odd to be sharing this personal moment with a roomful of people I have only just met. I feel like our relationship, all our vulnerabilities, are on display. Oddly, though, this helps me maintain composure. There's nothing like a crowd to ensure a steady performance. As instructed, I don't answer and call David back on the number that appears on caller ID.

It is a relief to hear my husband's voice, to know he is still alive. He sounds shaken, but his voice is strong, his thinking clear. This puts me at ease. I return the favor by maintaining composure for him. I realize this may be the only time we speak and I want to convey a sense that I am holding it together and will not give up, that I can handle this situation.

"Kristen?" David says, "Kristen?"

"David," I say, "It's Kristen, I love you."

"Kristen?" he asks.

"Yes?" I say.

"I love you, too," he says, "Write these things down, okay?"

"Okay," I say.

"Do you have a pen?" David asks.

"I have a pen," I say.

"I'm—we are being treated well," David says.

"Being treated well," I repeat.

"Number one," David says.

"Number one," I repeat.

"Number two," he says. "Deal for all three of us, all three of us, not just me. The driver and the translator also; it has to be a deal for all three of us."

"Deal for all three of us," I repeat. "The driver and the translator as well."

"Okay. Do not use force to try to get us," David says.

"Do not use force," I repeat.

"Four," he says.

"Yes," I say.

"Make a deal now or they will make it public," he says. "They want to put a video out to the media."

I repeat his words back to him.

"It will make it a big political problem," he says. "They want to do it now," David says. "They don't want to make it public. They want—they want to make a deal now."

"Want to make a deal now, okay," I repeat.

"'Cause they don't want, they don't want a big political problem with the leaders on both sides," he says. "They don't want the elders to know."

"Okay, they don't want elders to know," I say, "and they do not want problems on our side, okay."

"Make a deal, just make a deal quickly," David says. "Please make a deal quickly."

He pauses for a moment.

"They said I can't call you again," David says. "They want a deal now and I can't call you again."

"You cannot call me again," I repeat. "I love you. I love you, honey."

"I love you, too," he says. "Tell my family I'm sorry."

"Your family is here," I say. "Lee's here with me."

"I'm sorry," David says. "I'm sorry."

"Lee's here," I say, trying to reassure him.

"I'm sorry about all this," he repeats.

"It's going to be all right," I say. "I love you. I am praying for you every day."

I say I want to make sure I understand what they want. There is a pause and David relays a message from Atiqullah. He says the Kabul bureau should talk to him and negotiate with no one else. David says Atiqullah will call the Kabul bureau after we hang up and provide a list of demands.

"What is the deal? What is the deal?" I ask, trying to extend the call and get specifics. "Is it, what is the exchange? What do you want?"

David again says that Atiqullah will give his demands to the Kabul bureau.

"We are very concerned about you," I say. "And we love you and we're praying for you."

David repeats that Atiqullah will provide his demands to the Kabul bureau.

"Okay, okay," I say, "and how are you?"

There is a beep and the call ends abruptly.

After I catch my breath, our team reviews the conversation. I let them know which parts of the conversation were truly David—namely, the desire to make a deal for all three—and which seemed scripted. They are very optimistic about the call and my performance. I am patted on the back for my composure. It seems I have discovered a new skill set—one that enables me to be calm under pressure. My worst nightmare would be bursting into tears in front of a roomful of people.

At the same time, I feel completely enraged at my husband's captors and utterly confused. If they want to make a deal so quickly, why won't they list their demands? This is all part of a sick psychology on the captors' part: make the family feel totally responsible and utterly without control. Demand they meet demands, but fail to name them. I begin to wonder if the "make a deal quickly" was a signal from David, that perhaps he would be moved or sold up the food chain to a more powerful group of criminals or terrorists. This, I am told, often happens in kidnappings in Afghanistan.

My mind is racing, and I feel trapped. Our one-bedroom apartment is swarming with people. Mismatched dining and living room chairs are scattered all around. There doesn't seem to be enough space or air in our modest living room to accommodate them all. My mother steps in and urges everyone to clear out. She encourages me to go to work to take my mind off the situation—seemingly impossible—or at least to pass the time. I wonder how I can possibly do that.

Our case agents as always advise me to take care of myself. This, they say, is my number one responsibility. I will be better able to help my husband if I am in good physical shape. "Do not forget to eat, try to sleep. A call could arrive at any moment. You need to be prepared. This is the best thing you can do for your husband. David is going to need you to stay strong now and especially for when he returns." I will hear these directives repeatedly over the next few months.

As I walk to the subway, questions reel through my mind: Should I just jump on a plane to Kabul? Is it wrong for me to continue the routines of daily life? Am I being cowardly, or selfish, seeking refuge in my work? Practically speaking, I need to keep working. We have burned through our savings over the past few months between the wedding and honeymoon. And our country is facing the worst economic downturn in decades. Even in the fog of this crisis, I realize I need to keep my job as long as possible. In terms of my own sanity, I know it does me no good to stay in the apartment all day and sit by the phone. The last thing I want to admit to is that I am a victim as well, captive to a call that might or might not come. If I give up on daily activities, his captors will have succeeded in thoroughly disrupting our lives. I do not want them to win. Anger at the creeps holding David and his colleagues propels me forward.

I feel relieved when I ascend the subway steps to 57th Street in Midtown. I give myself a mental pat on the back as I approach the Hearst Publications building, where *Cosmopolitan* is headquartered, and pass through the shiny glass doors, past the security kiosks, and up the escalator. The office building has an air of glamour about it. It's modern, clean, bright. A waterfall serves as a calming backdrop in front of which the escalators ascend. The sound of cascading water soothes my mind. I feel like I have entered a sequestered world, one of well-dressed women and polite security guards. Everything is picture-perfect. Nothing need be explored or examined in too much depth. And you can start over again every month with some new outlook, style, or workout. I am able to skim the surface here and put the vortex of the last few hours behind me, momentarily. I breathe a sigh of relief and feel my energy restored.

An idea meeting has been scheduled for this afternoon. We will be discussing production and casting for our Man Manual shoot. This month it's "Bachelors in Their Boxer Shorts." I wonder if the Taliban wear boxers or briefs.

ALL THREE OF US

David, November 19, 2008

Standing in the remote darkness of Waziristan at the mercy of Taliban militants, I feel at peace. I have spoken to my wife for the first time in nine days. I expected panic or tears, but Kristen sounded collected and confident. Her words "It's going to be all right" will linger in my mind for months. Her composure will sustain me.

Atiqullah and Badruddin had driven us fifteen minutes outside Miran Shah, stopped the car in a dry riverbed, and turned off the engine. Leaving the headlights on, I called Kristen from a small handheld satellite phone Badruddin produced and followed their instructions to tell her we were being held in terrible conditions. I hope the tone of my voice somehow comforted her.

Now Badruddin and Atiqullah tell me to call *The New York Times* bureau in Kabul. Instead of ordering me to make specific demands, they instruct Tahir, Asad, and me to exaggerate our suffering. They also tell me to say that Atiqullah is not with us, even though he is standing beside me.

"We are in terrible conditions, Tahir is very sick," I tell Chris Chivers, a close friend and *Times* reporter who answers the phone.

Tahir then speaks to Chris and asks him to tell his family that he is alive and in good health.

"They keep telling me that if things go wrong they will repeat the story of Helmand," Tahir says, referring to the beheading of the Afghan journalist in 2007. "So I am just afraid they are going to kill me."

Asad then speaks in Pashto with an Afghan reporter in the bureau.

"I am fine, I am okay," he says. "Tell my family that we are in the mountains but we are okay."

The conversation drags on, with Atiqullah continuing to tell me what to say. He orders me to tell Chris that Asad and Tahir will be killed first.

I refuse. "Kill me first," I tell Atiqullah, "Kill me first."

Chris overhears me and interrupts.

"Nobody needs that, David," he says. "Nobody needs to die."

"They are threatening to kill the driver and the translator," I explain to Chris. "I have to tell you, I have to tell you. I don't want to tell you."

"We understand that they are making those threats," Chris says. "But that will not make our job easier."

Chris explains that if the Taliban kill anyone it will make government officials angry and make any deal even more difficult.

"Please don't let them kill the driver and the translator," I say. "Please don't let them kill the driver and translator. I am sorry about this," I add. "I apologize to everyone."

"David, this is not your fault," Chris says. He urges me to tell Atiqullah to keep calling.

I can tell Chris is trying to prolong the call, which drags on for twenty minutes. Growing impatient, Atiqullah and Badruddin order me to end the call.

"Okay, all three of us, Chris," I say. "It's gotta be all three of us. I gotta go."

I hang up the phone and Atiqullah and Badruddin order us back into the car. Worried that the call has been traced and a drone may be approaching, they quickly drive us out of the barren riverbed. Sitting in the back of the car, I am relieved. Kristen sounded calm. Chris said the paper was doing all it could. I feel that I fought for Tahir and Asad.

The car stops. With a scarf placed over my face, I am hustled into a new house. We have returned to Miran Shah.

I awake the following morning and I'm surprised by the quality of our new house. It is the finest of any we have been held in so far. The house has freshly painted white walls and regular electricity. We can wash our-selves with buckets of warm water. I receive a new set of clothes, a tooth-brush, toothpaste, and shampoo. Guards allow us to walk in a large dirt yard, which is roughly fifty feet by thirty feet and has a small patch of grass near the well. The weather is unexpectedly warm. We receive pomegranates and other fresh food. Nestlé Pure Life water bottled in Pakistan is delivered for me to drink. To my amazement, I am even brought English-language Pakistani newspapers. Delivered to a shop in Miran Shah, the newspapers are only a day or two old.

For years, the Pakistani military has portrayed the tribal areas to American officials and journalists as the deeply isolated mountain strong-hold of primitive Pashtun tribes. Instead, I find the tribal areas to be more developed than many parts of neighboring Afghanistan.

After breakfast, Badruddin visits us. He sits me down on the house's front steps and explains to me that the Haqqanis are loyal servants of Taliban leader Mullah Omar. He says that American military reports that the Haqqanis work with foreign militants and operate independ-ently are false. I don't believe him. His father, Jalaluddin Haqqani, is a legendary Afghan anti-Soviet mujahideen fighter who is believed to shelter Al Qaeda members on the family's territory here in North Waziristan. The Haqqanis are aligned with the Afghan Taliban but they have grown so powerful that they largely operate on their own. They personify how American support for fundamentalist fighters in the 1980s backfired.

During the anti-Soviet jihad, Badruddin's father, Haqqani was on the payroll of the CIA. Twenty year later, he and his sons are allies of the Taliban and operate the most lethal insurgent force the United States faces in Afghanistan. I also know that they are at the center of one of the most hotly contested debates in the American military and intelligence community. Is the Pakistani military—the United States' purported ally—covertly aiding the Haqqanis and other Afghan Taliban as they attack American troops?

Twenty-one years before I arrived in Miran Shah as a prisoner, an American congressman named Charlie Wilson met Badruddin's father here in 1987 and declared him "goodness personified." Jalaluddin Haqqani, the family patriarch, was the favorite Afghan mujahideen commander of Wilson, a garrulous, hard-drinking Democrat from the Houston, Texas, area who was famous for womanizing. Eager to exact revenge on the Soviet Union for American deaths in Vietnam, Wilson secretly funneled hundreds of millions of dollars in covert funding to the Afghan mujahideen.

Dressed in Afghan clothes and escorted by Pakistani intelligence officers, Wilson passed through Miran Shah in Pakistan's tribal areas and then secretly crossed the border into Afghanistan. For the next four days, he received a covert tour of mujahideen operations in the Afghan province of Khost from Haqqani and other Afghan commanders. Living in the mountains, Wilson ate dinner in caves with bearded gunmen he saw as the descendants of indomitable mountain warriors who stood their ground against vastly more powerful foreign armies. The Afghans' religious devotion seemed to give them no fear of death, Wilson later recalled. At one point, the congressman even gleefully fired a salvo of rockets at a Soviet base.

On the final night of Wilson's trip, Jalaluddin Haqqani apologized to the American politician for not having a good-bye gift for him. Haqqani demanded that Wilson name the gift he wanted. The congressman half jokingly replied that he wanted helicopter pilots shot down by American-provided Stinger antiaircraft missiles. Roughly thirty minutes later, Haqqani's men produced two terrified-looking Afghan pilots. Wilson expressed his appreciation but said he meant Soviet pilots. Haqqani promised to produce them in two weeks. The following morning, as Wilson prepared to leave, Haqqani had hundreds of mujahideen gather to say good-bye. One of the congressman's guides snapped a photo of a grinning Wilson sitting astride a white horse with four Kalashnikov-wielding Afghans behind him.

"I felt I had entered the ranks of the initiated," Wilson later recalled.

Wilson, like the other American architects of the anti-Soviet jihad, ignored the militant Islam that Haqqani and other mujahideen fighters fervently embraced. In the late 1980s, CIA officers viewed him as one of the most impressive, fearless, and organized Pashtun battlefield commanders. They trusted him with new tactics and weapons, including Stinger antiaircraft missiles, rockets, and even tanks.

Born in the village of Srana in the Garde Serai district of southeastern Afghanistan's Paktia Province, Haqqani was a deeply conservative rural Pashtun cleric. After studying in a local Afghan madrassa as a youth, he completed his religious studies at the hard-line Darul Uloom Haqqania, or "University for Education of Truth," in Pakistan's Northwest Frontier Province. Several other future Taliban leaders would attend the same school as well. The school banned televisions and music, taught young boys to memorize the Koran, and indoctrinated them in conservative Deobandi Islam.

In 1974, Haqqani took up arms against the Afghan government after the country's king was overthrown in a coup Haqqani perceived as left leaning. He left Afghanistan, crossed into Pakistan's tribal areas and based himself in Miran Shah. The town would serve as his headquarters for decades. His presence in Pakistan's tribal areas caught the attention of Pakistani intelligence officials, who began funding him. Later, they introduced him to CIA officials, who did the same. To the delight of his Pakistani and American backers, Haqqani and his men laid siege to Soviet and Afghan forces garrisoned in the Afghan city of Khost in southeastern Afghanistan.

Deft at cultivating support from various sources, Haqqani also spoke fluent Arabic and opened fund-raising offices in the Persian Gulf and Saudi Arabia. Already married to an Afghan woman, he married an Arab woman as well. Between both wives, he fathered nine sons. Haqqani's ability to build coalitions among a dizzyingly diverse array of resistance groups stood out among Afghan commanders.

At some point in the mid-1980s, Haqqani met Osama bin Laden, who had traveled to Pakistan to aid the Afghan resistance. Several months after giving Congressman Wilson his 1987 tour, Haqqani helped Bin Laden achieve his first battlefield victory. The two men and a few dozen of their fighters fought off a weeklong assault by two hundred Soviet paratroopers on a camp Bin Laden had constructed for Afghan and foreign fighters—called the Lion's Den. The following year, Bin Laden founded

Al Qaeda and built training camps in Haqqani-controlled territory in southeastern Afghanistan's Khost Province. Bin Laden would later call Haqqani a "hero mujahed sheikh" and "one of the foremost leaders of the jihad against the Soviets."

When the victorious mujahideen took Kabul in 1992, Haqqani was named justice minister, but fighting over the city quickly erupted between rival mujahideen commanders. Haqqani declined to join any side and returned to Khost, the largest city in his home region. His reputation for piousness and not engaging in the criminality and corruption rampant among other mujahideen commanders gained him standing among local Afghans.

When the Taliban emerged in southern Afghanistan in 1994, Haqqani apparently did not trust them. A year later, he joined the group, possibly after coming under pressure from Pakistani intelligence officials who saw the Taliban as a friendly proxy force against India. During Taliban rule, Haqqani served as the minister of borders and tribal affairs and governor of Paktia, the province in southeastern Afghanistan where he was born. He also commanded members of his Zadran tribe who battled anti-Taliban forces north of Kabul. By joining the Taliban, he greatly strengthened the nascent group whose leaders included many of his fellow graduates of Darul Uloom Haqqania religious school in Pakistan.

That same year, 1995, I visited religious schools in Pakistan while working as a reporter for *The Christian Science Monitor*. On my first visit to the country, I toured three madrassas and two Islamic universities in the city of Peshawar and found burgeoning fundamentalism. An estimated 200,000 Afghan and Pakistani boys studied in 8,000 madrassas, a 50 percent increase from seven years earlier. At one school, young Afghan teachers proudly stated that 400 of the school's students had gone on to join the Taliban. At the same time, Afghan refugees living in a fetid refugee camp accused the United States of mounting an "anti-Muslim" conspiracy to prevent the Taliban from establishing an Islamic government in Afghanistan. They also said the United States had "deceived" Afghans by convincing them to fight the Soviet Union and then abandoning them.

When I spoke with American diplomats, they played down the problem of fundamentalism. Pakistani prime minister Benazir Bhutto was exaggerating the problem, they said, to persuade the United States to lift sanctions it had placed on Pakistan for developing nuclear weapons.

"Pakistan is not a major link in an international terrorist conspiracy," an American diplomat told me in 1995.

A year after I departed, the Taliban took Kabul and began enforcing strict Islamic laws across Afghanistan. Mullah Omar, Jalaluddin Haqqani, and other Taliban leaders welcomed Osama bin Laden back to Afghanistan. With Haqqani's support, Bin Laden refurbished and expanded camps the Saudi jihadist leader originally built in Khost to support the anti-Soviet mujahideen. After Al Qaeda bombed two American embassies in Africa in 1998, the United States fired cruise missiles at the camps in a failed effort to kill Bin Laden. The missiles struck the camp where Congressman Wilson had slept during his tour of Afghanistan eleven years earlier.

A month after the September 2001 terrorist attacks in the United States, the ISI brought Jalaluddin Haqqani to Islamabad for a secret meeting with American and Pakistani officials. The ISI hoped Haqqani would join a new post-Taliban government that did not include officials they viewed as loyal to Pakistan's rival India. The Americans asked Haqqani to defect from the Taliban. Haqqani rejected the offer and complained that the United States had abandoned Afghanistan after the defeat of the Soviets. Soon after, American bombs destroyed three of Haqqani's homes in Afghanistan. He survived and is believed to have played a role in helping Bin Laden—his friend of fifteen years—escape from the battle of Tora Bora in eastern Afghanistan and cross into Pakistan's tribal areas in December 2001.

As they did during the anti-Soviet jihad, Haqqani fighters regrouped in Pakistan and then began launching cross-border attacks from Pakistan into Afghanistan with the support of foreign fighters. Assassinating and intimidating moderate tribal elders, the Haqqanis steadily weakened southeastern Afghanistan's Pashtun tribes. They told the Pashtuns that their primary loyalty should be to Islam, not to their tribe. Gradually gaining strength, they killed moderate clerics and beheaded Afghans working with Americans. Their long-standing ties with Arab militants brought them extensive funding from the Persian Gulf and an acceptance of suicide bombing, a tactic more moderate Taliban still questioned.

Between 2003 and 2007, I embedded with three different American military units that battled the Haqqanis in eastern Afghanistan. The first embed ended with a soldier having his lower leg blown off when our Humvee struck a mine five hundred yards from the Pakistani border. The second involved a unit trying to help a poorly equipped Afghan police chief who feared his own men would kill him because he was from the wrong tribe. And the third involved the Haqqanis beheading a tribal elder who American military officials hoped might work with a team of anthropologists they deployed to better understand Khost's tribal structure.

In 2004, the former NFL player Pat Tillman was killed in a friendly fire incident during an operation to block a cross-border infiltration route used by Haqqani fighters. Two years later, the Haqqanis used a teenage suicide bomber to kill Hakim Taniwal, a former sociology professor who returned from exile in Australia to serve as governor of two southeastern provinces. After killing Taniwal, they dispatched a second suicide bomber to his funeral, killing six more people.

By 2008, the Haqqanis had fielded several thousand fighters and were mounting complex operations in Kabul itself. They carried out a January 2008 assault on the Serena Hotel that killed six, an April 2008 assassination attempt on President Karzai that killed three, and a July 2008 attack on the Indian Embassy that killed fifty-eight people. American intelligence officials reportedly intercepted calls in which Pakistani intelligence officials guided the Haqqani operatives during the Indian Embassy attack. Pakistani officials denied the reports. American officials who were skeptical of the Pakistani military argued that the Haqqanis were still proxies that the ISI continued to use to prevent India from gaining influence in Afghanistan. They argued that the strength of the Haqqanis showed that the Pakistani military was playing a "double game" with the United States. Pakistan arrested Al Qaeda members in the country's cities, but continued to covertly support the Haqqanis and other Afghan Taliban.

After no public statements emerged from Jalaluddin Haqqani for several years, rumors circulated that he had died. His son Sirajuddin was said to have taken over day-to-day operations of the Haqqani network. In the spring of 2008, a frail-looking but ever-wily Jalaluddin Haqqani appeared in a video.

"This is not a battle of haste; this is a battle of patience," he said. "If a strong animal fights with a small and weak animal, the big animal uses all its power, not against the enemy, but against itself."

I had watched the video with a colleague in the newspaper's Kabul bureau after it appeared. I knew the Haqqanis were the Taliban faction with the closest ties to Al Qaeda. Now I am their first American prisoner.

In the day after my call to Kristen, Atiqullah and I discuss religion again. He wants to know how devout I am. I tell him that my parents took me to church when I was young, but I know little about Christianity and am not religious. I don't tell him, but my years of covering religious conflict has made me skeptical of organized religion.

Atiqullah asks me to recite the ten commandments and I struggle to remember them from the Episcopal Sunday school my mother had me attend. My parents were raised Episcopalian but my father became a fiercely independent Unitarian Universalist. In the end, I make up the final three or four commandments. When he asks me if I believe Jesus was the son of God, I say I believe Jesus was one of several prophets, including Muhammad. He tells me that he has sent for an English-language Koran for me to read. My religious beliefs appear to amuse him. I get the sense that he sees me as primitive. The following day, Atiqullah announces that he needs to return to Afghanistan, but that two of his men will stay behind to guard us.

"I will return in seven to ten days," he promises, then disappears.

One of the guards who stays with us is Akbar, the seemingly kind guard who brought us food in Afghanistan. The other is a heavyset young fighter who recites the call to prayer beautifully each day and rarely speaks to me. We nickname him Chunky. I am allowed to exercise in the yard, and I find that any exercise—no matter how small—raises my spirits. I walk back and forth dozens of times in the yard, which is strewn with bits of trash. Pakistani military helicopters occasionally rumble overhead. Airliners do as well. At certain times of day, I think I'm staring at the Dubai-New York flight I have taken home countless times.

One day, the guards buy a board game called Checkah, a Pakistani variation of Parcheesi, to help us pass the time. Instead of beating us, as I expected, our captors are trying to meet at least some of our needs. But as in so much of what will be seven months in captivity, reasons for optimism are overtaken by harsh realities.

At night, a stream of Haqqani commanders overflowing with hatred for the United States, Europe, and Israel visit us, unleashing blistering critiques that will continue throughout our imprisonment. As they enter the room, I stare at the floor as Tahir has advised me. By not looking at their faces, I hope I am being respectful and showing that I will not be able to identify them in the future to American officials.

First, teenage boys bring in large plates of rice, kebab, and spinach for dinner and place them on a plastic sheet on the floor. Our guards, Tahir, Asad, and I scoop up pieces of food with small sections of flatbread and eat it. There are no tables, chairs, or utensils. We sit on thin maroon floor cushions. Cans of Pepsi are brought in for me to drink. Grapes and pomegranates are served for dessert. I decline, fearing the water in the fruit will make me sick.

The commanders harbor many delusions about Westerners. But I also see how some of the consequences of Washington's antiterrorism policies had galvanized the Taliban. One commander demands that I be chained, citing the shackling of prisoners by American forces. Another commander says he was detained for months by Pakistani ISI intelligence agents in a dank underground cell. When American officials arrived to question him, he was brought to a clean, bright room with a bowl of fruit. When the Americans departed, the Pakistanis returned him to his dungeon.

All the commanders fixate on the deaths of Afghan, Iraqi, and Palestinian civilians in American air strikes as well as on the American detention of Muslim prisoners for years without charge. They all know of the physical abuse and sexual humiliation of Iraqi prisoners in Abu Ghraib and are infuriated by it. To Americans, these episodes are aberrations. To my captors, they are proof that the United States is a hypocritical and duplicitous power that flouts international law. America, Europe, and Israel preach democracy, human rights, and impartial justice to the Muslim world, they say, but fail to follow those principles themselves. When I tell them I am an innocent civilian who should be released, they respond that the United States has held Muslims in secret detention centers for years. Why, they ask, should they treat me differently?

Other accusations are paranoid and delusional. Seven years after the September 2001 terrorist attacks, they continue to insist that the attacks were hatched by American and Israeli intelligence agencies to create a pretext for the United States to occupy the Muslim world. They say the United States is forcibly converting vast numbers of Muslims to Christianity. American and NATO soldiers, they believe, are making Afghan women work as prostitutes on military bases. Their hatred for the United States seems boundless.

HUMAN RESOURCES

Kristen, November 20–December 15, 2008

I arrive at *The New York Times* building. The offices are bright and modern. The lively red walls seem a stark contrast to the intense and dour expressions among the employees working there.

David's brother Lee has once again set up camp in an office on the seventeenth floor. David McCraw, the newspaper's lawyer, has been assigned to help us work with the *Times'* crisis management firm, Clayton Consultants, and to coordinate the efforts in New York and Kabul to release David. We speak with him each day at noon for updates on the case, to assess different strategies—for example, whether the media blackout is effective or not—and to figure out our next steps.

Today, David McCraw, Lee, and I will interview a private security firm to work along with the people from Clayton. The head of Clayton is joining us for the meeting. We want his evaluation of the firm as well. We need to send someone to Kabul to represent our family during negotiations and relieve the pressure on the paper's Kabul bureau, which has been fielding the phone calls from David's captors and trying to get information related to the case. Since the FBI's hands are tied in terms of helping get David released, the paper, along with Lee and me, has decided to hire an outside security consultancy to conduct negotiations. The head of Clayton Consultants arrives and greets us. Most of the security contractors I have met so far are former employees of government intelligence agencies. He is no exception.

With sandy brown hair, a handlebar mustache, and a monotone demeanor, Clayton's representative is a walking caricature of an FBI agent—the kind you see on television. He looks vaguely familiar. Later he tells us he has actually portrayed an FBI agent in small parts on television shows.

He also explains that most likely this is a kidnap for ransom case. Our goal, he says, should be to draw out the process, decrease David's value in his captors' eyes, and maintain a dialogue with them. Over time the captors will lower their demands, until a realistic amount is agreed on. Prisoner exchanges are not possible, so he advises that we steer clear of this issue during negotiations with the captors. We expect that any haggling will occur over the phone. He says it is customary for families to think about what they might be willing to pay.

It is surreal to be putting a price tag on David. And trying to figure out what the markup might be when we include his two Afghan colleagues. The whole idea of the captors pricing human life like a perishable commodity is revolting. Yet I do not lose sight of the fact that this is a sad situation all around. I imagine life must be incredibly bleak in Afghanistan for kidnapping to be a viable business. Any potential funds we give them could be used to fuel future terrorist attacks or violence. This greatly disturbs us.

Even more upsetting is that I feel we do not have the luxury to debate this topic. While we hope for a ransom-free solution, we are not idealistic about the situation. There is no question that our family will raise funds in any way possible to protect the lives of David, Tahir, and Asad if it is the only means of seeing them alive again. We've decided to pursue this course in future communications with the captors.

At present, we are not in the same stratosphere: they are now asking for millions of dollars and the release of prisoners from Guantánamo and Bagram. Lee and I resign ourselves to trying to reach an agreement when the captors diminish their demands to a reasonable amount. We have no idea how long this will take, and at this point we also know that it is nearly impossible to apply logic and reason to an irrational situation.

Lee, McCraw, Clayton's representative, and I are seated around a conference table in a corner meeting room, tucked away behind the stairwell and removed from the flow of office traffic. The interview begins. We hear from the leader of the private security consulting firm American International Security Corporation, or AISC, which has been recommended to us by a former special operations soldier.

Mike Taylor, the head of the firm and a special forces veteran as well, explains that he has experience "in the field, on the ground." He is very fit and seems to be in his forties. He never cracks a smile and at first appears put off by our questions. Quiet but hyperalert, he seems to be taking in the details of our surroundings as he seats himself a few feet away from the table.

He proclaims that his agency has never paid ransom for a hostage. "We've never exchanged funds," he says. Awkward silence. Lee and I glance at each other.

We are all a bit baffled by this statement. We thought the private security team would be providing a negotiator. We ask what exactly he means. Mike replies that his team has contacts on the ground, through a local network of informants in Afghanistan, and the region. They have the ability to move money and evacuate hostages. They are not opposed to paying ransom, he says, but have never needed to do so in previous kidnapping cases.

Uncomfortable pause.

I ask bluntly how it is possible to get someone out if no money is paid.

"Snatch and grab," he says, referring to a rescue. "Or an exchange of another sort," he says, adding that we may be able to barter with other goods—medical supplies, vehicles.

Lee and I step out for a moment to share our impressions while the Clayton and AISC representatives talk privately.

I'm a little hesitant because it seems to me that AISC might take a bit of a bold approach. Lee has the same concern but asks me, "If you knew this could be solved quicker, would you be opposed to a more aggressive approach?" We both feel we are in a race against time. I worry that each moment that ticks by is taking a chunk of David's sanity along with it.

When we return, the head of Clayton is very confident that AISC is a good choice. "They bring a different set of assets and skills to the table," he says archly. "We've checked out their bona fides," he adds. "They are the real deal. We feel comfortable working with them."

On the basis of this recommendation, we set aside our fears and decide to hire AISC. They will send a negotiator to Kabul to represent our family and to work alongside a kidnap expert from Clayton. We will come to refer to this duo as Team Kabul. We will be in regular contact with them, along with McCraw, on a daily noon conference call.

Both teams advise us to keep "the bureau," or the FBI, out of it. They are useful for some things, but cannot deliver funds, release prisoners, or provide direct negotiations when discussions involve ransom. They are strictly an information-gathering agency.

I've confided in several of David's closest friends at this point. Each of them offers unwavering emotional support. A few also provide invaluable practical advice. One longtime friend, Samantha Power, suggests that I reach out to Richard Holbrooke, a former official in the Clinton administration who knows my husband and is aware of our situation. Rumor is he will be assuming a diplomatic position in the incoming Obama administration, with a focus on Afghanistan and Pakistan. While our friend admits that Holbrooke is often referred to as the diplomatic equivalent of a "bull in a china shop," he is also smart, passionate about causes, well respected, and personally moved by our situation.

As fate would have it, David had introduced me to Holbrooke and his wife, Kati Marton, several months ago at Samantha's wedding. We sat next to each other at the church service. David respects him, but is a bit embarrassed in his presence because of their history.

Thirteen years ago, Holbrooke played a key role in negotiating for David's release from Serbian authorities. During the Dayton peace talks in 1995, which Holbrooke had convened to help end the bitter civil war in Bosnia, ten members of David's family showed up and threatened to protest on the street outside if the Clinton administration did not pressure the Serbs to free David.

I call Holbrooke in the evening to ask his advice about what more I can be doing to get assistance from the United States government and to hear his thoughts on our decision to keep David's case out of the public eye. He responds with a reference to the wedding.

He reminds me that he orchestrated David's release in Bosnia. "I put our peace talks on hold for three days to work for the release of your husband, simply because it was the right thing to do," he says. "What were my parting words to David this past summer—do you remember?" Holbrooke reminds me that when he learned David would be going back to Afghanistan soon after our own wedding, he half jokingly told him, "Don't get captured again."

Holbrooke ruminates as he speaks. You can hear the wheels turning. His speech is deliberate, thoughtful, and slightly muffled. I have to strain to hear him. As a result, he has my undivided attention. He tells me he has been turning this over for quite some time—especially the thought of whether to go public or remain quiet. "Given that we are not dealing with a legitimate government, I think you are right to keep this private. You are dealing with a set of unpredictable, ruthless individuals.

"I am sure you have Googled the Haqqani family, and if you've done your research, you know of the connection to the ISI. So, you might want to think about reaching out to them. Rumor is I may be working with the new administration, but I won't assume my post until January. I promise to work on this, to make this a priority when I assume my post. Until then, I suggest you stay in close contact with Condi Rice. Have you contacted her? It would be good to check in with the State Department on a regular basis in case anything can be done, any pressure applied on the diplomatic front to keep this on the radar of the Pakistanis."

Before we say good-bye, Holbrooke emphasizes that it is a good sign that David has survived the first few weeks. He reassures me David will come home.

Atiqullah continues to call the Kabul bureau of *The New York Times* regularly, reiterating his possession of "our three," as we have come to refer to them. Since the beginning of the case, the FBI has been sending negotiations experts to the Kabul bureau to assist in communications and record these phone calls.

On November 21, Atiqullah calls with a grim message for Chris Chivers, the reporter who has been fielding the calls: If the demands are not met, they will go public with the case and set a three-day deadline. They will kill Asad first and then Tahir. We know there is no way we can meet their demands but we must keep them talking. Coached by the FBI, Chris pleads with Atiqullah to keep our three alive until we can reach an agreement. We realize that if the kidnappers publicly announce a deadline, they will have to carry it out. In Afghanistan, never losing face is paramount. We anxiously await the next phone call.

On Thanksgiving eve there has been no word from David's captors in five days. Heightened security in the wake of a car bomb prevents the FBI from getting to the Kabul bureau in time to take a call from Atiqullah. The FBI experts advise Chris to delay speaking with Atiqullah until they are present. In truth, Chris is poised by the phone.

By the end of the day, Atiqullah has not called back the Kabul bureau. Apparently the delay has upset him and made him skittish. We have no new information about our three. This reaffirms our decision to hire a private security firm.

I am completely exhausted, on edge, and angry at the FBI agents in Kabul for scuttling our communications with David's kidnappers. I pace back and forth in our small galley kitchen, then collapse on the living room sofa. I turn on the television, hoping to take my mind off our situation.

CNN presents an emergency newscast of an unfolding tragedy. I watch in horror as our honeymoon spots from a weekend in Mumbai— the Taj Hotel, the Oberoi, the harbor—are in chaos and smoke. Mumbai is burning. It is sad to see our recent history in flames and disturbing to see that India has been hit by terrorists.

Lee and I immediately personalize this horrifying event: How will it affect David? Does the recent silence in his case relate to the bombing? Once again, we question whether to make the kidnapping public. I check in with our various advisers. The FBI votes yes, but cannot provide specifics as to why they take this stance. I disagree. Our private security team advises us to keep it private. Bill Keller, the *Times'* executive editor, sends me an e-mail suggesting that we revisit the situation.

This is the first of many long periods of silence.

It is also our first holiday as a married couple, and we will spend it apart. My family has rallied to my side in New York. I am thankful for their presence but feel a mix of emotions. I was single for thirty-nine years, and now, confronted with my first married Thanksgiving, I am disappointed that I am still the odd girl out—the only one without a date.

I have been restless of late. The stress of the situation is starting to have a physical impact. My arms are often numb. It's disturbing not to be able to reach out to David and help him in a tangible, immediate way. I have gained weight around my middle, which I attribute to the buildup of the stress hormone cortisol, a natural by-product of sustained tension. My chest is wound up. I liken my mental experience to the moment when a jetliner touches down and the engines are at full force but the brakes are engaged. Everything has come to a screeching halt momentarily. Suspended animation. Fear. No sense of what will come next. Not knowing whether we will move forward or spontaneously combust. My entire mode of being is stuck in the moment of not knowing, waiting, having no control over the next moment. Life is simultaneously in intense overdrive and stalled. The only thing to do is to surrender and trust that some greater benevolent force is at work. Many people have told me that this journey will be a marathon, not a sprint.

My mother, Mary Jane, is still living with me and brings some levity to the situation. One of her volunteer projects in her community back home in Maine is to make "dishware gardens" for shut-ins—patients, the elderly, and the disabled. As I look around the room, I see she has applied this practice in my own apartment. I notice that several of our spider plants have new companions. She has been cooking up a storm of late and placing the seeds and pits remaining from our meals in planters around the apartment. I am somewhat amused to find an avocado pit beginning to sprout among the leaves of a spider plant. I point this out to her.

"I thought it would be a positive way to mark time," she tells me. "It's good to bring new life into the situation. Let's see if he's home before it bears new fruit."

"Thanks," I tell her, and then admit to myself: I officially feel like a shut-in, albeit an emotional one. Thank you very much. Still, I have to smile.

This is one of the reasons I love my mother—she always maintains a positive outlook and an offbeat sense of humor, and she never lets anything go to waste. Once when I was home from college, after a breakup with a serious boyfriend, I found her on the back step with a carton of expired eggs. "They are wonderful for the soil," she said, launching one at nearby tree. "It's good exercise. And, it's very satisfying when you are feeling frustrated and want to channel your energy in a positive way."

She was right—hurling a few eggs through space at a nearby target was incredibly satisfying, especially when faced with the reality that romance had gone rotten.

There is always a certain wisdom hidden in her somewhat quirky behavior. I have no doubt there is a koan or parable embedded in these actions somehow. She can nurture anything, including my now improving mood. On the windowsill above the would-be avocado plant, she has created a miniature "zen garden" that consists of a glass vase, pebbles, and a plant. It sounds completely tacky, but it is actually quite beautiful to behold. Several friends inquire about it during their visits. They think it is exquisite. I derive great joy in revealing the punch line to these Manhattan sophisticates: That beautiful piece of zen art is the remains of a sweet potato.

I receive a call from Secretary of State Condoleezza Rice. As Holbrooke suggested, I have been trying to reach out to her in an attempt to have regular contact with the State Department. She is aware of David's case and has agreed to speak with me. I've spent most of the morning preparing a list of questions. She is warm and forthcoming. I ask if the captors or anyone else connected with David's case is making political demands that perhaps we are not aware of. She denies this. No demands have been made to our government, she says. She advises us to keep the situation quiet. She reiterates what others have said: that we are not dealing with a legitimate government, and that the group holding David is immune to moral pressure.

I pray that David, Tahir, and Asad will have the strength to endure this uncertain period and find peace of mind. I make the same request for me and all our families. I was raised Catholic, so my go-to device for all situations beyond my control is prayer. I try to view this through a larger lens: Why is this happening? What am I meant to learn from this situation? Patience. Surrender. These things spring to mind. Patience is my least favorite virtue, but I am certain this is the lesson I am meant to master through this harrowing test. And I am torn between feeling completely responsible for our three and realizing I may ultimately have no control over the outcome of this situation. I pray for the strength to not give up and, simultaneously, the ability to surrender. My prayer does not take a traditional or eloquent form of incantation. I do not have the strength for this. I merely express the words, "Help me, help us." These seem the most fitting and easiest to access.

Yet at the same time, I am having great difficulty acknowledging my own vulnerability. It must be a trick of the mind, a survival tactic. My thoughts wander to David. Is he being held with other people, or are they keeping him in a hole somewhere, underground? Does he know what day it is, how much time has passed? Has he found his own way to cope? I know it is futile to try to imagine his circumstances. Speculation only leads to a downward spiral. I am confident he will know what to say and do to keep himself and the others alive as long as possible. I worry more about his peace of mind. What is he doing to ease his own boredom and lack of control?

David's religion is the pursuit of the truth. An agnostic with a Unitarian-Episcopalian upbringing, he does not hold to one religious ideal or path. His reporting experience covering atrocities related to religious bigotry have made him skeptical of organized religion. With this in mind, I hope he is able to find some sort of comfort during this time—some personal expression of faith and a belief that some higher force will look out for him.

SPEAK GOOD WORDS TO AN ENEMY

David, Late November–Late December 2008

Atiqullah promised to return in seven to ten days. Yet ten days pass and he does not appear. Instead, in a worrying sign, Badruddin Haqqani now seems to be in charge. A dozen members of his family have been killed by American drone strikes. He himself is a primary American target.

Badruddin moves us to a far smaller, dirtier house five minutes away by car. Transported at night, again with a scarf placed over my face, I have no idea where our new home lies in Miran Shah. We are confined to two small rooms in the back of a large traditional Pashtun family compound with mud-brick walls. An old man and a young boy bring us meals three times a day, often with meat that appears several days old. We sleep on dust-covered mattresses.

One room has posters on the walls. One shows a Swiss chalet in the snow-covered Alps, a setting often used in Indian movies. Another features a majestic Ottoman mosque in Istanbul, a city I have visited with Kristen. The other room holds sleeping bags and camping equipment apparently used by Taliban fighters when they enter Afghanistan. A large radio antenna perched on a nearby rooftop is part of a seemingly sophisticated Taliban communications system in Miran Shah.

We are allowed to walk in a small courtyard that is the width of a city sidewalk. Direct sunlight reaches it for a few hours each morning.

Throughout the day, we hear children playing and laughing on the other side of the walls but never see them.

Akbar—the seemingly kind guard—departs. Qari—the unstable guard who nearly shot Tahir—arrives with a new Taliban fighter in his early twenties named Mansoor, who speaks broken English.

During our first night here, the Taliban commander who owns the house introduces himself to us. At first, he is polite and respectful. He promises to update us every three days on negotiations for our release. As the conversation continues, though, my optimism fades.

He proclaims that he was held in American detention and I am receiving vastly better treatment than he endured. Then he complains that the Taliban released the group of Korean missionaries they kidnapped in 2007 far too quickly. I had covered that kidnapping. The Taliban first demanded that the Afghan government free twenty-three Taliban prisoners in exchange for twenty-three Koreans. President Karzai flatly refused, citing the blistering domestic criticism he came under for releasing five Taliban prisoners for the Italian journalist four months earlier. In response, the Taliban executed two male Korean missionaries.

The Korean government then carried out direct negotiations with the kidnappers, who released the remaining twenty-one hostages after six weeks in captivity. The Taliban triumphantly announced they had been paid a ransom of roughly $20 million. Afghan officials said the actual number was closer to $1 million. American and NATO special forces units later hunted down and killed the Taliban leaders involved in the kidnapping. The commander tells me the Taliban mishandled the case. If they had held the Koreans longer, he believes, the Taliban could have forced the world to accept them as Afghanistan's legitimate government.

"The elders should have listened to me," he says. "I could have gotten the Emirate recognized."

I think to myself that we are in a giant insane asylum. Next, he asks me if I support the American government. I respond that I am an independent journalist and try to explain that American government and military officials frequently do not like journalists and are often angered by our stories.

"Who did you vote for in the presidential election?" he asks.

Sensing a trap, I tell him that I did not vote in the American election because I was in Afghanistan at the time. In truth, I voted by absentee ballot. He says that if I had voted in the election it would mean that I am personally responsible for the actions of the American government, including drone strikes carried out in the tribal areas. He promises to give us an update on the negotiations in three days and leaves. We will not see the commander again for months.

In our first days in the new house, I try to engage Mansoor in more in-depth conversations. Mansoor is short—roughly five foot six inches tall—but stocky and strong. He has dark hair, a thin beard, and a boyish face. He and Qari occasionally wrestle each other to pass the time. Mansoor wins every time.

Our talks do not go well. During one, Mansoor complains that when he got married in Afghanistan, American warplanes circled over the large crowd that formed in his village in a pro-Taliban part of Afghanistan. His family was terrified that the group would be seen as Taliban fighters and bombed. During another, Mansoor agrees with me that he will teach me Pashto and I will teach him English. He buys me a notebook in one of his trips to the local market. For a few days, we give each other brief lessons. Then we both lose interest. Mansoor and I fail to connect on a fundamental level. What interests me—the outside world and my wife and family—does not interest him. What interests Mansoor—religion and jihad—does not interest me.

Qari increasingly unnerves me. He spends hours each day memorizing verses in an electronic Koran. Seated on his knees, he holds the small device—which looks like a digital camera—in his hands. As a computerized voice repeats verses in Arabic, he rhythmically recites them. Rocking back and forth, he seems to be in a trance. After each session, he gently kisses the electronic device, recites a blessing, and wraps it in a small cloth. He then carefully places it on a shelf to ensure it does not make contact with the ground. Qari is polite to me but we rarely speak. I fear provoking him and have no interest in trying to understand him. He has no interest in trying to understand me.

When we hear over the radio of the November 26 terrorist attacks on luxury hotels in Mumbai, our guards are elated. Mansoor cheers as the carnage drags on for three days and 173 people are killed. I ask him why he is celebrating. Mansoor declares that the luxury hotels are dens of prostitution, alcohol consumption, and debauchery. The guests deserve to die because they are sinners.

Another week passes and it becomes clearer that Tahir and Asad will be separated from their families for Id al-Adha—a major Muslim holiday on December 8 that marks Abraham's willingness to sacrifice his son and show his devotion to God. They are more and more frustrated.

Tension is also growing among me, Tahir, and Asad. They are angry with me for my promises to Atiqullah on the second night of the kidnappings that he would get prisoners and millions of dollars for us. I tell them I was trying to save our lives. They say I have vastly raised our captors' expectations.

My attempts to play sick are going nowhere. I have made myself vomit in the new house but the guards do not appear worried. Qari says that I am intentionally making myself sick. December 10, the one-month anniversary of our kidnapping, is approaching. There are no signs of a deal. After taking Tahir to a local doctor several times for stomach and skin problems, the guards stop taking him to the doctor without explanation.

Becoming more desperate, Tahir and I talk over what we can do to create pressure for our release. We settle on a hunger strike, an option we have both been considering for weeks. We have no idea if it will work, but are running out of options. That night before dinner, Tahir announces that he is going to stop eating food. I decide to stop eating food and drinking water, hoping it will make the guards think I will die quickly. Asad does not join us.

The following day, I lie on the mattress where I sleep, staring at the ceiling for hours at a time. I think of the hunger strikes I have read about over the years but cannot remember how long a person can survive without water. I experience less pain than expected and I am pleased by the initial results. At the end of the first day, our guards panic and beg us to eat dinner. We refuse. Relatives of the commander who owns the house beg us to eat as well. It is an enormous shame to them, they say, to have guests who refuse to eat. We decline.

As the second day comes to a close, my stomach begins to ache, my throat is dry, and I have cottonmouth. Pressuring our captors, though, elates me. I am finally doing something concrete to relieve the suffering of my wife and family. That night, the guards announce that Atiqullah has called and said a deal for our release is imminent. It only needs the approval of Karzai, who is on a foreign trip. The French aid worker whose video I was shown when we first arrived in Miran Shah has been released, they say. We are next.

Tahir says we should continue the strike. As a Pashtun, he does not want to show weakness by stopping without achieving our goal. Asad urges us to begin eating again. He says we are angering our captors, not pressuring them. I am torn. A recent radio news broadcast confirmed that Karzai is, in fact, at a meeting abroad. I worry that our continued defiance will cause our captors to refuse to compromise and scuttle a final deal that could be days away. Recent kidnap cases in Afghanistan have ended in four to eight weeks. I hope our month-old case will end in that range as well.

I tell Tahir that we should end the strike. He has kidney problems, is in intense pain, and I worry about his health. The guards have promised to begin taking Tahir to the doctor again if we begin eating. At first, Tahir refuses. We receive a second call from Atiqullah, who swears our release is days away. Tahir relents and we eat for the first time in forty-eight hours.

Instead of releasing us, Badruddin moves us to a nicer house. It is larger than the previous one but feels more like a prison. Twenty-foot-high brick walls covered in peeling white paint surround a thirty- by thirty-foot concrete courtyard. We have a freshly painted blue bedroom to ourselves and the guards sleep next door in a room of their own. Three times a day, a boy from the family who brought us food in the previous house arrives with our meals. When the electricity goes out and the house's water pump has no power, another boy brings us barrels of water for washing.

After several days, the guards announce that we must begin cooking our own meals. The family that has been preparing our food will no longer do so. With cash from Badruddin, the guards buy food from the local market and order Asad to cook it. I try to wash the dishes, but the guards initially urge me to stop, saying it is shameful to have an elder clean for them. We agree that I will wash only the breakfast dishes. At dusk each day, Asad sautés onions over a small propane burner before adding rice. There is a momentary sense of good cheer among us. The food, at least, is fresher, cleaner, and better tasting. But cooking for ourselves gives a worrying sense of permanence to our imprisonment.

Our lives settle into a monotonous routine of meals, washing our clothes, and Checkah board games. While washing the dishes one morning, my wedding ring falls off my finger. I frantically chase it across the courtyard, grab it, and put it back on. Later, it falls off as I take a bucket shower in the bathroom. I am losing weight, but I wonder if this is a sign that something is wrong with Kristen. Worried I will lose the ring, I take it off before I wash in the bathroom, kiss it, and carefully place it in the pocket of my baggy local pants for safekeeping. The narrow gold band with KRISTEN engraved on its interior is the only physical connection I have to the outside world.

Boredom and claustrophobia begin to take a toll on the guards. Qari tears the Checkah board to shreds after he loses several games. Then Tahir and Asad rip up two Checkah boards out of frustration when they lose as well. I worry that Qari will shoot Tahir if he loses another game.

Each day, I spend hours walking in circles in the walled courtyard alone. In my mind, I relive happy memories of my times with my family, friends, and wife. I play out trips I took with Kristen to Europe and South Asia, our wedding, and our honeymoon. I remember the small, everyday beauties of life with her, such as having coffee together each morning. I pretend I am walking beside her down the Hudson River bank at dusk as we do in New York.

As time passes, I realize I must control my thoughts to fight off depression. Certain actions immediately raise my spirits, such as walking, talking with Tahir, and reliving moments with Kristen. Other actions leave me discouraged, such as conversations with the guards. Strictly managing my day and my thoughts becomes a survival tool.

For the first time in my life, I begin praying several times a day. I struggle to remember the Lord's Prayer and don't know if I'm reciting it correctly. Resorting to prayer heightens my sense of desperation, but it also gives me something to do each day, a task the guards cannot stop me from silently completing. In the months ahead, I will realize that prayer is something they can never take from me.

One day I pray in front of Mansoor and Qari, trying to demonstrate that I, too, have faith. They seem unmoved by it. I shift to silently praying as I walk in the yard. I don't know if some higher being is hearing my prayers, reaching down and comforting me, or if prayer is simply a psychological trick that gives humans a false sense of control. I decide it does not matter. Whatever is happening, prayer centers and strengthens me.

Badruddin visits us intermittently at night and promises that negotiations are continuing. He is generally polite and respectful. During one visit, he gives me a woolen Afghan blanket to stay warm. During another, he gives us a Chinese-made shortwave radio with a hand crank to generate electricity when the batteries run out. It is familiar to me. The American military has distributed thousands of these radios to Afghan villagers in the hope of winning their support.

To my amazement, Badruddin arrives with a laptop computer one evening, opens it, and plays *Taxi to the Dark Side*, an American documentary film that won a 2007 Academy Award. The film recounts how two of my colleagues from *The New York Times* exposed that American soldiers had beaten to death a young Afghan taxi driver in the main American detention center in Bagram, Afghanistan. I am elated. The film is a perfect opportunity to explain American journalism to Badruddin.

As Badruddin and the guards watch, the documentary recounts how the American military initially stated that Dilawar, a twenty-two-year-old Afghan taxi driver, died of natural causes in 2002. One of my colleagues then visited his family in Khost Province and discovered an American military death certificate that declared the driver's death a "homicide." His brother could not read the document, which was in English.

"My friend!" I shout, as my colleague describes confronting the commanding American general in Afghanistan. "My friend!"

A still photo of two men arrested with Dilawar in his taxi that day flashes across the screen.

"I found those two men in Khost," I say, explaining that I helped write a follow-up story. "I interviewed them and took that picture."

The next segment describes how another colleague obtained a 2,000-page American military report that confirmed Dilawar was innocent and had been beaten to death. A final segment recounts how the same American military police unit was transferred to Iraq's Abu Ghraib prison where similar abuses occurred. Photographs then flash across the screen of a female American soldier, Lynndie England, smiling as a naked Iraqi prisoner masturbates in front of her. Other images show naked Iraqis stacked in pyramids and England's boyfriend, Specialist Charles Graner, giving a "thumbs up" over the body of a dead Iraqi prisoner.

Badruddin and the guards grow visibly angry. The images reinforce their view of Americans as malevolent hypocrites who preach human rights but torture privately. I try in vain to explain that American journalists, in fact, exposed the Abu Ghraib abuses. My explanations do not matter. My captors pick the information that fits their worldview and ignore the rest. I realize that Badruddin does not fit the Western caricature of a Taliban fighter—a cave dweller who rejects modern technology. Instead, he and other young Taliban embrace technology and use it to strengthen and spread their worldview. Globalization impacts their lives and exposes them to vast amounts of new information, but does not moderate them.

At the end of the film, autopsy photos of dead prisoners appear. Each prisoner is naked. I am sure the film's director included the images to force American viewers to face the reality of the abuses. To an Afghan audience the images further insult the dead. For Afghans, public nudity is deeply humiliating.

After the film ends, the guards complain that none of the American prison guards were seriously punished for the abuses. I have no answer for them.

We reach mid-December and I find myself hanging on to each word uttered by Badruddin. We have not heard from Atiqullah for weeks. Badruddin is increasingly unpredictable. During one visit, he declares the Taliban will not kill me.

"You are the golden hen," he says, expecting me to lay a golden egg.

I ask him to promise not to kill Tahir and Asad. Speaking directly to me in broken English, he says the Taliban have decided to kill Asad if their demands are not met in a week. Then he leaves the house. I panic. Our worst case scenario is unfolding.

When we tell Asad about the deadline, he is fatalistic. Escape from our current house—with its twenty-foot walls—is impossible.

"The Afghan always gets fucked," Asad says.

Over the next two days, I frantically try to think of ways to save our young driver. Since we were abducted, I have spent hours talking politics, religion, and survival with Tahir, but I can barely communicate with Asad. I speak little Pashto, he speaks little English. I try to help him with chores, searching the rice for stones each day before it is cooked. When an English-language newspaper arrives, I show him photos and try to explain what they are about. He laughs, but I feel like a monster. Asad is an impoverished, hardworking father of two—and I am going to get him killed.

On the third day after Badruddin's visit, I tell Mansoor that I am willing to make a video—or do anything they want—to save Asad. Mansoor says he will check with Badruddin. The following day, Mansoor announces that it has all been a misunderstanding. There is no deadline to kill Asad. I feel enormous relief but do not know what to believe. The lies from our captors are constant and, it seems, intentional. While researching my book, I had heard a Pashto saying that described lying as a tactic of war.

"Speak good words to an enemy very softly," the proverb says, "then gradually destroy him root and branch."

Several days later, Badruddin arrives to make the video. He tells Asad that he had recently watched the video of the beheading of Sayed Agha, the Afghan driver kidnapped with the Italian journalist in 2007.

"I've decided that I don't want to do that to you," Badruddin says with a smile.

He promises us that the video will go only to our families, but what he instructs us to say makes me think it will be released publicly. As we sit in the room where we normally sleep, Mansoor and Qari put scarves over their faces and point assault rifles at our heads. Badruddin aims a handheld camera at me. Following Badruddin's orders, I call for President Bush and President-Elect Obama to meet the Taliban's demands.

"If you don't meet their demands," I say, "they will kill all of us."

Tahir and Asad then make similar statements in Pashto. Badruddin departs, and I tell myself that our families will at least know we are alive.

Several days before Christmas, Atiqullah and Akhundzada appear. Atiqullah has spectacular news.

"We are here to free you," he declares, wearing no scarf over his face for the first time. "We have come here to release you."

Atiqullah is bald and his face is pudgy. He is not the dashing Afghan warrior that Americans idealized during the anti-Soviet jihad. Delivering the news of our release, though, his round face looks sincere to me. I am euphoric. My confidence in Atiqullah is not misplaced. He is a moderate and reasonable Taliban leader who will release us.

Two of Atiqullah's younger brothers accompany him as well. They also make him seem more moderate. One is a respectful young man in his late twenties named Timor Shah. The other is in his early twenties and says he is a fan of American wrestling. He lifts weights and says his favorite wrestler is John Cena.

After dinner, my conversation with Atiqullah turns menacing. Before we are released, he says, we must answer his questions.

"We've investigated you," he declares. "We know every interview you did. We've analyzed every stamp in your passport."

I tell him I have nothing to hide and to ask any questions he wants. Atiqullah announces that on the morning we were kidnapped the American military had mounted an operation to arrest Abu Tayyeb, the Taliban commander who had invited us to the interview. Stunned, I tell Atiqullah I know nothing about a military operation.

He accuses me of sending text messages from my cell phone to Saudi Arabia before the interview, to tip off the American military about Abu Tayyeb's location. I tell him I have no idea what he is talking about.

Finally, he declares that I am a spy, along with other employees of *The New York Times* in Afghanistan. His men have prepared a suicide attack on the paper's Kabul bureau, he says, which he could set off with a single phone call. His men nearly kidnapped another one of our reporters, but they left an interview just before the Taliban arrived, he says. I know he is probably lying on both counts, but I fear he is telling the truth.

Finally, Atiqullah begins asking me a series of questions about the time I lived in New Delhi and served as the newspaper's South Asia bureau co-chief. He demands to know exactly how many times I met the American ambassador there. I answer truthfully, saying that I spent the vast majority of my time in Afghanistan and Pakistan and met the American ambassador in New Delhi once at a group interview and once at a holiday dinner. Atiqullah scoffs at my reply.

Our imprisonment, I think, has reached a low point. Our captor believes I am a spy and my colleagues in Kabul are now in danger as well. Atiqullah's talk earlier in the day of our imminent release seems farcical. The following morning, Atiqullah insists that there is, in fact, a deal. At one point, he says we will be exchanged within "days." He toys with me, asking which flights I will take back to the United States and how many television cameras will be at the airport. He asks me what I will say to Kristen when I see her.

By this point, I have begun to doubt everything he says. Then I learn that he has lied to us from the beginning.

In separate conversations when our guards leave the room, Tahir and

Asad each whisper to me that Atiqullah is, in fact, Abu Tayyeb. They have known since the day we were kidnapped, they say, but dared not tell me. They ask me to stay silent as well. Abu Tayyeb has vowed to behead them if they reveal his identity.

Abu Tayyeb invited us to an interview, betrayed us, and then pretended he was a commander named Atiqullah.

I am despondent and left with only one certainty: We have no savior among the Taliban.

VIDEO GAMES

Kristen, December 22, 2008–Early January 2009

Around noon I receive a call at my office at *Cosmopolitan* from Jim, the Joint Terrorism Task Force FBI agent assigned to our case. The kidnappers have made a video of David. Jim cannot say how the FBI obtained the video, but offers to bring it to me for a private screening. The FBI is honoring our family's request to see the footage first, before the newspaper and security team, in a discreet setting. Everyone involved in the case has been jockeying for my trust of late. This is clearly a gesture on their part. Jim and his fellow agents tell me to look for the blue car parked outside Starbucks on West 57th Street, not far from my office in Midtown Manhattan. I find this slightly amusing as I recall a similar scene from a *Sopranos* episode.

I am so thankful my office has a door. This is not typical at women's magazines. A glass wall separates me from the rest of the photo department—very convenient when planning a clandestine meeting with federal agents. From the exterior cubicles, I can be seen but not heard. This is a great advantage in terms of keeping my situation secret, although the isolation the secrecy fosters leaves me feeling like a lone fish in an aquarium at times.

I'm only a month into my new job, but I regularly fail to arrive at the office before 10 A.M., delayed by phone calls and updates, and then I usually need to leave well before 7 P.M. My associates must be thinking the new girl is a real prima donna. While I have informed the top editors at the magazine of my predicament, the rest of the staff is unaware of my unusual situation. As a newlywed, I am often asked about my husband: Do I have a photo from the wedding I can show? When will I be bringing him to the office for a visit? Has he returned from his reporting trip? I find new and inventive ways to respond to or, in effect, not answer these questions.

I meet Jim, Cathy, and another agent for a private screening in their four-door sedan. This gives new meaning to the phrase "drive-in movie," I think. Jim produces a silver laptop. I assume the video has been intercepted somehow, but do not know from where. The video is poor quality black-and-white footage. David sits between two men Jim tells me are Tahir and Asad. Immediately I notice David is wearing his glasses. This is a huge relief. I was worried they had been confiscated. He is nearly blind without them, and I have spent nights tossing and turning over this fact.

Two Taliban gunmen frame the image, each with a Kalashnikov. One of them has a scarf over his face. The other is cropped out from the neck upward.

David speaks first.

"I am David Rohde, a journalist for *The New York Times*," he says. "I was detained on November 10 and have been held captive for thirty-four days. It's very cold, very difficult. They are moving us around the mountains of Afghanistan and we are not allowed to make calls."

"I ask my office, President Bush, and President-Elect Barack Obama to meet their demands," he says. "If you do not meet their demands, they will kill all three of us. Please meet their demands. Please meet their demands. Please meet their demands."

Tahir and Asad repeat similar speeches in Pashto and plead to Afghan president Hamid Karzai in addition to the American government. All three look remarkably calm, which surprises us. The guns remain pointed at David throughout.

It's the first time I have seen my husband in a month and a half. He seems like a foreign object to me. His expression is a little vacant and glassy-eyed. He is well groomed, cleaner than I expected. He wears a salwar kameez, the baggy pants and shirt that are the local dress. A woolen blanket covers his shoulders. I try to discern information, signals from his eye movements. His hands, concealed by the blanket, are behind his back. I have no idea if they are bound or free. I am struck by the fact that his beard is neat. I was expecting unkempt hair akin to John Walker Lindh, the American who was captured fighting for the Taliban in 2001.

The world within the video feels so removed from my own—distant, foreign, staged. It is not every day one sees one's husband videotaped by terrorists. I find it difficult to absorb this fact. I am at once enraged and relieved. It incenses me to see David used as a mouthpiece. Yet it is comforting to see that he has not been physically mishandled. And, odd as it seems, I am simply relieved to have contact with him. No one has heard a word from him or his captors in over a month. I interpret any form of communication, after this long a silence, as a sign of hope.

And yet there are no specific demands being made in the video. I worry that the Taliban are directing their vague message to the United States government. In addition to being a disturbing situation, it is also bad timing. We are between administrations—in political limbo. The old guard is on its way out; the new is not yet able to step up to the plate.

I watch the video over and over. I can't stop looking at it. One of the drawbacks to clandestine meetings in cars on 57th Street in the middle of Manhattan is traffic. Someone bumps the fender. A traffic cop arrives and threatens to issue a ticket. Jim has to produce his credentials—apparently even the FBI is not exempt from traffic laws. The irony and humor of the situation is not lost on Jim. Months later, when we review the list of communications received from David's captors, he will refer to this one as "the car bump video."

I head back to my office to complete the day, a difficult proposition given that I am now thoroughly distracted. Composing shoot budgets, editing film, and sketching storyboards provide me with a momentary, tangible sense of control, order, and escape. But my solace is fleeting as my mind wanders back to the dubious messages in the video. A few days before Christmas, this was not the holiday greeting I was hoping for.

Back at home, from our apartment window I can see the Christmas trees lined up on the corner for sale, a singular ritual of city life. Cheerful white lights illuminate an overpriced selection of firs and pine trees from

Vermont, Maine, and upstate New York. An enormous plastic snowman flashes a red candy cane and green top hat.

I've been trying to come up with positive ways to reinforce my connection with David during his absence. I decide to go ahead and buy our first Christmas tree as a married couple. A close friend comes over and we drown our holiday sorrows in cheese fondue. Just what the doctor ordered. Then we proceed to the tree stand on the corner. I ask the vendor what I can buy for $40. He produces a sparse sapling, barely a foot high.

"That's one sad-looking Charlie Brown tree," I say.

"Not even!" he admits.

I point to another tree that is a few feet taller, fuller, and more hopeful. Then he tries to sell me a nine-foot tree. "Just sold one of these to Mrs. Gandolfini," he says proudly, referring to the wife of the *Sopranos* star. It's $300. We settle on the smaller but hopeful-looking tree and some stringy tinsel.

At home, we set it up in David's office alcove. We add lights and miniature ornaments, including one David and I bought on a recent trip to Paris. I also pull out every religious relic I can find. There is the "longevity" charm we picked up at the Takstang Monastery in Bhutan, a scared heart from Sacré-Coeur in Paris, and a Buddhist prayer bracelet from Varanasi in India.

Along the window ledge of the living room, I set up all the cards we've received from relatives still unaware of our situation, wishing us a happy first Christmas together. I want to inject as much positive energy into this space as possible in hopes that it will somehow reach David. For the first time in weeks I feel more connected to my husband and hopeful that he will return. I notice a sense of peace I have not felt in quite some time.

Ruhullah, David's former translator in Afghanistan, who is now a college student in the United States, stops by for a visit. After years of working together in tense situations, David and Ruhullah are very close. David treats him like a younger brother. He helped bring Ruhullah to the United States after the work he was doing for David and *The New York Times* bureau made him a target of the Taliban. Ruhullah is headed back to Kabul for the holidays and has offered to remain there to work on David's case.

I tell him David would be very upset if he knew Ruhullah was missing school because of him. Maybe he can think of something more I should be doing, or some type of message I should be trying to send as David's wife. What would a Pashtun woman do?

Ruhullah begins to write a plea for me in Pashto to send to David's captors. "It is a popular saying in my culture: My husband is my veil. Please return him to me." Ruhullah underscores the significance of this phrase: "It means my husband is my honor and you are denying me my honor by keeping him away from me. It is shameful for Afghans to do such a thing. I think this will help."

I scan and e-mail the note to our consultants who are in the process of setting up a base in Kabul, suggesting that they keep it on file for a time when it is possible to send it.

On New Year's Eve I get a call from Jill Abramson, Bill Schmidt, and Craig Whitney—senior employees at the *Times*—all of whom are working late. They have been following David's case and are calling to wish me a happier New Year. While their New Year's Eve has been less than stellar, they all agree mine is probably worse.

We have assembled our consultants in Kabul: Team Kabul.

The team consists of two patient individuals who are tasked with fielding phone calls from the captors, a job that is mostly a waiting game. One of them is a Clayton kidnap expert; the other is an AISC consultant. After much deliberation, the newspaper, Lee, and I have decided to move the operation out of the *Times*' bureau there. The newspaper does not want to endanger its staffers. We also want to shift the kidnappers' perception that *The New York Times* is handling this case. The security team also feels the bureau is not a secure location. They prefer to work from an anonymous compound.

We want to encourage direct contact with our family. And because some people at the Kabul bureau are opposed to the payment of ransom, we do not want them to be the ones to negotiate on David, Tahir, and

Asad's behalf. We also do not want the FBI to oversee our negotiations, because the terms they could discuss are very limited, but we do update them periodically on the status of our communications. We have stuck with David's request to negotiate for all three together. We want the kidnappers to realize that our family, Lee and me, is the correct point of contact for negotiations. We hope the change in venue will achieve this. The phone number the captors have been calling is forwarded to this location.

The downside of moving the call center is that the personnel from AISC and Clayton who will man it rotate out every month. The other disadvantage is that once we move, we won't have nearly the same access to David's colleagues at the Kabul bureau and their enormous expertise in the culture and politics of this region. They have completely dedicated themselves to working for the release of our three, desperately trying to gain on-the-ground intelligence from their local network of sources. They have contacted local tribal elders, the Quetta Shura, and Afghan officials in hope of coming to a resolution that will not involve ransom. One of David's colleagues e-mails daily updates on their progress. This journalist has also researched Abu Tayyeb's background in hopes of gaining insight into his motives, and provides updates to the families of Tahir and Asad. David's colleagues are hesitant to move the call center, but are under pressure from superiors. And they are exhausted, having also to continue to provide daily news coverage of events in the region for the *Times*.

The security team is skeptical of the Kabul bureau's actions. They want to limit outreach done on David's behalf, as they feel it creates confusion about who is running the negotiations and raises his value as a hostage.

Chris Chivers, another reporter in the Kabul bureau and a friend of David's, has returned to the States. He has graciously brought me the laptop and notebook David left behind at the bureau when he set out for the interview on November 10. It is chilling to flip through David's notes. Written on the last page of a small Moleskine are the words *Abu Tayyeb*. This was the Taliban commander David was due to meet that fateful day. The computer, too, is unaltered since David last used it. The November 9 front page of *The New York Times* Web site pops up, an eerie reminder of all the time that has passed while our life together remains on hold.

I have one new friend and confidant, the enigmatic Irishman Michael Semple. He and I have developed a rapport over Skype. He is gracious enough to provide his assessment of how the case is going from time to time on an informal basis. I trust Michael. He knows an enormous amount about what is happening on the ground in Afghanistan and Pakistan and has been brought up to speed on our case by a reporter in the Kabul bureau. He is fluent in several local dialects and understands the complexities of the tribal structures in the region. And he is familiar with members of the Haqqani network, which most people involved in our case now think is responsible for David's kidnapping.

Michael has worked on other kidnapping cases on an unofficial basis, so I hope he has some sense of how this might play out. I value his insight and appreciate his eloquence, which is always tempered with a healthy dose of Irish humor.

I have forwarded the scan of the plea to the captors that Ruhullah wrote in Pashto. Michael promises to pass it along to a mullah who is known to have contact with the Haqqani family. Michael feels that even though the man who has been identifying himself as Atiqullah has been the point person on the phone, it is unlikely he has much authority in striking a deal for the release of David, Tahir, and Asad. Michael, along with our security team, think that Sirajuddin Haqqani is the person ultimately in charge of David's fate.

I have heard of Siraj—the elusive second son of Jalaluddin Haqqani, the mujahideen warrior who helped the United States drive the Soviets out of Afghanistan but then later aligned with the Taliban after 9/11. Siraj rarely grants interviews, eschews photography, and is often referred to as bipolar or schizophrenic. I do not know if this is a clinical term or merely hyperbole. At any rate, he is viewed as erratic and unpredictable. I Google him and learn that he is "so elusive that only a sketch exists of him." The FBI has informed us that one of the captors' voices on the phone—perhaps Atiqullah himself—is Badruddin Haqqani, Siraj's younger brother. Badruddin is believed to be in charge of orchestrating kidnappings for the Haqqani network. We now think "Atiqullah" is the alias that both Abu Tayyeb and Badruddin use when they call us. They are working in tandem.

Every day at noon, we conduct a conference call during which we receive updates on David's case from Team Kabul and discuss the way forward. My day is scheduled to allow for this. As I duck into my office at *Cosmopolitan* and shut the door, I secretly hope my assistant thinks I am talking to my husband or negotiating photography contracts. I phone into an assigned number on a private call box.

A beep precedes the announcement of each participant. We have a lot of cooks in the kitchen. Our noon calls include me, Lee, McCraw, Team Kabul, and an AISC employee in the United States. Michael continues to advise me privately, but does not participate in the daily group calls. Lately, personalities have begun to clash. A kind of turf war, perhaps inevitable, is starting to break out. The security consultants feel all other inquiries and activities, namely the Kabul bureau's outreach to local government officials and elders, should stop. I am hesitant about this, but Lee, McCraw, and I support the suggestion because we feel it will give the new team a chance to establish one clear, direct channel to our family.

Team Kabul has received word, via rumor, that the Taliban want $25 million and ten prisoners in exchange for David. We also hear that David is not well. He is sick from the food and other conditions of captivity. Michael Semple assures me not to be alarmed. "Every hostage is, quote, 'gravely ill' or 'suicidal.' This is merely a way to assert pressure on you." In the meantime, a reporter in the Kabul bureau has gotten in touch with the International Committee of the Red Cross to see if they can make contact with the people holding David in order to send medicine or assistance. The Red Cross informs us that it may be able to act as an intermediary if we want to write letters to our three. Everyone agrees this is a good idea.

At home, I once again Skype with Michael. He assures me that many of his contacts are continuing to inquire about David and are working for his release. Ever the poetic Irishman, he tries to buoy me up. The Afghans have a saying, he tells me: "The fruit of patience is sweet." He encourages me to keep this in mind. Then adds, "Think of yourself as Helen of Troy. Many ships have been launched for your cause." This is rather intriguing, and sustains me for a moment. But when I log off, my mood drops. All illusions aside, my hope is stranded: Afghanistan is a landlocked country.

FUTILITY

David, Late December 2008–Mid-January 2009

T he day after Christmas, Abu Tayyeb announces that his negotiator in Kabul—a man they call the engineer—has reached an
agreement to exchange us for female prisoners from the Afghan
national prison in Pul-i-Charkhi.

"Don't you think it's wrong to hold women prisoner?" he asks me.

"Yes," I say, playing along.

I pace in the yard, telling myself not to believe him. He has lied to us
from the beginning, inviting us to an interview, kidnapping us, and then
masquerading as someone named "Atiqullah." Yet he continues to treat
us well physically, and I find myself unable to stop daydreaming about
our release. Again, my mind seems to be instinctively drawn to a narrative of survival, not death.

Our living conditions have improved again. On Christmas night, Abu
Tayyeb moved us to a larger, more modern house in Miran Shah. The
next morning I was allowed to lie on a cot outside and soak up direct
sunlight. The owner of the house, a tall Afghan Taliban commander
named Sharif, is friendly and encourages me to walk in the yard. The
house's eight-foot walls allow the courtyard to be flooded with sunlight.
It is the most modern house we have inhabited since being abducted. It is
a one-story, five-room structure built in 2005, according to a date scrawled
in one corner of the concrete floor. It has metal doors and window frames,

two bathrooms, and an electric pump that fills a rooftop water tank on the intermittent days when Miran Shah has electricity.

Bedspreads manufactured by a Pakistani textile company for export to the United States cover the floor of the room where we sleep. They are emblazoned with characters from the American television shows *Hannah Montana* and *Littlest Pet Shop,* and the movies *Spider-Man* and *Cars.* My blanket is a pink Barbie comforter. Our guards have never heard of any of the characters. Each night, all of us curl up beneath icons of American pop culture.

Abu Tayyeb spends a few days with us in the new house. He says I am confined for my own safety. If word spreads that an American is being held prisoner in Miran Shah, he says, Arab or Pakistani militants could demand that I be executed in revenge for a drone strike. One night, he returns home and announces that there is an agreement to release us in exchange for seven male prisoners from the Afghan national prison. The exchange will happen in "days," he says.

The following morning, Abu Tayyeb vanishes again. Timor Shah, his younger brother, is now our chief guard. He seems amiable and respectful. To my relief, Qari departs and Mansoor stays. Sharif and one of his gunmen live with us as well.

The next night, Badruddin arrives and shatters my hopes of release. No agreement has been reached for the exchange of seven prisoners from the Afghan national prison, Badruddin says. And the Taliban are continuing to demand a $15 million ransom in addition to prisoners. His description of how our captors are conducting negotiations, though, demoralizes me most of all.

Their negotiator in Kabul—"the engineer" mentioned by Abu Tayyeb—is an Afghan man whom the Haqqanis kidnapped along with his son several months ago, according to Badruddin. At some point, the Haqqanis decided to keep the engineer's son in captivity, release the engineer, and tell him that if he obtained the desired prisoners and ransom in our case, his son would be released. If not, the engineer's son would remain in captivity.

I tell Badruddin their demands will never be met and that blackmailing a man into serving as a negotiator will never succeed. Badruddin says he has no choice. The Afghan government arrested the negotiator the Haqqanis used in their last kidnapping. Badruddin departs and I am livid. I am desperate to speak with Tahir about what to do, but the guards insist we go to bed. Unable to sleep, I grow increasingly angry. I want to punish Badruddin for his obstinacy. I want to show our captors that we will not wait forever for an agreement.

I decide to fake a suicide attempt the following morning. Before dawn, I hear Sharif and one of his gunmen walking around outside. They are performing ablutions before waking the others for predawn prayers. I get up, grab the Afghan scarf my captors gave me to cover my face, and walk out of the room where we sleep with our guards. The gunman greets me and I motion to him that I am waiting for the bathroom, which Sharif occupies. The gunman walks into the yard to perform ablutions at a spigot around the corner.

I push the cot the gunman sleeps on up against a wall, step onto it, and tie one end of the scarf to a metal bar I have seen during the day. I tie the other end of the scarf around my neck. When I hear the gunman walking back toward the house from the yard, I step off the cot, hang in the air, and start kicking my feet.

"Sharif!" the guard shouts. "Sharif!"

Seconds later, someone places me in a bear hug and lifts me up. The scarf is loosened from around my neck. Tahir rushes out of the bedroom and starts shouting.

"David! David!" he thunders. "Can you hear me? What are you doing?"

His voice is filled with anger, not sympathy. All the guards rush out of the bedroom and glare at me. Tahir leads me back into the bedroom, tells me to lie down, and asks me why I did this.

"I have no hope because of Badruddin," I say, and break into false tears. I do my best to look depressed and desperate to Sharif and the guards. Tahir and the guards speak in Pashto. I am left alone for several minutes with Asad and one of the guards watching me. Asad walks over to me, tugs my beard, and embraces me. I tell him that I'm sorry.

Tahir returns to the room and is irate. "Are you a child?" he shouts. "Why did you not speak to me before doing this?"

He explains that attempting to commit suicide confirms that I am guilty in the eyes of our captors. The Taliban believe that if a human being is truly innocent, they will patiently wait for God to save them. If they try to kill themselves, they are guilty. My head spins. Another rash decision by me has endangered us. I ask Tahir to forgive me. He says he no longer trusts me.

Badruddin arrives an hour later. As he walks through the door, I stare down at the floor. He slaps me on the shoulder and shouts, "Sit up straight!" Incensed, he turns to Tahir and accuses him of telling me to attempt suicide. Tahir denies it but Badruddin does not believe him. Everything I do is blamed on Tahir. I apologize to Badruddin, tell him I have made a terrible mistake, and promise not to do it again. Seething with anger, he leaves.

Timor Shah takes away my scarf and issues new orders. I am not allowed to leave the bedroom at night without the permission of the guards. I must ask them before walking from room to room and going to the bathroom. And when I am in the bathroom, I must leave the door open at all times so the guards can watch for a suicide attempt.

Abu Tayyeb arrives several days later. He tells me that if I do this again my life will end.

"If you want to die," he says, "this is a very easy place to die."

I apologize to him and again promise nothing will happen. Abu Tayyeb says we will now be guarded by three of his men at all times. Chunky will be joining us as well. The following morning, he departs again.

Tahir tells me the attempt has exponentially increased our captors' suspicions of me. Sharif does not think it was real. If I was serious, I would have tried in the middle of the night when no one would find me. Tahir's disappointment devastates me. I have let him down in a way I never intended.

Trying to regain the trust of the guards, as well as Tahir's and Asad's, I comply with all the new rules and sheepishly ask for permission to do the smallest of acts. I do more chores to show my loyalty. Along with washing the breakfast dishes, I sweep the floors, and look for stones in the rice before Asad cooks it.

Trying to stay patient, I multiply the amount of praying I do. Three times a day, I silently pray for Kristen, my family, Asad, and Tahir, confess my sins, and ask for forgiveness and for our freedom. I repeat each one-line prayer forty-one times, the number of years I have lived. I count the prayers on my fingertips while I'm walking in the yard, varying the order depending on what seems most dire that day. If I have made a mistake with the guards, I pray for forgiveness first. If there is a recent threat of Asad's or Tahir's being executed, I pray for them first. If it is a holiday or family birthday, I begin with Kristen and family. I sense that I am becoming compulsive about praying, but it continues to give me a sense of control when I have none.

I know the guards would find it blasphemous that I dare formulate my own prayers. The hard-line Wahhabi Islam they follow focuses on exacting ritual. Sharif and the guards wear their hair, beards, and clothes precisely as they have been told the prophet did. Mustaches are neatly trimmed to prevent food from gathering in facial hair. Beards are not allowed to grow longer than the width of a man's fist. Pants hang three to four inches above the ankle. As the prophet did, they brush their teeth with a miswak, a twig from an arak, or peelu, tree that contains natural disinfectants.

The guards' five daily prayers themselves are soothing. As they rhythmically confess sins and appeal for mercy in Arabic, they press their foreheads to the ground and supplicate to God. The tremendous discipline they show is impressive, but the rigidity of their interpretation of Islam rings false to me. If there is a higher being, I believe it will hear a sincere and humble prayer no matter how it is delivered.

In early January, Asad tells Tahir that he is going to try to escape on his own. I am elated by the news. By dutifully cooking our meals and essentially serving as slave labor, Asad has gradually gained the trust of the guards.

Tahir, by comparison, is defiant. He refuses to do any chores. His attitude toward the guards is a lesson in Pashtunwali. He refuses to show weakness.

"They can't touch me," he says.

Tahir's powerful tribe—the Luddin—will take revenge on anyone who harms him, he believes. The man who kills him will die along with ten members of his family. I admire his bravery. I know Afghanistan's tribal structure has weakened over the years. The Taliban do not fear Afghanistan's tribes as they once did.

Asad believes that Tahir is being reckless and his escape plan is simple. The guards have started taking Asad with them on regular trips to Miran Shah's busy central market to buy food. On a recent trip, Asad slipped away and met a taxi driver who said he would drive Asad to the Afghan border. Asad returned to the guards and apologized for getting separated. He now plans to slip away again from the guards on his next trip to the market, jump in the taxi, and head for the Afghan border. Tahir, who brought several hundred dollars in cash to our ill-fated interview, gives Asad extra money to pay the driver.

The following morning, Asad departs with the guards. The thought of his being reunited with his wife and two sons is thrilling to me. I pray he will succeed. Several hours later, there is a knock on our compound door. Asad enters ashen faced. The guards are nowhere to be seen. Asad whispers to Tahir that he evaded the guards in the crowded market and reached the taxi. But when the driver tried to leave Miran Shah, Taliban fighters stopped the taxi at a checkpoint. When the Taliban grew suspicious, Asad had the taxi return him to Miran Shah and walked back to our house.

The guards return from the local market and berate Asad for getting separated from them. Asad tells them he got lost. We return to our bleak daily routine. All of our attempts to fight back have proven futile

MULTITASKING

Kristen, Early to Mid-January 2009

"Nothing to report" has become the standard daily update from Team Kabul as we endure the quiet winter months.

Today's noon call is a surprising exception. Team Kabul informs us that they have been contacted by Atiqullah and that they have made an offer to counter his demands for $25 million and ten prisoners. We are all a bit stunned, because our family has not preapproved any amount. "What did you offer?" we ask. They tell us.

You can hear a pin drop. While it is nowhere in the range of what the kidnappers are demanding, it is much more than we ever intended to offer up front. We have been told to offer low, in hopes of lowering expectations. For weeks we have been debating with Team Kabul what this might mean. We were forewarned about offering too little—we need enough on the table to keep David and his colleagues alive. But this number seems way too high.

We have no intention of paying any amount, at this time, but we hope the offer will keep the conversation going. It does not.

Word comes back from the kidnappers that our offer is offensively low. They turn their phones off. We do not hear from them for several weeks. The Clayton consultant who made the offer did so with the best intentions. He valued all three lives equally. We think he was going for a slam-dunk. But, clearly, this has backfired. He rotates out of Kabul and does not return for a second rotation.

It's been several weeks since we've heard from David's captors. Despite the fact that phone communication has come to a halt, the two-man Team Kabul remains in place. Each day they try the mobile phone numbers that Atiqullah had previously given to us. No answer.

One day, a person who identifies himself as "the engineer" shows up at Team Kabul's compound with a bold claim. The Haqqanis have sent him to negotiate a deal for the release of our three, he says. The engineer is a former Afghan military official who once worked with Americans. He himself was kidnapped several months ago by the Haqqanis. He was released in exchange for his son, who is now in captivity. He announces that the Haqqanis want prisoners and money in exchange for David, Tahir, and Asad—as well as several prisoners to gain his son's release.

We are skeptical as to why he would help us. Does he have a side agenda? Can we trust him? Team Kabul meets with him on numerous occasions and reports that the engineer appears to be well educated and genuine. He does not ask for money for any of his efforts.

Team Kabul decides to take him up on his offer. He begins to contact representatives for the Haqqanis and relays messages back that our family is working to resolve this issue, but will never have the amount of money they are asking for.

Back in New York, our noon updates continue with *The New York Times*, Team Kabul, and AISC, the private security contractors. Weekends are no exception. This particular weekend I am checking in on a *Cosmo* cover shoot a few blocks from my home. We are photographing one of the *Gossip Girls* at a loft studio in Tribeca. Everything—the floor, the ceiling, the furniture—is stark white. The space is a mix of modern and vintage architectural details. We have also put up a backdrop of colorful seamless paper.

All morning the actress has been getting *Cosmo*-ready: full hair, makeup. Racks of designer dresses and platform shoes line the dressing area. Pop music blares in the background. Push-up bras, pins, and cleavage enhancers are on hand.

I'm hoping we will start shooting before my noon call so I can duck out to listen to the latest update from Kabul. No such luck. Instead, I phone in to our call box from the set and look for a quiet corner.

The update is horrific. A messenger was sent in to obtain recent proof of life from David's captors. He has not resurfaced. We receive news that he never returned and might have been shot en route. It is not clear whether the incident was due to his attempt to help us or random fire. The border area is a war zone, after all. We are not quite sure which route he took or his intended final destination, only that he claimed to be able to make contact with people in proximity to David. A death might have occurred as a result of our case. I feel nauseated.

The call continues. Mike, the head of AISC, weighs in on the latest speculation on David's whereabouts. Another individual who AISC brought onto the case has recently begun to frequent our noon calls. Until now he has been working behind the scenes. We hear from him next. A gruff voice proceeds to tell us what he has learned from an American government official with contacts in the region. I have not met the owner of the voice on the other end of the line, so I have yet to match a face with the speaker. But his voice is distinct and he seems to be quite the mastermind, able to think of long-term connections and associations of the Haqqanis. The gravelly older voice on the end of the line, with a hint of a New England accent, is Dewey Clarridge. Over the course of the next few months, his colorful personality emerges. We quickly learn that Dewey has two modes: grumpy and "grandfatherly." He shifts between the two periodically, occasionally offering me heartfelt encouragement: "We're gonna win this thing, kiddo!" And at other times, he is disgruntled and tells me to take up needlepoint. He often punctuates his point by hanging up on the noon calls or telling us all to shut up. McCraw refers to the softer side of Dewey as "Grandpa Dewey."

Dewey seems to be a sharp strategist and savvy operator. I consider his opinions, though I do not always appreciate the delivery. Today he informs us as to how he thinks David's case might play out. If David or his captors are still in Afghanistan, the winter storms will be kicking in, followed by the spring offensive—this is a period of time during which the Taliban fighters regroup and redouble their efforts—typically in April.

On the basis of this pattern, he estimates David will not be released before May.

May! I am outraged—inconveniently so, as the photo shoot is beginning to take shape in the background. The actress is finished with hair and makeup and is getting ready for her close-up.

"May is thoroughly unacceptable," I respond, my imperious fashion editor voice creeping in. "How can you tell me this? David has been gone for two months. Every day he sits there takes a toll on his sanity."

I realize this is a business on both sides and wonder what the incentive is to get him out quickly if our security team is paid by the day. I say as much, which thoroughly offends and pisses off half the team. The rest of the group is silent, understanding it's my prerogative as the hostage's wife to lose my cool now and then. I am disgusted at the prospect of facing more months of uncertainty. I am also tired of dealing with a virtual roomful of men. Not the eager-to-please pinups we exhibit in *Cosmo*, but the macho former-intel and military types who comprise our team. As Dewey interrupts to tell me to calm down—and shut up—I hang up. I do not want to incur more damage. And my tolerance for speculation coupled with chauvinism is exhausted.

The shoot gets under way and seems on track, so I head home. It has begun to snow. The cool air is a calming relief. No sooner do I round the corner than I get a call from someone at the shoot. Lunch has arrived. Shrimp. And the publicist has neglected to tell us that the actress is allergic to shellfish. What should the crew do? I suggest ordering extra sandwiches. They inform me the water for tea is cold. *You've got to be kidding me,* I think. Yet it's my job to manage every detail of a shoot, large and small, from budgeting and location down to gastronomic minutiae. The big picture and the smallest detail. But given the fact that I have been told that someone surrounding David's case may have been shot and that I should expect to face the cold winter months without my husband, I find it impossible to care.

Trudging back to the apartment I hit an all-time low. I am exhausted to the point of tears. I don't see how I can juggle my work life and the demands of the kidnapping. Pleasing a celebrity and chewing out a security team are incongruous and perhaps irreconcilable activities.

At home, my mother encourages me to get some rest, but my mind is on overload. I find no peace in sitting still. I glance at the avocado plant my mother has been growing in the apartment since Thanksgiving. It is now a hearty sapling and has sprouted several leaves.

"I should leave work," I say. She encourages me to hang on. Work, she says, while stressful, provides a sense of stability and routine. And, oddly, a respite from being completely consumed by crisis. I am frustrated because I am unable to give 100 percent to work. I have to resign myself to the fact that my energy is finite. If working at half speed is all I can do right now, I need to accept it. The magazine has recently offered to let me hire a freelancer to fill in for me a few days a week. My mother encourages me to take advantage of this and rest when I can.

My mother and I have made very different choices in life. She married young and had three children. Motherhood was a priority for her in her twenties and thirties.

I am nearly forty and have just gotten married. I hope to have a family, but other things were more important to me until now. I regret to admit that the clock is now ticking full force. In fact, the alarm bell rings every hour. One subtext to all this uncertainty and waiting is that I wonder if David and I will miss the opportunity to have a family together.

My mother and I are quite different, yet I know no one feels my pain more than her. It's tough for her to see me in distress. She has been a real trouper, doing her best to conceal her own sadness and fear. This alone is a huge service. I often feel I have no room for anyone else's emotion. I am constantly barraged with well-meaning but often tearful inquiries about David. Calls from friends and family once a comfort now feel like an added responsibility. I do not know what to tell them. I have hit full saturation. It's all I can do to keep myself composed, let alone comfort someone else.

At this point, David's colleagues, other news organizations, the United States government and close relatives are aware of the situation. Yet most of my colleagues, with the exception of the top editors at *Cosmopolitan* and a few close friends, are still in the dark.

My mother tells me on occasion that she does not quite know what to do to help me. I reassure her that just her presence is enough—the fact that she has kept the apartment in order, reminded me to eat and rest. These things, while so basic, are so easily forgotten in the midst of crisis. She is also quite handy, I have learned, and regularly assigns herself home improvement projects, executing them flawlessly. They involve everything from putting a closet door back on track to repairing floor tiles and managing the plumber when the faucet leaks. As I look around, the apartment seems brighter. She confesses that she has painted the hallway. "When?" I ask, astonished. "While you were at work one day, just some minor touch ups," she replies. I am exhausted by the thought of her seamless productivity around the home. Exhausted and thankful.

If nothing else, I have a newfound respect for my mother; not just her efficiency, but her strength and her complete willingness to be my silent hero. I appreciate the power her presence has to make everything seem like it will be all right. My father, too, has been a strong support, shuttling my mother between New York and Maine and visiting on the weekends. He has been a selfless advocate, willing to accommodate my mother's long absences as he knows her presence has been an essential part of my ability to cope with the daily challenges of the kidnapping.

I never wanted to be the spouse stuck at home, waiting for someone to return. For years, I chose a career that would enable me to be the one off having adventures, often at the expense of my personal life. In David, I chose a partner who had taken a similar path. Our desire to reform our solitary lives and build a home life seemed to converge. I recall our first meeting in New York, or the first meeting I remember. I had met David briefly in college, at Brown where we were both students. He had bright red carrot-top hair, was always dressed in khakis and an oxford shirt, and never said a word to me. He swears we met in New York five years or so after graduation when he stopped by my apartment with a mutual friend. I have no memory of it. The same friend suggested we meet in June 2006.

We exchanged e-mails and met at a restaurant in my neighborhood. At any rate, the David of 2006 breezed into the restaurant, only a few minutes late.

I didn't consider our dinner to be a date, but merely two people with a mutual friend, meeting for a casual meal. He had just finished a day of reporting. I'd just come from a still-life shoot for *Self* magazine, where I was working as a photo editor.

I was pleasantly surprised. For starters, David was taller than I remembered. I was in heels and he still had a few inches on me. He was also friendlier, more talkative. And he was a good listener—probably a side benefit of his job, or perhaps the reason he was so good at it. We spoke freely. He told me he had recently returned to the States from a reporting posting in Delhi. He was looking to slow down a bit, maybe settle down. He asked how I felt about my life now. I said I had spent a lot of time thinking only of me. I was ready to share my life with someone else. This was risky for a first nondate, but I was tired of game playing: I was ready to think about someone else for a change. I wanted to start a family. We also shared a mutual connection to Maine. By coincidence, his father lives twenty minutes from my parents. We each treasured our fond memories of spending time there.

At the end of the night, I kissed David on the cheek. He told me he was headed off to Afghanistan, but would call from there. The very notion of calling me from a war zone seemed a bit improbable, impractical. To my surprise, that is exactly what he did, on a regular basis during his monthlong assignment.

I remember saying good-bye to David that night and rushing home to call my mother. "I met the most interesting man," I told her.

THE TALIBAN TRUST
THE RED CROSS

David, Mid-January 2009

Badruddin arrives for another visit. He walks into the room and I greet him respectfully, shake his hand, and sit on top of my pink Barbie bedspread. He formally greets everyone else in Pashto. As he makes small talk, I am on my best behavior and trying to regain the trust of the guards. I brace myself for the bad news that seems to come with each of Badruddin's visits.

After several minutes, he pulls papers from his pocket that bear the seal of the International Committee of the Red Cross. "Red Cross Message" is printed just below the seal, followed by a blank form where prisoners or refugees give their name, date, and place of birth as well as other details that prove their identity. I'm going to be allowed to write a letter to my wife. My fake suicide attempt may, in fact, have placed some pressure on our captors.

For weeks, I've been practicing what I would say to my family if given the chance. I want to communicate far more than I did in the first video. Someone produces a pen and I stare at the form. Badruddin and the guards stare at me.

The form asks the prisoner to list the full names of their mother, father, and grandfathers. I hesitate, fearing that listing names could endanger my family. At the same time, I know that if I refuse to name them or give false names it will raise my captors' suspicions.

I write down their names, hoping my family will understand the rationale that has gradually solidified in my mind. Crying on videos, begging
my family for money, and obeying my captors' commands is justifiable if
it saves the lives of Asad and Tahir. My wife, family, and friends are strong,
I tell myself, and they will able to bear this burden.

I begin writing the letter. To make it seem like I have nothing to hide,
I describe each sentence to Badruddin before writing it on the form in
clear capital letters.

"Thank you for our wonderful wedding on September 6, 2008," I
write in clear capital letters that I hope will be easy to read. I try to include innocuous details that will both prove I am, in fact, the author of
the letter and bolster my wife's spirits. "Memories of that wonderful day
and our beautiful time together keep me strong here."

I tell Kristen I love her "so very, very, very much" and thank her, my
family, and my friends for all they are doing to help us. Then I try to ease
any guilt they may feel. I know I might not have another chance to communicate with them and I want to give them closure if our case ends badly.

"Simply do the best you can," I write. "That's all I ask.

"I accept the consequences of my actions and thank you all for all of
the joy you've given me," I write. "I thank you and love you all so much."

Badruddin declares that the next portion of the letter should focus on
the Taliban's demands. We briefly argue over what those should be. I
insist they are vastly too high. He says he is already compromising.

"The Taliban started out asking for 10 prisoners and have reduced their
demand to 5 prisoners from Pul-e-Chargi prison," I write, using the spelling for the government prison that Tahir gives me. "They have reduced the
money from $25 million to $15 million."

The figures deeply depress me. They refuse to reduce them further.

Badruddin will not allow Tahir and Asad to write letters to their families. In mine, I insist that their release must be part of any agreement.
"Any deal must be for all three of us," I write. "Again, any must be for all
three of us."

"Please tell the International Red Cross to tell Asad and Tahir's family they are alive + well," I write, using a "+" to save space. "Tell Asad +

Tahir's family to please send messages to them through the International Red Cross. They love their families very much."

I urge my family to negotiate through the Red Cross. I want to somehow shift Badruddin's and Abu Tayyeb's attention away from the *Times'* Kabul bureau, which I worry is still the focus of their paranoia. I am also desperate to find a middleman who they believe will not steal any ransom.

"The Taliban do not trust and are very angry + suspicious of the office," I write, referring to the bureau. "You should negotiate through the Red Cross only. All negotiations and transactions of any kind should be through the Red Cross. The Taliban trust the Red Cross."

Hoping to increase the pressure on my family, Badruddin orders me once again to falsely state that we are in the mountains of Afghanistan. Hoping to tip off my family that I'm being ordered to lie, I write: "They are telling me to tell you that we are in a mountain area in Afghanistan with cold weather, snow and Afghan food + water that make me sick." Badruddin then dictates more lines. "They say that if their demands are not met they will kill the three of us," I write. "They are telling me to tell you to hurry up + meet their demands."

There are only a half dozen blank lines left on the small form. I try to communicate the argument I've been making to our captors. "I've said I'm a journalist who has spent my career writing to help Muslims but they say you must meet their demands," I write.

Three lines remain on the page. I scribble my final words.

"Please, please, please help us," I say. "I'm so sorry. I'll pay back anyone who helps us for the rest of my life."

"I'm so, so sorry," I repeat. "I apologize to you, my family and friends."

I scrawl "I love you!!!" in large letters and sign my name.

Badruddin takes the letter and has Tahir slowly translate each passage to him. When he hears the phrase "they are telling me to tell you," he grows suspicious. I immediately offer to blot those words out with the pen. He agrees and then departs. For hours afterward, I berate myself for how I constructed the sentence. I need to be humble and patient and think small. Haste had gotten us into this disaster. Being impatient will only make things worse.

Roughly two weeks pass and we hear nothing from Badruddin. Then he arrives without warning and tells us we are going on a picnic. At first, I think he is joking. The guards tell me to cover my face with a scarf, follow Badruddin outside, and get into his pickup truck. After a five- to ten-minute drive, I am allowed to take the scarf off and look around.

Dust-covered hillsides surround us as we wind our way up a valley somewhere outside Miran Shah. There are no trees or discernible landmarks. We could be anywhere in the tribal areas. As we drive, I ask Badruddin if he has any response to my letter. He says the International Red Cross will not act as an intermediary for negotiations. My hopes fade. Badruddin stops the truck and we walk up a barren hill. I ask him how the negotiations are proceeding. He says he has nothing new to report. What has he been doing all this time? I ask. He says the problem is on my side. He scoffs at the amount of money they are offering for our release.

Badruddin asks me if I want to fire one of the guard's Kalashnikovs. I decline. If I look like I know how to fire the rifle, I will appear to be a soldier. And if I take the rifle and try to shoot Badruddin and the four guards who are with us, I'm unlikely to kill all of them before they shoot me. Asad walks to a nearby hillside and fires a Kalashnikov with one of the guards. Badruddin has the most advanced Kalashnikov, which has a grenade launcher mounted on the end of it. For entertainment, he fires a grenade at a nearby hillside and it detonates loudly, and he and his men watch to see if it frightens me. I try to show no reaction.

Badruddin, the guards, Tahir, and Asad then spread scarves on the ground and perform afternoon prayers. After they finish, Badruddin invites me to sit down. I oblige him. Unsure when I will see him next, I again tell him he will never get five prisoners and $15 million for us. He vows that he will and tells me the United States freed seven Serbian military officers in exchange for my 1995 release in Bosnia. Amazed by his statement, I tell him that is absolutely false. He responds that I told him that when we first arrived in Miran Shah.

"You said I was slow," he says, smiling. "You said seven prisoners were released for you after only ten days."

He is lying, apparently for the fun of it. No Serbian prisoners were released for me in 1995. The Haqqanis have turned my arrest for helping to expose the massacre of 8,000 Muslims into a liability in my case, not an asset. We sit in silence for several minutes.

"I could shoot you here and end this now," Badruddin offers with a smile.

I do not respond.

He again ridicules the ransom being offered for us. "I will sell your bones to your family" for that amount, he says.

Again, I do not respond.

We drive back to the house in silence. The following day, I learn that the guards are angry with me. They say Badruddin took me on a picnic and I was rude to him.

As January progresses, events in the outside world become a growing source of tension. The Israeli attack on the Gaza Strip infuriates the Taliban. Along with monitoring Western news broadcasts on Afghanistan, our guards closely watch world events as well. As the number of Palestinians killed spirals to 1,400—as compared with 14 Israelis—the Taliban seethe. Our guards see the campaign as the latest example of Muslims being slaughtered by an arrogant, hypocritical West. I wonder if we will be killed on videotape in retaliation. A second date also hovers: January 20, the inauguration of Barack Obama. I worry that the "blood message to Obama" that our kidnappers promised on the day we were abducted will finally be delivered.

The Israeli assault on Gaza ends on January 18 and Obama's inauguration passes without incident two days later. I read about it in one of the Pakistani English-language newspapers the guards bring me once or twice a week. The newspapers continue to be a godsend. I have begun reading each newspaper cover to cover to pass the time. I find myself drawn to stories that I glanced at in the past. Reading them transports me to another place. Editorials condemning the Taliban remind me that most Pakistanis oppose the group. A book review on a study that examines the history of religion states that human beings create gods when confronted by forces greater than themselves. Science section stories bolster my belief that human civilization is progressing. A paid advertisement printed on the day of Obama's inauguration shows me another side of the Pashtuns.

It is a historical piece about a nonviolent Pashtun political leader known as the Frontier Gandhi. The political party he founded purchased ad space to print a biography of his life on January 20, the eleventh anniversary of his death. The party's version of his life is glowing and I know from things I have previously read that much of it is true. The existence of a pacifist Pashtun seems improbable. Their fighting skills are what has made the region so forbidding.

Born in 1889, Khan Abdul Ghaffar Khan was a devout Muslim and lifetime follower of Mahatma Gandhi's philosophy of nonviolent resistance. A towering figure who was six and a half feet tall and had a hawk nose, Ghaffar Khan founded a 100,000-strong movement called the Servants of God, or Red Shirts, in the 1920s. Its members were famous for their willingness to stage nonviolent strikes to protest British colonial rule—and die by the hundreds in the process.

A friend and compatriot of Gandhi's, Khan had the goal to free South Asia from British colonial rule and establish one independent, secular state where Muslims, Hindus, and people of all faiths could live peacefully. Later in life, he also campaigned for the reunification of the Pashtuns divided by the despised British-dictated border between Afghanistan and Pakistan.

Before dying at the age of ninety-eight, Ghaffar Khan achieved one of those goals but failed at the two others. Colonial India won independence from Britain in 1947 but was divided into two countries—a predominantly Muslim Pakistan and a predominantly Hindu India. Pashtuns in Afghanistan and Pakistan also failed to be reunited. The partition of British-controlled India into two nations sparked one of the greatest and bloodiest mass migrations in human history. Over the course of several months in 1947, 14 million Hindus and Muslims crossed the newly created borders in the hope of finding a safer life in the country where they would be in the religious majority.

To the dismay of Ghaffar Khan and Gandhi, cataclysmic religious clashes erupted. As many as one million Muslims and Hindus perished on both sides of the new border. Two months after independence, war broke out after the Hindu ruler of the majority Muslim state of Kashmir said it would join India, not Pakistan. It was the first of four wars that India and Pakistan waged between 1947 and 1999.

Since arriving in the region in 2001, I had seen how the rivalry between the two countries fueled instability in Afghanistan and the wider region. For sixty years, partition colored nearly every move by India and Pakistan. Since 2001, India had backed the Karzai government with vast aid programs and record numbers of Indians living in Kabul. Threatened by what it saw as India encroaching on its flank, Pakistan's military quietly maintained its longtime support for the Afghan Taliban. Over time, I came to see the fighting in Afghanistan on one level as a proxy war between India and Pakistan, with American soldiers caught in the middle.

As I finish reading the story, Ghaffar Khan emerges as a tragic figure. In some ways, he reminds me of the educated Pashtun moderates I have followed in "Little America" since 2004. Their efforts to promote reform were hampered by religious conservatism and regional rivalries as well.

Instead of being hailed as a hero after Pakistan achieved independence in 1947, Ghaffar Khan was repeatedly placed under house arrest or jailed by the military-dominated Pakistani government. His fealty to Gandhi was seen as loyalty to India, not to the principle of nonviolence. All told, he spent more than twenty years in Pakistani and British detention. Ghaffar Khan died in Peshawar in 1988 and retained some popular support among Pashtuns for his campaign for Pashtun reunification. He asked to be buried in Afghanistan to show his continued devotion to the goal of unifying the Pashtuns.

His pro-Gandhi and pro-socialist stance, though, took a toll on his popular support on both sides of the border. Pakistani nationalists marginalized him by declaring him pro-India. Afghan's mujahideen accused him of supporting the Soviet Union, the country's atheist occupier. In the decade after his death, the Taliban in Afghanistan and hard-line religious parties in Pakistan proclaimed themselves the true leaders of the Pashtuns. A moderate Pashtun nationalist political party founded by Ghaffar Khan's son gained only limited electoral support from Pashtuns.

In February 2008, I covered elections in Pakistan's Pashtun-dominated northwest that pitted the secular Pashtun nationalist party of Ghaffar Khan's descendants—the Awami National Party—against Pakistan's hard-line religious parties. In 2002, conservative parties had won control of the provincial government for the first time, but subsequently failed to deliver economic growth, clean government, and security. In the 2008 elections, the moderate party of Ghaffar Khan triumphed. Now led by his grandson, Asfandyar Wali Khan, the moderate Pashtuns defeated hard-line religious parties and won control of the provincial government. The question I posed in 2001 about how best to counter religious extremism seemed to have an answer: electoral politics.

Yet after taking office the moderate Pashtuns struggled to effectively govern. Stepped-up Taliban suicide attacks and kidnappings ravaged Peshawar, the largest Pashtun-dominated city in northwestern Pakistan. In the newspapers I received from our guards, story after story described public disappointment with the moderate Pashtuns' inability to stop suicide bombings and abductions. Rumors of corruption hovered over the government as well. The pattern was similar to what I had seen in Afghanistan.

After decades of neglect, moderate Pashtuns were weak and poorly organized. Trying to reverse decades of shortsighted American, Saudi, and Pakistani support for hard-line Pashtuns was enormously difficult, slow moving, and bloody. Yet it was vital. To me, finding ways to more effectively support Pashtun moderates was the key to stabilizing Afghanistan and Pakistan.

LOVE LETTERS

Kristen, Late January 2009

D avid McCraw has become a stable, regular character in my life. His calm and wholesome midwestern manner is paired with a savvy wit and deep intelligence.

He, David's brother Lee, and I talk all the time about everything from conflicting reports and information to media strategies and personal frustrations. McCraw is also thoughtful enough to contact me in advance of the noon call on days when updates may be unpleasant. A few weeks ago, McCraw forewarned me that in response to our request for proof of life, the captors responded: "We'll give you a finger." (My mother was present while I took this call. She was quick to point out, "A finger is not proof of life.")

Today, McCraw is calling with the latest rumblings from the Afghan rumor mill. A tribal elder who knows the Haqqanis has relayed a message to the paper's Kabul bureau. Rumor is that David is on a "ransom farm" in Afghanistan with as many as sixty other hostages, including the engineer's son. The elder claims that David has his own room, but keeps Asad and Tahir with him at all times. He is free to move about the compound and chat with other captives. It sounds like he is at the Club Med of hostage camps. It seems too rosy to be true. We have heard stories of other people currently being held hostage, among them a Polish hostage, and several aid workers from the World Food Program. It is difficult to know if this information is accurate or merely a fabrication, though the messenger did not request money.

A few days later, on January 24, the International Committee of the Red Cross delivers a letter to the Kabul bureau. We have no idea what route it has traversed or how many hands it has passed through. It bears no date. One of David's colleagues scans it and forwards it to my e-mail.

I know instantly the letter was written by him.

"Thank you for our wonderful wedding on September 6, 2008. Memories of that wonderful day and our beautiful times together keep me strong here. I love you so very, very, very much and thank you for all the joy you have given me. Thank you for all you and my friends and family are doing to help us. Simply do the best you can. That's all I ask."

It's incredibly moving just to see his handwriting.

The demands have dropped from $25 million to $15 million. And from ten prisoners from Guantánamo and Bagram to five from Pul-i-Charkhi, a less-secure prison in Afghanistan. But David's captors are still in a different stratosphere from us.

Pul-i-Charkhi. This is interesting, as the newspaper's Kabul bureau has found out that Atiqullah's real name is Najibullah Naeem and he also goes by Abu Tayyeb. Abu Tayyeb has twice been a prisoner at Pul-i-Charkhi, but was able to bribe his way out. He lived for years in Zabul Province, the same as Tahir. We are now certain that the Taliban commander David went to interview is also his captor. To add to the intrigue, the FBI has "declassified" the identity of Atiqullah. They claim Atiqullah is an alias for not one, but two individuals working in tandem: Abu Tayyeb and Badruddin Haqqani. They think Abu Tayyeb originally abducted David and perhaps sold or handed him over to Badruddin Haqqani.

David insists that this be a deal for all three. The letter also states: "The Taliban do not trust and are very angry and suspicious of the office and the head of the office in Kabul. You should negotiate through the

Red Cross only. All negotiations and transactions of any kind should be through the Red Cross. The Taliban trust the Red Cross."

Something has been obliterated and is unintelligible, followed by: "We are in a mountain area of Afghanistan with cold weather, snow and Afghan food and water that make me sick. The conditions are very difficult. They say that if their demands are not met they will kill the three of us. They are telling me to tell you to hurry up and meet their demands. I've said I'm a journalist who has spent my career writing to help Muslims but they say you must meet their demands. Please, please, please help us. I'm so sorry. I'll pay back anyone who helps us for the rest of my life. I'm so, so sorry. I apologize to you, my family and friends. I LOVE YOU!!!"

I spend the next few days in my apartment writing a response, and then rewriting it. I show drafts to Lee, McCraw, our security team, and the FBI for feedback. Their responses are typically contradictory: I do not feel there is one channel giving Lee and me clear and authoritative advice. Our team members are sometimes at odds because of their background, agenda, and viewpoint. I spend days fine-tuning the letter. I want to include enough personal information to put David at ease, without revealing any additional information to his captors. This means omitting the names of family and friends—and referring to them simply by relationship. As a team, we debate content, word choice, as well as etiquette. The competing strategies are becoming clear. Some feel we should play on the captors' sense of honor by thanking them for treating David well. Other members feel they have no honor and should not be praised for their behavior. I'm trying to strike a balance between cultural sensitivity and authenticity.

Our team debates the merits of including a counteroffer within my letter, even though we have already been told by the head of the International Red Cross in Kabul that the organization will not participate in or facilitate negotiations. They will not carry a letter containing negotiation points. This is very frustrating. Why would the Haqqanis select the Red Cross as an intermediary when they are not permitted to act in this manner? We compose two letters—one that is personal and a second that also contains a counteroffer. We are mentioning it to keep the conversation going, until we are in striking distance of their demands. Or, no matter how improbable, until the FBI can get a fix on David's location and facilitate a rescue attempt. We also send a backup message through the engineer.

We also debate the meaning of David's reference to "the office in Kabul." The security contractors claim this is the paper's Kabul bureau. The *Times* thinks it refers to the security contractors. A jousting match ensues. McCraw steps in to referee.

One of the Clayton kidnap experts on Team Kabul has worked on many cases in Colombia. While the negotiation strategies do not always translate across cultures, his knowledge of what will help sustain a hostage does. He advises me to put something in the letter that lets David know we will never give up and asks him to promise to do the same. He advises me to tell David that I am well and that he must promise me that he will do his best to keep himself in good spirits. In my letter I say, "You must promise me you will not give up. You must be strong, because I am strong." I carefully write the entire letter out in longhand, and I sign it "Love always." I underscore the always.

In the letter, I refer to our respective families—the Mulvihills, the Rohdes—as one unit: our family. One of the side effects of the last two months is that I've gotten to know my in-laws—and my brother-in-law Lee in particular—quite well. Mary Jane and Lee have been my intermittent roommates. Lee makes frequent trips to the city. I marvel at the irony that I have spent more time at home with Lee than I have with my husband. While Lee has taken on the role of updating David's siblings and parents with daily text messages, I also speak regularly with Erik and Laura. Both families have rallied to support me, emotionally and at times geographically. I feel we are one family now. I think this is something David would be proud to hear.

On January 24, I scan and e-mail the letters back to the International Red Cross in Kabul and copy all our team members and our FBI case agent, Jim. Copies are translated and read to the families of Tahir and Asad and they are encouraged to write their own replies.

The letter containing negotiation points is rejected by the Red Cross director in Kabul. The first, more personal letter is passed along. We have no idea how or when it will reach David.

While we wait for a response to our letter, McCraw receives another confounding message from an Afghan source. A person who identifies himself as a relative of Afghan president Karzai claims that the Haqqanis want to use him as a middleman to secure a deal for our three. He says the Haqqanis have not been satisfied with the engineer—they feel he is too sympathetic to our family. This person, who also says he is a former mujahid, asserts that five parties have a stake in our three. Each expects to be compensated—$5 million apiece—in the event of a negotiated release. The five parties include the original kidnapper, the Haqqanis, Baitullah Mehsud, a tribal shura, and a Pakistani government agency. In addition, Siraj Haqqani is demanding the release of Taliban prisoners.

Even though this explains the astronomical nature of the initial demands, it does not bring us any closer to securing a clear communication channel. When McCraw tries to follow up with this source, he is told that while the Haqqanis would like the mujahid to work on their behalf, he will not be able to do so. According to him, the five parties have not been able to reach an agreement on what they are willing to settle for. Once again, we feel we are just chasing shadows.

In the meantime, Team Kabul begins to draw up an exit strategy in the event David is released. Given that we've still had no phone contact with the captors for over a month, this seems premature. But it keeps our spirits up. We appreciate their foresight. We all know that if or when a release happens, there will be a mad rush to get David home and reunite Tahir and Asad with their families. Team Kabul and the other consultants in the United States advise us to make private arrangements for David's transport home. We should not count on the United States government to get him home. With two wars going on, extracting David from the region may not be their top priority. Also, they tell us not to rely on the FBI because they cannot guarantee assets, such as helicopters, when needed. They add that they might want to keep David at the embassy in Kabul or Pakistan for questioning, as it is their duty to gather information in hopes of prosecuting this crime in the future.

Lee and I are beginning to wonder if we should leverage the U.S. government to do more to help us during David's captivity. We're still optimistic about their influence. Later on, we will become all too aware of the limits of their power in that part of the world. One of the many useful contacts in David's e-mail is Zalmay Khalilzad. He is the former United States ambassador to the United Nations and also an Afghan. I decide to set up a meeting.

Khalilzad is a large man, with a Cheshire cat grin and a mastery of the sideways glance. He is also very astute. "What you need is a high-level advocate, someone to represent your family, someone in the U.S. government, who can assign tasks to members of foreign governments and also keep abreast of what U.S. agencies are doing." He suggests someone well respected, with a bit of gravitas and experience in the region. Hillary Clinton and Richard Holbrooke are his suggestions.

With this in mind, Lee and I decide to take a day trip to Washington to meet with officials at the State Department as well as Senators John Kerry and Joe Lieberman, both of whom have expressed an interest in helping in David's case. We want to put a face to our issue. Our hope is to find an advocate within our government to keep our issue at the forefront and possibly to coordinate information coming in from various agencies: FBI, CIA, State Department. We hope this advocate will be Clinton or Holbrooke.

We arrive in D.C. on a snowy morning and walk from Union Station to the Senate offices in the Russell Building. The place is in transition. Office furniture is stacked in the hallways: camelback sofas, Chippendale chairs, dark wooden desks. It looks like an Ethan Allen showroom exploded.

Our first meeting is with Senator Kerry and his chief investigator for the Senate Foreign Relations Committee, Douglas Frantz. Doug is a former investigative reporter who worked at *The New York Times* and knows David. Doug is the one actively keeping our case on the senator's radar.

My mother has given me a recent photo of David and me that was taken at my brother's wedding last year. We look very happy and relaxed.

She has put the photo in a paper frame and suggests I show it to everyone I meet with from now on as a way to humanize our issue. Most people are moved by the fact that we are newlyweds. Our apparent happiness in the photograph underscores the sadness of our current situation.

Senator Kerry is a tall, imposing man. He looks exactly like he does on television. "Your husband certainly likes to push the envelope," he says, referring to David's decision to interview the Taliban commander. He then asks us for an update on the situation, apologizing for not knowing more about the case. He agrees that it is best for us to keep David's case out of the media.

He'll be in touch with Pakistani officials about the case, he says, and will get back to us. Senator Lieberman's aide suggests that he and his colleague compose a letter to Hillary Clinton, telling her they feel this is a matter that deserves her attention as secretary of state. It is surreal but reassuring to have former presidential and vice presidential candidates in our corner. Over the next few months Lee and I remain in touch with Doug Frantz, who informs me that the letter drafted by the senators was received by Secretary Clinton. Senator Kerry continues to follow our case and informs us soon after our meeting that he has raised the issue with Pakistani officials and will continue to do so.

From the Senate office building, Lee and I rush off to meet with Richard Holbrooke, now the special representative to Afghanistan and Pakistan, for lunch. We had assumed this meeting would be top secret. Holbrooke has selected the venue: the Four Seasons restaurant in Georgetown. Lee and I arrive early and request to be seated at a quiet table in the lounge. Holbrooke arrives soon after. A large man with piercing blue eyes, he breezes in, complete with State Department badge and binder. He gives me a bear hug, then requests we move tables, to the middle of the restaurant, where we can order a meal.

He asks us where things stand. We give him a brief update, including that we now think David is in Miran Shah, Pakistan, the stronghold of the Haqqani Taliban network. The FBI has traced earlier calls and video communications to this region. Holbrooke promises to check with the FBI and CIA. He will be traveling to the region soon and says he will raise David's case with Pakistani officials. We think this is the most efficient use of his energy, as we believe the Pakistani intelligence agencies may be able to get word to the Haqqanis and pressure them to release our three or prompt a resolution to negotiations.

The Pakistani intelligence agency, the ISI, has been linked with the Haqqanis. There is an assumption that Siraj Haqqani, the head of the faction, is considered to be an ISI asset. If he is indeed financed by the agency, they may be able to apply pressure on him to release David. Holbrooke also suggests I get in touch with the United States ambassador to Pakistan, Anne Patterson, who is also following David's case. He promises to raise our case with her on his upcoming trip as well.

When I'm back in New York, the following day, Michael Semple, my chief confidant, writes to me that he's learned from Pakistan contacts that a mullah with links to the Haqqani family is moved by my personal plea. He is referring to the Pashto note that David's friend Ruhullah had composed for me to give to the captors: "My husband is my veil, my honor. Please return him to me."

Michael suggests a brazen move: that I come to Pakistan and visit the mullah's mosque in Swabi, just outside of Peshawar. Atiqullah and Badruddin are the ones holding David, but Michael feels the real authority to release our three lies with Siraj Haqqani. He feels the mullah can make contact with Siraj Haqqani or a close family elder and create one clear negotiation channel.

Peshawar. David visited the city several times, always with the utmost caution. Despite my desire to see David home soon, I have no wish to don a headscarf and travel to Pakistan alone. Everything in my being feels opposed to this. I tell myself I am just being a wimp—maybe fear is clouding my judgment. Still, I cannot ignore the sinking feeling in my gut. I turn to others for a reality check.

Lee is immediately opposed. I do not ask him to consider joining me. He has a two-year-old daughter. I mention it casually to my sister, which leads to a flood of calls and e-mails from her begging me not to go. "It is enough that David is in harm's way. You do not need to make the same mistake," she says.

McCraw, at the *Times*, is also skeptical, but tells me the paper will help facilitate my transportation within Pakistan if I decide to go. He advises,

though, that it might be best to hold off on a trip until we have reestablished contact with the captors or are somehow close to a release of our
three. He suggests I consult Jane Perlez, another correspondent and colleague of David's who is based in Islamabad. Jane tells me to stay put. She
says there is a lot of anti-American sentiment in Pakistan at the moment
and adds that all the local news people are aware of David's case. The
minute I arrive, the story of David's kidnapping will most certainly become
public. This is the most persuasive argument against visiting Pakistan.

Nevertheless, I contact Ambassador Anne Patterson at the embassy in
Islamabad. She reluctantly agrees to put me up at the embassy if I decide
to take the trip, but advises me that I will not be able to come and go
freely. Basically, I would be under "house arrest." She cannot guarantee
my safety. She informs me that a member of her staff was nearly abducted recently. The woman was only able to avoid capture because her
driver had recently taken an evasive driving course.

I am concerned it may look suspicious if I am a guest of the United
States Embassy. Many Taliban think that all American journalists are
spies. A jaunt to the embassy on my part could be misconstrued to mean
that either David or I work for the government. If word got out that I was
a guest at the embassy, the captors might think David is indeed a spy. I
also know that airfare to Pakistan is not cheap. I do not want to send a
message that we have money to spare.

Even though I have more than a dozen sane excuses for not traveling
overseas, I secure a visa and purchase a ticket to Islamabad for the first
week in February, less than a week away. Flights are scarce and fill up
quickly. I will see what transpires in the next forty-eight hours, then I'll
make my decision to stay put or head east.

WORDS AND PICTURES

David, Late January 2009

Tahir and Asad ask me to make our case public as the end of January approaches. The American and Afghan governments have forgotten us, they believe, and public pressure is the only way to get them to act. I believe going public could result in the Taliban's setting a deadline and first Asad, then Tahir, and finally me being killed. Tahir and Asad say they are ready to die. I defer to their wishes and tell Timor Shah that I want to make a video for the news media.

For the next several days, we receive contradictory reports on when and how the video will be made. At one point, our guard Akbar suggests that a local prisoner be brought to the house. With cameras rolling, the prisoner would be executed in front of us. Hoping to prevent an execution, I offer to weep on camera instead. Over the next few days, I silently prepare for the video, memorizing sentences I plan to say to Kristen and my family. I sit in the sun for long stretches, hoping sunburn will make me look healthy.

Badruddin arrives several days later with a video camera and, to my relief, no prisoner for execution. Instead, white sheets inscribed with the seal of the Islamic Emirate of Afghanistan and a verse from the Koran are taped onto the wall of the room where we sleep. Our Barbie and Hannah Montana comforters, my stack of English-language Pakistani newspapers, and my bottles of Nestlé Pure Life bottled water are moved out of the shot.

Tahir, Asad, and I sit side by side on the room's red-checkered carpet. We wear salwar kameezes, jackets to make us look cold, and prayer caps to make us look devout. Two guards with scarves over their faces stand on either side of us pointing machine guns at our heads. Badruddin turns on the camera and motions with his hand for me to speak. Tahir stares straight ahead. Asad looks at the floor. I say my name, identify myself as an American journalist, and give the date of our kidnapping. Then I recite the words that Badruddin specifically demanded.

"Our lives are in great danger," I say. "I ask President Barack Obama, I ask Secretary of State Hillary Clinton, and I ask special envoy Richard Holbrooke to please meet the Taliban demands."

I try to convey a message to our families and tears well up in my eyes. I'm more emotional than I expected. On one level, it's a relief. I worried I would be unable to cry on cue. As he holds the camera, Badruddin nods. He is happy with my performance.

"I want to apologize from the bottom of my heart to the families of Asad and Tahir," I say, beginning the message. "I'm so sorry that they are going through this.

"And I apologize from the deepest part of my soul to my wife Kristen," I say. "And to my parents, and to my siblings, and to all my family and all my friends.

"I love you all very, very much and I thank you for all the joy you've given me throughout my life," I add. "I've lived a very blessed life because of you.

"I'm so sorry that you have to see this video and I'm so sorry that you're going through this again," I say. "If we are released I promise to spend the rest of my life doing absolutely everything I can to pay you back. And to do absolutely everything I can to somehow make this up to you. I apologize to you all."

Badruddin continues filming. I am thrilled that I have been able to express a message that I hope will console Kristen and my family if we die. I then repeat my call for Obama, Clinton, and Holbrooke to meet the Taliban demands.

"I beg you, I'm so, so sorry, I beg you, please, please meet their demands," I say, hoping this will satisfy Badruddin. "Please save the three of us. Please save the three of us. Please save the three of us."

I bow my head and Tahir introduces himself. He speaks in Pashto and appeals to Afghan president Hamid Karzai to please help us. Asad does the same. After the video, the guards quietly snicker at me for weeping on camera. I don't care and feel relieved. I hope my words will comfort Kristen and my family.

Badruddin says he will be back in two days. He returns a week later. After several minutes of small talk, he casually pulls a white envelope from his pocket, places it on the floor, and announces he has Red Cross letters for all three of us. The envelope is like a talisman. Tahir, Asad, and I stare at it eagerly. It holds words from our families.

Badruddin hands me the envelope. I give Tahir and Asad their letters and suddenly find myself staring at Kristen's unmistakable handwriting. Her words flood my mind. "It was wonderful to hear from you," she writes. "I am warmed by memories of our marriage and time together with our family."

She apologizes to our captors and asks them not to be angry with her. "I am also frustrated with this process," she writes. "Trust and a clear channel of communication are both important to all of us."

She encourages me. "There is hope. No matter how long it takes, we will not give up and we will not forget about you. Not a moment goes by without us trying to bring you, Tahir, and Asad home."

She talks about the effort to free us. "Our family is doing all we can, as quickly as possible, but some things are beyond our control. We will keep trying."

I am not sure, but believe she is referring to prisoners.

"But, you must promise me, that you are going to do your best to survive this ordeal," she writes. "You must be strong because I am strong."

Kristen says she will meet soon with my mother and siblings to continue working for our release. She says my brother and father have been strong. I am touched. She knows news of my family will buoy me.

"Your father is grateful to the men holding you because they are keeping you safe," she says. "He asks for their patience."

I am impressed. She is clearly trying to navigate Pashtun culture. She is making requests herself but also having my father—the patriarch of my family—pose them as well.

Her next line is an attempt to comfort Tahir and Asad. It touches me that she shows respect for them, their lives and families. "I will relay your message to the dear families of Tahir and Asad," she states. "Please tell them *salaam alaikum* and they should not lose hope."

She concludes the letter with her trademark positivity. "I know God is watching over all three of you. I hope your spirits will be strengthened by this," she says, her words echoing her cheery voice. "Thank you for writing to us! Love always, Kristen."

I am disappointed by the seeming lack of progress in negotiations, but heartened by the letter's eloquence. Tears come to my eyes. Her words will strengthen me for months.

Tahir translates the letter to Badruddin, who is disappointed that it contains no offer of high-level prisoners and millions in cash. I again tell Badruddin that it is impossible for my family to produce five prisoners and $15 million. He pays no attention.

Badruddin inspects Tahir's and Asad's letters as well. Tahir's eldest daughter has written that she and her siblings deeply miss their father. Asad's father has written that Asad's two sons miss him but are well. At the end of the note, Asad's father makes a seemingly casual comment. "People say you're in Miran Shah."

Badruddin explodes in anger. He is furious that our location is known and quickly departs. The momentary bliss generated by our letters evaporates.

Later, the guards tell us Badruddin has decided not to send our video to the news media. Instead, we will shoot a new scene that will prove we are being held in Afghanistan, not Pakistan.

I spend my days doing chores and saying my prayers. I place Kristen's letter in the left-hand pocket of a vest I wear every day, close to my heart. A week later, the guards ask for all three of our letters and say Badruddin wants to copy them. The letters are never returned.

In late January, Badruddin arrives and announces he is going to drive us to a remote, snow-covered hillside to shoot the final scene of our video. Roughly ninety minutes after we leave the house, Badruddin sees a group of trucks stopped on the opposite side of the road and quickly pulls over. A nervous-looking Pakistani soldier points a rocket-propelled grenade at our pickup truck. Mansoor, the guard sitting beside me and Tahir in the backseat, loads his Kalashnikov and orders me to put a scarf over my face. A group of Pakistani civilians standing nearby moves out of the way, anticipating a firefight.

The soldier is in the lead vehicle of a Pakistani army supply convoy in North Waziristan. After surveying the road, the soldier gets back in his truck, and the convoy rumbles forward.

Running into a Pakistani army resupply convoy at first appears to be an enormous stroke of luck. As I watch the convoy drive toward us, I hope that the Pakistanis might somehow rescue us.

I wonder if we should make a run for it, but quickly realize Tahir and Asad will never make it. I am seated in the left rear passenger seat and can open my door and jump out of the truck. Tahir is in the middle of the seat and will be shot by Mansoor if he moves. Asad is riding in a car behind us and I have no way to signal him.

Frustrated, I watch in dismay as Badruddin gets out of the truck and calmly stands on the side of the road. As trucks full of heavily armed government soldiers roll by, he smiles and waves at them.

After the convoy disappears, Badruddin seems amused.

"Do you know who that was?" he asks me.

"No," I say, playing dumb.

"That was the Pakistani army," he responds.

Badruddin explains that under a cease-fire agreement between the Taliban and the Pakistani army, all civilians are required to get out of their cars when an army convoy approaches. For Taliban vehicles, though, only the driver has to get out. The practice, I realize, allows the Taliban to hide kidnapping victims and foreign militants from army convoys.

As we continue our journey, we pass a half dozen government checkpoints that have been abandoned by the Frontier Corps, a tribal militia that is supposed to police the tribal areas. Badruddin says that under the cease-fire agreement, only unarmed militia members can stand at the checkpoints. He is correct. As we drive, I occasionally see members of the militia standing on the side of the road without guns. Some casually chat with local tribesmen.

The trip confirms suspicions I have long harbored as a reporter. The Haqqanis oversee a sprawling Taliban ministate in North Waziristan with the acquiescence of the Pakistani military. A 2006 truce the Pakistani army signed with militants has given them complete control of North Waziristan. Repeated Pakistani army claims to the contrary are false. The Haqqanis are so confident of their control of the area that they take me—a person they consider to be an extraordinarily valuable hostage—on a three-hour drive in broad daylight to shoot a location scene for an outdoor video.

For years, dozens of Pakistani, Afghan, foreign journalists, and I have written about the systematic takeover of the tribal areas by foreign militants and the Afghan and Pakistani Taliban. After being driven from Afghanistan by the 2001 American invasion, Uzbek and Arab militants began slowly reorganizing themselves. The foreigners rented compounds from local tribesmen who fought alongside them in Afghanistan, sympathized with their cause, or were in search of money and security. The foreign fighters paid two to three times the normal rate for rent in the impoverished area. The Haqqanis—my kidnappers—welcomed Arabs and Uzbeks.

Surrounded by high mud-brick walls, the Pashtun family compounds are oases of privacy and protection for conservative tribesmen. The high walls prevent strangers from seeing—and dishonoring—Pashtun women and shelter families from attacks from rival clans. They also hide the inhabitants' identity.

In some ways, the Arabs and Uzbeks are returning home. Many of them used the tribal areas as a base during the anti-Soviet jihad of the 1980s. Dozens of Arabs and Uzbeks married local women.

In the spring of 2002, CIA officials began reporting to Pakistani army commanders that large numbers of foreign fighters appeared to be hiding in South Waziristan. Pakistani military officials were skeptical. In an interview nine months before I was kidnapped, a former Pakistani military official who served in the tribal areas told me that he did not believe large numbers of foreign militants had settled there. "There were conflicting figures about the number who crossed the border," he told me. "Nobody was sure. It was all guesswork."

General Ali Muhammad Jan Aurakzai, a tall, commanding Pashtun whose family hailed from the tribal areas, was Pakistani president Musharraf's main adviser on the issue. After serving as the military commander of the region from 2001 to 2004, he served as its civilian governor from 2006 to 2008. For years, he argued that American officials exaggerated the threat in the tribal areas and that the Pakistani army should avoid sparking a tribal rebellion at all cost.

The former senior Pakistani military official defended the army's record to me, contending that the Pakistani military had doubled the number of troops in South and North Waziristan from roughly 2,000 to 4,000 in September 2002. He said Pakistani soldiers also pushed into dozens of square miles of "no-go" areas that Pakistani or British forces had never before entered but "found nothing."

American officials said that Pakistani army sweeps, though, were slow moving and easily circumvented by militants. A former CIA official who served in Islamabad told me that Pakistani generals were "dismissive" of the reports because they feared sparking a tribal rebellion.

"Aurakzai and others didn't want to believe it because it would have been an inconvenient fact," the former official recalled. "Going out there, rooting around, trying to root out foreigners was going to cause real problems for them."

Another American official was blunt. He derided Aurakzai as a "snake oil salesman" and "the Neville Chamberlain of Pakistan," a reference to the pre–World War II British leader who downplayed the threat from Nazi Germany.

Throughout 2002, officials in Washington largely ignored a chorus of warnings from American officials in Afghanistan that the Pakistani tribal areas were becoming the Afghan Taliban's new base of operations. Instead, they downplayed the group's importance and praised the Pakistani government for arresting Al Qaeda members in Pakistan's major cities.

A conversation with one American diplomat in Islamabad illustrated the mentality. He told me that the Afghan Taliban no longer represented a national security threat to the United States while Al Qaeda remained one. When I contended that the Taliban and Al Qaeda worked closely together, he dismissed my argument.

In December 2002, I visited Miran Shah on a reporting trip. At that time, it was still under Pakistani government control. Escorted by members of the Frontier Corps, the government-paid tribal militia, I found the tribal areas simmering with anger at the United States. On the roads leading to Miran Shah, men carried Kalashnikovs. On the roofs of houses, flags of Pakistan's hard-line religious parties fluttered. And in front of religious schools, fierce-looking young students strung ropes across the road, stopped cars, and demanded donations.

"Mosques, mosques, mosques," I scribbled in my notebook. "This is a completely different world."

We first stopped at a border crossing between Pakistan and Afghanistan fifteen miles outside Miran Shah. Members of the Frontier Corps went through the motions of checking cars as they rolled across the border. An officer told me it was impossible to control the border because smuggling routes blanketed the surrounding hills.

In Miran Shah itself, I met the Pakistani government–appointed political agent charged with governing North Waziristan. He said anger was simmering in the town because of a recent joint Pakistani-FBI raid on the sprawling Manba Uloom madrassa the Haqqani family had built north of the city in the 1980s. No foreign militants—and no Haqqani family members—had been found.

Rumors abounded that the FBI agents wore boots into madrassas and mosques, an insult and desecration to Pashtuns. Furious local tribesmen fired rockets at an abandoned technical school where the Americans were believed to be staying. Six local tribal elders gathered by the North

Waziristan political agent fumed. They denied that any Afghan Taliban or foreign militants were in North Waziristan.

"The Americans have fifteen to twenty times disgraced our soil and our sacred mosques," one tribal elder told me, vastly exaggerating the number of raids. "They cannot produce a single man from the fourteen or fifteen attempts."

The elders believed that the American bombing of Afghanistan in 2001 had killed 50,000 Afghan women and children. They said the United States had invaded Afghanistan to control the oil and gas riches of the Middle East and Central Asia. Asked about the 9/11 attacks, they said there was no proof who had carried them out.

"People have actually started believing Osama never existed," one elder told me. "They think it is a conspiracy against us."

I later learned that Americans—most likely CIA operatives—had, in fact, raided the Haqqani madrassa and found nothing. Before the raid, the Americans intercepted communications in which a local Pakistani official called the madrassa and warned the occupants that the Americans were on their way.

My trip was part of a sophisticated campaign by Musharraf's government to show that the Afghan Taliban were not using Pakistan as a base. The Pakistani military ferried American journalists, diplomats, and intelligence officials to the tribal areas and told them the area was ungovernable. In many ways, the trips mirrored the tours the Pakistani military conducted in the 1980s for Congressman Wilson and other American government officials. The only difference was the message. Now, the Pakistani military said it could not control the tribal areas.

Evidence that the Afghan Taliban were, in fact, reorganizing inside Pakistan abounded. In September 2003, I interviewed two Afghan Taliban members in the southwestern city of Quetta, which lies several hundred miles south of the tribal areas. Afghan officials had long charged that Taliban leader Mullah Omar was based in the city.

Hajji Abdul Majid denied that the Afghan Taliban were receiving support from Pakistan. A wizened Afghan Taliban commander who had lost his right leg fighting Soviet troops, he appeared completely at ease in Pakistan. He and the other former Taliban commander met me in the basement of the office of a local radio reporter. He predicted the United States would eventually fail in Afghanistan. He said Afghans initially supported the Russians to "take their money" and then turned against them.

"The same case will be the Americans," the Taliban commander told me confidently. "For two or three years, they will support the Americans for their money but after that they will leave them."

Hostility toward Westerners simmered in Quetta as well. The same false stories of American bombs killing tens of thousands of civilians swirled. During a subsequent reporting trip to Quetta, a young Pashtun spit in my face as our car drove past a religious school. My translator, who was also a Pashtun, profusely apologized. He was ashamed that a Pashtun would do such a thing.

Complaints that Pakistan was failing to crack down on the Afghan Taliban reached the White House in October 2003. In a principals meeting, American military and diplomatic officials based in Afghanistan said that Pakistan had become a major safe haven for the Afghan Taliban. They presented their argument that Musharraf was playing a "double game," periodically arresting Al Qaeda members but allowing the Afghan Taliban to regroup on Pakistani territory.

Bush, Secretary of State Colin Powell, and Deputy Secretary of State Richard Armitage believed the allegations that Musharraf was playing a double game were false. In meetings with senior American officials and interviews with me and other journalists, Musharraf vehemently denied the charges.

Armitage insisted that Musharraf did, in fact, break the ISI's ties with the Taliban from 2001 to 2005. "There was little contact between the ISI and the Taliban other than liaison," Armitage told me when I interviewed him for my book.

Armitage said that during those years the administration focused its efforts on persuading Musharraf to end the ISI's support to two Pakistani militant groups targeting India: Lashkar-e-Taiba and Jaish-e-Muhammad. The two groups had carried out a December 2001 attack on India's parliament that nearly sparked a war between nuclear-armed India and Pakistan.

Armitage, who left the Bush administration with Powell in early 2005, said that he believes the ISI reestablished its ties with the Taliban later that year when the ISI saw the Taliban successfully reorganizing and the American-led military effort flagging. "My personal view is that the ISI began increasing support for the Afghan Taliban when they started to see the Talibs regrouping," Armitage said. "ISI was coming of the view that the coalition might not prevail."

In 2005, the Haqqani network and other Taliban did gain strength, doubling American deaths in Afghanistan from fifty-two in 2004 to ninety-nine in 2005. American military officials requested permission to carry out commando raids into Pakistan's tribal areas. Military officials argued that as long as the Taliban safe havens existed in Pakistan, American troops could not stabilize Afghanistan.

American troops carried out two cross-border raids into the tribal areas in 2006 and 2008, but they sparked an immediate outcry from the Pakistani army. Bush opposed further operations inside Pakistan. He worried that unrest could topple Musharraf or derail his personal efforts to persuade the Pakistani leader to take off his military uniform, become a civilian president, and reinstate democracy in Pakistan. As part of his commitment to spreading democracy abroad, Bush had privately and repeatedly lobbied Musharraf—who was both Pakistan's president and army chief—to resign from his army post and become simply president.

CIA officials based in Pakistan argued that it was far better to have Pakistani troops carry out such operations. The arrival of American troops in the tribal areas would confirm Islamist conspiracy theories that the United States planned to occupy Pakistan, the world's only predominantly Muslim country with nuclear weapons.

In an attempt to get the Pakistani army to be more aggressive in the tribal areas, the Bush administration backed a loosely monitored billion-dollar-a-year reimbursement program where the United States paid fuel, ammunition, and other costs incurred by Pakistani forces in the tribal areas. The massive program was by far the largest source of American funding to Pakistan.

American military officials detected that the Pakistani military was inflating their claims under the program and receiving tens of millions of dollars in fraudulent reimbursements. They also warned of a more dangerous problem: The Pakistani army was so weak, they warned, that it could not defeat the Taliban and Al Qaeda if it confronted them.

For the next three years, that appeared to be true. The Pakistani military fought brief operations against militants in the tribal areas and then struck two peace agreements. Each cease-fire further emboldened the militants, who killed more than 200 tribal elders they saw as potential rivals in 2005 and 2006. The army signed a third and final cease-fire agreement—known as the Waziristan accord—in Miran Shah in September 2006. In exchange for militants promising to halt attacks in Pakistan and Afghanistan, the Pakistani army agreed to withdraw its forces from all checkpoints in North Waziristan. The Taliban ministate that I later inhabited was born.

Militants in other parts of Pakistan were emboldened. Students in the Red Mosque, a hard-line mosque and madrassa in the center of Islamabad, demanded that local stores stop selling DVDs they considered indecent. Then they took a local woman hostage in July 2007 and accused her of operating a brothel. Security forces surrounded the mosque and after an initial gun battle stormed it, killing roughly 100 people. Pakistani militants claimed that 1,000 students—many of them women— were killed in the attack.

Enraged, they declared war on the Pakistani government. In the tribal areas, the Haqqanis played a central role in brokering the creation of a powerful and unprecedented alliance of Pakistani militant groups—the Tehrik-i-Taliban Pakistan, or Taliban Movement of Pakistan. Founded in December 2007, the alliance of previously disparate groups fielded an estimated 5,000 fighters. They unleashed attacks that killed former prime minister Benazir Bhutto in 2007 and killed or wounded 5,000 Pakistanis in 2008.

As I received newspapers from my captors in January 2009, more Pakistanis were dying in terror attacks than Afghans or Iraqis. The Pakistani Taliban had seized control of all seven agencies that made up the tribal areas and a famed tourist area sixty miles from Islamabad known as the Swat Valley. Declaring a complete ban on girls' education, the Pakistani Taliban destroyed or damaged 175 girls' schools in Swat.

I recalled a meeting I had with a retired senior official from the ISI four months after the storming of the Red Mosque. Asking that he not be named, he was the first senior ISI official to admit to me that some ISI officials had been playing a "double game."

He said that while he and other ISI officials arrested Al Qaeda operatives and impressed American officials, other ISI officials turned a blind eye to the Afghan Taliban and Pakistani militants they thought could be useful proxies against India. With suicide bombings besetting Pakistan's largest cities, the former ISI official admitted that his agency had lost control of the militants it had nurtured for the last thirty years.

"We indoctrinated them and told them, 'You will go to heaven,'" he told me. "You cannot turn it around so suddenly."

After a two-hour drive in Badruddin's truck, we arrive in a snow-covered valley with towering pine trees. The hills and snow, he hopes, will convince the world we are being held in Afghanistan, not in a bustling town in Pakistan.

The drive has been a delight for me. After nearly three months of living in walled compounds, I relished looking out the window as we drove through towns, villages, and open spaces of North Waziristan. Much of the landscape is dry, desolate, and reminiscent of the American Southwest. Other areas have the rolling hills and soaring trees of the Rocky Mountains.

Badruddin orders Tahir, Asad, and me to put on new black Chinese-made high-top basketball sneakers he has purchased. I fold my pants into the tops of the sneakers and wrap the blanket Badruddin gave me months ago around my neck as a scarf. I hope both steps will make the video look more ridiculous than frightening. Badruddin tells his men to set up a tent he has purchased as a prop on the hillside. His men can't figure out how to assemble it. I think about helping them but decide not to.

As a backup plan, Badruddin instructs us to walk up a snow-covered hillside with a half dozen guards. Scarves cover their faces and each carries a machine gun or Kalashnikov. Timor Shah leads the way. He peers through a tiny pair of binoculars Badruddin has given him. We follow him up the hill, and I exaggerate my movements to try to make the video appear staged.

We are led into a small cave where one of Badruddin's men has lit a fire. Badruddin orders us to say we are sick and in the mountains of Afghanistan. I do so but try to show little emotion. As I speak, I place my left hand over my right, hoping my wife will see that I am flashing my wedding ring at her.

Outside the cave, we sit on the hillside and Badruddin orders me to again call for President Obama to meet the Taliban's demands. I do so but add a new line. At Tahir and Asad's request, I explicitly ask journalists to publicize our case.

"We ask journalists to please help us," I say. "Please write stories about us. Please don't let us be forgotten."

I fail to cry. After the last video, I am less willing to placate our captors. Badruddin does not seem to care. After a few more minutes, he stops filming. Our location shoot has taken roughly thirty minutes.

As we walk down the hill, the guards get into a snowball fight with Tahir and Asad.

A FRENCH STREET GANG

Kristen, Early to Mid-February 2009

A rumor has spread that an unidentified person has a video of our three and is shopping it around Kabul to American and foreign news organizations. The BBC and several others refuse to purchase it. Al Jazeera Arabic allegedly buys it for an undisclosed amount.

Michael Semple and I are now in daily contact. He tells me not to panic—this is most likely what he refers to as "a midterm fund-raising effort." Most likely the captors have raised a few thousand dollars from the sale of the video footage, he says. Kidnapping is a group endeavor and the individuals guarding and feeding David, Tahir, and Asad need to be compensated for their time and effort. Michael has been the one consistent presence in this experience—in advice and in manner. For this reason, I have come to trust his opinion above the others.

A colleague of David's in Kabul, Dexter Filkins, tracks down an Al Jazeera representative and asks to see a copy of the video. While he isn't permitted to copy it, he and his translator are allowed a viewing and type up notes.

His transcript serves as a preview for Lee and me. We are struck by a few observations he makes, namely that David looks old and "his shoes are not his own." This seems odd. How would Dexter know this? Soon enough, we understand.

Al Jazeera Arabic airs a snippet of the video a few days later. It is a twelve-second segment in which David, Tahir, and Asad appear outside, against a snowy backdrop. This is the promotional teaser to a full-length broadcast scheduled for that day.

The New York Times comes to our rescue. Bill Keller, the executive editor, calls the head of Al Jazeera's station in Doha and requests that it refrain from showing the video in its entirety because of our safety concerns. Al Jazeera agrees to pull it off the air. We are terrified the video will be leaked and end up on the Internet. Our main concern is that a public airing will give the captors the attention and acclaim they seek in holding an American.

We do not want David's value to become that of a political spectacle. We do not want him to be used to test or challenge the new Obama administration.

With the video taking up my attention, I cancel my flight to Pakistan. I will stay put.

Keller's office alerts me to expect a call from Secretary Clinton. She has heard about the Al Jazeera segment. I am told she wants to console me and provide reassurance.

I am at home when she calls. I am struck by her appealing combination of warmth and composure. Helpful and efficient, she assures me that David's case is being worked on "at the highest level."

"My heart goes out to you," she adds. "I can only imagine—actually, I cannot imagine what you must be going through."

I ask her if David's captors have made additional demands—political demands—that perhaps we as a family are not aware of. She reassures me that no one in our government has received communication from the group holding David. Holbrooke will be making a trip to the region soon, she says, and I should stay in touch with him.

"I am a longtime admirer and supporter of yours," I say, thanking her. "I feel very confident knowing you are at the helm and aware of this issue." I can't resist adding, "And, frankly, I am so thrilled and relieved to have another woman in the mix!"

She bursts into laughter. "Oh, dear," she says, "I know *exactly* what you mean!"

The next day, February 7, I receive a call from a journalist in New York who has obtained a copy of the video. The sound is still spotty but the visuals are clear. The journalist offers to meet me at the United Nations building.

I have spent the last few days agonizing over my decision not to travel to Pakistan. Tonight I am thankful that my gut check was right: I am relieved to be in New York to view the only communication from my husband in six weeks.

Lee flies in to join me. He is able to do so on a moment's notice because he runs a corporate aviation consulting company. He's constantly flying somewhere for work and often makes last-minute pit stops in New York. This also serves as his cover with business associates and some family members who are not yet aware of David's situation. Our immediate family knows, but the extended family—cousins, uncles, nieces—do not.

It is 5 p.m. on a snowy, cold Saturday. The journalist meets me at the security gate and assures me that while I cannot obtain a copy of the video, I can make arrangements for our security advisers to view it.

Apparently, our security advisers don't want to wait that long. AISC has overnighted to me a pen that doubles as a camera. They suggest I use it to take covert footage of the video. I was expecting something worthy of James Bond—perhaps a chic, ultra slim version of a Bic pen. Instead, a large heavy fountain pen, the size of a small telescope—or an engorged Mont Blanc—arrived this morning. It looks like a sight gag from a Peter Sellers film.

It has a hole toward the top and a small blue light the size of a pinhead that lights up when it's filming. I call the security team and tell them that while I appreciate their efforts, I do not feel comfortable with their plan. I do not want to be busted by UN security for packing a suspicious fountain pen.

I breeze through security. They do not X-ray me. I could have gotten the pen in no problem, I say to myself. Lee, however, is asked to submit to a full security screening. At six feet tall, with a buzz cut and military training, he looks like a contractor or government agent.

The journalist ushers us into an elevator, then through increasingly narrow corridors to a small, carpeted room at the end of a neglected, dimly lit hallway. The windows of the room overlook the East River. The three of us cram into the tiny room and gather around a small monitor.

The video is rather surprising, and long—twelve minutes in total. It begins with David. "I want to apologize, from the bottom of my soul, to my wife Kristen," he says. I am moved by this genuine expression. Soon after, it is followed by an obligatory plea and what look clearly like fake tears. David makes it obvious he is reading from a script. He is dressed in a salwar kameez, prayer hat, and jacket. His hands are unbound. He is still wearing his wedding ring. A banner hanging behind his head bears the emblem of the Islamic Emirate of Afghanistan and an Arabic slogan that says "There is no God but Allah and Muhammad is his prophet."

We note that Tahir is wearing a large gold watch. Dexter had made reference to "handcuffs" in his account of the video. It turns out he mistook the watch for a shackle. We are relieved and slightly perplexed. It is surprising that the money-grubbing Taliban would not confiscate valuable personal items like the wedding ring and watch.

Once again, gunmen flank the edges of the video frame, but they appear at ease. Tahir speaks next in Pashto. Asad makes a brief statement as well.

The video then cuts to a strange clip of our three walking up a hill in what looks like suburban Westchester County in New York. The incline is not steep, but the camera is tilted at an angle to make it appear more precipitous. They are surrounded by ten men in turbans, pajama-type pants, and camouflage jackets. Everyone sports oversize black basketball high-tops with thick white soles—Chinese knockoffs of Reebok. David has tucked his pants into his sneakers and the result is a somewhat comical fashion statement. They look more like a French street gang than a bunch of terrorists. The camera cuts to David and he explains that they are in the mountains of Afghanistan, where it is cold and difficult. In a matter-of-fact way, he adds that the food and water are making him sick.

"I thought he might convert to Islam, but I never dreamed he'd go hip-hop," I tell Lee. He smiles and adds: "Clearly they are feeding him. There's no way he has diarrhea." David appears to have gained weight. Maybe it's the full beard. He looks like a burly mountain man. Grizzly Adams springs to mind. His beard, although thick, is well groomed. His face is tan. We are relieved to see this, and our relief takes the form of humor. We actually have a laughing fit over the footwear and general attire, which is incongruous with David's traditional New England style: khakis and an oxford cloth shirt.

In the next segment of the video Tahir laments, "It's so cold, so cold." Yet they all have their jackets unzipped and the tree branches are bare— the snow is clearly melting. One of the Taliban fighters sports opera glasses and pauses occasionally to survey the area.

In the final portion David appeals to "President Obama, Secretary of State Hillary Clinton, and special envoy Richard Holbrooke to meet the Taliban demands." He also asks that journalists write stories about them so that they will not be forgotten. I do not think this is coming from David as he is clearly reading from a script and staring blankly ahead as he relays this sentence. "Please meet the Taliban demands. Please save the three of us, please save the three of us, please save the three of us." He adds the word "again" before restating this plea, as if repeating the cameraman's directions to him.

We watch the video several times, obsessing over details. We are not quite sure who its producers consider to be the target audience: our family, the government, or the public. We ponder this as we head back to the apartment in lower Manhattan.

It's been quite a day and we decompress in the living room over diner food. We call Lee's wife, Christie. Lee says Christie insisted that he join me in New York so I would not have to watch the video alone. She has been a source of strength and calm throughout this ordeal, willing to accommodate Lee's last-minute trips to New York and Washington in support of David and me. We tell her about the video and admit that we are baffled by its somewhat comical staging, which seems at odds with its disturbing message.

We discuss our impressions of the footage, briefly laughing as we recall the more absurd moments—the release is crucial, given the confusing reality of the situation. The captors have not made explicit demands in the video. We have no idea what, if anything, they plan to do next.

We worry the video will surface on the Web and make our case public. Due to its political undercurrent—the mention of Obama, Clinton, Holbrooke—we feel more strongly than ever that we should keep the case quiet. While our government and the journalism community are well aware of the case by now, the public at large is not. I alert Holbrooke to the contents of the video and forward him my notes and a written transcript.

Two days later, the FBI alerts me that a video execution of a Polish hostage is on the Internet. I'm haunted by the idea that we may one day receive similar footage of David.

The New York Times agrees that we should remain silent, but wants us to have a plan in place in the event that another news organization or blogger is less amenable than Al Jazeera in respecting our choice.

As part of the preparation, the newspaper's public relations office arranges for Lee and me to receive media training. Defensiveness training is actually a more accurate description. The goal is to learn how to deflect questions. Neither one of us has any desire to appear on television. We decide Lee will be the family spokesman should the story ever break. He assumed this role before on behalf of David when he was imprisoned in Bosnia. He is the perfect choice. My mother often refers to Lee as "the epitome of an officer and a gentleman." He has quite a fan club among our media experts and FBI agents because he projects both strength and calm. Cordial and soft-spoken, he could easily disarm reporters.

We arrange for two separate sessions. I meet the training crew at a glass office building in Midtown after I finish work. A chair, video camera, and monitor have been set up in the corner of a conference room. In the mock interview, I feel like a deer in the headlights. A tired looking deer at that. I glance at myself in the monitor. I've aged several years in the last few months, I think. I am wearing a gray button-front crocheted sweater. I look like a tired old lady, a gray presence with circles under my eyes. My interviewer comes to my rescue and suggests the cameraman back up a few feet—"Give her a break," she says.

The public relations team has compiled a notebook of talking points and suggested answers. We role-play through them.

Who is working on David's case?

Answer: Many people and agencies are involved in working toward his release.

Have you spoken to David?

Answer: Yes, but I am not going to discuss additional details.

Do you have any indication of what the abductors want?

Answer: We are not going to discuss details.

Why has the *Times* not reported on this?

Answer: We were told by his abductor that the safety of David and his colleagues would be in jeopardy if we discussed this publicly.

Then the interviewer asks me a series of more personal questions:

What is your husband like? How are you getting through each day, how are you not falling apart? Is there something you'd like to say to David or to his captors?

This is no one's business, I think. My voice gets notably more formal as the questions get more personal. It's impossible to define my husband and our relationship with a sound bite. It throws me off kilter to talk about David in this format. I have expended so much energy trying to stay positive and strong. Once again, I feel the desperation of our situation.

I have no desire to sit across from Matt Lauer. Ever. I do not wish to be comforted by Ann Curry. I keep this in mind as I practice thwarting direct questions about ransom, government agencies, communication with captors.

While I am no screen goddess, I am a quick study at deflecting questions and, after several takes and critiques, I am given permission to call it a day.

I talk to Lee on the phone afterward to compare training stories. It's past 11 P.M. and I have just polished off some leftover pizza. He has flown home and is back in New Hampshire.

He informs me he was caught off guard during the training session. Normally cool and composed, he choked up when confronted with questions about David. Neither one of us has had a chance to stop and reflect. He confides that this is the first time he has really felt the depth of his sadness over his missing brother.

ARE YOU THERE?

David, Early to Mid-February 2009

In the first week of February, our hopes plummet. An American who works for the United Nations is kidnapped on February 2 in the Pakistani province of Baluchistan. Gunmen open fire on the car of the worker, John Solecki, kill his driver, and abduct him. Solecki, a career humanitarian aid worker, leads the United Nations refugee office there. Over the next several days, I learn about the details of his case from radio and newspaper reports.

A previously unknown group calling for Baluchistan to become an independent country—the Baluchistan Liberated United Front—claims responsibility. Secular nationalists, they have no relationship with Pakistan's Islamic militants but their demands are just as astronomical. They threaten to kill Solecki if 141 women they say are being held captive by the Pakistani government are not released. The Pakistani government responds that it does not have 141 women in custody. In the perverse world of ransom demands, their call for the release of 141 female prisoners—who may not even exist—makes my captors seem reasonable.

Five days after the kidnapping of the American UN worker, a Pakistani Taliban group beheads a Polish hostage. Piotr Stanczak is killed after the Pakistani government refuses to release twenty-six Taliban prisoners. He is the first foreign captive to be executed in Pakistan since the murder of the *Wall Street Journal* reporter Daniel Pearl seven years ago. I never met Stanczak but immediately grieve for him and his family. I assume Stanczak, like me, spent months pacing in a small yard, dreaming of release and trying to reason with his captors. In the end, none of it mattered.

His abduction and execution are a symbol of the growing reach of the Pakistani Taliban. They kidnapped Stanczak, a geologist who was surveying oil and gas fields, an hour's drive outside the country's capital in September 2008, two months before our abduction. They shot his driver, guard, and translator and took him into the tribal areas.

Stanczak's killing calls into question the logic of the one instruction I remember from my hostile environment training course: prolong a kidnapping. A kidnapper is hypothetically less likely to kill a hostage after investing funds, manpower, and time into their care, according to experts. They want to recoup their investment, in a sense, after spending time and resources on the prisoners. In Stanczak's case, his captors held him for five months and then killed him. They received no money or prisoners in return for their effort. As I read about it, his case presents a different logic.

The Pakistani Taliban seemingly want to defy the Pakistani government, show its weakness, and generate widespread press coverage of their brutality. While a criminal is in search of ransom, militants may be simply interested in generating publicity. I don't know which path our captors will follow.

Evan after Stanczak's death, the Pakistani Taliban find a depraved way to still make money off his case. Echoing Badruddin's threat to sell my bones to my family, Stanczak's executioners vow to hold the Polish geologist's body until the Pakistani government pays a ransom for it.

His execution leaves me grasping at straws. In an earlier conversation, Badruddin told me that the Haqqanis had decided to never set a deadline in our case. I don't believe him. As an American, I don't know if they see me as worth more alive or dead. Stanczak was Polish and hailed from a small country with several hundred soldiers in Afghanistan. I am American and hail from the nation the Taliban view as their central enemy. My captors' demand for five prisoners is small in comparison with the demand of Stanczak's captors for twenty-six prisoners.

Other cases in Pakistan involving foreigners set no clear precedent. Over the last several years, the Pakistani Taliban had kidnapped four Chinese engineers in an effort to embarrass the Pakistani government and deter foreigners from coming to the country. Two were released, one was still in custody, and one had escaped. None of the Chinese had been executed within days like Daniel Pearl.

Throughout my captivity, I often thought of Pearl. I never met him but had many colleagues who passionately liked and respected him. I had become close friends with the *Wall Street Journal* correspondent who succeeded Pearl as the newspaper's South Asia bureau chief. Pearl was tricked into going to an interview as well. A British-born militant of Pakistani descent, Ahmed Omar Sheikh, first held a friendly meeting with Pearl in the northern city of Rawalpindi in January 2002 and won his trust. Then he promised Pearl an interview with a senior militant accused of involvement in the case of Richard Reid, the British "shoe bomber" who tried to blow up a U.S.-bound passenger jet in December 2001.

I wrote about Pearl's case. I visited the site of his captivity and execution—a small tree nursery several hundred yards from a conservative religious school in Karachi. I saw the perimeter wall Pearl tried to scale when he attempted to escape. Five years later, I know that the only thing that separates me from Pearl is luck.

In mid-February, Timor Shah, our chief guard, informs us that Badruddin has sent the video to Afghan and foreign media outlets but that only Al Jazeera has broadcast it. The news frustrates Tahir and Asad, who had hoped that the video would be widely broadcast and stimulate negotiations. I am not surprised and assume my colleagues believe that my request to publicize our case was coerced. Incensed, Badruddin washes his hands of us. Timor Shah says that Badruddin has declared me "worthless" and will no longer pay for our food.

Desperate to spark negotiations, we ask Timor Shah to call Abu Tayyeb and beg him to help us. To our relief, Abu Tayyeb says he will return to

Miran Shah in a few days. He promises to take charge of the negotiations and finally secure our release. After so many lies, I doubt he will actually do it.

Several days later, on February 14, two missiles fired by an American drone kill thirty people in South Waziristan, the area to our south. Most of them are Uzbek militants, a development that infuriates our guards and others around us. The guards say the Uzbeks were teaching the Afghan Taliban how to make roadside bombs.

Four weeks into the Obama administration, it is clear that the United States is not decreasing drone attacks. In fact, it is increasing them. Several times a week, drones circle over Miran Shah. Tiny specks in the sky, the whir of their propellers announces their arrival. They sound like single-engine Piper Cubs circling overhead for hours at a time. Seemingly surprised by the escalation, the Taliban bitterly criticize President Obama, who is the focus of more hatred from the Taliban than President George W. Bush.

I am not sure of the exact number, but it seems like roughly a half dozen drone strikes have been carried out in the three months since we arrived in Miran Shah. Based on the reaction of the guards, the attacks appear to primarily kill militants. Yet the Taliban exaggerate the number of civilian casualties killed and use the strikes to attract more recruits. A stalemate has emerged between the United States and the Taliban. The Americans kill top leaders and inhibit their movements with drone strikes, but the Taliban slowly generate new leadership. Neither side is able to win a decisive victory. To me, the deadlock will continue until the Pakistani army ends its cease-fire and moves into the tribal areas in force.

The drones also represent an entirely new form of warfare. The United States is able to carry out assassinations thousands of miles away without deploying American troops. No declaration of war is required. The American public hears little about the attacks. And no American lives are lost. The military itself is not necessarily involved. Some drones are operated entirely by the CIA. An agency employee sitting in an office in northern Virginia can guide the drones remotely and fire its missiles.

Our guards believe I am a target of the drones. United States officials want to kill me, they say, because my death will eliminate the enormous leverage and credibility the Haqqanis believe a single American prisoner gives them. Whenever a drone appears, I am ordered to stay inside the house. The guards believe that its surveillance cameras can recognize my face from thousands of feet above.

A week after he promised to return to Miran Shah, Abu Tayyeb, to my surprise, actually arrives and says he will allow me to call Kristen. The engineer, who is still acting as a liaison between the captors and my family, has brokered a deal to exchange us for five male prisoners from the Afghan national prison, Abu Tayyeb says. A lingering disagreement is over money, but he promises to lower the Haqqanis' demand from $15 million to $7 million. The figures are still astronomical, but I cannot keep from yet again seeing him as a potential savior. He is bound to settle for far less in direct talks with Kristen.

Later that night, Abu Tayyeb toys with me again. He and Akhundzada, his intelligence chief, announce that I am good friends with Obama's new envoy to Afghanistan and Pakistan. They ask me his name. I play dumb. They have apparently Googled my reporting in Bosnia and seen that Richard Holbrooke was the American diplomat who pressured the Serbs to release me in 1995. Fearing this moment, I have not mentioned Holbrooke's name since we were kidnapped. In January, he was named the Obama administration's special representative for Afghanistan and Pakistan. In my captors' eyes, this proves yet again that I am a "big fish." In truth, I felt that Holbrooke has been mildly irritated with me ever since I complicated his Bosnia negotiations. Each time I have seen him since then he has reminded me not to get myself kidnapped again. I have repeatedly promised him it would not happen.

The disappointments continue the following day. Instead of leaving early in the morning to call Kristen, we are delayed because no phone is available. Finally, several hours late, we depart with Abu Tayyeb for a spot near the Afghan border where we will make the call. On the way Abu Tayyeb tells me what to say. I make a detailed list in the battered reporter's notebook that I brought to what I thought would be a Taliban interview. I also have a plan. With Tahir's encouragement, I have compiled a list of the first names of friends I believe can help Kristen raise money. The vast majority of them are reporters with limited resources, but thoughts of my family selling their homes haunt me. By giving her the names I will ease the burden on Kristen.

We arrive at a remote location near the Afghan border. Badruddin is already there in a separate car. Apparently, they hope to get close enough to the border that a cell phone tower in Afghanistan will handle the call and disguise our location inside Pakistan. Badruddin gets in our car and hands me a cell phone. The phone's display shows that it's on an Afghan cellular network. I think it might be midnight in New York. Abu Tayyeb orders me to give Kristen their cell phone number and have her call us back. They are demanding $7 million in ransom but are too cheap to pay for the phone call.

I dial my home number and the answering machine picks up. I hear Kristen's joyful voice ask callers to leave us a message.

"Kristen, it's David," I say into the machine. "Kristen, are you there?" No one picks up.

"Kristen, can you hear me? Kristen, Kristen, can you hear me?" I repeat, thinking she might be asleep. "I'm calling, I'm with the Taliban. We're calling to try to negotiate."

"Kristen, are you there?" I say, increasingly worried we will miss this opportunity. "Kristen? Kristen?"

Abu Tayyeb orders me to end the call. Fearing I won't be able to call again, I blurt out "I love you" and hang up. We sit in the car for roughly fifteen minutes. Abu Tayyeb and Badruddin are nervous that the calls are being traced. They fear our car will be targeted in a drone strike. I ask them to let me try one more time. I dial our home number. Again, the answering machine picks up.

"Kristen, Kristen, it's David, can you hear me?" I say. "Kristen, Kristen, Kristen, are you there? Kristen, are you there? Please wake up."

"Kristen, it's David," I say. "Please wake up, Kristen."

MY FUNNY VALENTINE

Kristen, February 15, 2009

I hear a man's voice calling my name as I stand outside the front door. "Kristen, Kristen, are you there?" For a brief moment, I think some strange guy has broken into my apartment and is now pleading to be let out. Then I realize it's David!

My mom has gone back to Maine for the week, and my brother and his wife are here for the long Presidents' Day weekend and Valentine's Day. On Sunday we go out to dinner and a movie, something I have not done in a long time. It's more apparent to me that I have become a captive as well. This experience is shifting from a crisis to a lifestyle.

I rush to get the key in the door, stumble over to the answering machine and pick up just in time. "David, David!" I say breathlessly. "Can you hear me?"

"Yes," he replies.

"I love you, honey," I add.

"Can you get a pen and paper. I am going to give you a number to call me back on," he says tensely, adding, "do not trace the call. Do not let anyone trace the call. Do not let the government trace it."

GOLDEN CHANCE

David, February 16, 2009

The phone rings. Kristen is calling back. I am elated: there will be negotiations. I answer and immediately begin dictating from my notes. "Write this down," I say. "I cannot talk for very long. You cannot try to call me back."

"Okay," Kristen says, "I will write this down."

I look over the list of things Abu Tayyeb has ordered me to tell her.

"Okay," Kristen says again. "Hello?"

"Okay, this is the last call," I say. "This is my last chance."

Kristen repeats what I say.

"She's writing it down," I tell Badruddin and Abu Tayyeb.

"Okay, do not trace call. Don't use force to try to find us," I say, as Kristen repeats after me. "It puts us in great danger. We are in the mountains of Afghanistan."

"Uh-huh," Kristen says.

"It's very cold," I say.

"Yep," Kristen responds, sounding unimpressed.

"There's snow and I am very sick," I say.

"Yeah, okay," Kristen responds again.

"It's very difficult for us," I say. "And the video is on Al Jazeera."

"Al Jazeera overseas?" Kristen asks.

"I don't know," I reply.

"Okay, I do," Kristen says. "Okay."

"It was shown once," I say.

"Yes it was," Kristen replies.

"We called Atiqullah, the commander that arrested us," I explain.

I continue to call our captor by his false name, even though I know Atiqullah is Abu Tayyeb. Tahir and Asad still fear that Abu Tayyeb will decapitate them if he learns they revealed his true identity to me.

"Yes," Kristen says.

"He has come back to help us. He is a very big commander," I say, trying to play to his ego. "He took many, many risks, he came very far through many, many checkpoints so he could come and he is going to leave now."

"Okay," Kristen says.

"And I asked him to let me call you," I say, my voice cracking.

"Thank you," Kristen says.

"Because I thought it was the best thing to do," I say.

"Yes, it is," Kristen says, reassuring me.

"Okay, Atiqullah will negotiate with the family about money," I say. "And then the office in Kabul should negotiate with a man called Engineer." I explain to her that the engineer is their representative for negotiating prisoners.

"I know who he is," she says.

Kristen then asks me if Atiqullah is aware of the ransom offer. I say yes and then ask Kristen if she knows anything about an agreement for five prisoners.

"I am not aware of that," she says. "I am not aware of that."

"Have you heard—do you think that's not true or you don't know?" I ask, devastated by her response.

"Uh, I don't think it's true," Kristen says.

My chest tightens. We have been lied to yet again. There is no agreement for prisoners.

Kristen tries to set a time for the next phone call.

"We're running out of time," I say, repeating what they're telling me. "Atiqullah is willing to make a deal now for $7 million. Instead of for $15 million, he will drop to $7 million. And that's their last offer—and five prisoners."

I explain that the Taliban say the current ransom offer is "a joke." They claim that $38 million was paid for the French aid worker whose video I saw. They also believe that the Italian journalist was exchanged in 2007 for prisoners and $15 million in cash.

Kristen says that the U.S. government will not exchange prisoners or pay ransom. "Our government does not do that," she says.

Abu Tayyeb interrupts us and tells her to speak with the engineer about prisoners. He says any ransom payment must be done through the International Red Cross. Kristen thanks him for trying to work with our family but says that is not possible.

"I just want him to know the ICRC will not help us negotiate," she says. "I don't think they will carry funds. So I just want to make sure he knows that."

Abu Tayyeb says he will call her.

"Don't let this opportunity end," I say, repeating one of the points Abu Tayyeb dictated to me. "It's only a short time. He would like to finish everything within a week. If not, he will leave. He'll take his guards away from us and we'll be left with these other people who will kill us."

I start giving Kristen the names of the people who I think could raise ransom money. Abu Tayyeb says he will call again in four days, but will not name a time.

"She can't have a translator sitting in her house twenty-four hours a day," I say. He promises to call on Thursday.

The phone starts beeping. I know some Afghan mobile phone companies charge for receiving international calls. Even though Kristen called us, our phone will soon run out of minutes.

I quickly tell Kristen the remainder of the names.

"Honey," Kristen says, "we're doing everything we can."

The line goes dead. The phone has run out of credits.

MIDNIGHT

Kristen, February 16, 2009

I 've just gotten off the phone with my husband. I am surprised that the Taliban let him stay on the phone that long. Then again, I am footing the bill.

I feel a mix of elation and desperation. From what I could gather, David knows nothing of the ongoing negotiations. While I tried to assure him we would not give up, I also had to alert him to the fact that the Red Cross cannot assist in any negotiations. And that a prisoner exchange is not possible.

David's voice sounded strong. He was also very lucid in his thinking. This is the upside. And I have a promise that his captors will call back in a few days. We even have an assigned time.

"Midnight," I say triumphantly. Midnight on Thursday.

Midnight? Now I realize that this is the worst choice possible. Does it mean midnight on Wednesday, the very beginning of Thursday? Or the end of Thursday? I exhale an expletive.

GIFT FROM GOD

David, February 16–20, 2009

As we drive back to Miran Shah, I am shattered. There is no deal for prisoners, the Red Cross will not handle a ransom payment, and Abu Tayyeb is refusing to budge from $7 million and five prisoners. Worst of all, I have placed my wife in a horrific position—she is now directly negotiating with our captors. She will feel that she holds our lives in her hands.

Abu Tayyeb asks how I'm doing. "We're fucked," I say. Before the call, I had let myself believe that his false name, Atiqullah, "gift from God," might be a sign he would still somehow save us. Yet again, I am wrong.

We return to the house and the guards stare at me as I walk through the front gate. My face is ashen and my clothes are covered in sweat from lying under a blanket in the back of the car. I sit down next to Asad and tell him in broken Pashto that the call went badly. He pats me on the back and urges me to wash. I take a bucket shower in the bathroom, change clothes, walk in the yard, and try to gather my thoughts.

The call was a disaster. If Abu Tayyeb abandons us and Badruddin sets a deadline, we will be killed one by one.

That afternoon, I watch Asad as he prepares dinner for us. He had no idea how to cook when we were abducted three months ago but has proven to be a fast learner. As a means of survival, he is making himself useful to our captors. He and I still struggle to communicate but connect in small ways. Asad jokes with me when we are alone in the kitchen.

Tahir has become my only companion and my only attachment to reality. We have become close friends, encouraging each other in our lowest moments. He continues to fight like a lion, haranguing our kidnappers for hours at a time and threatening vengeance from his tribe.

In recent weeks, I have started encouraging Tahir and Asad to escape on their own. As Pashtuns, they have a chance of making it to the Afghan border if they can somehow slip out of our compound. Tahir adamantly refuses to leave without me. Under Pashtunwali, I am his guest and abandoning me would shame him for life. As soon as he departs without me, Tahir says, the protection of his tribe will be lifted and the Taliban will kill me.

When the guards leave us alone, Tahir whispers to me about how much he misses his seven children. He is determined to educate his daughters and is unabashedly proud of his eldest girl, who is an excellent student. Asad's two boys are younger but his face brightens each time he speaks of them. I think of how Tahir and Asad's nine children will fare without them. As adult males, they are their families' main providers. If they die, their families will be destitute.

My own death is a growing possibility as well. As the months pass, though, that prospect is gradually becoming less frightening. I tell myself that I will simply go to sleep. On a few days, I accept my death, relish the life I've had, and silently relish the idea that our greedy captors will get nothing for me. On most days, I am heartbroken at the thought of never seeing Kristen, my family, and my friends again.

What haunts me most is picturing Kristen as a widow at forty. She is dressed in black, a color she rarely wears, and her sunny countenance is dark. Her glow—the radiant smile that drew me to her at our first dinner together—is gone. I promised her a new life and a family. Instead, I have given her this.

Abu Tayyeb joins us that night for dinner. I ask him to promise that he will stay in Miran Shah until there is a resolution to our case. He does. For the next four days, we wait for him to call Kristen back. Our conversations leave me doubtful that he will ever compromise in a case involving an American.

He weeps at a radio news broadcast about civilian deaths in Afghanistan. A guard explains to me that Abu Tayyeb reviles the United States because of the civilian deaths he believes it causes. Abu Tayyeb says that Americans fixate on wealth, comfort, and fame and ignore the crimes the American government commits abroad. My captors see me—and seemingly all Westerners—as selfish, morally corrupt, and focused on pursuing the pleasures of this world. They believe Westerners will pay staggering sums to keep a kidnapped family member from being executed. They believe that Westerners' fear of death is their fatal weakness. They are convinced the Taliban will prevail because they do not fear death.

Abu Tayyeb and our guards see the American-led reconstruction effort as a giant fraud scheme designed to enrich Westerners and shortchange average Afghans. They say the American-backed Karzai government is enormously corrupt. And Akbar, our friendliest guard, says he has heard stories that American companies intentionally build low-quality bridges in Afghanistan so they can be awarded lucrative repair contracts in the future. He says Americans came to Afghanistan to enrich themselves, not to help average Afghans.

For years, I have reported on the shortcomings and waste of the American-led reconstruction effort, but I also knew the Taliban caricature of the endeavor is exaggerated. Yes, Afghan expectations of a sweeping reconstruction of the entire country were raised and then not met. And yes, corruption in the Afghan government is a staggering problem.

Evidence of how flawed the American effort is even lies on the floor of our bedroom every day. One of the machine guns our guards have was apparently given to the Afghan army or police force and then sold to the Taliban or captured by them. The gun has a tag on it with handwritten instructions in American English that tell users which settings to use when firing the weapon. Our guards ask me to translate the words for them.

At the same time, Abu Tayyeb and his men ignore the fact that the United States has built hundreds of miles of paved roads in Afghanistan and more than a thousand schools and health clinics. They deny widespread news reports that the Taliban have burned down scores of newly built schools to prevent girls from getting an education. And they ignore the Taliban's killing and kidnapping of dozens of Afghan and foreign engineers and road workers.

He complains that foreigners have not kept their promise to rebuild the country. But the Taliban, in fact, have done more to thwart the reconstruction effort than any other group. In conversations with him, I argue that the United States is not the menacing, predatory caricature that he believes it to be. I also try to counter his belief that all Americans are astonishingly rich hedonists. Nothing I say, though, seems to change his view. He sees himself as the noble defender of a culture and faith that are under assault.

PEACE BE UPON YOU

Kristen, Late February–Early March 2009

Getting a Pashto translator is not as daunting a task as it might seem, at least not in New York. With the help of David's colleagues at the newspaper, I am able to track down a translator who lives in Brooklyn and will come over to my apartment on Wednesday and Thursday night, when I'll be waiting for the next phone call from the captors. By this point we have opted to conduct negotiations privately, but we continue to send tapes of phone calls to the FBI in case they are able to pinpoint a call location or provide voice recognition.

I recorded my phone call with David three nights ago. I play it back for Lee, David McCraw, Team Kabul, and our AISC consultants. I send a recording to Michael, in Pakistan, who instructs me to forward the upcoming call to the man he works with in the tribal areas, who asked to be identified in this book as John. John has worked with Michael on prior kidnappings. We will direct all calls with the Taliban to him. At Michael's request, John has traveled to the region as our family's representative to meet with a mullah at Swabi who has connections to the Haqqanis. Now he will serve as our primary negotiator. The security consultants agree. I should not be pressured with the responsibility of negotiating directly with the Taliban on my husband's behalf. This is typical protocol—it's far too easy for captors take advantage of direct contact with family to frighten or threaten them and thus extort even more money.

Lee comes back to the city to join me in waiting for the impending call, which we plan to relay to John in hopes of making him the primary negotiator. "I thought my days of sitting and waiting by the phone for a man to call would end with marriage," I joke as I greet Lee.

Our translator arrives at 5 p.m. on Wednesday. He is a Pashtun from southern Afghanistan who has lived in the United States for several years. I serve an eclectic feast of tea, pizza, salad, and snacks—a far cry from the well-balanced cuisine Lee and I have become accustomed to during my mother's visits. "When does Mary Jane return?" Lee asks with a hint of humor.

To pass time as we all wait, I turn on the television. A *Top Chef* marathon is on. Our translator is transfixed by the host, Padma Lakshmi. "Excuse me," he asks. "Who is she? What show is this?" Then a revelation: "This is cable," he says happily. "I have cable. I could watch this at home, too?" Lee looks up at me from his computer and rolls his eyes. "Yes," I say, "in the privacy of your own home."

We share our recent histories. Our translator is from Kandahar. "This is a very interesting case for me. I left Afghanistan because my family wanted me to join the kidnapping business," he tells me. I don't know if this is true, but it doesn't seem far-fetched, given how dire the situation is abroad. He also explains that in Pakistan and Afghanistan, people with relatives in the United States are often kidnapping targets, as it is believed anyone lucky enough to be living in America has money or access to it.

We talk about photography, and he asks me about the famous photograph of the Afghan girl that appeared two decades ago, on the cover of *National Geographic.* The one with the terrorized, intense green eyes. "What was so compelling about it?" he asks. "She looks like every other Afghan girl."

I tell him my husband has been held since November 10, just over three months. He says I am a brave woman and is amazed I am not a puddle of tears. I think brave is overstating it—I have no other option, I respond. And thanks to a hefty share of defense mechanisms—denial, distancing, humor—I'm still able to function.

For some reason—most likely stress—I am incredibly exhausted. I take a nap. One would think it would be difficult to sleep under the circumstances, but I have learned to sleep when I can. Rest is an essential part of staying sharp. I have been on an adrenaline rush since David's call and am now experiencing the downswing. The hours tick by: 1 A.M., 2 A.M., then 3 A.M. We have well surpassed our midnight deadline. At 3:30 A.M. we tell the translator he can leave and that we will see him again tomorrow evening.

Lee settles in on the couch and I retire to the bedroom. At 4:30 A.M. the phone rings. I jolt out of bed and run into the living room. Lee is in his running shorts and a T-shirt, looking equally startled and disheveled. I pick up the phone. Lee reads and records the phone number off the caller ID. The area code indicates a Pakistani number. He texts it to the FBI.

"Hello, *salaam alaikum*," I say. This is a Muslim greeting which means "Peace be upon you." It never hurts to be polite.

"Alaikum asalaam," or "The same to you," the caller responds. What a gentleman, I think.

"Call me back, this number," the voice says before the line goes silent.

Several rings later, a small eternity, our call resumes.

"This is Kristen, can you understand?" I ask. I hope.

"No speak Eng-leeesh," he exaggerates. "Only Pashto."

Oh no. I am concerned they think I slacked off on finding a proper translator. Screw it, I say to myself, and proceed to speak in English, without making any apologies. They will either understand me or they won't. I tell them to call John's number in Afghanistan and that he will be representing the family in negotiations. This is Michael's contact. The captors have long stopped calling the security experts that make up Team Kabul for fear that they are government agents. They have also shunned *The New York Times* bureau, because we have convinced them that this is a family matter.

Michael suggested I use specific wording in conveying information to the captors. I recite the phrases I have memorized: "My representative, my friend, John, is in Afghanistan and he is authorized to help you. He is the only one you should speak to."

For the next five minutes, a somewhat comical exchange ensues as I relay numbers to Atiqullah and he repeats them back to me. He is oddly polite and somewhat cheeky. I laugh triumphantly when he gets all the digits correct and in proper sequence. Lee looks somewhat quizzical as he witnesses this exchange. Lee calls Michael on the other line to alert him that his contact should expect a call.

Luckily, Atiqullah knows his English numbers. Within minutes, Michael calls to alert us that Atiqullah has already made contact with John. I hope passing Atiqullah on to this negotiator is the right decision.

It's now early March and my mother has returned to New York with my father, Jim, for a visit. My parents have been happily married for over forty-five years. Seeing them together gives me a sense of comfort, but also makes David's absence more palpable.

Two weeks have passed since my call with Atiqullah. Our noon updates continue. Atiqullah had at first made repeated calls to our contact, John, then stopped abruptly. John informs me and Lee over Skype that during the initial calls, Atiqullah said he would kill David on the spot, a threat John found ludicrous. "I knew there was no way David was with him," John tells us. "It would be too risky." When John remained unfazed, the kidnapper's tone once again shifted to "Let's make a deal." John says they have come down from $7 million to $5 million and that they are trying to arrange to meet face-to-face in a few days. To my knowledge, this never transpires.

A few days later, on a Sunday morning, my phone rings at 7:30 A.M. Unfortunately, I've left the cordless handset in the living room, where my parents are sleeping.

I wish this was not happening in front of them. My father has not yet been subjected to a call from the captors. I know he would do anything to protect me. Proactive and sensitive, seeing me go through this ordeal and feeling he cannot remedy the situation is a strain on him as well. I motion for them to leave the room to avoid distraction. I hit the record button attached to my answering machine.

"Hello, *salaam alaikum*," I say.

"*Alaikum asalaam*," he responds.

"This is Kristen. Who is this?" I ask, trying to buy some time to catch my breath.

"This is the translator for Atiqullah. So what is the progress?" he asks.

My heart is racing but I try to sound as calm and casual as possible and stick to the talking points outlined by our security team. I continue: "I gave Atiqullah the phone number of John, our representative in country. We are still working on raising money. It has been difficult to raise money because it is illegal to do so, so people have been, you know, a little hesitant." I chastise myself for the stupidity of this statement, then add, "I have a friend in country now who could arrange to get it to David's hosts." The line goes dead.

I phone Michael to alert him that I have just received another call. I ask him why they are contacting me when John is still in Afghanistan. He tells me to stonewall them if they call again. "Keep referring them back to John," he advises. "Also, tell them you are shocked they are speaking with you directly. You are a woman and it is dishonorable for them to be speaking to you. It goes against all they preach."

I wait several minutes for Atiqullah's translator to call me back, then take matters into my own hands, realizing once again they are going to stiff me for the cost of the phone call. I dial the number from caller ID. "Hello," I say. "This is Kristen."

"Hello, hi," he says, seemingly surprised to hear from me. "Yes, go on. So you continue." he adds casually.

I am struck by the conversational way the translator speaks English. I realize he's fluent in "American."

"My representative in country. Atiqullah has talked to him before," I say. "He can tell you more specifically what we can do. Do you need his phone number?" I ask.

"Listen, listen. Master John is not good man, he is creating problems," the translator responds.

I take this to mean John has stood firm and not agreed to give them $5 million. Lee and I have decided to stand firm on our offer. AISC has advised us to stand fast, too. Increasing the amount while our captors remain at an unmatchable level on both money and prisoners is futile, and they claim it will only further extend our ordeal. They are of the "give them an inch and they'll ask for a mile" school of thought. Anyway, we don't have this kind of money and have no intention of trying to raise it.

"And your husband has said that you speak directly to my wife," the translator claims.

I try to thwart this idea. "I am very concerned, but I am a woman. I am surprised you are calling me direct," I say.

"Well," he says a bit sheepishly, "we are interested to hear from you, what progress you have made. So far your husband is in good condition but over time anything can happen."

"The newspaper will not help me and our government will not pay. Our government is very different from the Italian government or the Korean government," I inform him, knowing that those countries had recently paid ransom in Taliban kidnappings. "So we will keep trying. Five million is a lot. We will never have it. We have a certain amount now and we can get it to you very quickly," I add, as I have been instructed to do by John and Michael.

"Yes. You know our circumstances," he explains. "Everybody is putting nose in. We should not talk all the time because it is dangerous. So try to keep it limited."

I agree with him and add, "That is why our representative is in the country. He can talk to you and the government cannot trace the call."

"Atiqullah says to you he is the only authentic representative for this issue," he adds.

"Okay, for the money issue?" I ask.

"Yeah, yeah," he confirms.

I am relieved he has not made any mention of prisoners.

"Okay," I repeat. "John is my only rep in country. Can we have him and Atiqullah talk again? He knows my father. He is a family friend. He also knows Afghanistan. That is the connection between us." I know invoking one's father is a form of credibility in Pashtun culture. I also don't want to let on that we think David and his captors are in Pakistan.

"Listen, you just try to prepare to arrange the money, then we will talk to you. You try to prepare the money as quietly as possibly," he states.

"Okay, we will keep trying," I say, to let them know more funds may be available if we keep talking. "We have an update about funding in the country, if you want to contact John he should know about it. He has access to the money and can get it to you."

"Yeah, we are going for praying," he says, wanting to get off the phone, in just one of the absurdities of the situation. He may be a criminal and a kidnapper, but he's observant. "After two days we will have another conversation, *inshallah*," he adds. God willing.

"Okay, Tahir and Asad—they are okay?" I ask. I know their families are worried sick. And I want to reinforce the idea that they must be part of the deal.

"Yeah, yeah, completely well. There is no problem," he says. "Is okay— one hundred percent."

"Okay," I add, "and tell David I love him and I pray for you all. I pray for you *all* every day." I hope in some bizarre way this will play on their sympathies, if only momentarily. There is a muffled pause, a fumbling in the background.

"God bless you," he responds.

Michael alerts me he will be traveling to Washington in a few days, and I plan to meet him there. We exchange text messages and set a meeting point: the bookshop at Union Station, just in front of Au Bon Pain. At this point, we have only seen each other in miniature during our telephonic computer exchanges on Skype. I tell him I will be wearing a red scarf.

I have no idea what to expect beyond the sandy brown hair, prophet-length beard, and broad smile I have seen on my computer screen. I have heard rumors about Michael. Mystery precedes him. A Google search reveals he was expelled from Afghanistan by President Hamid Karzai in 2007 for trying to negotiate with the Taliban. He has worked in the region for the United Nations and the European Union as a diplomat. Some speculate that he is a member of British intelligence. This is most likely wild rumor fueled by the fact that he has worked in Afghanistan and Pakistan for the last twenty-five years and is fluent in several local dialects and well versed in the nuances of tribal structures and custom. He is an expert on Taliban leadership. Two former hostages I met claim he was their lifesaver. The Kabul bureau trusts him and uses him as an analyst. David viewed Michael as a well-respected expert on Afghanistan and Pakistan. I have found him to be an insightful and articulate Skype correspondent.

He arrives on time. I'm relieved to see he is somewhat older than I expected and slightly professorial in his demeanor. A tall man with a warm smile, he greets me with three kisses, alternating cheeks. There is an awkward charm about him and something fatherly that puts me at ease. He is quite sensible, respectful, decent—and every bit as eloquent in person as on a computer screen. He's married and has a normal family life outside the business of kidnapping. He informs me he has just been offered a fellowship at Harvard and seems genuinely surprised by the honor. Michael says he is in Washington on business. He occupies quite a niche: a person who has talked to the Taliban. He jests that Karzai has done wonders for his brand.

"I should tell you, your husband was due to interview me before this unfortunate incident. Did you know this?" he asks as we settle into the lobby coffee shop of a nearby hotel.

Of course I do. I've scoured David's e-mail account for references to Michael and found out he was indeed going to meet with him in Pakistan, the day after his fateful interview with Abu Tayyeb. "David would be slightly upset knowing I have now scooped him on several interviews, including you," I joke, recalling my brief chats with Condoleezza Rice and Hillary Clinton.

Michael says he still believes that Atiqullah is not the ultimate decision maker in the kidnapping and that he does not have the authority to release our three. Michael is pushing for John to meet with a relative of Siraj face-to-face to try and strike a deal. Upon parting he praises my patience. I think this is a dubious honor. I have been beating myself up for days with the thought that if I were truly doing a good job, David would be free by now. Michael counters that the United States government cannot find Siraj Haqqani. Why should it be any easier locating David and securing a deal for his release? He adds that Siraj cultivates a self-image of being moral, but in reality heads a criminal conspiracy. "When you're dealing with one of the world's most formidable characters," Michael tells me, "things take time."

AN ALTERNATE UNIVERSE

David, Late February 2009

Abu Tayyeb calls Kristen to negotiate and informs me that she told him to speak with someone in Kabul. Then he disappears again. I am relieved in a way. At least Kristen is not negotiating herself. Over the next several weeks, we receive contradictory reports from our guards about the negotiations. On one day, they say an agreement is close. On another, they say there is no progress.

Our existence reverts to its old pattern. Each day consists of the same tedium: prayers, meals, naps, and depression. Tahir and Asad grow more and more pessimistic. I tell them to be patient. They shake their heads at me.

My mind-set is gradually shifting. For the first three months of captivity, I tried to find ways that I could somehow help engineer our release. Now, as we begin our fourth month, I tell myself it is my job to wait as long as it takes for our release. I am sure that Kristen and my family are doing all they can to free us. My part of the bargain is to be patient and strong and do nothing rash. We are being treated well compared to other hostages, many of whom spent far longer in captivity. I think of Terry Anderson, the American journalist held for seven years in Lebanon. I try to look at my time in captivity as a jail sentence that I must serve until release. At the age of forty-one, I have twenty to thirty years of life ahead of me. A few more months of imprisonment in exchange for decades of happiness are worth it.

The question I posed about who represented the true Taliban in the first days of our kidnapping now seems silly. In my mind, Qari, the unstable guard who nearly shot Tahir and our kidnapper who uses multiple false names are one and the same. As I come to know the alternate universe the Haqqanis have created in Miran Shah, I grow more and more dejected. Our captors are unwavering in their belief that the United States is waging a war against Islam.

It is a universe filled with hypocrisy. My captors bitterly denounce missionaries, but they press me to convert to their faith. They complain about innocent Muslims being imprisoned by the United States, even as they continue to hold us captive and try to extort money from my family. They rail against American, Israeli, and European mistreatment of Muslims, but they celebrate suicide attacks on mosques that kill dozens of Muslim worshippers as they supplicate to God. Those living under Afghanistan's and Pakistan's apostate governments, they say, deserve it.

Yet in our day-to-day existence, when commanders are absent, some of our guards show glimpses of humanity. These moments give me hope that we may somehow be able to talk or reason our way to freedom. I do not know if they are simply humoring me so I will remain an obedient and patient captive. I do not know which side of our contradictory captors is real.

Over the last three months, I have gradually gained a clearer sense of our guards and their backgrounds. They are mostly Afghan men in their late twenties and early thirties. Some have grown up as refugees in Pakistan. All have the equivalent of elementary or junior high educations from government or religious schools. None have seen the world beyond Afghanistan and Pakistan.

Waging jihad seems to give them discipline, self-respect, and a sense of belonging to a greater cause. They see the United States military as the latest foreign force trying to subjugate Afghanistan and Islam. Akbar believes he must have many children because they will be needed to fight Afghanistan's next foreign invader: China.

I talk the most with Akbar, who seems to illustrate how the United

States lost the initial popular support in Afghanistan in 2001. In the first years after the fall of the Taliban, Akbar worked as a painter on some type of construction project. Over time, he turned against the United States as American forces arrested local leaders, searched houses, and, in his mind, humiliated Pashtuns. He also embraces wild conspiracy theories about the United States. He is convinced the American military uses some type of weapon that sterilizes Muslim men. Several of his Afghan friends, he tells me, are unable to have children.

He praises the Taliban for cracking down on warlords, combating corruption, and delivering law and order. He despises the Pakistani army. In Miran Shah, he spends many afternoons using a Taliban radio scanner to discover the frequency used by nearby Pakistani forces. Speaking in Urdu, he lures soldiers into a conversation and then curses them in Pashto and English. He seethes with hatred toward what he sees as an apostate army that oppresses their fellow Muslims in exchange for Western cash.

He and the other guards speak of the foreign militants in the tribal areas with reverence. In conversations, they refer to Osama bin Laden with the honorific "Sheikh Osama." For several weeks, they take turns attending bomb-making classes from Uzbek militants in Miran Shah. They set off enormous explosions but Pakistani forces never come off their base to investigate. The only signs of a Pakistani military presence are planes and helicopters taking off from an airstrip somewhere to our east.

Timor Shah—our chief guard—is particularly proud when he comes home one day from bomb-making class with skinned knees. He set an explosive but did not give it a long enough fuse. As he ran away from the bomb, he dove to the ground as the blast erupted behind him. In some ways, the guards remind me of young soldiers anywhere. They enjoy playing with guns and testing their own strength. Chunky enjoys taking apart and cleaning his machine gun over and over. When I tell the guards my pen is my weapon, they laugh.

Day and night, they monitor American-funded Voice of America Pashto-language service radio and celebrate reports of the deaths of Afghan and American soldiers. Whenever a guard hears a news bulletin describing a major Taliban suicide bombing, he excitedly calls for the other guards to come listen. Hunched around the shortwave radio, they shout "God is great!" in unison after the number of dead is announced.

I try to get to know one of Sharif's fighters, a young Pakistani Pashtun named Hamid who is training to be a suicide bomber. In his twenties, he has a slim build, brown hair, and brown eyes. He graduated from a high school in Pakistan and at one point hoped to become an engineer. He never attended college but is relatively well educated compared with the other fighters.

Conversations with him help me understand how hard-line Islam's focus on the next world eases the training of suicide bombers. Taught that their relationship with God is all that matters, young recruits are slowly distanced from their families. When I ask Hamid why he wants to die, he replies that living in this world is a burden for any true Muslim. Heaven is his goal, he says. Earthly relationships with his parents and siblings do not matter. Music, laughter, and idle chatter are seen as distractions from worship. Life is a flat, colorless existence that is something to be endured, not enjoyed. Days are spent studying the Koran, praying, and fearing judgment day. If he successfully carries out a suicide bombing, he believes he will die as a martyr and ensure he goes to heaven, not hell.

Hamid speaks a smattering of English, and my own beliefs seem to interest and amaze him. During our six weeks together, he asks me a series of questions. Is it true, he asks, that a necktie is a secret symbol of Christianity? Is it true that Christians want to live a thousand years? Is it true that American soldiers hunt wild pigs—animals that Muslims consider unclean—and feed them to their commanding officers?

Sharif, a tall, burly, and imposing figure, tells me that the Taliban have been unfairly portrayed by the Western media. He says that the Taliban would have allowed girls to attend school when they governed Afghanistan, but security problems prevented them from doing so. Once security improved, he insists, girls would have been allowed to enroll in classes. He expresses dismay at the United States, a country he considered an ally against the Soviets. The 2001 American invasion was unjustified, he says. The Taliban should have been allowed to try Osama bin Laden on its own and determine if he was guilty of the 9/11 attacks.

When I ask him about my captivity, he tells me that each day the Taliban hold me they deliver "massive political blows" to the American government. When I tell him that my case is not public and Americans don't know I'm a prisoner, he insists that my case is still consuming American government time and resources.

When we discuss journalism, he declares that he is an enemy of *The New York Times* because it supports secularism. He says that secularism is the Taliban's adversary and religion must govern all aspects of life. He flatly rejects my compromise suggestion that strict Islamic law be enacted in Afghanistan's conservative rural south, while milder forms of Islam be followed in the comparatively liberal north.

Citing the Taliban's interpretation of Islam, Sharif says it is every Muslim's duty to try to stop others from sinning. If one person in a village commits a sin, God will also punish those who witness it and do not stop him. The concept of God judging us as individuals does not seem to exist for him. To ensure that he goes to heaven, Sharif believes he must persuade others to become strict Muslims as well.

One day, I receive a Pakistani English-language newspaper with a photograph of Barack and Michelle Obama dancing at an inaugural ball. For weeks, Sharif has looked through the newspaper and used a pen to scribble out women's faces from photographs. Any portrayal of the human form is an affront to Islam, according to the Taliban's interpretation of the faith. Hamid burns newspapers after I have read them, seemingly convinced that their removal cleanses the house. On the day I receive the newspaper with the photo of the Obamas dancing, Sharif flips through the paper and stops at the picture of the Obamas. He stares at it briefly and then spits on it.

One morning, two of our guards leave for bomb-making class and Mansoor leaves for the market. As one guard naps in Sharif's bedroom, Hamid announces he is going to pick up bread for our lunch from a nearby madrassa. He departs and I realize we have a chance to escape. I find Tahir and tell him that we can close the door to the room where the guard is sleeping, slide the bolt on the door's exterior, and lock him inside. If we act quickly, we can take his rifle and radio and walk out of the compound.

Tahir rushes to Asad and the two speak feverishly in Pashto for several seconds. Asad picks up a machine gun that is lying on the floor and I don't understand what is happening. We do not need the machine gun. It will make us more conspicuous and slow us down. We need the Kalashnikov. The Taliban and local tribesmen consider any man walking through Miran Shah without one suspicious.

"He is acting strangely," Tahir says, referring to Asad.

The two speak again in Pashto. If we do not act now, Hamid or Mansoor will soon return. Tahir walks outside to see if anyone is nearby. He walks back inside the compound and again talks with Asad. Finally, Tahir announces that Asad thinks it is too dangerous for us to simply walk out of the compound. Tahir agrees with him. The area is filled with Taliban, he explains. We will quickly be shot or arrested. We decide to wait.

Their judgment proves wise. A few minutes after our conversation ends, Mansoor walks through the front door. He says he was walking home from the market and saw Tahir step out of the compound. He demands to know what happened. Tahir says he stepped outside to get water from a nearby stream to wash clothes. Mansoor remains suspicious.

Later, Tahir tells me that he is worried about Asad. Our driver is having, long secretive conversations with the guards. When Tahir asks him what they are speaking about, Asad does not give clear answers. I do not worry and assume that Asad is pretending to befriend the guards in order to keep himself alive.

As February comes to an end, the guards demand I stop washing the group's dishes because they do not want to catch my diseases. They believe the intermittent diarrhea I suffer stems from being an inherently unclean non-Muslim, not from unhygienic food.

Sharif begins repeatedly pressing me to convert. In excruciatingly long conversations, he tries to get me to agree with him that there is only one

God. He asks me to repeat after him in Arabic "There is no God but Allah and Muhammad is his prophet"—the words uttered by someone converting to Islam. He orders me to read a passage of the Koran each day and discuss it with him at night. He dismisses my arguments that a forced conversion is not legitimate. He and the guards politely say they feel sorry for me. If I fail to convert, I will suffer agonizing pain in the fires of hell.

Whether or not I read the English-language Koran that Atiqullah gave me has become a source of tension. Some guards argue that I should not be allowed to touch a Koran because I am an unclean non-Muslim. Barring nonbelievers from reading the Koran baffles me. I do not understand how a non-Muslim is supposed to learn about Islam if they are not allowed to read its holy book.

Sharif believes it is permissible for me to touch the Koran Abu Tayyeb gave me because it includes Arabic, Urdu, and English script. An actual Koran, he says, is written only in Arabic. In a compromise, he tells me to not touch the part of the pages of the Arabic, Urdu, and English Koran that contain Arabic script. That part of the pages, he says, is sacred.

Each time I touch the book I fear I will accidentally drop it. Each time I turn the paper I fear I will tear it. Either act will be seized upon by my guards as blasphemous. In an effort to show respect, I place a scarf over my hands to prevent my flesh from making direct contact with their holy book. Before I pick up the Koran, I whisper "In the name of Allah, the most merciful and beneficent" in Arabic as they do. After Mansoor accuses me of insulting Islam by pointing my feet—which Muslims consider unclean—toward Mecca while reading, I sit cross-legged. Eventually, I copy passages into a notebook so I can read them in peace.

The English-language Koran I have been given has a brief biography of the prophet Muhammad as its introduction. It describes Islam's founder as a great social reformer of his time. He called for equality, justice, and an end to the tribal feuds and greed that beset the Arabian peninsula in the seventh century A.D. Most of all he calls for honesty, piousness, and justice.

"O ye who believe! Be steadfast witnesses for Allah in equity, and let not hatred of any people seduce you that ye deal not justly," reads one verse. "Deal justly, that is nearer to your duty. Observe your duty to Allah. Lo! Allah is informed of what ye do."

To me, Muhammad's calls for honesty, humility, charity, compassion, and confession of sins echo the tenets of all the world's faiths. Instead of making me want to join their cause, reading the Koran makes me believe our captors are not following his core teaching. The dishonesty, injustice, and greed they show in my case are the opposite of what I am reading.

Since arriving in the region in 2001, I have come to see the West and the Taliban as competitors in a race to put in place a government system that can produce noncorrupt leaders who provide security and jobs for their people. The Taliban argue that implementing their strict version of Islamic law—replete with beheadings—is the best way to do so. The United States and its allies argue that free-market democracy is the answer.

My time living in India has shown me that steadily implemented, indigenous versions of free-market democracy can work. India is a place of hope for me. While not perfect, I see it as a relative success story that may offer lessons for Afghanistan and Pakistan.

Based on my reporting there, I feel that religious extremism is a problem among all faiths in India, but the country's messy and chaotic democracy generally tends to slowly mollify it. When allowed to vote freely, impoverished, illiterate Indians show remarkable savvy in choosing leaders. Minority groups often feel they receive some airing of and response to their grievances. Elections are generally considered credible in India due to the vital role played by a handful of strong, independent institutions: a national supreme court, an independent election commission, and a free news media, among others. Corruption and poverty remain crippling across India, but the country's free-market economy and educational institutions are steadily growing.

Pakistan, on the other hand, remains hugely fraught with ethnic and political divisions and handicapped by inconsistent economic growth. The country's powerful army continues to quietly manipulate politics, and the three institutions that play a central stabilizing role in India—the supreme court, the election commission, and the free press—remain only partly independent in Pakistan. Coups and manipulations by the military have resulted in no democratically elected government serving its full term since Pakistan won independence from Great Britain in 1947. In the army's defense, the country's civilian political class has also performed poorly. Unlike in India, no comprehensive land reform has been carried out in Pakistan to break the lock on civilian power enjoyed by the country's landed oligarchs. Pakistan's current president, Asif Ali Zardari, is ineffective, surrounded by cronies, and widely viewed as corrupt, according to Pakistani newspaper editorials I receive.

Afghanistan is in an even more dire state politically. After thirty years of war, the country's institutions have been shattered. Deep suspicion divides its ethnic groups. Its most basic form of government, its tribal structure, has been severely weakened. And President Karzai is seen as increasingly mercurial, opportunistic, and unwilling to control corruption.

A question that has hovered over many other developing countries I have covered lingers over Pakistan and Afghanistan: Is a messy, unstable democracy better than a stable one-party or military-led government? Judging by my reporting in India, I still agree with moderate Pakistanis and Afghans who see an imperfect, locally created representative democratic system and education reform as the best hope of creating long-term stability in their countries. It may take decades to achieve in Pakistan and Afghanistan—as it has in India—but it can work.

Living in the tribal areas has made me even more convinced. Compared with the dynamism of New Delhi, Islamabad, and Kabul, Miran Shah seems frozen in time. An incessant focus on the next world has led to intolerance, zealotry, and stagnation in this one.

On some days, the virulence I see among the Haqqani foot soldiers eases. Amid the monotony and tension are moments of kindness and levity.

When no commanders are present, Mansoor allows me to walk in a small walkway between the house and perimeter wall. If I follow the narrow path, I can walk in large circles around the house. For a few moments during each loop, I am momentarily alone. Since my fake suicide attempt in late December, I have been constantly under the watchful eye of a guard. Moments of solitude are blissful.

Taking advantage of the privacy of walks around the house, I sometimes touch a spot on the wall where I imagine Kristen's face is. On others, I run back and forth in the small alleyway, eager for endorphins that will raise my spirits.

To my relief, on one afternoon, the guard we have nicknamed Chunky leads me through the jihadi-version of calisthenics. He and I perform deep knee bends in the yard as Tahir, Asad, and the other guards guffaw. I look like a white-bearded, geriatric militant, but the exercise—and laughter—are a godsend.

With the guards' approval, Asad buys a volleyball in the local market one afternoon. For several weeks, the guards, Tahir, and Asad play volleyball in the small, dirt-covered yard. During the games, they spike the ball at one another's head as powerfully as they can. They invite me to join them but I decline. Eventually, they hit the ball so hard it careens into a neighboring compound and is never seen again.

For several weeks, Tahir is allowed to play in a local pickup soccer game held near our house and Asad is allowed to hunt birds in our yard. He and Akbar construct a crude cage out of slats of wood and chicken wire, stand it on its side, and spread bird food on the ground. When birds come to feed, they pull the cage down with a string. Each day, they spend hours waiting for birds to be lured into their trap. They eat the handful of birds they manage to catch. Tahir and I oppose the hunting. We argue it is wrong to kill anything simply for sport. I have an irrational fear that God will punish us for Asad's bird hunting and prolong our imprisonment.

On one Saturday night, Akbar helps me find an Indian music station that plays Western music. In broken Pashto and English, I try to explain the meaning of the INXS song "Beautiful Girl" and the Lenny Kravitz song "Fly Away."

One young Talib even tells us that his commander has ordered him to kidnap a foreigner working in Afghanistan, but he refuses to do so. If a foreigner has come to help the people of Afghanistan, he says, they should be treated well. He suggests I read a passage from the Koran each day for comfort.

"Allah tasketh not a soul beyond its scope," it says. "For it is only that which it hath earned, and against it only that which it hath deserved. Our Lord! Impose not on us that which we have not the strength to bear! Pardon us, absolve us, and have mercy on us, Thou, our Protector, and give us victory over the disbelieving folk."

At night, Sharif and the guards search for ways to break the monotony. If it weren't for us, they say, they would return to Afghanistan and help prepare spring offensives. After dinner, Sharif often tells long jokes. He tells one joke involving a man who stutters in Pashto so convincingly that I find myself laughing while not understanding a word he says. On many nights, he seems to sincerely want to cheer us up.

Still trying to gain their sympathy, I reenact my wedding for Sharif and the guards one night. I have Akbar stand beside me and play the part of Kristen. They seem fascinated as I describe how Kristen's father walked her down the aisle and gave me her hand. They listen intently as I explain how Kristen and I placed rings on each other's fingers and recited our wedding vows. When I take Akbar's hand and pretend I'm sliding a wedding ring on his finger, they howl with laughter.

During the wedding reenactment, I decline to mention other details that will paint me as a hedonistic nonbeliever. I do not say that the service took place in a church and ended with the bride and groom publicly kissing, a scandalous act for Pashtuns. I know it is odd to share my wedding with my captors, but I am still trying to humanize myself in their eyes.

The activity Sharif and the guards love most, though, is singing Pashto songs after dinner. My voice and Pashto pronunciation are terrible, but our guards urge me to sing along. The ballads vary. On some evenings, I find myself reluctantly singing Taliban songs that declare, "You have atomic bombs, but we have suicide bombers."

On other nights, at Sharif's urging, I switch to American tunes. In a halting, off-key voice, I sing Frank Sinatra's version of "New York, New York" and describe it as the story of a villager who tries to succeed in the city and support his family. I sing Bruce Springsteen's "Born to Run" and describe it as a portrayal of the struggles of average Americans. When

I sing John Lennon's "Imagine," Sharif shows little interest in the lyrics and asks for something livelier.

I realize that my guards, too, need a break from our grim existence. But I feel like a performing monkey when they tell me to sing in Pashto for visiting commanders. I know they are simply laughing at me.

I intentionally avoid American love songs, trying to dispel their belief that all Americans are hedonists. Despite my efforts, romantic songs—whatever their language—are the guards' favorites.

The Beatles song "She Loves You," which popped into my head soon after I received my wife's letter from the Red Cross, is the most popular. For reasons that baffle me, the guards relish singing it with me. I begin by singing its first verse. Timor Shah, Akbar, and Chunky, along with Tahir and Asad, then join me in the chorus.

"She loves you—yeah, yeah, yeah," we sing, with Kalashnikovs lying on the floor around us.

A GOAT WILL NEVER BE A COW

Kristen, Early to Mid-March 2009

I receive a text on my BlackBerry from an American who works with local journalists in Afghanistan and Pakistan. He has heard of our alleged communications with Siraj Haqqani. "Siraj is hopeful," he claims. How he knows this, I am not quite sure. He asserts that a local journalist has just interviewed Siraj and inquired about David.

I relay this to the team in our noon call. Our team has been on a cultural sensitivity kick of late, perhaps influenced by information from John and Michael. After four months of this nightmare, we want to deliver the message to Siraj that enough is enough, urging him to accept what has been offered, an amount well below what the Taliban are asking.

The gruff voice of Dewey Clarridge chimes in and tells us we need to be mindful of the local culture. "We need to say it in the Afghan, Pashtun way: 'What you have is a goat and a goat will never be a cow.' This is the Pashtun way of saying things," he states plainly.

Frustrated with the lack of progress, I simply cannot resist, and chime in, "Then tell those jackasses to let my husband go." Dewey is clearly amused. "That's pretty good," he admits. Dewey and I have had a love-hate relationship over the phone. This is one of our lovelier moments. I think back to the very beginning of this ordeal. The captors referred to David as a "golden hen." Tahir's father sent me a moving letter in which he thanked our family for continuing to work on behalf of our three, adding that without our help he would be like "a blind rooster." I also recall a recent interview with Siraj that was e-mailed to me by a local Afghan journalist. In it Siraj notes the similarities between the Obama and Bush administrations by stating, "They are two ears of the same donkey." It seems the only common and consistent thread in our communications—and cultural exchanges—has been the repeated reference to barnyard animals. A mildly amusing but sad comment on our state of affairs.

The divided agendas in our team are starting to turn into a full-fledged schism. Consultants from Clayton, the security team on contract for *The New York Times*, disagree with AISC, the private security team we have hired, and vice versa. One of the contractors calls me and claims that McCraw is giving Dewey a hard time because of his role in the Iran-contra affair. Lee, David McCraw, and I are constantly having to weigh contradictory opinions. Clayton has years of kidnapping negotiating experience, but very little of it has been in Afghanistan or Pakistan. The private security team has contacts within the region and within the governments there. AISC is often skittish about sharing information with Clayton. The lack of transparency, maintained with the intention of protecting sources, has at times led to division and mistrust among our team members. At times we have considered jettisoning some or all the consultants. But we feel that starting from scratch would only confuse the kidnappers and prolong David's captivity. The one player who seems to get along with everyone is Michael. He is also the only one who actually lives in the region. He does not try to divide and conquer. I don't know what his larger agenda might be, but at least it doesn't get in the way here.

We are told by Michael that contact from the captors will be imminent. Someone who identifies himself as Atiqullah has started calling John again. Back in January, the FBI told us that Atiqullah was an alias used by both Badruddin Haqqani and Abu Tayyeb. They also told us that as the head of the Haqqani network, Siraj is ultimately the one in charge.

Michael maintains that Atiqullah is just a middleman. He is uncertain as to whether it is Abu Tayyeb, Badruddin, or some third party trying to take a cut of the money for himself. Michael believes the real point of contact needs to be Siraj Haqqani or a family elder close to him. He continues to push to have our guy on the ground meet face-to-face with them. But each time a meeting is set to take place, there is a delay. The weather turns foul, or it's suddenly time for a hajj to Mecca, or an elder simply fails to show up.

I have learned through months of dashed hopes, bizarre video communications, and misinformation to embrace the old adage, "Believe half of what you see and none of what you hear." Privately, Lee and I speak with the other members of our team one by one and get their recommendations. Should we increase our offer, and if so, when?

John insists it should be at a face-to-face meeting and that the captors need to come down and name a price we can match. The Clayton team advises us to raise our offer preemptively. We are told by John that it seems we are close to reaching an agreement.

My fortieth birthday is March 9, also the four-month anniversary of David's abduction. It's a dreaded milestone—not so much in terms of my age, but because it has been a time the family looked forward to, thinking surely David would be home by then. I now fear I will be a widow at forty, after only six months of marriage.

To boost my spirits, I decide to pack a suitcase. If David is indeed released, I am to meet him in Dubai. Lee will come along to fend off the press. We have had the "evacuation strategy" in place for months. The situation has been so unpredictable, I haven't been getting my hopes up, but I also cannot let myself wallow in sadness.

I recall my conversation with Alan Johnston, a BBC journalist who was held hostage in Gaza for nearly four months, in 2007. I remember thinking four months was an unfathomable amount of time.

Alan reached out to me a few weeks ago and his words of wisdom linger. "This situation is going to run its course. You will not have control over the outcome," he says. "It will have the same outcome whether you spend fifteen hours a day worrying about it—or whether you try to make the space and time to relax and find some joy in your life." He encouraged me to find and embrace the moments that sustain me—time with friends, family—and not to feel bad for continuing to find those moments of happiness in my life. He told me that during his own captivity, he learned a lot about how his mind worked. He quickly realized which thoughts would boost him, and which ones would lead him down a negative spiral. He trained himself, over time, to extend the positive thoughts. He encouraged me to do the same. He added that he was certain, judging from his own experience, that David would want me to do this. He also reminded me that in some ways, the situation is worse for the family.

"David knows his circumstance. He will adapt. And he can imagine what your life is like back home," Alan said, pointing out that for me and other family members, everything about David's experience is an unknown.

BIRTHDAY WISHES

David, Early to Mid-March 2009

In early March, Badruddin arrives for a visit. We have not seen him for weeks. At this point, I'm entirely dubious of him. He is either making impossible demands or telling outrageous lies, both of which I find infuriating.

He sits down and we exchange pleasantries. Each meeting is more formulaic than the last. I pretend to be meek and respectful; he pretends he is seriously negotiating for our release. He tells me that the engineer's son has been released. I am delighted for the engineer's family, but see this as another setback. The engineer is out of the picture. Another negotiation channel has failed.

Tensions continue to simmer between Tahir and Asad. One day, they come to blows and none of us is sure why. Asad said that Tahir insulted him. Tahir accuses Asad of the same.

March 9—a day I have dreaded for months—arrives. It is Kristen's fortieth birthday, and I have visions of her alone in New York. I spend the morning praying for her and then, to my surprise, Timor Shah takes Tahir and me on a rare drive outside the walled compound. In reality, it's not simply a magnanimous gesture. A drone has been circling over Miran Shah all day. Fearing a missile attack, Timor Shah hustles me into the back of the station wagon and speeds away from the house. Once we are outside town, I am allowed to sit up, remove the scarf from my face, and look out the car's back windows.

My first trip outside in weeks instantly raises my spirits. I watch the Waziristan countryside roll by and relish its arid beauty. Farmers tend fields of wheat and rice surrounded by networks of irrigation canals amid rock-strewn hillsides. While thirty years of conflict have devastated Afghanistan's infrastructure, Pakistan's infrastructure appears comparatively intact. The canals were one of the products of limited Pakistani, American, and British development programs designed to pacify the tribal areas.

I had recently found out that our house-turned-prison was as well. To my surprise, Tahir informed me that our house was built by the Pakistani government in 2005 to serve as a health clinic. When I looked at our bedroom, I saw it was a waiting room. The two adjoining bedrooms were examination rooms. The construction of the clinic was likely part of a government campaign to win the support of the local population. After the Taliban seized control of Miran Shah in 2006, Sharif took over the clinic and made it his house.

As we drive past more of the irrigation canals, they appear similar to ones I have seen in Helmand Province, the part of southern Afghanistan that was the focus of my book and site where the United States built "Little America." I have fond memories of the province, which fascinated me. As I completed my research, I had come to see Helmand as a case study of how the American and Afghan governments had grown vastly weaker between the Cold War and the war on terror. The post-2001 effort in Helmand was a shadow of the endeavor there in the 1960s and 1970s.

After the fall of the Taliban, the only foreign troops to deploy to Helmand, a province twice the size of Maryland with a population of one million, were several dozen American Special Forces soldiers. They built a base in the center of the province in 2002, hired several hundred Afghan gunmen to protect them, and focused solely on hunting Taliban and Qaeda remnants.

Helmand Province's voluble young governor, Sher Muhammad Akhundzada, was largely left to do as he pleased. The son of a famed local commander who fought the Soviets, Akhundzada entered Taliban-controlled Afghanistan in 2001 at Karzai's request and won control of

Helmand with the help of American Special Forces. Rumors abounded about the boyish governor. In interviews with journalists, Akhundzada said he was in his early thirties and a high school graduate. Afghan aid workers said he was in his late twenties and illiterate.

Whatever he may have lacked in administrative skills, he made up for in muscle. As the head of Helmand's largest and most influential Pashtun tribe, the Alizai, he commanded several thousand gunmen. As time passed, other Pashtun tribes grew frustrated with Akhundzada. First, tribes accused him of falsely declaring his potential rivals Taliban and having American troops arrest them. Then they accused him of funneling land, reconstruction projects, and cash to his own tribe. Finally, reports began to reach the American officials in 2003 that Akhundzada himself was promoting the growth of opium poppy, the raw form of heroin.

After the fall of the Taliban, poppy growth had exploded in eastern and southern Afghanistan, fed by poverty and weak law enforcement. An epic five-year drought made poppy—a lucrative cash crop that required little water—a talisman to farmers in Helmand. Partly in response, American officials expanded their development effort in Afghanistan in 2003, increasing American assistance from $962 million to $2.4 billion. In Helmand, a field commander in the new development effort was Charles Grader, the contractor who first brought me to Helmand in 2004. Twenty-five years after running USAID's Afghanistan office, he was back at the age of seventy-two, managing a $130 million U.S. government contract to revitalize agriculture and slow the growth of poppy.

Grader's career was a marker of how the American approach to development had changed since the 1970s. No longer a government worker, he was now a private contractor paid $130,000 a year by Chemonics International, a for-profit consulting firm based in Washington. Short on personnel, USAID hired the company to implement and manage its agricultural development program across Afghanistan.

In 2004, I was with Grader when he toured a USAID-funded demonstration farm bursting with cotton, pomegranates, and other crops designed to show farmers they could make a legal living. Grader asked the Afghans who ran the farm what would persuade others to stop growing poppy. Their responses had little to do with agriculture. They said the biggest problem was poverty and corruption. Farmers, they said, no longer believed the government would punish them for growing poppy.

"There is an inverse relationship between security and poppy growing," said a local engineer trained in Lashkar Gah by the Americans in the 1970s.

A local farmer was more blunt. "We don't have law. This is a warlord kingdom."

Grader discussed creating public works projects that would repair the province's irrigation system and employ large numbers of farmers. But four months later, he resigned after clashing with USAID officials over the direction of the program. He was not alone. High turnover rates among aid agency officials, contractors, and the military were common. Americans generally arrived in Helmand on twelve- to eighteen-month tours. Determined to make a mark, they announced new projects or revamped existing ones. The result was a constantly shifting array of Americans and projects that to Afghans produced few tangible results.

Some American projects did get under way in Helmand. And an alternative-livelihoods program put 37,000 Afghans to work cleaning hundreds of irrigation canals. By 2006, a dozen new or refurbished health clinics were opened, more than a hundred wells dug or deepened, and ninety miles of highway paved. Overall, USAID spent about $180 million in Helmand between 2001 and 2006.

Over time, though, the American-funded development projects did not provide enough jobs for Helmand's 100,000 farmers to counter the lure of growing opium or joining the Taliban. In addition, a popular perception took hold that after foreign contractors and subcontractors took their cut of aid money, little cash was left for average Afghans. Locals grew suspicious of the foreigners who lived in heavily guarded compounds with electric generators and satellite televisions while local people lacked regular running water and electricity. Afghan government officials were seen as corrupt as well.

One Afghan working on an American agricultural development program declared both Americans and Afghans corrupt. Americans made their money through high overhead and expense rates, he said. Afghans made their money through old-fashioned kickbacks and bribes.

"For you, it's white-collar crime," he told me. "For us, it's blue-collar crime."

Along with the stepped-up reconstruction effort, the United States deployed one of eight new military units known as Provincial Reconstruction Teams in Helmand in 2004. The units tried to integrate efforts to provide security, mount small reconstruction projects, and help Afghan government offices deliver schools, health clinics, and jobs. The units were recognition that the various efforts were interconnected. Over the next two years, the team spent $9.5 million to build, refurbish, or equip twenty-eight schools, two police stations, two orphanages, a prison, a hospital ward, and twenty miles of roads.

A few hundred yards from the Provincial Reconstruction Team base on the edge of town, the United States built a women's job-training center for Fowzea Olomi, the Afghan woman educated by American teachers in the 1970s who was one of the people I was following for my book. The Americans provided dozens of computers and sewing machines and even set up a mock beauty salon so women could learn marketable skills.

In May 2006, Taliban gunmen on a motorcycle shot dead Fowzea's driver as he drove through Lashkar Gah. False rumors had been spread that the center's female students were being taken to the nearby American military base and forced to have sex with soldiers. The center was closed for security reasons. The attack was one of several by the Taliban that shut down American projects across the province, including the canal-cleaning project that employed 37,000 men—perhaps the Americans' most successful undertaking in Helmand to date.

Security quickly emerged as the single most important factor in developing Helmand, but the country's nascent army and police force were unable to deliver it. The first units from the new, American-trained Afghan National Army arrived in Helmand in 2005, but they comprised only several hundred soldiers and carried out few operations. A new provincial antinarcotics force was created that year, but it consisted of just thirty officers.

Police training also lagged. Police from Helmand attended a two- to four-week training course in Kandahar run by contractors from DynCorp International, an Irving, Texas, company, hired by the State Department.

European officials derided the classes as "conveyor-belt courses." In 2006, two retired American sheriff's deputies arrived in Lashkar Gah to serve as advisers to roughly 2,000 police in Helmand. One was from Santa Cruz, California, and had trained police in Bosnia, Indonesia, and the Philippines. The other was from a small town in Wyoming and before arriving in Helmand had never been east of Wisconsin. Security was so bad that the two advisers could not leave Lashkar Gah to visit any of the province's thirteen districts.

The Bush administration, meanwhile, declared success in Afghanistan and handed over responsibility for security and development in Helmand to the British. One of the foreign occupiers most hated by Pashtuns, the British were still despised for dividing the Pashtuns between Afghanistan and Pakistan. Their arrival appeared to boost Taliban recruitment.

More than 3,600 British troops arrived in Helmand in 2006, ten times the number the United States had deployed there, and set up bases across the province. In response, the Taliban launched their largest offensive since 2001, killing twenty-nine British and dozens of Afghan police. Scores of schools and courts were also shuttered.

As a condition of their arrival, the British demanded that Sher Muhammad Akhundzada, the province's young governor, and the local police chief, Abdul Rahman Jan, be removed from power. Both were reported to have links with the narcotics trade. Karzai agreed to the move but it added to growing suspicions he held that the British—and later the Americans—planned to weaken the Afghan leader and remove him.

Muhammad Hussein Andiwal, the other moderate Afghan from "Little America" who I was following for my book, became Helmand's new police chief in 2007. Educated by American teachers in Lashkar Gah High School in the early 1970s, he represented the kind of moderate, educated Afghan that Western officials hoped could do an effective job running the province. At first, he did. Lashkar Gah residents lauded Andiwal—whose name means "friend" in Pashto—for arresting a 13-member kidnap gang that had been abducting local children. He and his men intercepted 11 suicide bombers before they carried out their attacks. Most important, he arrested 117 police on corruption charges, displaying the rule of law that Afghans craved.

British advisers hailed Andiwal as well, but they said he was "in command but not in control" of Helmand's roughly 2,000 police. Outside Lashkar Gah, police were loyal to their local tribe. Worst of all, the former governor and police chief tried to win back their jobs by sowing chaos and undermining their successors.

In September 2008, the Taliban took two strategic districts outside Lashkar Gah—Marja and Nad Ali—and panic spread among Afghans that Lashkar Gah itself would fall. Police who were members of the former police chief's tribal militia reportedly handed over the districts without firing a shot. Officials in Kabul blamed Andiwal for the loss of the two districts and fired him after fourteen months on the job. An ally of the former police chief replaced him.

On the night before going to my Taliban interview, I met with a frustrated Andiwal in Kabul. He said officials in Kabul were not interested in fighting corruption and the British were not aggressively confronting the Taliban in Helmand. Disgusted by the level of Afghan government corruption and angered by British and American raids that killed civilians, most of the people in Helmand were beginning to support the Taliban.

"They are completely dissatisfied with the government," Andiwal said. "In my lifetime, I have never seen such a corrupted government."

The Taliban, meanwhile, stopped some of their harshest practices from the past and promised to create law and order. In the two districts they seized outside Lashkar Gah, residents reported that the Taliban were not enforcing unpopular, pre-2001 edicts against television, radio, kite flying, shaving beards, or growing poppy. They also reported a major improvement in security under strict Taliban rule.

In October 2008, in my last interview with her before the kidnapping Fowzea told me she feared that the Taliban would take "Little America" itself. Two years after her driver was shot, the American-built women's center remained closed due to poor security. Eight years after the fall of the Taliban, Lashkar Gah still lacked regular power.

"The situation that I see now, it's not 'Little America,' it's a village," Fowzea lamented. "'Little America' had schools and roads and electricity."

Americans, meanwhile, expressed frustration with corruption among Afghans. One American aid worker who had served in Iraq and several other countries told me that the corruption in Afghanistan was the worst he had ever seen. Police and government officials demanded bribes for the most basic of services.

"It just seems to be endemic in the whole society," he said. "They just don't seem to have any compunction about it."

Four years after I first visited it, "Little America" highlighted the worst of Afghanistan and the United States. After thirty years of chaos, Afghans took whatever they could whenever they could for their families. With no strong institutions and a weakened Pashtun tribal structure, they had no guarantee how long they would hold their posts or that merit would be rewarded.

Helmand acted as a mirror for the United States as well. It showed how the American government's ability to devise and carry out complex political and development projects had atrophied. Since the cold war USAID had shrunk and the American public's desire for quick solutions had grown.

With the Taliban on the doorstep of "Little America," the United States deployed 2,200 marines to the province in 2008 to aid the British. I embedded with an American marine company dispatched to the town of Naw Zad in northern Helmand to train police. Instead, the marines found themselves engaged in heavy combat, short on helicopters, and suffering heavier casualties than they did in Iraq.

While most of the Taliban they fought were local Afghans, they heard militants they battled in one corner of Naw Zad speak a foreign language. It was Urdu, the national language of Pakistan. The marines nicknamed the area "Pakistani alley." Like American soldiers I had occasionally embedded with since 2001, they expressed frustration at the Taliban safe havens in Pakistan.

The final blow to the troubled American and British effort in Helmand was the ability of the Taliban to carry out a ruthless insurgent campaign.

More than anything else, relentless Taliban attacks derailed the American effort to re-create "Little America." With their safe havens in Pakistan, the Taliban could not be stopped.

Our afternoon drive in Pakistan's tribal areas continues. At one point, I see furtive figures clad in burqas crossing a distant field. It is the first time I have seen a woman since arriving in Waziristan four months earlier. Women are virtually invisible in public.

Like so much else, they are surrounded by contradictions. According to the introduction to my English-language Koran, Muhammad expanded the rights of women. He urged his followers in seventh-century Arabia to stop the widespread practice of burying baby girls at birth. He increased women's inheritance rights.

Yet the Taliban are accused of reducing women's freedoms. In our conversations Abu Tayyeb argued that the Taliban protect women from dishonor, sexual exploitation, and other harm. Women in the United States are forced to wear revealing clothes, he said, and define themselves solely as sex objects. To him, the Taliban treat women better than Americans do. I realize that I do not fully understand his views, but this core difference between us seems irreconcilable.

On the ride home, I see groups of teenage boys and young men playing cricket and volleyball. They appear to meet at dusk and celebrate the end of the day with a game at a local park. In some small ways, life inside the emirate is no different than life outside it.

We stop and watch a local soccer game. Several dozen men sit around a dirt field with virtually no grass. Young male soccer players battle furiously on the field for the ball, like young men in any corner of the globe. Pakistani and Afghan jihadists dot the crowd of spectators. They have long hair and beards, wear camouflage jackets, and relax as they watch the game.

For me, the drive cements my belief that the Haqqanis run a Taliban ministate in North Waziristan. Taliban policemen patrol the streets, Taliban road crews carry out construction projects, and Taliban religious teachers indoctrinate young boys in local schools. Haqqani commanders and foreign militants stroll the streets, comfortable and confident in their sanctuary.

We return to the house at dusk and are greeted with horrible news. Sharif announces that the negotiations have failed. Tahir, Asad, and I will be moved to South Waziristan, he says, the stronghold of the Pakistani Taliban that lies roughly fifty miles south of Miran Shah.

South Waziristan is a worst case scenario. We will be under the control of Baitullah Mehsud, the leader of the Pakistani Taliban, the man blamed for the assassination of Benazir Bhutto, and the mastermind of suicide attacks that have killed hundreds of civilians. For months, Tahir has heard rumors of an underground prison there where other hostages are being held in caves. Now we will join them.

Our departure from Miran Shah is deeply depressing, the clearest sign yet that the negotiations for our release have failed. Our captors, I assume, refuse to lower their demands. I walk in the yard and let my mind yet again come up with rationales for why the situation is not, in fact, hopeless. I have none. I think of Kristen, who is likely just now rising in New York, where it is her birthday morning. Our chances of surviving will be much lower in South Waziristan.

That night to our delight, Sharif tells us that our move to South Waziristan has been canceled. Overjoyed, we tell ourselves that this may finally be the breakthrough in negotiations that we've been waiting for. I again somehow think Kristen has managed to give me a gift on her birthday.

A week passes. Sharif announces that we will definitely be moving to South Waziristan. Again, nothing is as it seems. The following morning, we silently load our sleeping bags, clothes, and pots and pans into the back of an Afghan police pickup truck that has been captured by the Taliban. A green Ford Ranger with an Afghan flag painted on the door, the truck is one of hundreds of American-made pickups the United States has provided to the Afghan police as part of the American police training effort.

I lie down in the back of our station wagon, on top of blankets that our guards have placed there for me. The guards—Timor Shah and Akbar—insist they will continue living with us and we will not be handed over to the Pakistani Taliban. As we drive away, I feel an emotion I never expected: I long for Miran Shah.

For the next several hours, we drive south down a modern, two-lane asphalt road in broad daylight. I stare out the window at the green tree-covered hills. The landscape again reminds me of the Rocky Mountains.

We cross into South Waziristan and enter the territory of Baitullah Mehsud. At dusk, our car pulls into the parking lot of a large government building or school. Sharif says good-bye. "We're bringing you here because you're going to cross back into Afghanistan," he says. "Ten days, ten days."

A Pakistani Taliban commander politely ushers all of us into a room at the rear of the compound. I am told again that no one must know that I have arrived in the area. If local Arabs find out an American hostage is present, they will kill me. We are given fresh tea, rice, and bread for dinner. As we eat, the Pakistani Taliban commander stares intently at me. I'm sure I am the first American he has ever seen up close. The zoo animal phenomenon is happening again but I don't care. As the months pass, the experience has become normal. After sharing a cup of tea with him, we drive in the darkness to a house that will serve as our new prison.

Over the next several days, it becomes apparent that the Afghan Taliban have not handed us over to their Pakistani counterparts. Instead, the two groups work seamlessly together. The Pakistani Taliban are giving the Haqqanis a remote house where we can be imprisoned. In military terms, they are providing logistical support for their Afghan allies.

Our new house has a half dozen rooms and is the largest we have been imprisoned in. It is also the most primitive. All the floors are dirt. There is no running water. Within days, fleabites begin appearing on my skin.

I feel for the family that normally lives here. A cowshed with heaps of drying manure is located inside the compound. Pots, pans, and other utensils in the mud-floored kitchen appear to be poorly washed, apparently due to the lack of water. Piles of ash show where they cooked food over an open fire. The people of the tribal areas are destitute.

GREETING CARDS FOR
THE MUJAHIDEEN

Kristen, Late March–Early April 2009

My suitcase has been packed for nearly three weeks, but there has been no word from the captors.

Silence is torturous. Our imaginations run rampant when things are quiet. This leads to all kinds of impossible schemes. The latest: AISC, the private security team, wants to bribe David's guards. They also want to enlist the help of the United States military to retrieve David. By official policy, our government will not interfere in Pakistan.

The FBI continues to maintain that David is in the tribal areas of Pakistan, specifically an area called Miran Shah, known to be a Haqqani stronghold. But the private security team says David continues to be moved between Miran Shah and surrounding border areas of Afghanistan. We spend hours on noon calls and follow-up calls debating these issues. It passes the time, but gets us nowhere.

There are three tracks our team is simultaneously pursuing: the moral track, which consists of pressuring the mullah in Swabi to continue to plead for the release of our three on humanitarian grounds; the monetary or negotiation track, which at the moment has come to a standstill; and the bribery track, which seems highly unlikely since none of us know for sure exactly where David is.

Word comes back to us from John that Siraj and the kidnappers are now demanding $5 million and prisoners. They are sure that we actually have the $5 million. They will not settle for less. This is a far cry from the report a few weeks ago from an Afghan journalist that they were "hopeful" about a deal. Someone has apparently told the kidnappers we have $5 million. Something has happened to stop communications.

Soon after, we find out that the State Department has recently raised the bounty on Siraj Haqqani's head from $200,000 to $5 million. This is a stunning example of the lack of communication between government entities. How hard would it be for one agency to touch base with another? We have kept the State Department and FBI aware of our progress and of the captor's slow decline in demands. The State Department and the FBI clearly have no plan to keep each other updated on current cases. We know the captors are Internet savvy, despite their archaic beliefs. It's quite possible they set up a Google alert and found out about the increase in bounty that way.

The private security team blames the FBI. The FBI claims another agency has set the government's bounty and that they are not responsible. I fire off an e-mail to Richard Holbrooke, asking what the State Department was thinking—is this a tactic or negligence? He says he had no idea they'd raised the bounty. He calls me soon after to tell me in no uncertain terms that any other course of action beyond family negotiations is futile at this time. He feels the contractors are grossly misleading us and "playing a dangerous game" with David's life in considering alternative options. A rescue operation is out of the question because our government believes David is in Pakistan. And the diplomatic approach, meaning pressuring the Pakistanis, has yet to yield a tangible result. Holbrooke advises me to ignore the advice of AISC. "You are the only person in this situation who has David's interest purely at heart. Everyone else has to worry about setting precedents."

I appreciate his candor, but I am frustrated by our exchange. I feel caught between a rock and a hard place. Even if we do raise some substantial money, what good is it going to do if we can't communicate with the kidnappers?

At this point, I am going to work three to four days a week and dedicating the rest of my time to David's case. I feel like I am living a double life, experiencing global terrorism at the most personal level. There is a constant influx of information and misinformation. Sifting through it proves to be exhausting, maddening. Each entity involved in David's case—the newspaper, the government, the security team—has its own bias and agenda, despite their good intentions. I do not fully trust any of them. My own agenda is simply to secure my husband's release. I listen to all opinions, but trust no one. It is not unusual for me to spend entire days on the phone or computer, contacting government officials, sharing concerns with Lee and McCraw, and following up with Michael Semple. Days have lost their significance. I am stuck in a seamlessly never-ending season of waiting. I feel I am in the middle of a complex game in which time and silence are my opponent's greatest weapons. I have no control over the situation. Despite the collective efforts made on David's behalf, only the captors have the power to release him. I am increasingly convinced that our fate lies in their hands.

On March 22 we receive a message from Team Kabul concerning the engineer, the go-between whom the Haqqanis dispatched in David's case. The plan was that the engineer would work on a negotiated resolution for our three as he made his own attempts to free his son, who was also being held by the Haqqanis.

The message from Team Kabul is that the engineer's son has been released. Their report reads: "Approximately two weeks ago the engineer was finally successful in resolving his son's situation. He was able to convince the Haqqanis that he had no power to enable prisoner release and that the governments were not going to help. In addition to whatever had been paid on his release, he was able to negotiate a payment of $60,000 for his son (down from $100,000)." The update continues: "The engineer continued to make efforts to call Atiqullah on behalf of Team Kabul/David. He states that Atiqullah has not taken his calls for approximately sixteen days. He states he will continue to try."

Not a good development. And local negotiations through John have produced no better results. The kidnappers have turned off or dumped their cell phones. Michael still tries to create a channel directly to Siraj, the older brother of Badruddin whom the FBI has identified as one of

David's kidnappers and who he believes has the authority to strike a deal for our three.

I have spent most of my work day securing a location for an upcoming celebrity cover shoot. I have successfully negotiated a 20 percent discount on the day rate for a Malibu beach house and booked an on-set chef to cater a vegan meal. I have also learned that in addition to being an avid vegetarian, the young actress is very concerned about our environment and requests that she be chauffeured to the shoot in an environmentally conscious vehicle—a Prius or similar.

Meanwhile I worry David is stuck in a cave somewhere, eating nothing but rice, or that he is being shuttled through a war zone. It is amazing to think our two disparate worlds coexist. And that my life is now in a constant state of tug-of-war between the two.

At home, bills mark the passage of time: another maintenance check, an outstanding invoice, a payment to a trauma therapist. March is nearly behind me. In an attempt to spark communication once again, Michael asks that I compose several letters: greeting cards for the mujahideen.

I have accumulated a strange arsenal of pen pals. "Pals" is a misnomer; it implies a two-way communication. I send letters out into the great void, hoping they will have some impact on David's release.

The men Michael has suggested I write to are Haqqani elders in Afghanistan and Pakistan, including the mullah who may have direct contact with Siraj. The others are to Siraj's uncle and to an aspiring politician who was once an underling to Siraj's father, Jalaluddin. I have no idea if these messages will reach the intended targets. If they do, most likely the recipients will reject them, for fear they are sprinkled in a magic dust that doubles as a tracking device. I am told by American officials and security consultants that the Taliban believe such things, including that beacons are placed on objects like letters to guide drone attacks. These beacons, they think, can take many forms: liquid, solid, particles.

I have mixed emotions about this task. On the one hand, it is hugely time-consuming and a bit unorthodox. Yet it makes sense to try to establish a point of contact and seems no less plausible than other channels we have tried. Now that the engineer seems to be out of the equation and no one is contacting Team Kabul, I feel I have nothing to lose. I wonder if this is merely a way to keep me occupied and optimistic—if so, this is perhaps one of the kinder agendas I am tasked with in these long months.

It is impossible to apply logic to any considerations at this point, given how irrational the whole situation has become. The strangest of my "greeting cards" is to Siraj himself. Michael has advised me to "just briefly make the moral case."

"You should use a slightly anonymous form of address instead of his name so that our contact does not feel vulnerable carrying it," Michael writes to me in an e-mail. "I suggest something like 'Dear Brother in God'—Charm him! We use the letter to establish direct connection and a lever that our contact can work on. In other words, you do not have to agonize too much about the wording—it's our contact's job to advocate."

I have no idea if this is an exercise in futility, but I compose the following and ask David's young friend Ruhullah to translate it into Pashto for me. It may read like a second-rate soliloquy, but it is certifiably culturally sensitive:

> Dear Brother Mujahid,
>
> I am the wife of David Rohde. As a woman whose protector has unjustly been taken, I implore you to use your influence to return him to me. We believe in the same God and have faith that he rewards such acts of righteousness.
>
> David is a decent man and an honest journalist who has dedicated most of his career and life to writing good things about Muslims. By your act of goodness you will free him to continue to use his pen to defend the rights of others who have suffered injustice, so many of whom are Muslims.
>
> Thank you for your kind consideration.
>
> May God bless and protect all who struggle in his name,
>
> Kristen

I cannot help thinking what the Hallmark equivalent might be, imagining a category for "Captives and Their Handlers" somewhere between Birthday and Sympathy cards. This strikes me as precisely the kind of art project that would garner a rave review in the New York edition of *Time Out* magazine.

Michael also suggests that I write a letter to David, in case one of the elders has the ability to pass it on. I will also e-mail a duplicate to the International Red Cross, even though they have been unable to confirm the status of my previous letters. In it, I refer to a conversation David and I had the day after our wedding along a rocky coastal park in southern Maine. Following the torrential arrival of Hurricane Hannah at our reception, the day after the wedding was calm, sunny, and clear.

> *Dear David,*
>
> *I write this with no other agenda than to simply tell you I love you. Please promise me you will stay strong and have hope.*
>
> *Remember our wedding vows: "One day at a time."*
>
> *I have not forgotten this promise. And, I continue to look forward to our shared calm after this storm.*
>
> *Our family and friends love you and send prayers and support. This has been an endurance test—but, hopefully one that leads us all to find our better angels.*
>
> *I pray you find strength, peace, and your way home. Thank you for the joy you have given me, my dear.*
>
> *Love Always,*
>
> *Kristen*

In addition to pursuing a negotiated release, AISC, through the use of their local Afghan network, is also trying to infiltrate the guards. A few days later, a report comes in from AISC. Their local sources claim that David is being guarded by as many as ten people. They rotate in and out and include several foreign militants. Our security team's informants on the ground claim they have succeeded in bribing David's guards to walk him out when the time is right. They also claim that David has been separated from Tahir and Asad and is being held at a village named Kharcin along the Afghanistan-Pakistan border.

Their report is rather detailed. They add that some of David's guards are so young that they are devoid of facial hair. The specificity of this report temporarily gives us hope in its veracity; they even send us coordinates of the village and a Google Earth map to match. Still, I decide not to hold my breath on this one. Misinformation and false reports from local Afghans has been rampant. While we have received information of a potential location, we have not received proof of life. The FBI still maintains that our three remain in Miran Shah in the tribal areas of Pakistan—far from the border—and that they have been there since my first phone call with David in November. They say there is no benefit for the kidnappers in moving David over the border and into Afghanistan, where they would be vulnerable to surveillance, rumors, and military intervention.

A week later, we hear from our team's Afghan network that David has been moved and is once again being held with Tahir and Asad. They are now in a village called Shinkay. The number of guards has increased from ten to twelve. One of the bribed guards has agreed to bring in a beacon to show their exact location. Once again we are reminded that he is standing by to walk our three out.

At the beginning of April, a third update comes in from the local network. Our three have been moved to a house in Miran Shah. Their guards have changed and now include young men from Chechnya and the Pakistani province of Punjab. Later we will learn that most of the reports from the Afghan network are wrong.

It has been five months since David was abducted. We have spoken only twice. I make a list in my journal of all the things he's missed, from holidays to disasters and personal milestones: Thanksgiving, the Mumbai attacks, Christmas, Gaza, New Year's, the inauguration of Barack Obama, the miraculous landing of a plane on the Hudson River, Valentine's Day, my fortieth birthday. We are nearing Easter. More important, we are nearing the six-month mark. I feel this as an ominous shift: from months to a half a year. I fear this will drag on indefinitely.

The security consultants have told us to sit tight and wait. But Lee and I feel we need to expand our outreach once again to the United States government. If David is indeed in Pakistan, they can continue to pressure the Pakistanis to find him and pressure for a release, assuming they can get word to the kidnappers. It is tough to accept that the American government can do so little to effect change.

A STONE WILL NOT BECOME SOFT

David, Late March–Late April 2009

Two deafening explosions shake the walls of the compound in South Waziristan. My guards and I dive to the floor as chunks of dirt hurtle through the window.

"Dawood?" one guard shouts, saying my name in Arabic. "Dawood?"

"I'm okay," I reply in Pashto. "I'm okay."

The plastic sheeting covering the window hangs in tatters. Debris covers the floor. Somewhere outside, a woman wails. I wonder if Tahir and Asad are alive. Chunky grabs his rifle and orders me to follow him outside.

"Go!" he shouts, his voice shaking with fury. "Go!"

Our nightmare has come to pass. Missiles fired by an American drone have obliterated their target a few hundred yards from our house in Makeen, a remote village in South Waziristan. Dozens of people are probably dead. Militants will call for our heads in revenge.

Outside, shredded tree leaves litter the yard, but the house and its exterior walls remain intact. Tahir and Asad look worried. No one is hurt, but I know the three of us may not survive for long. It is March 25, and for months the drones have been a terrifying presence that has unnerved and angered the guards.

In the courtyard after the missile strike, the guards clutch their weapons and anxiously watch the sky. Fearing a direct attack on our house, Timor Shah orders me to cover my face with a scarf and follow them outside the compound. I know that enraged Arab militants or local Waziri tribesmen can identify me once I am outside, but I have no choice.

They hustle me down a hillside to where our station wagon is parked between rows of trees. Opening the rear door, they order me to lie inside and keep the scarf on so passersby cannot see my face. Then they disappear.

I lie in the back of the car and silently recite the Lord's Prayer. In the distance, I hear men shouting angrily as they collect their dead. For months, I have promised myself that if they tape our execution I will remain calm for my family and declare our innocence until the end.

After about fifteen minutes, Timor Shah returns to the car and leads me back to the house. The missiles have struck two cars, killing seven Arab militants and local Taliban fighters. I feel a small measure of relief that no civilians have been killed. But I know we are still in grave danger.

For the next two hours, I do my best to placate the guards. I do not walk in the yard. I do not speak unless spoken to. I praise God for saving us. Later, I learn that one guard was so enraged that he called for me to be taken to the site of the attack and ritually beheaded as a video camera captured the moment. Timor Shah rejected his suggestion after Tahir argued furiously with him and again threatened retribution from his tribe if I was harmed.

Several days later, we hear that foreign militants have arrested a local man. After the militants disemboweled the local man and chopped off his leg he purportedly "confessed" to being a spy. Then the militants decapitated him and hung his body in the town bazaar as a warning to the local population.

In the days after the drone strike, my focus begins to slowly shift. Instead of thinking I need to be patient, stay calm, and serve out my time as a captive, my goal becomes simply to survive.

Nestled in the mountains, Makeen is colder than Miran Shah, and frequent rain and frigid temperatures create miserable conditions. Hailstorms are common and viewed as punishment from God by our guards.

Timor Shah gives me additional chores. Along with sorting stones from our rice before it is cooked and the Sisyphean task of sweeping dirt floors, I fill the barrel in the bathroom with water twice a day so that we can clean waste from the toilet, a porcelain hole in the floor. Using a tube the guards placed in a nearby stream, I fill two fifty-gallon plastic drums with water once or twice a day. As we quickly use up water for ablutions, cooking, and cleaning, I see it more and more as a magic elixir that I took for granted when it surged out of a pipe in New York at the twist of a knob.

The chores are demeaning, since elders are normally treated with reverence in Pashtun culture, but I do not care. The tasks help me pass the time and appear to give the guards the sense that I am loyal.

Rarely allowed outside the house, I see my world shrink to a few dozen square feet. Training my mind to stay optimistic becomes more difficult. Walking back and forth in the yard is complicated by the drones. Tahir struggles as well, telling me at times that he can no longer remember the faces of his seven children. "This is not life," he says. "I want to die."

I urge him to be patient. He prays more and memorizes larger portions of the Koran. He prepares for salvation no matter what happens to us. His faith seems to give him peace and strength. To me, it is an example of religion as a positive force. Tahir has no fear of death because he is absolutely certain he will go to heaven.

Two weeks go by and Sharif's promise we would be crossing into Afghanistan proves to be another lie. With each passing month, we feel increasingly forgotten by Abu Tayyeb and Badruddin Haqqani. Abu Tayyeb talks with our guards by phone but refuses to speak with us. One day, Timor Shah speaks with Abu Tayyeb by phone and tells us there is an agreement for our release. We are elated. The next day, Timor Shah says there is no agreement.

We are now at the mercy of the young guards who control our daily existence. Soon after we arrive in Makeen, Timor Shah begins pocketing some of the money given to him by Badruddin to buy our food and supplies. He dares us to try to escape so he could end our captivity with "one bullet." He complains that "great mujahideen" are dying in the drone strikes yet enormous attention is being wasted on one American prisoner.

When I show Timor Shah several dozen fleabites on my stomach and arms, he buys a farm pesticide and suggests that I put it on my sleeping bag. Fearing it will make me sick, I decline. When the bites continue, I show Mansoor, our other guard. His response is to show me his own stomach, which has no bites on it.

"I never get sick while I'm on jihad," he says.

The guards begin blaming me for things I did not do. Someone places a piece of toilet paper in a bucket the guards use for ablutions and I am accused of putting it there. Mansoor announces one day that I was about to pick up the machine gun when he walked into our bedroom. In truth, I had been sweeping the floor and was startled by his arrival. Another Pashto expression I researched as a possible book title refers to Pashtuns' reputation for tenaciously fighting their enemies. "A stone will not become soft," it says, "nor an enemy a friend."

For hygienic reasons, I decide in Makeen to cut my hair for the first time in four and a half months. I had refused to do so because I felt cutting my hair was an acknowledgment that we were still many weeks from being released. Asad cuts the hair on my head but we do not trim my beard. The guards urge me to grow the beard until it is the length of my fist, the way the prophet wore it. My beard is gray, like my father's and grandfather's before me. I look like an elderly man but relish it. I want the guards to feel ashamed for kidnapping an old man.

Several hourlong conversations between Tahir and me have prompted the guards to accuse us of planning an escape. As a result, we speak less and less. Some days, we talk only for five to ten minutes. At the same time, the guards are furious that I have not converted to Islam despite reading the Koran for several months. I stop reading it in an effort to decrease tensions. As these sources of stimulation disappear, I become lost in my own thoughts, and memories of the world I had known begin to fade.

Trying to stay connected, I begin listening to the BBC's shortwave radio broadcasts for hours at a time. I hear my colleague from the newspaper, Jane Perlez, interviewed by the BBC in Islamabad. I know she is roughly a hundred miles away, but I feel physically farther and farther away from the world I knew.

News stories about New York make my heart leap and I instantly think of Kristen. I relish an arts program called *The Strand*, a celebration of human creativity. I follow English soccer teams, something I have never done in my life.

I listen to an interview with a Baghdad-based mediator who tries to resolve kidnapping cases. He says that cases involving foreigners can drag on for years. I do not tell Tahir what I have heard.

On weekends, I try to catch a show called *The Forum*, in which British hosts discuss contemporary thought and life. In one program, a guest declares that humanity has finally reached an age where people expect to work at jobs that fulfill them. Human existence has moved beyond simply subsistence toiling to feed one's family, they say. The comment—and my surroundings—make me realize how truly disconnected some Americans and Europeans are from the rest of the world.

On another BBC program, a writer describes how there are two narratives in life. There is the narrative that we actually experience each day and the narrative we create in our minds of how it occurred. I wonder what narrative I will construct of our captivity if we survive.

The BBC broadcasts raise my spirits each day, but they also give me the sensation of being in a coma. I can hear how the world is progressing but cannot communicate with anyone in it.

The video image is grainy but I immediately recognize the Polish hostage.

"Hello, Peter," an off-camera questioner asks. "How are you?"

"Fine," answers Piotr Stanczak, the Polish geologist who was kidnapped by the Taliban six weeks before us.

"Fine?" the questioner asks.

"Fine," Stanczak answers, nodding. Two masked militants holding Kalashnikov assault rifles stand on either side of him. A black sheet with jihad slogans in Arabic is tacked to a mud-brick wall behind him.

I read about Stanczak's execution in a Pakistani newspaper a month ago. Our guards have somehow gotten a copy of one of the videotapes made of him while he was in captivity. They are playing it for me, Asad, and Tahir on a small DVD player that Mansoor has bought.

"You feel good?" the questioner asks.

"Yes," Stanczak answers, again nodding. He is soft-spoken and appears to be in his forties.

"Okay," the questioner answers. "And what is your message for your people, for the people of Poland?"

"I would say to my people, to people from Poland, to make pressurize for my government," Stanczak replies in broken English. "Because government send too much army, too much soldier to Afghanistan, and to Muslim country. And I want stop this fight."

Seated on a plastic mat, Stanczak appears calm. He holds his hands in his lap and occasionally glances to his right as he speaks. He is dressed in tan local clothing. He wears a dark brown winter jacket as well. His clothes are more or less identical to mine.

"Okay," the questioner answers. "And what is your message for the government of Poland?"

"My message to my government of Poland is don't send more army for Muslim country," Stanczak replies, clearly trying to play along with his captors. "Because Muslim people they fight with, with another army."

"And now, what you want to give a message to your country?" the questioner asks. "What will they make their relationship with Pakistan country?"

Stanczak stares at the camera. "I would say to government of Poland break, break relation with Pakistan because, because government of Pakistan nothing do for me," Stanczak replies. "I am here four months and nothing do for me.

"Nothing contact with me," Stanczak adds, as the camera slowly zooms in on his face. "I am self here. Not, not security. This country is not safety for me."

"And what do you think about the people of Pakistan, who kidnapped you, the surrounding people?" the questioner asks, apparently referring to the men with Kalashnikovs.

"About people, yes, of Pakistan?" Stanczak replies.

"Yes," the questioner says.

I realize this is the second tape made of Stanczak, not the first. The tape will end in his beheading.

I immediately stand up and begin walking out of the room. I do not want to see it—or give Mansoor the satisfaction of watching me see it.

"I would say people of Pakistan is very good, people is very good," Stanczak says as I walk out the door and into the yard.

Each time we think our captivity has reached its low point it somehow gets worse. The videos are the latest example. They are impossible to avoid at night, when I am confined to the room where we sleep alongside the guards. Instead of singing after dinner, we watch jihadi videos that are little more than grimly repetitive snuff films.

The Taliban execute local men who they have declared pro-American. Taliban roadside bombs blow up Afghan government trucks and American Humvees. Taliban plunder the limp bodies of dead Afghan policemen. The moment of a sniper firing a shot or a roadside bomb exploding—the moment of death—is shown over and over in slow motion. As I silently watch, Mansoor repeatedly asks me what I think of seeing American soldiers killed on the screen in front of us.

"All killing is wrong," I say.

The high-quality sound tracks include prayers, religious chants, and computer-generated gunshots. To aid foreign viewers, English subtitles and computer-generated graphics have been inserted. An arrow indicates which Humvee is about to be incinerated. A circle shows how a roadside bomb tosses a human torso in the air like a rag doll. Snipers gun down American soldiers and veiled women donate their jewelry to aid insurgents in Iraq. In other videos, unidentified young boys miraculously recite vast portions of the Koran. Men compete in Koran recitation competitions and Taliban prisoners in Afghan government jails recite the Koran together. One video features dozens of images of the word "Allah" miraculously appearing on clouds, mountainsides, rocks, flowers, gourds, and other objects.

On some nights, we watch American movies and television shows apparently downloaded from the Internet. In a movie called *Windtalkers*, Nicolas Cage battles Japanese soldiers in World War II. In an HBO series, *Band of Brothers*, American and German soldiers fight the Battle of the Bulge.

We are also shown a popular—and heavily edited—YouTube video of George W. Bush stuttering as he tries to make a statement at the White House. To an American, the video makes fun of President Bush's halting oratory. To the Taliban, it is proof that God is on Islam's side.

"He is trying to insult Islam," Mansoor says. "But Allah is stopping him."

The longest videos—and the most popular among our guards—document the final days of suicide bombers. Most are young men in their twenties. The videos follow the same formula. In the first scenes, the bomber happily receives military training, jokes with friends, and explains why he is eager to die. Then he builds the bomb that will kill him. Finally, he bids his friends good-bye, hugs them, and climbs behind the wheel of the vehicle and drives into the distance. His car or truck is shown speeding toward its target. The vehicle detonates and the cameraman shouts "God is great!" as an enormous plume of smoke rises in the air. As they watch the explosion, my guards utter the same phrase. Finally, a computer-generated graphic lists the number of American or Afghan soldiers killed in the attack.

Other videos show dead American soldiers in Afghanistan and Iraq, wreckage from downed American helicopters and drones, and frenzied Taliban fighters pounding a captured Humvee into small pieces with hammers. My guards rejoice at each image of American impotence. The videos—and their reactions—are evidence of how desperately the Taliban want to exact revenge on Americans—and how valuable a prize I am in their eyes. A constant theme is that the United States and NATO underreport the number of their soldiers who are dying in Afghanistan. Overall, the videos create a false, pro-Taliban narrative of the war in Afghanistan. My guards denounce journalists for reporting American military "lies."

"How can only one or two people have died?" Mansoor scoffs, as we watch a dust cloud from a roadside bomb engulf an American Humvee. "The vehicle was completely destroyed."

The videos are not limited to the conflict in Afghanistan and Pakistan. Images of dead Palestinian, Kashmiri, and Iraqi civilians deliver the message that vast numbers of Muslims are being slaughtered across the globe. A series of flags flashes on the screen—American, Israeli, Indian, British, French, German, and United Nations—representing the international Judeo-Christian conspiracy against Islam that they believe exists. Finally, bearded men dressed as seventh-century Muslim warriors are shown galloping across the desert on horseback wearing conical helmets and carrying scimitars. Young Taliban are taught that they are Muslim warriors battling crusader Christian armies that have again invaded the Middle East.

The tapes strike me as jihadi versions of Western music videos. Militant groups compete with one another to produce the most sophisticated and gruesome scenes. Our guards cannot get enough of them. For the few hours each day that electricity is available in our house, they watch the videos over and over. The constant images of violence seem to numb our guards to the idea of death. Over and over again, human beings are killed on the small screen in front of us. To me, the videos are cynical efforts by Taliban commanders to brainwash their foot soldiers. While death is ignored in the West, it is embraced in the videos. Death, the message goes, is not a distant fate. Instead, it is a friendly companion and a goal.

Our guards share a book that glorifies martyrdom. Several hundred pages long, it makes saccharine promises of fruit juices, sumptuous food, and seventy virgins in heaven. One of the guards reads haltingly, pronouncing each word out loud as if he were an elementary school student.

Most worrying of all, I fear that the videos are brainwashing Asad as well. After we move to Makeen, he seems friendlier toward the guards and begins carrying a Kalashnikov rifle they have given him. He also stops smoking, which the guards say is forbidden under Islam. According to Tahir, Asad has told the guards that Tahir encouraged him to make his failed escape attempt in January. He also told the guards how we nearly walked out of our compound when our guard fell asleep in February. Asad has also told the guards that I am playing with Islam and not serious about studying the Koran.

In mid-April, Abu Tayyeb strides into our compound just before dinner in an expensive white tunic. We haven't seen him in the eight weeks since he had me call Kristen. Akhundzada accompanies him. In Makeen, I have learned that our guards are related to either Abu Tayyeb or Akhundzada. Mansoor is Akhundzada's son and Akbar is Akhundzada's nephew. And Timor Shah is Abu Tayyeb's younger brother. The disclosure makes me realize that a small group—many of whom are related to each other—has kidnapped us. We are being guarded by Abu Tayyeb's closest relatives. They seem to function like an organized crime group. Abu Tayyeb is a young leader—or capo—who tries to impress his Taliban commanders with his schemes. My case is one of them.

Abu Tayyeb sit downs in the room where we sleep with the guards and immediately begins toying with me, raising our hopes that negotiations are progressing.

"Dawood," he asks, "what would you say if I told you that you could start your journey back to New York tomorrow?"

"That would make me incredibly happy," I say, trying to be polite.

He tells me to get a notebook and pen and orders everyone else to leave the room except for his intelligence chief and Tahir.

"Your family has been very slow," he says. "Write this down."

"This is my proof-of-life video," he dictates. "Maybe another video will come that will be very bad."

He pauses and tries to think of his next line.

"If this message does not help," he says. "I cannot say what will happen to me."

I realize he is not here to complete a deal. He is here to make another video to pressure my family. When we called Kristen in February he demanded $7 million and five prisoners. I have no idea what his demands are now.

Calmly sitting across the room from me, he dictates more lines.

"If you don't help me, I will die," he says. "Now the key is in your hand."

He pauses for a moment.

"Please save me, I want to go home," he adds. "Don't you want me to stay alive with you? Hurry up. Hurry up."

Then he tells me I must cry. I look at Tahir. I can barely contain my contempt for Abu Tayyeb and what he is doing to my wife and family. At the same time, if I refuse to make the tape, the Taliban might kill Tahir or Asad to drive up a potential ransom payment. Tahir is the father of seven children. Asad is the father of two. I agree to make the video.

Akhundzada, a man who appears to be in his fifties, places a scarf over his face and picks up the guards' .50-caliber machine gun. He points it at my head, and one of the guards turns on a camera.

During the filming, I try to convey that I am reading a prepared statement by intentionally looking down at the pad of paper. I sob intermittently but no tears flow from my eyes.

I read the message word for word and Abu Tayyeb announces that I haven't cried enough. He orders me to read the message a second time. Standing behind the guard holding the camera, Abu Tayyeb waves his hands in the air, as if he were a film director. He wants me to sob louder. I try to cry in such an exaggerated fashion that my family will recognize that none of it is real.

Later that night, Abu Tayyeb announces that the Afghan government had agreed to free twenty prisoners in exchange for our release. The problem, he says, is that my family will not agree to pay a $5 million ransom.

"My family does not have $5 million," I tell him angrily, making the same point I did after we called Kristen eight weeks earlier. "Why you think we have been here for so long? Do you think they're sitting on $5 million and just playing a game? If they had the money, they would offer it."

Abu Tayyeb ignores me. He smiles and tells me I am a "big fish." He says my brother is the president of a company that manufactures jumbo jets. If my brother would sell one plane, he explains, my family could pay the ransom.

He has clearly looked up my family on the Internet. My brother is, in fact, the president of a small aviation consulting company, but it consists of four full-time employees and manufactures nothing.

Abu Tayyeb goes on and appears completely convinced that he is right. He claims that the American government paid $10 million for the release of John Solecki, a United Nations worker kidnapped in Pakistan in February. As I have for months, I tell him that the American government does not pay ransom.

Ignoring me, he says that the head of the FBI's office in New York has traveled to Afghanistan to secure my release. He vows to force the United States government to pay the $5 million.

"You know where the money will come from," he says. "And I know where the money will come from."

I tell him that he is delusional and that he should just kill me. Tahir refuses to translate my words. "Don't provoke him," he whispers.

I tell Abu Tayyeb we will "be here forever" if he does not reduce his demands.

"You are a spy," Abu Tayyeb declares. "You know that you are a spy."

I respond that he is absolutely wrong and that I am a journalist. Then I try to shame him in front of his men.

"God knows the truth," I say. "And God will judge us all."

THE GIRL WITH THE SAD STORY

Kristen, April–Early May 2009

Walking to the subway one night after work, I notice a news flash on the JumboTron in Times Square: US DRONE ATTACKS TARGET BAITULLAH MEHSUD. The news feed feels like an oversize text message intended just for me. I now have a new fear: David and his colleagues will be killed by friendly fire.

Pakistan seems to be rapidly deteriorating. The Taliban are closing girls' schools by force in Swat Valley. I have read that drone strikes are targeting the Haqqani network in North and South Waziristan. The rumor from ground intelligence is that our three may have been moved to this area. We fear they may have been handed over to Baitullah Mehsud, the Taliban commander responsible for the murders of Benazir Bhutto and, most recently, the killing of the Polish hostage Piotr Stanczak. The latest strike occurred in a place called Makeen. I have been checking David's e-mail each day and reading the automatic updates he still gets from the American military spokesmen in Afghanistan that detail targets and casualties—a far cry from *Women's Wear Daily*.

I've acquired some unusual new habits and routines. The most out of character: I've taken to watching C-SPAN religiously from my couch in the evenings. I actually find it enjoyable, as I now recognize many of the players related to Afghanistan and Pakistan. I marvel at how familiar it's all become to me: Pakistan's Federally Administered Tribal Areas, or

FATA, the area where the Taliban took David after kidnapping him in Afghanistan; Miran Shah, the capital of the North Waziristan tribal area and the town where David is most likely being held hostage; and the ISI, which has done so little to help our three. This is a sharp contrast to the tabloid reports I'm required to follow for my day job: the latest celebrity hookups, the newest reality show starlets, and recent fashion dos and don'ts from Hollywood awards ceremonies. I'm being pulled into a deeper direction, a broader world.

The confirmation hearing of the new American ambassador to Afghanistan, General Karl Eikenberry, is televised. My mother, Mary Jane, and I spend several late evenings watching the proceedings. "He looks and sounds more like a college professor than a general," Mom observes. Eikenberry seems to be an interesting man—with degrees from Harvard and Stanford and the ability to speak fluent Mandarin. The general was to have been a character in David's book. David interviewed him several times before the kidnapping. I wrote to the general's wife, Ching, when I first learned of David's abduction, knowing she would recognize my name from David's recent visit to their home. After seeing the confirmation hearing, I e-mail Eikenberry directly and explain the current situation.

> *Ambassador Eikenberry,*
>
> *Congratulations on your new post. I am certain the region will benefit under your guidance.*
>
> *David Rohde is my husband. We were engaged and married soon after his visit with you in Brussels. He spoke fondly of you and your wife Ching and was excited about including you in his forthcoming book. And, he enjoyed your visit to Waterloo immensely.*
>
> *As you know, David was abducted in Logar Province on November 10. We have since been working to get him released, but it has been a slow process.*
>
> *I spoke with David several weeks ago. He has called home twice. His captors have contacted me on numerous occasions. I*

*have a representative in the region who has also spoken with the
Haqqani representatives.*

*Please let me know if you have any suggestions or insights into
what more I could be doing to secure my husband's release. This
has proven to be quite an endurance test akin to a marathon for
myself, my family, and most of all for David. I appreciate any
advice or information you might be able to offer.*

All the best to you and your family,

Kristen Mulvihill Rohde

He responds immediately, e-mailing to ask for my phone number and
then calling to invite me to two upcoming events: his retirement from
NATO and his swearing in as the new ambassador to Afghanistan. I
receive his call while I'm at Whole Foods. It is distinctly strange to be
talking to a soon-to-be-retired general, soon-to-be ambassador in the
middle of the whole grain cereals and gluten-free desserts aisle. I am
slightly embarrassed and amused by the background music—"Waiting
for You" by Seal is playing. How appropriate.

Eikenberry informs me that he originally planned to invite David to
these events, but requests that I attend in his place. He promises me, "Rest
assured, not a day goes by without my thinking about your husband."

I appreciate his reaching out to me in this personal way. Of all the
government institutions we have consulted, the military seems to be the
most understanding about what it means to be separated from a loved
one who is in harm's way. I accept his offers, thinking this will be a good
chance to bump into other government officials, namely Secretary Clinton, and refocus their attention on David's case. My hope is that they will
apply pressure to Pakistan's intelligence agencies as well as our own.

Eikenberry's aide follows up with a call to explain protocol for a Pentagon event, and to forward information about the general's swearing-in
as ambassador, which will take place at the State Department. I have not
completely lost touch with my once fashion-conscious self. What does one
wear to a military service? I muse. This is quite an unusual fashion di-

lemma, and it provides a momentary escape to be able to focus on solving a mundane problem. I settle on a gray skirt suit, black pointy-toed pumps and a simple blouse with a slight ruffle—conservative business attire, softened by a touch of "damsel in distress" detailing.

Throughout this ordeal, I have been conscious of the fact that people look to me, to my moods, tone of voice, and even appearance, to gauge the status of our situation. If I appear pulled together, this gives other people confidence that I am hopeful and that David will return. This proves essential when catching up with friends and David's colleagues. His mother, Carol, informs me that she also looks for cues in the sound of my voice when we speak by phone.

I am taking a week off from work. It's becoming increasingly difficult to straddle both worlds. I go into the office often on weekends—only to end up taking calls on my cell phone from security consultants and others in the case. The kidnapping has invaded every space I inhabit. It has become an unwanted occupation. On my computer desktop are photographic files of the latest fashion trends: denim biker chic, minidresses. A click away are several files of letters to the kidnappers and others translated in Pashto, as well as Google Map images of David's rumored locations.

I find myself jumping every time the phone rings past 9 P.M. or before 9 A.M., thinking it will be a call from Atiqullah. I've learned to recognize the numbers of various government agencies on my office and home caller ID: 646 is FBI, a lot of zeros usually indicates State Department, and a consecutive series of ones is the unmistakable calling card of *The New York Times* office. My mind has to shift between the kidnap strategies: pursuing a humanitarian release; negotiating a ransom; or bribing David's guards. The security consultants' claim that their local network bribed the guards and that David would be released "within days" is beginning to look false. I have no doubt they are well intentioned. But I have become skeptical of their sources on the ground. Interspersed among these moral dilemmas are the issues of how to illustrate the stories sitting in my desk inbox: "What a Guy's Butt Says About Him." "How to Be a Lucky Bitch." And "The One-Hour Orgasm." Haggling over the beach house location for the upcoming cover shoot in Los Angeles while contemplating the value of my husband's life has proved to be quite jarring.

Exhaustion has set in. Sadness has become a permanent resident and has morphed into physical pain: backaches, sore arms, and the occasional migraine. The stress also weighs heavily on my mother, who has thrown her back out and returned to Maine to recuperate for a while.

At work, the circle of people who know about my situation has expanded. I am often asked about David. I feel stigmatized. In my own mind, I am rapidly becoming the girl with the sad story. I find it hard to relate to normal conversations: exchanges about weekends, home life, celebrity gossip—normal office banter. It all feels like a remote foreign language—one I studied as an adolescent but have now forgotten. My situation has also taken a toll on my co-workers' schedules. I have missed two trips for our spring and summer issues, the first to Miami in February, the second to Los Angeles in early April. David's release would be imminent, I was told. A generous art director filled in for me. Time, too, has lost its meaning. Months and events all blend into one endless season of uncertainty, waiting, and loneliness.

I miss the everyday moments most couples share: coffee in the morning, grocery shopping, sleeping intertwined. Occasionally, I hear couples arguing on street corners—this is a common occurrence in New York City, where much of one's private life is lived in public. Sometimes I think, *What a waste of time.* In other moments I wish I had the luxury of being able to argue with David over some small detail. I try to escape by going to the movies, attending a yoga class. But I am averse to fabricated violence or intrigue and have no patience for a well-intentioned, three-part breath.

On April 27, I pack my carefully chosen outfit and catch a train to Washington for General Eikenberry's swearing-in ceremony. On the way, I call my sister, Karen, for advice on my job. I do not think I can keep working, but I am hesitant to make David's abduction my full-time occupation. I have briefly discussed the option of taking a leave of absence with the magazine's managing editor. I was relieved and surprised that they were willing to accommodate a leave and would later welcome me back. Karen encourages me to take them up on the offer.

I meet up with my brother, Jason. His apartment will become home base for my numerous visits to Washington over the next four weeks. I will only be in town for two days on this trip, but will return with David's brother Lee in another week to meet with Pakistani officials.

The next morning is overcast. I take the metro to the Pentagon stop for General Eikenberry's reception. I am nervous as I ascend on the escalator and proceed to the security line, where I am to be met by a military escort. I chat with other attendees, many of whom have known Eikenberry for decades. I am vague when asked about my connection. I say that my husband is a journalist who is friendly with Karl and Ching and that he is currently overseas, so I am attending in his place.

We walk upstairs to a reception hall with blue carpeting, a small platform, and fold-up chairs. Seating is assigned by name tags. I have been given a prime view, an aisle seat in the third row. Eikenberry nods and smiles at me as he proceeds down the aisle to the stage. A military band plays "The Army Song." Admiral Mullen, chairman of the Joint Chiefs of Staff, presides over the ceremony. There is a formality and sense of tradition to it all. Eikenberry is given a retirement plaque.

After the ceremony, we convene as a group in a small, modest reception room. Coffee, tea, cookies, and Middle Eastern appetizers are served buffet style. I thank Eikenberry for the invitation. He informs me that David e-mailed him just prior to his fateful interview. Eikenberry tells me David's e-mail remains in his inbox and that he will not let David be forgotten. I chat with his wife, Ching. She asks a family member to take our photo. She will be joining her husband in Kabul. "This is in case I see David first," she says, optimistically. "I will show him this photo." I appreciate her kindness and hopefulness. I know she truly understands what it means to have a spouse in a high-risk job that demands time in dangerous places.

In the evening, I join a friend of David's for dinner. Kay McGowan worked for the State Department in Afghanistan for several years. Two years ago, her fiancé, a microfinance expert working with the World Bank, was murdered at gunpoint in Kabul in an attempted kidnapping. She was eight months pregnant at the time and has since rebuilt her life.

I admire her courage and appreciate her kindness. She has helped me make contact with government officials on numerous occasions.

Tonight, we meet at an outdoor café in downtown Washington, and she introduces me to her friends. Among them is a young man named Philippe Reines, a senior adviser and spokesman for Hillary Clinton. Philippe is well aware of our case, as are most government officials here. Washington, after all, is very much a rumor mill. Any bit of information spreads like wildfire in this one-industry town. In many ways, it has come to remind me of Los Angeles—a city I have spent a good deal of time in over the last few years on photography shoots. Philippe will be at Eikenberry's swearing in tomorrow. He tells me to look for him when I arrive. He will do his best to give me the opportunity to speak with Clinton in person to update her on the progress, or lack of, on David's case.

The next morning, I get up early, anxious about the upcoming ceremony. I arrive at the State Department. The midcentury-modern lobby gleams. Through the courtyard window I see the *Man and the Expanding Universe* fountain. A mythical figure sits astride the universe. I am ushered to the Benjamin Franklin reception room on an upper floor. Its colonial moldings and furnishings are in sharp contrast to the modern lobby below. The crowd is composed of foreign and American dignitaries, journalists, and friends of Eikenberry's. A colleague of David's from the newspaper recognizes me and keeps me company before the ceremony begins.

The Pakistani ambassador to the United States approaches me. "I am so sorry about David. We will do everything we can to help get him released. But you know, David is in Afghanistan," he says, kissing me on each cheek before rushing off. I feel violated by this outpouring of superficial concern and casual dishonesty. We have known for the last five months that our three are in Pakistan. David's colleague is speechless.

The swearing-in ceremony proceeds. Clinton is dressed in a bright red suit. A receiving line forms and Philippe, her senior adviser, waves to me from across the room. He brings the secretary over to say hello after the line disperses. Clinton is petite but charismatic. I am struck by her warmth. She immediately takes me by both hands and asks for an update. I inform her that David has been in captivity for six months. We have had no word from his captors in six weeks. "We need to get them to call you again," she says, cutting to the heart of the matter. I tell her, with all due respect, that the move by the State Department to increase the bounty on Siraj Haqqani may have interfered with our ability to make a deal. She looks aghast and pulls me into a conversation between General Petraeus and Richard Holbrooke, the State Department representative. Tough and articulate, she does not mince words. "This has gone on long enough," she says, seemingly feeling my frustration. "Her husband has been gone for six months. This needs to be a priority. I mean it." She all but adds "boys" to the end of her remark. I am thankful to have her as an advocate. She is so focused and determined.

I am told Holbrooke will once again be traveling to the region and will continue to raise David's case. Later, he informs me that several Pakistani officials will be in D.C. in early May for the Afghanistan-Pakistan summit. He suggests that I make a return trip to Washington to meet with these officials on David's behalf and offers to facilitate these introductions. This has been the best opportunity I've had so far to spotlight David's case. I spot Eikenberry across the room and thank him for inviting me. He smiles knowingly.

Back in New York a few days later, we deal with the threat of publicity once again in what normally would have been a jubilant occasion. David and several of his colleagues have won a team Pulitzer Prize for their reporting in Afghanistan and Pakistan. David's stories focused on the failure of Pakistan to confront militancy inside its own borders.

The newspaper has alerted us that another news organization may decide to write a story. The *Times'* preference is to maintain silence. The paper will only issue a statement if prompted by another news organization. David McCraw, the paper's lawyer, proposes that the public relations department at the *Times* prepare a low-key statement confirming the kidnapping and stating that we kept the matter quiet because of concerns for our three's safety. Lee and I agree.

I receive a copy of the press release, which contains the following statements:

David Rohde, forty-one, a correspondent for *The New York Times* who is on leave to write a book about Afghanistan, was abducted south of Kabul on November 10, along with a local reporter, Tahir Luddin, and their driver, Asadullah Mangal. Rohde had been invited to an interview with a Taliban commander in Logar Province and never returned. Information indicates that Rohde and his Afghan colleagues are being held by the Taliban. The families of the three men are doing everything they can to secure their release and we are working closely with them.

From the early days of this ordeal, the prevailing view among David's family, experts in kidnapping cases, officials of several governments and others we consulted was that going public could increase the danger to David and the other hostages. The kidnappers said as much. We decided to respect that advice, as we have in other kidnapping cases, and a number of other news organizations that learned of David's plight have done the same. But now that other news organizations have chosen to report on the case, we have little choice.

The statement goes on to include a brief section on David and Tahir's professional bios. It ends: "The families, wives and children, friends and colleagues of all the men await their safe return." To our amazement and relief, no other news organization reports on David's being part of the Pulitzer Prize–winning team. Once again, we are able to keep David's case off the public radar.

April is coming to a close, and this is my final photo shoot. *Cosmopolitan* has been quite gracious. They have agreed to let me take a three-month leave of absence, basically a maternity leave minus the baby. I spend my last few days tying up loose ends on an upcoming issue, which features stories entitled "Stalking Danger," "How Yoga Can Help Your Sex Life," and "Confronting Your Gyno Fears."

Our crew consists of a hairstylist, a makeup artist, their two assistants, a fashion stylist, a photographer, two photo assistants, a prop stylist, and five models. We base ourselves out of a photo studio in Tribeca. We shoot the dramatic stalking scene "cinema verite" style on the surrounding streets. We dress the models—a hunky male model and a svelte brunette—in black, white, and shades of gray. This is what we refer to stylistically as "colorless color."

For the yoga piece, the prop stylist arranges a mattress, pillows, and mosquito net in the center of the studio—everything in shades of purple. We photograph a couple in this setup using only available light to evoke the sense of twilight. The entire crew contributes suggestions for sexy and slightly suggestive yoga poses, though, looking around the room, it's safe to estimate half of us have not been to the gym in quite some time, me included. The female model has never done yoga. Our male model saves the day, as he is über-fit and able to hold poses for a long time.

The gyno setup is the most elaborate. We assemble a medical exam table and props in the corner of the all-white studio, using a modern paneled wall partition as a backdrop. It all looks rather convincing. The prop stylist stands in as the doctor, complete with lab coat and stethoscope. We dress our model in a pink exam robe and pull her long blonde hair into a loose ponytail. Her nails have been painted a tasteful buff. Her skin glows, thanks to a healthy application of shimmer lotion. She is the chicest gynecological patient I have ever seen. I am relieved she does not leave the room in a panic or call her agent to complain about the content of our story. We assure her we will crop out part of her face to protect her anonymity.

Most of today's crew does not know anything about my personal life. It has been difficult to live with this burden, but I've learned to artfully dodge questions about my new husband.

By day's end we have achieved our goal of capturing convincing moments in a digital frame. The work provides me with a sense of control, even if it is only for a brief moment. I am sad to be leaving this job, but know there is no other option. I have to ration my energy. I can no longer accept the fact that my husband is not yet home—not that I have ever accepted this. Next week will be six months since the abduction.

My first week of full-time devotion to David's case begins today with another trip to Washington. This time I am accompanied by Lee and a new addition to our small lobbying unit. We hope to meet with senior Pakistani and Afghan officials who are in town for a summit and who may be able to influence David's case.

I am nervous about this visit. I will be out of my element. Then again, after years of working at fashion magazines, I am used to smoke and mirrors and discerning illusion from reality. I reassure myself that this skill will serve me well. Lee and I are exhausted. I convince him we need extra support on this trip. We are both so good at staying calm—Lee in particular. I think we need someone who can make a fuss, create a scene, and be emotional without consequence. We need backup. We need Carol.

David's mother has been ready to spring into action since day one. She is smart, spirited, and attractive. She is also a social creature and very good at managing people. Lee, Carol, and I meet up at 8 A.M. on May 4 at the Monaco Hotel in downtown Washington. Our morning begins with a visit from two *New York Times* reporters who are colleagues of David's. Coffee is interrupted by an urgent e-mail from Nic Robertson, a senior international correspondent for CNN.

We have exchanged e-mails a few times over the last few months. I contacted Nic after I found an e-mail from him in David's inbox. It was simple and heartfelt. He repeated the words "you are not forgotten" several dozen times. He and his wife have offered their emotional and professional support. Nic agrees that it is wise to keep David's case out of the public eye. He has been discreet in his inquiries, but keeps David in mind when meeting with sources in Pakistan and Afghanistan.

Today Nic informs me that he has just interviewed a Taliban spokesman in Afghanistan who seems to know quite a bit about David's case. I am skeptical, as many Afghans have come forward with information regarding David in the past, very little of which has proved accurate. The Taliban claim that David is a "friend of Obama's," Nic informs me, and that they are demanding prisoners for his release. If true, this is a massive setback. Our security consultants and the FBI have been saying for months that the case could only end with ransom, not a prisoner exchange.

I e-mail back to Nic and tell him I think his source may not be reliable. I cannot believe I am criticizing Nic Robertson's source. He is a seasoned journalist, but the demands don't match our current understanding. I am suspicious that this is merely a false channel and also don't want to believe that the demand for prisoners is real.

Soon after, the FBI calls my cell phone. They have received a new video of David, along with a written list of prisoners that the Taliban demands be released in exchange for his freedom. The local FBI agents offer to show us the video in their Washington headquarters in the Hoover Building.

When we arrive we are ushered through the lobby security checkpoints and into the counterterrorism office. The agents warn us that some of the content is disturbing, but they assure us this is not an execution video.

The video was dropped off by a source in Kabul, someone who claimed to have access to David. It was delivered to the FBI at the American Embassy there, along with a request for $8 million and four of eleven prisoners named on an attached list. The FBI cannot reveal their source, but tell us they are willing to send a message back through the channel to the kidnappers. They do not produce the list of prisoners. Despite our repeated inquiries about it, we are never permitted to view it.

We watch what we will come to refer to as "the crying video." Shot in black and white, with harsh lighting, and from a slightly elevated angle, the video's content is in fact disturbing. David appears to have lost weight, his face is ghastly white, perhaps enhanced by the blown-out lighting, but the effect is upsetting nonetheless. He is clean, but gaunt. The language is inflated, like a bad snuff film.

"It's April 20, this is my proof of life video," David says. "Maybe another video will come that will be very bad. If this message does not help, I cannot say what will happen to me."

He is sobbing as he speaks. An unseen gunman points a machine gun at his head. Tahir and Asad are nowhere to be seen. We fear they have been killed and that is why David is so upset. For a moment, I think David has gone insane.

"If you don't help me, I will die," he says. "Now the key is in your hand.

Do you want to kill me or do you want to save me?" he says. "If you do not meet their demands you will be responsible for my killing, not the Taliban." He urges us to hurry up, says this is his last video, and pleads for us to help him.

"I am so, so sorry," he says. "Please help me, please help me. I love you all very, very, very much."

The video enrages me—the ridiculous language, the sense that David is at fault. I also think my husband has crossed a threshold. He appears completely distraught and broken in the footage. Carol feels the same. Lee stands by, speechless.

"Sorry to say this in front of you, Carol," I inform everyone, "but my husband has definitely crossed a line. He looks like crap—that is a man that has not seen daylight in quite some time."

I am also angered that David's appearance does not match the description our security consultants provided recently through intelligence from Afghan and Pakistani local sources: that he was being treated well and allowed outside while being held in a small village on the border between Afghanistan and Pakistan. I feel completely duped. The insistence from the consultants—and the FBI—that the case could be solved with only money now seems utterly false. The situation feels hopeless. Securing $8 million and the release of four prisoners will be impossible.

Carol is in tears. Until now, we have shielded her from the harshest portions of the other videos and communications. I pound my fists on the desk in the office and demand that everyone see the video—President Obama, the head of the FBI, Holbrooke, Secretary Clinton—in the hopes of sparking an urgent response. I feel staying calm has gotten us nowhere. Time to try a different approach. Lee remains silent. I worry that he has been caught off guard by the extreme display of emotion in the video and in Carol's and my reactions.

The lead FBI counterterrorism agent chimes in. "I notice there are no tears in David's eyes," he says. "When he cries, does he typically produce tears?"

Carol and I both shoot him looks that say, "How dare you."

The agency promises to accommodate our request to send copies of the footage to high-ranking American officials. They suggest we take a few days to craft the message they will send back through their channel to the kidnappers. They emphasize that the FBI will not get involved in the negotiations; they are simply relaying the video and our response. The family must conduct negotiations privately.

We press them about their source and whether he is close to the Haqqanis. An agent will tell us only that the source is someone who has access to the Haqqanis and to David. This is assuming that David is indeed still under the control of the Haqqanis, the agent adds. I take this to mean that perhaps they think David has been moved or sold to a different group. I ask them if this is the case. They cannot say.

We make arrangements for local agents to show the video to David's father in Maine and to his sister, Laura, and younger brother, Erik, in their home states. I talk to Laura and Erik to forewarn them that the content is disturbing and that unlike previous footage, David does not look well. I send them the transcript as a preview but discourage them from actually viewing the footage, admitting that images from the video will haunt me indefinitely.

Our private security team is furious to learn of our meeting with the FBI. When we call to inform them of the latest video communication, they chastise us, claiming that our outreach to government officials has "put the stamp of USG on the case." This will set us back, they claim. It's difficult to know whether it was merely a coincidence that the video emerged during our visit to Washington. Dewey adds that my generation as a whole is impatient and all about immediate gratification. Then he suggests I consider "taking up needlepoint." I fire off an e-mail telling him I can stomach any offense he throws at me—except needlepoint. Later we will learn that David made the video on April 20—a week before either of my trips to D.C. Still our outreaches appear to be another lesson in futility.

I relay the contents of the video to Michael. He considers it a setback, but recommends that we move forward with our plan to meet the Afghan and Pakistani officials and continue to push for contact with Siraj Haqqani.

"Up until now the kidnappers have been relatively sedate in their communications," Michael says. "I am sorry you have to deal with this now—no one should ever have to go through this."

Exhausted and upset, I go over to Jason's apartment for the evening, but I can't sleep. Around 1 A.M. he finds me sprawled out on the couch in the living room. We talk about the video and my growing sense of hopelessness. "I'm embarrassed that I have not been able to bring David home," I tell him. "I feel like I have failed him." Jason assures me I am doing everything possible in the face of an impossible situation. Then we sit in silence for the next half hour.

The next morning, at 8:30, I meet Lee and Carol at the Willard Hotel, the site of the Afghanistan-Pakistan summit. It is a grand old hotel, with a touch of European flair. We set up camp in one of the seating areas along the wide carpeted corridor that connects the lobby to several conference rooms. The walls are mirrored and the hallway is punctuated by love seats, coffee tables, and upholstered chairs. It's a rainy day and the air-conditioners are on full force, adding to the already uncomfortable atmosphere.

We wait for several hours before finally meeting with a senior Pakistani intelligence official. As we ascend the elevator to the top floor and follow the circuitous security detail, I try to catch my breath. Holbrooke told me that this man has a soft spot and that I should not hold back from showing emotion. Several Pakistani security guards and aides line the hall. I recognize one of the aides from Eikenberry's confirmation.

We join the intelligence officer in a large suite. He is affable and courteous. "Up until now, we have thought that David was in Afghanistan," he says, a hint of surprise in his voice. "My American friends informed me today that he is in Pakistan."

We all keep quiet, having heard this excuse before. It's all I can do not to blurt out, "No kidding." He adds that David is being held by "the most despicable people," not referring to the Haqqanis or the Taliban by name. He adds that Pakistan's ISI does not talk to these people directly, but can reach them through intermediaries. He says he sent a message regarding David a while back, but that the captors responded that one order of business needed to be cleared up before they could move onto David.

"They wanted us to pay for the dead body of the Polish hostage," he states plainly, referring to Piotr Stanczak, who was executed on video two months ago. It is believed Piotr was under the control of Baitullah Mehsud, a Taliban commander affiliated with the Haqqani network.

My heart sinks. I feel sick to my stomach. Tears well up in my eyes as I realize how gruesome and twisted this situation is. The Pakistani official notices and stops for a moment, realizing the impact of his words. He asks his aide to bring me a glass of water. He looks a bit teary-eyed himself and seems choked up by my sadness.

"Do you have children?" Carol asks.

"Yes," he replies.

"Well then you know how horrible this is," she says.

This is Carol's go-to comment, part of her emotional arsenal. She asks this of all officials and it always allows room for a thoughtful pause and then an empathic response.

Shortly after, the Pakistani official resumes, adding that his agency will do what it can. We should not lose hope. At the end of the conversation, he turns to Carol and says, "Don't worry, ma'am. You will have your son back." Then he adds, "And when he gets back, I personally think you should spank him."

This odd comment takes us all by surprise. After showing sympathy, he jokingly admonishes David for the situation and the grief he has caused his mother. It is the latest example of the contradictions and unpredictability we have grappled with for months.

After we depart and convene in the elevator, I say, "Carol, I think if you offered to spank David in front of that guy, he'd be out tomorrow!" We all have a laugh.

At the end of the evening, we meet with another Pakistani government official, a man who has been personally touched by terrorism. He offers little hope, beyond encouraging the three of us to "draw upon the power of the universe." Think positive. This is a surreal comment, coming from a senior official of a conflict-torn country. And yet it is perhaps the most sound advice I have received to date. It is the only thing over which we have any sense of agency—our own ability to maintain hope. To possess blind faith that there will be a positive outcome. This by far is a more appealing endeavor than merely flying blind.

The following day, we drive to a hotel near the Pentagon for a meeting with another high-ranking American military official. I have exchanged e-mails with him over the last few months, but this is our first meeting. Lee, Carol, and I are greeted by his assistant and ushered into a conference room off the lobby. The officer arrives with several aides and analysts in tow. As promised, the FBI has given him a copy of the latest video of David, the "crying video." He offers his sympathy and shares what he knows.

Thoughtful and straightforward, he proceeds to tell us that this is a very complex situation. He believes David is in the tribal areas of Pakistan. "We believe he is on the Haqqani compound in Miran Shah, but do not have a fix on a specific location. Anyone that tells you they know exactly where your husband is is lying."

While I appreciate this honest admission, I am crushed. I had hoped the lack of information from government officials was due to secrecy. I hoped there was some greater knowledge of David's case or plan in the works to secure his release. In the movies, our government's intelligence and military institutions always have a card hidden up their sleeves. This, sadly, is not reality. I have been hearing about the Haqqani compound for weeks. "Exactly how big is this compound?" I ask.

"About twenty square miles," he says, referring to the Miran Shah area. He goes on to tell us what he knows about the Taliban group holding David, stating that the different groups function much in the way syndicated crime families do. There are different factions, including the Haqqani network, Baitullah Mehsud, Lashkar-e-Taiba, and Hizbi-i-Islami. "They compete with each other, but they also help each other out—guarding each other's prisoners, etc." He reiterates that the United States military cannot intervene if David is in the tribal areas. Once again, we are confronted with the reality that our only means of getting David out will be through private family negotiations.

Back at the hotel over dinner, Carol concedes: "You two have done everything possible. I feel at peace knowing that all avenues have been pursued. Our government can't do anything. They don't even know where David is." I agree. I am increasingly convinced that my energy should be expended elsewhere, namely in maintaining my sanity. If negotiating doesn't get us anywhere, all I have to fall back on are faith and prayer.

LIES

David, Late April–Early June 2009

O n April 24, we are told that we are moving back to North Waziristan. Elated, we depart Makeen on my brother Lee's birthday. As we leave the house in the darkness, I pray that this is somehow the beginning of our journey home.

After driving for several hours, we arrive in an area roughly twenty miles south of Miran Shah. Later, I will learn that we are in Dosali district. Our new prison is a school that was built by the Pakistani government to teach local women how to make textile weaving and other skills to support themselves. It has been taken over by the local commander who is overseeing our imprisonment. The school has concrete floors and is a vast improvement over our house in Makeen, but the basic circumstances of our captivity are not changing. We continue to be lied to constantly and have no idea what negotiations, if any, are taking place.

Over the next four weeks, we receive contradictory reports. First, our guards repeat Abu Tayyeb's story that an agreement has been reached to exchange us for twenty Taliban prisoners. Then they say my family is not offering enough money along with the prisoners. Finally, they tell us that only sixteen of the twenty prisoners have been agreed on.

I am horrified that the Taliban may receive sixteen prisoners for us. The deal would set a terrible new precedent that will encourage future kidnappings.

I ask Tahir if there is any way we can escape from the house at night. A set of power lines runs nearby that we could potentially follow. Tahir laughs at me and says it is too remote and too far from the Afghan border. I decide to wait.

Tahir and Asad are barely on speaking terms, and I increasingly distrust Asad. He continues to carry a gun and according to Tahir is bad-mouthing me to the guards. He tells them that I am the dirtiest foreigner he has ever worked with, according to Tahir. He also brags that he stole money from the foreign journalists he worked with in the past.

My hopes of ever leaving the tribal areas are slowly fading. From the yard of the house, the remains of a nineteenth-century British army post can be seen on a hillside. According to villagers, 1,000 British soldiers were killed in a battle there. I assume the figures are exaggerated, but the story is one more episode in the history of fierce Pashtun resistance to foreign occupation.

During one of the trips I made with Kristen to India, we visited St. Paul's Cathedral in Calcutta. Built by British merchants during the height of the British raj, the walls of the Anglican, Gothic revival church are lined with marble plaques praising the heroism of British soldiers who died in Afghanistan and the tribal areas. A century later, the plaques are largely forgotten.

On another nearby hillside, a newly constructed health clinic appears to sit unused. I had read that many doctors and nurses fear working in the tribal areas. Even before the rise of the Taliban, rumors circulated that medical vaccines for children are secret efforts to sterilize Muslims.

News broadcasts continue to serve as Rorschach tests for our odd group. In early April, our guards cheer an attack on an immigration center in upstate New York that kills thirteen people, firing their Kalashnikovs in the air in celebration. The Pakistani Taliban leader Baitullah Mehsud claims a Muslim he recruited carried out the attack in revenge for American drone strikes in the tribal areas.

When subsequent news reports say the gunman is a disgruntled Vietnamese immigrant who has no links to terrorist groups, our guards are puzzled. Having little knowledge of the world beyond Afghanistan and Pakistan, they ask me if Vietnamese people are Muslims.

When swine flu begins spreading across the globe later in April, our guards see it as God's punishment to people who eat pork, a practice forbidden by Islam. On May 4, they excitedly cheer a news report that says masked men gunned down forty-four people at a wedding in south-eastern Turkey and assume it is a terrorist attack that shows the steady spread of jihad. Later reports say the attack was the result of a blood feud between two local families.

The guards continue to assail the Pakistani army. Akbar and Chunky say they were nearly killed by a Pakistani army resupply convoy that opened fire on a group of civilian vehicles. They curse the army and say it fires wildly and needlessly endangers civilians.

Anecdotal evidence of Afghan and Pakistani Taliban using the tribal areas as a safe haven and embracing a jihad that spans the Muslim world continues to unfold before me. We are told that Mullah Dadullah, a widely feared Taliban commander whose men beheaded the Afghan journalist Ajmal Naqshbandi and driver Sayed Agha in the 2007 kidnapping, used a nearby house as a base. While in the tribal areas of Pakistan, Dadullah organized the Afghan Taliban's first group of suicide bombers.

On another night, I meet Mullah Sangeen, a Haqqani network commander who oversees their operations in Afghanistan's Paktika Province. He accuses the United States of launching an unprovoked war on Islam and sees the conflict as a global struggle between faiths. He tells me our release is close and departs. I know he is probably lying, but cannot stop myself from feeling hopeful for the next forty-eight hours.

Young Taliban fighters visit and express the same support for a jihad that spans the Muslim world. They discuss a prophecy that an army carrying black flags will someday emerge from Khorasan—the ancient name of Afghanistan—and liberate the holy cities of Mecca and Medina from foreign occupation. One of them said if it was up to him he would take me outside and give me one last chance to convert to Islam. If I refused, he would shoot me.

The only bright spot is a local man who visits the house and is compassionate toward us. He seems to embody the positive side of Islam and Pashtunwali that I remember. While our guards see me as dirty and refuse to share a plate of food with me, the local man scoffs at their bigotry. He announces that he would happily reach into my mouth and eat a morsel of food I had started chewing.

"He is God's creation," he says.

In late May, we move back to Miran Shah, and Sharif, the tall Taliban commander, informs us of a final deal. All that is needed, he says, is for the two sides to agree on where the prisoner exchange will take place. The next day, Sharif announces that there is no agreement.

We see Badruddin for the first time in three months and he is utterly contemptuous of us. He claims he has no idea what is happening with the negotiations and then leaves. Everyone is sick of us. Yet no one will free us.

We are visited by two teenage boys, one of whom is a computer wiz who apparently edits jihadi videos for the Taliban. Using his laptop, he shows us a PBS documentary called *Return of the Taliban*, which documents the group's resurgence in the border area. The teenage boys cheer each time one of their commanders appears on the video. The film presents detailed evidence that the Pakistani military continues to support the Afghan Taliban. It features experts who say the Haqqanis—the group that is holding us—have been an asset of the Pakistani intelligence since the 1980s. I know that no Pakistani rescue mission will be arriving to save us.

The dirt room where we are being held is the most cramped of our captivity. We inhabit one fifteen-foot-by-ten-foot room and are not allowed to leave it. Throughout the day, children come to the well in our yard to fill up buckets of water. They are covered in dirt and fleabites. Human waste flows down a drainage ditch that runs through the center of the yard. We chat with children to pass the time.

One afternoon, a student who appears to be roughly ten years old arrives from one of the local hard-line religious schools. When I ask him what he wants to be when he grows up, he says he wants to be a suicide bomber. When I ask him his second choice, he says he wants to be a mujahideen or "freedom fighter." When I asked him his third choice, he says he wants to be a Muslim.

On June 4, Abu Tayyeb reappears without warning. He announces that the American government is now offering to trade the seven remaining Afghan prisoners at Guantánamo Bay, Cuba, for us. I tell him that is ridiculous. For months, Abu Tayyeb has been vastly exaggerating my value. I am furious that he will not stop. He insists that I am best friends with Richard Holbrooke.

"Then why am I still sitting here after seven months?" I ask him.

He smiles. If I make one more video, he says, I will be released. Ashamed of my previous video and convinced that Abu Tayyeb is lying yet again, I refuse.

"This is all about you," I say, raising my voice. "You are demanding millions of dollars so you can make yourself look good to the other commanders. You are the problem."

He declares that he is doing everything "for the jihad." Visibly angry, he again tells me to make the video and leaves the room. Thirty minutes later, he returns and says that making the video is not a choice but an order. The half dozen guards in the room stare at me. Once again, Abu Tayyeb repeats his order, and I say no. I know it's reckless, but standing up to him feels enormously liberating after months of acquiescing.

Sensing that Abu Tayyeb and his men are about to beat me, Tahir and Asad step in. "Just do it," Tahir says. I relent, but I am determined to turn it into an opportunity to console our families, not worry them. Abu Tayyeb has no guards pointing guns at my head. I refuse to cry.

"My name is David Rohde. Today is Thursday, June 4, 2009," I say calmly. "Myself, Tahir, and Asad are alive and well. Please tell our families that we are alive and we miss them very, very much and we are so sorry for the pain they are feeling.

"I want to say to my wife Kristen that what you said in your January Red Cross letter still helps me. I am strong because you are strong," I continue. "Your love helps me so much during this time. And the love of Asad and Tahir's family has helped us during this time."

"However this ends, Kristen and all my family and friends should live in peace with yourselves," I say. "I know you have all done absolutely everything you can to help us.

"I am responsible for this situation," I add. "And I apologize to you all from the bottom of my heart and thank you for all you have done for us."

I finish with several lines Abu Tayyeb asks me to include. Without them, I fear he may not actually send the video. "Please do all you can to release us as soon as possible," I say. "We are in a very difficult situation. Please help us, please help us now. Please help us as quickly as possible. Please free us soon. Please."

Abu Tayyeb departs and I feel at peace for the first time in months.

HOME MOVIES

Kristen, Early May–Mid-June 2009

We spend days crafting and redrafting a message to the kidnappers that the FBI says it will channel through the source who provided the "crying video." Despite the fact that the letter will be arriving via the FBI, we are advised by them to remove any references to the United States government. We are also advised by our private security consultants not to respond with a specific offer of money. A low offer could endanger the lives of our three; a high offer could extend captivity by increasing the expectation that more money could be raised the longer this drags out. We are told merely to ask for proof of life and state that we are ready to settle this matter through communication. We include Tahir and Asad in the letter.

> *This is a message from David's family:*
> *We want to bring David home. Please allow us to come to an agreement that returns David to his wife and family. David is a journalist and a good man. We are very concerned about David, Tahir and Asad. Please let David phone home so we know this is the authentic way to get him released. We are available and ready to communicate. We respectfully await your reply.*

We list the local contact numbers for John and for Team Kabul. Lee sends a copy of the statement to the rest of our family via text message. The letter is dispatched on May 9, a few days before Mother's Day. Then we wait.

I spend the rest of May in our New York apartment, feeling no further along than when I left for our meetings in Washington. At times, I glance at our wedding photo, which sits on a console in the hallway. It's an exuberant photo—my mouth permanently shaped into a wide-open smile. David, too, is beaming. The background is marsh grass and fog—the fog gives the image the feeling of a dreamscape. I stare at my expression and think how easily this open-mouth laugh could be reinterpreted as a scream, should our situation end in tragedy. The fog, too, takes on an eerie quality. It's difficult to know which world or reality will prove true. The idyllic marsh or the eerie fog. I recall Munch's painting, *The Scream*, and cringe thinking that this will forever be my association with this photo should things end badly.

I try to think of a way to maintain a positive connection to David. I remember our wedding service. One of the songs we chose was based on the prayer of St. Francis, entitled "Make Me a Channel of Your Peace." I have a prayer card of it, at the back of my nightstand drawer. I pull it out and tuck it into the photo frame.

It reads:

> Lord, make me an instrument of Your peace.
> Where there is hatred, let me sow love;
> Where there is injury, pardon,
> Where there is doubt, faith,
> Where there is despair, hope,
> Where there is darkness, light,
> And where there is sadness, joy.
> Divine Master, grant that I may not so much seek to be
>   consoled, as to console;
> To be understood, as to understand;
> To be loved, as to love with all my soul;

For it is in giving that we receive—
It is in pardoning that we are pardoned;
And it is in dying that we are born to eternal life.

I decide to say this prayer each night for me and for David as a way to stay connected and centered until he returns. I can no longer find this positivity within myself. I rely on this prayer and hope its recitation brings us both some peace, strength, and acceptance. Faith is an old resource of mine. Having gone through decades of exploring, questioning, and rediscovering my religion, I am still a practicing Catholic. And these are the words that feel most genuine as I surrender to a need for something beyond me. Prayer and positive intention offer me the ability to let go without feeling like I am giving up. Reciting prayers I knew from childhood provides me with a sense of continuity.

More than ever, I realize the need to take care of myself. That means reaching out for help, and then embracing the help that is offered to me. I have been obsessed with David's well-being for the last few months. Yet the only thing I have the ability to maintain is my own sense of wellness.

In late May, one of our Clayton team members in Kabul puts me in touch with Dr. James R. Alvarez, a hostage negotiations specialist and psychologist whose writing appears in the book *Trauma Psychology: Issues in Violence, Disaster, Health and Illness*. Alvarez's chapter, "Psychological Impact of Kidnap," addresses the stress and emotional issues experienced by kidnap victims and their families. While it is not an uplifting read, it is a life preserver of sorts. Reading it, I feel less isolated. It gives voice and perspective to our situation and to my own conflicted feelings, which Alvarez claims are "normal reactions to an abnormal situation." I e-mail a digital scan of the chapter to Lee and the rest of our family.

Throughout the case, I've heard periodically from the FBI's victim specialists. Their job is to provide support to family members as well as prepare them for the return of their loved one—and introduce the idea that there may be aftereffects from captivity, namely posttraumatic stress.

While I don't take this idea lightly, I do marvel at the fact that David was kidnapped in a country that has been at war—civil and otherwise— for the past three decades. Afghanistan and the neighboring tribal areas are home to millions of PTSD sufferers and survivors—almost none of whom, in all likelihood, are in therapy. It seems a Western notion to deal with a disorder before one has even been affected by it.

Physical numbness and pain have proved to be chronic side effects of dealing with the emotional pressures and uncertainties of the past few months. However skeptically, I decide to see a somatic therapist to ease my own growing physical discomfort. Needless to say, finding a therapist in Manhattan is even easier than locating a Pashtun translator. Despite my skepticism, the treatment technique called somatic experiencing proves to be a welcome release and a way to feel grounded in my own body again. The method, developed by the psychophysiological theorist Peter Levine, is based on the concept that the body stores memories and that we respond to trauma with fight, flight, and fright response—much like predatory animals. The idea is that traumatic events can leave you immobilized. The body needs to release this blocked energy to prevent chronic ailments and to find a new vocabulary that emphasizes support and groundedness.

During our first meeting, the therapist asks me about my situation, and interrupts as she notices physical tensions and movements that may indicate that my body's natural defensive systems have been activated. She tells me to identify the parts of my body that feel most supported and at ease. Then apparently because I have acknowledged places of safety and solidity, when I'm guided again to notice where I'm tense, subtle releases take place. She also asks me to do some visualization. This proves to be quite satisfying; I'm comfortable working with images. These practices will turn out to be invaluable tools that enable me to manage my stress and carry on over the next few months.

Several days later from the other side of the globe Michael e-mails to say he has spoken to the mullah, the religious figure in the Swabi district in Pakistan that claims to have contact with the Haqqanis. Michael complained to him that the kidnappers do not know how to negotiate and settle this. Our letters were ignored because the Taliban thought they were spoofs. According to Michael, the mullah advises that I make a video to prove the communication is indeed from our family. The mullah has said that the kidnappers have provided us with videos and it would be fitting to respond in kind.

Michael asks that I film the footage as soon as possible and e-mail it to him. He will have it translated into Pashto and give it to the mullah to deliver to the "Waziristan brothers," a.k.a. the kidnappers Siraj and Badruddin Haqqani. Michael jests that he had considered sparing me this activity by wrapping himself in a headscarf and making the recording himself, but thinks it best that I do it.

"It will be helpful to David because we'll use it to establish clarity in our communication, demonstrate the family is ready to settle, and point to the channel they must use to settle," Michael says. "We are herding them towards the final deal."

I am skeptical, but I defer to Michael's judgment and agree to make a video. My friend Josh comes over to my apartment the next day. It's a sunny afternoon in late May. I have known Josh for more than twenty years. We were classmates at Brown and sat next to each other in film class. We moved to New York around the same time, following graduation. He is now an independent filmmaker who also produces and edits for TV shows. His latest project is editing the reality show *The Real Housewives of Atlanta*.

We set up a makeshift studio in the living room, removing paintings from the wall to create a neutral backdrop, one that provides no clue as to my whereabouts or circumstances. I prop myself up on the back of the sofa, against the wall. Josh frames my face, cropping the image at my shoulders. My wardrobe is a maroon pashmina that David purchased for me during a trip to Islamabad. I wrap it around my head loosely. Michael has advised me to emulate Benazir Bhutto when it comes to styling a headscarf. I am to gently cover the top of my hair and let the fabric drape around my neck. I overthink this process every step of the way. Maroon, a relatively sedate color, now seems a bit brazen in this context.

"Is this too racy?" I ask Josh.

Josh assures me my wardrobe will not offend anyone. "You look like a Connecticut housewife in a headscarf."

I laugh at the accuracy of his description. I never could have imagined that I would consider this a reassuring statement or affirmation of my styling abilities. Nonetheless, we decide to convert the footage to black and white, just to be on the safe side. Despite the humor, I can tell Josh feels bad for me.

"This is the latest act of desperation," I say.

It's true. It all seems so futile, but I am willing to try anything. I have written the script in consultation with Michael and now recite my lines as Josh signals that the camera, a portable Flip video recorder, is rolling:

"*Salaam alaikum.* My name is Kristen. I am the wife of David Rohde. Our family wants to settle this situation. We have been ready to settle this for quite some time and are concerned that you have not contacted our representative in country, John. To settle this immediately, please contact John. His phone number is on this CD. Please contact him so that the long wait may be over for all of us. Thank you."

Looking at the footage later, Lee remarks that as a newlywed couple, David and I have compiled quite a unique DVD collection over the past six months.

Carol and I remain in close touch. She has invited me to visit her at home on the Connecticut coast. Up until now I have been too busy or exhausted to accept. I have also had reservations about staying in her home. The last time I did so was with David, en route to our wedding in Maine. While I have only happy memories of that visit, I do not know how I will react to staying in the guest bedroom alone.

It's a sunny Saturday, and I take the local train to New London. Carol greets me. I am glad to see her. She and her husband, George, make dinner, and we reminisce about happier times and talk about how we plan to move forward when David returns. David's captivity has been a strain on all of us, but it has also brought us closer. Of all the support Carol has provided, I am most grateful for the fact that she has respected my position as David's wife. She has been willing to step aside and let me and Lee take the lead, while also remaining at the ready to jump in and offer support on a moment's notice. This is something I imagine must be difficult for a new mother-in-law to do, and it is a testament to her strength.

I retire early and am surprised to find that it is comforting to be in the familiar wicker bed that I last shared with David. I fall asleep quickly and awake feeling closer to my husband. In the late morning, Carol and I visit St. Edmund's Church on Enders Island, an idyllic waterfront retreat and chapel located a few minutes from her home. Carol is not a Catholic, but she takes time each week to go to mass at this church, light candles, and say prayers for David, Tahir, Asad, and our families. She says it gives her a sense of peace.

I've visited Enders Island before with Carol and David, and once on my own as a teenager, when I attended a mandatory retreat before making my Confirmation. In addition to a traditional church, the island also has an outdoor chapel that abuts the water. It consists of three modest stone walls. The front of the chapel is open and faces the ocean. The floor consists of natural stone that gradually descends into the water. Its modesty is reassuring and calming. The chapel contains a small altar cluttered with prayers, stones, charms—memorabilia of loved ones, written requests left by former visitors. Carol and I decide to say a prayer for David and leave symbolic personal items to help him find his way home.

Carol has been concerned about David's eyesight throughout his captivity. With this in mind, she leaves a bottle of Visine on the altar as a symbol of protection, to help him see clearly—as well as to ease any tears.

Before David departed New York for Kabul back in October, I gave him a sacred-heart charm I had purchased on our honeymoon in Paris from Sacré-Coeur in Montmartre. I wear an identical charm around my neck. I recall that David looked at me quizzically when I gave it to him, because he is neither Catholic nor religious. But being somewhat of a reticent romantic, he took it with him. I was shocked at my own insistence that he do so, because I had never before given him anything to carry as a memento or good luck charm. Still, I wanted him to keep it in his pocket or duffel as a reminder of our recent time together and as reassurance that there would be cheerful times ahead.

I now remove the matching charm from the chain around my neck and fasten it to one of the branches of the twig cross that is centered on the altar. I hope that David and I will one day return to retrieve it together.

Back in New York, on June 8, I am surprised by a Google alert about David. It links to the *Huffington Post,* which has put up a story titled "U.S. Journalists Arrested, Kidnapped Abroad." It's a roundup of American journalists detained in the past and present and includes a short bio and photograph of each: Daniel Pearl, kidnapped and murdered in Pakistan in 2002; Jill Carroll, kidnapped and eventually freed in Iraq in 2006; Roxana Saberi, charged with espionage in Iran and recently freed on appeal; Euna Lee and Laura Ling, detained in North Korea in March and recently sentenced to twelve years in a work camp for "hostile acts." I am mortified to see that David is included as "still missing." A photo accompanies his bio. I am shocked that the Web site did not consult our family before posting this. While it is not the best-kept secret in town, it's also common knowledge among the journalism community that David's case has been kept out of the news as a safety precaution.

Lee and Ling have been in jail for three months. Recently, their families have gone public, making a plea to the North Korean government on *Larry King Live* and holding a candlelight vigil in Rockefeller Center. My heart goes out to their families. The decision to go public seems to be helping in their case because they are able to appeal to an established, albeit unreasonable, government. Recent press coverage of their case has sparked renewed interest in the issue of journalists' safety and the role of diplomacy. It has also begun to draw attention to David's plight.

I contact Lee and David McCraw at the *Times* and alert the paper's vice president of communications, Catherine Mathis. Catherine has done an expert job of tracking media activity and requesting the removal of any content that may endanger David. I tell her I have no qualms about contacting Arianna Huffington and holding her accountable should anything happen to David because of the publication of this piece. But there is no need to do so. The *Huffington Post* honors Catherine's request and immediately removes David's name and portrait.

The main side effect of being on leave from work is that I now have twenty-four hours a day to devote to obsessing about David's case. This is a blessing and a curse. My mother, Mary Jane, returns in mid-June after a six-week absence. She is in good spirits, but still limits her movements and activities because of the healing slipped disc in her back.

I have no idea if the family's message sent through the FBI or my video has made it to any of our intended targets. But we receive word that another video of David has emerged through the FBI's unnamed contact, the same one who provided the crying video. The FBI, along with a member of our private security team, plan to meet with the source of the video, who will travel to Dubai in the next few days.

As always, I am reassured by the agency before I watch that this is not an execution video and that David appears to be in good condition. They add that this video is not as menacing as the last. My mother and I huddle together on the sofa and watch it on my laptop. The sound and image do not sync up. I have to periodically stop and resume by hitting the play/pause button. The audio is clear, and David's voice is strong, but the video is stilted and appears as a series of stills. David seems at peace as he sits on a cushion with a full white beard, wire-frame glasses, and a white salwar kameez. He looks like John Lennon. He seems to have come to some inner resolution. He is clean and calm. His words are personal.

"My name is David Rohde. Today is Thursday, June 4, 2009. Myself, Tahir, and Asad are alive and well. Please tell our families that we are alive and we miss them very, very much and we are so sorry for the pain they are feeling."

He addresses some short comments to me and the family and then concludes by asking us to help them. "Please help us as quickly as possible," he says. "Please free us soon. Please."

It is a relief to know he has received my Red Cross letter—and that he knows he has not been forgotten.

I find the video reassuring: David's message is largely personal. I take this as a good sign, as it seems his captors have permitted him to speak freely. I am comforted to hear him repeat the words in my letter. He has not given up. It is a relief, too, that he realizes the futility of our situation on the outside and trusts that we are doing everything possible to bring him home. He is composed, a striking contrast to the seemingly broken subject in the "crying video" we saw in Washington. So much for the previous video being "his last."

I begin to realize there is a pattern to the captors' communication. Six to eight weeks of silence, followed by some form of contact. It seems that communications will resume again. Although it is tough to think in terms of eight-week cycles of waiting, it is somehow reassuring to know the captors may actually be following some kind of thought-out strategy. My greatest fear now is not that they will harm or kill David, but that they will hold him indefinitely.

A few days later, I receive an e-mail from a friend and colleague of David's in Pakistan, Beena Sarwar. She has been in touch with me several times over the last few months to check on David.

It seems I am not the only one who is looking for an alternative, positive outlet. Beena and some of David's colleagues have come up with a meaningful way for people to reach out to David. Beena's e-mail explains:

> *Dear Kris,*
>
> *Just want to let you know that David has many friends here and elsewhere who are all thinking of him. I was online with a reporter just now and she wanted me to let you know that the mood in Pakistan is changing, too, and things will come right. That is what I believe, too.*
>
> *So here's a bizarre notion I'll share with you which sounds very silly—but the idea is basically for all those who know and care about him to spend ten minutes, all at the same time on the same day, all over the world, thinking of him and sending good vibes, goodwill, reiki, whatever, all at the same time. It can't hurt. And it may comfort friends and family members if nothing else.*

We were thinking a good time would be when it's morning in the U.S. and evening here—say this Sunday (June 14) 10 a.m. EST, 8 p.m. in Pakistan.

We don't need to go public on it if you don't want but just let everyone who already knows to spend ten minutes at that time, like a kind of a worldwide mental vigil.

Let me know what you think.

With very best wishes and hopes that you and the rest of the family remain strong and positive.

Beena

This is a lovely sentiment, and I write back to her to thank her and tell her I support her efforts.

A few days later, I hear from Michael Semple. John has made contact with the uncle of Siraj and Badruddin Haqqani and claims that they are willing to settle for much less money than what they have been demanding. Lee, McCraw, and I are skeptical, because the FBI's point person, the one who has provided the last two proof-of-life videos, is still asking for $8 million and four prisoners.

The FBI and Team Kabul meet with the FBI source in Dubai twice over the next two days. On day one, he claims he can get David released and would be willing to carry funds should the family be able to raise them. He adds that the kidnappers are willing to be "flexible" and settle the deal for reasonable money. Day two, he changes his story, stating that he will not be able to facilitate an exchange and that the Taliban still want prisoners in addition to money. The family must work through a third party.

Similarly, we have recently heard from Karzai's government in Afghanistan, which says the Taliban are asking them for three Taliban prisoners in exchange for David. Michael has forewarned me about these pleas. He tells me to ignore them because both channels are false. He believes John's contact has the ability to cut a deal, even though this channel has produced no proof-of-life videos. We are told that if John's source is correct, we should expect to hear back for instructions on how this will proceed.

Still on leave from *Cosmo*, I keep myself busy at home and sort through a clutter of papers in an attempt to restore some semblance of order to my life. My dining table overflows with notes pertaining to David's case, updates or "sit-reps," from our security team, and thoughtful letters from extended relatives—all of whom are now aware of our situation. Amid the random pile is a prayer card from Mother Teresa's mission in Calcutta, a place David and I visited together during my first trip to India a year ago. Mother Teresa's calling had always intrigued me, and we had flown in specifically to see her orphanage and home for the destitute. For me, growing up Catholic, there seemed to be only two cool contemporary female role models: Madonna and Mother Teresa. Together their various behaviors seemed to define what was possible within the realm of my faith.

I am a big believer in the power of intention, and in writing things down. With this in mind, I compose a written prayer to Mother Teresa, who died in 1997 and is on the road to sainthood, having been beatified by the Church. In doing so, I feel I am recruiting a higher entity to share in the responsibility for David's release. Over the past few months I have written to my husband, government officials, CNN reporters, former CIA officials, newspaper editors, Taliban elders, religious extremists, and Siraj Haqqani. By now, writing to a Catholic icon on her way to sainthood doesn't seem far-fetched in comparison. And it doesn't seem any less likely to produce a response. It's a surrender of sorts. A last-ditch effort.

I ask for the safe return of David, Tahir, and Asad, by whatever means possible. I believe in and would welcome a miracle.

In the days ahead, I make an effort to fill my time with activities that will boost my spirits—catching up with friends, talking with family, walking along the Hudson River—which is particularly meaningful because David and I did this weekly. I recall David's romantic marriage proposal, and how nearly a year has passed since then. My only comfort is the realization that nothing is permanent. Things are inherently ephemeral. At some point, this situation will change—it will end. I desperately hope it resolves with David's release and our reunion, but if it ends otherwise, there is some small relief in knowing that this suffering will cease. We have been in limbo for far too long.

PASHTUNWALI

David, June 19–20, 2009

I lie awake in the darkness and wonder if the guards have fallen asleep. Their breathing is heavy and regular but I cannot see them. I blink over and over in the darkness but see no difference when my eyes are open or closed. I turn around and look at the orange light on the swamp cooler—an antiquated version of an air-conditioner—to make sure I can still see.

It is roughly 1 A.M. on Saturday, June 20. After seven months and ten days in captivity, Tahir and I have decided to try to escape. I fear that the guards will wake up and catch us. I fear even more that our captivity will drag on for years.

The confidence I felt while walking around Sharif's house—the belief that we would be released if we were patient—has faded. The determination to survive in Makeen, the willingness to wait as long as it took, has been replaced by a searing rage at our captors. As my abject hatred for Abu Tayyeb, Timor Shah, and Badruddin has grown, my judgment has weakened and my patience has wavered. As I lie in the darkness, I wonder if trying to escape is another rash decision that will have disastrous consequences.

I try to calm myself by praying. In February, Sharif told me that if I said "Forgive me, God" a thousand times each day, our captivity might end. I have done as he suggested for the last four months with no results. But I do not care. As it has for months, prayer soothes and centers me.

Each day, I stare at the ceiling and say, "Forgive me, God" a thousand times while the guards take naps. Counting on my fingers, it takes me roughly sixty minutes to reach one thousand. Tonight, as I wait to make sure the guards are sound asleep, I ask God to forgive me two thousand times.

That day, Tahir and I were told yet another lie regarding the negotiations for our release. Timor Shah said that an Afghan government negotiator had failed to show up at a scheduled meeting in the Pakistani city of Quetta. Instead, he had departed on a religious pilgrimage to Saudi Arabia. The negotiator was supposed to be finalizing the deal that Abu Tayyeb had told us about on June 4: the exchange of all remaining Afghan prisoners in Guantánamo Bay for the three of us. Tahir and I knew Timor Shah's claim was absurd.

Since we returned to Miran Shah, we have been talking about trying to escape, but disagreed on exactly how to do it. Infuriated by Timor Shah's lies that day, we finalize our plan. I will get up first, go to the bathroom without asking the guards for permission, and wake Tahir as I leave. If the guards remain asleep, Tahir will follow.

Following our plan, I slowly stand up and creep across the room. I pass Timor Shah on my left and then crouch down and tug Tahir's foot. Tahir groans and I fear the guards will wake up. But their heavy breathing continues.

To my right, Akbar is sleeping with his head a few feet from the door's hinge. I worry that opening the door will wake him, but I have no choice. I'm desperate to proceed with our plan. If Akbar wakes, I will tell him I was simply going to the bathroom. I open the door and the roar of the swamp cooler and ceiling fan seems to drown out the noise. I slowly step outside and gently close the door behind me.

I slip on my sandals, walk to the bathroom, and wait for Tahir to emerge. My heart pounds. Twenty feet away, on a shelf outside the kitchen, is a car towrope we plan to use to lower ourselves down the ten- to fifteen-foot wall ringing the compound. I had found it two weeks earlier on a shelf beside motor oil and car wrenches. Compulsively cleaning as I had in every house, I placed some old clothes on top of the rope to prevent the guards from seeing it. The discovery, I thought, was the first stroke of good luck in our seven months in captivity.

Several minutes pass, though, and Tahir does not come out of the room. I stare intently at the door—roughly fifteen feet away and directly across the courtyard—still Tahir does not emerge. When I pulled his foot to rouse him, he had groaned and I assumed he was awake. As the minutes pass, I'm unsure what to do. I stand in the darkened bathroom and wonder if Tahir has changed his mind. If the guards catch us, they might kill me, but they will definitely kill Tahir. Part of me thinks it was wrong even to have asked him to do this. I wonder if we are still capable of making rational decisions.

Even if we make it over the wall, we will have to walk for fifteen minutes through Miran Shah to reach a nearby Pakistani base. The town is full of Afghan, Pakistani, and foreign militants. Whoever catches us might be far less merciful than our current guards. And we are not necessarily safe once we get to the base. We could fall into the hands of members of the ISI who are sympathetic to the Taliban. They could simply hand us back to the Haqqanis. Months ago, our guards had told us that the Pakistani tribal militia had handed back one escaped prisoner to the Haqqanis and they had executed him. A week ago, another worrying sign of cooperation had emerged. The Afghan Taliban in Miran Shah had apparently received orders from Haqqani commanders to not fight the Pakistani army if it tried to regain control of Miran Shah. Instead, the Pakistani Taliban would fight them.

But I desperately want to see Kristen and my family again. And I want our captors to get nothing in exchange for me. The last video I filmed with Abu Tayyeb was enormously liberating for me. I felt I had signaled to them that if I died they should feel no guilt and move on. I alone was responsible for the situation.

In the three weeks since taping the video, I've felt more and more willing to take risks and plan an escape. I started performing tests in the last house we inhabited. In the middle of the night, I got up and walked to the bathroom without asking for permission from the guards. To my surprise, they stayed asleep. Then I walked to the compound door, pulled on the handle, and found it locked. When I told Tahir about my test run the next morning, he said I was crazy to try such things. Along with finding the rope in our current house, I found a set of padlock keys and tried to see if they opened the padlock on our compound's exterior doors. None of them worked.

Now, standing in the bathroom, I try to decide what to do. I could walk back in the room and go to sleep, or I could follow a seemingly foolhardy backup plan that Tahir and I had devised to make sure he woke up. Telling myself that we may never have another chance to escape, I push ahead.

In the darkness, I step out of the bathroom and pick up a five-foot-long bamboo pole that's leaning against the adjacent wall. I walk to the living room window and peer inside to make sure the guards are still asleep. I slowly open the window beside the cooler, point the pole at Tahir's side, and poke him. I quickly close the window, walk back to the bathroom, and lean the pole against the wall. I step inside the bathroom and wait again. Still Tahir does not appear. I am convinced that he has changed his mind. It isn't fair of me, I think, to expect a man with seven children to risk his life.

Then like an apparition, Tahir's leg emerges from the window. His upper body and head follow and, finally, his second leg. As he stands up, I rush out of the bathroom to meet him and accidentally kick a small plastic jug used for ablutions. It skids across the ground, and I motion to Tahir to freeze.

Tahir and I stare at each other in the darkness. The cooler roars. No guards emerge from the room. Taking a few steps forward, I whisper in Tahir's ear. "We don't have to go," I say. "We can wait."

"Go get the rope," he says.

Inside the room, Asad is sound asleep with the guards. This afternoon, Tahir and I made the gut-wrenching decision to leave without him, fearing he would inform the guards of our escape plans—as he had repeatedly in the past.

Two weeks ago, after Abu Tayyeb had me make the last video, Tahir had whispered to Asad "Let's escape" at night while the guards slept. Asad did not reply, according to Tahir. Instead, a guard told Tahir that he had heard Tahir was talking about trying to escape. Finally, Asad had seen me trying the keys in different padlocks in our current house and told the guards, according to Tahir.

Our rupture with Asad has become the darkest aspect of our captivity. Over the months, the solidarity the three of us shared immediately after the kidnapping frayed under the threat of execution and indefinite imprisonment. Yet Tahir and I also know that Asad is under enormous pressure. He may be cooperating with the guards in order to save his life. In the end, though, we decide we cannot trust him. If Asad tells the guards, we will squander an opportunity for freedom we might never have again. We know that this house is closer to Miran Shah's Pakistani military base than any we have been held in.

Since we arrived in the house two week ago, we have been trying to think of ways to flee. When the guards let me sit on the roof with them as they prayed at dusk, I noticed that a five-foot-high parapet surrounded it. If we could hoist ourselves over the wall, I thought, we could use the car towrope I had found to lower ourselves the ten to fifteen feet to the street.

At the same time, Tahir had surveyed the area around the house when the guards took him outside to buy food and watch cricket games. He plotted a route to the Pakistani military base. Finally, a few hours after Timor Shah lied to us about the negotiations, electricity returned to Miran Shah for the first time since fighting cut power lines six days earlier. We knew electricity meant the swamp cooler and ceiling fan would help conceal any noise we made when we fled. Unsure when we would have power again, we decided to make our attempt that night. We also added one last touch. We agreed Tahir would try to keep the guards up late playing Checkah. If they were tired, they would sleep more soundly.

Our plans for how to get over the wall were in place. Unfortunately, we disagreed about what to do next. Tahir believes the militiamen who guard the military base will shoot us if we approach them at night or hand us back to the Haqqanis. He says we should hike the roughly fifteen miles to the Afghan border. I do not think we could ever make it that far without being caught. Going to the Pakistani base is a risk we have to take. If we surrender to an army officer, I told Tahir, he will protect us.

One of our guards then walked into the room and Tahir and I stopped speaking. For the rest of the evening, we were not alone again. Our plan still had no ending.

After Tahir and I meet in the courtyard, I retrieve the rope and we slowly walk up a flight of stairs leading to the roof. Threading the rope through a drainage hole in the bottom of the five-foot parapet, we tie the rope to the wall and throw the long end toward the street below. Placing his toe between two bricks, Tahir climbs to the top and peers at the street below. He steps down. "The rope is too short," he whispers.

I shift the knot on the rope to give it more length, pull myself up on the wall, and look down. The rope does not reach the ground, but it appears close. I glance back at the stairs, fearing the guards will emerge at any moment. "We don't have to go," I repeat to Tahir. "It's up to you."

He signals that he wants to try again. I get down on my hands and knees. Tahir steps on my back and lifts himself over the wall. I hear his clothes scrape against the bricks, look up and realize he is gone. I grab his sandals, which he left behind, and stuff them down my pants. I climb over and momentarily snag a power line with my foot as I slide down the wall faster than expected. I land in a small sewage ditch. I look up and see Tahir striding down the street in his bare feet. I run after him.

For the first time in seven months, I walk freely down a street. Glancing over my shoulder, I don't see any of our guards coming out of the house, which looks even smaller than it felt like inside. We head down a narrow dirt lane with primitive mud-brick walls on either side of us. Makeshift electrical wires snake overhead in what looks like a densely populated neighborhood. I have no idea where we are or where to go.

I follow Tahir and we walk into a dry riverbed and turn right. I keep slipping on the large sand-covered stones and feel punch-drunk. I catch up to Tahir and hand him his sandals. "My ankle is very painful," Tahir whispers as he slips them on and continues walking. "I can't walk far."

A large dark stain covers his lower left pant leg. I worry that he has ripped open his calf on his way down the wall. At the same time, my left hand stings. I notice that the rope has made a large cut across two of my fingers.

"Where are we going?" I whisper to Tahir as we quickly make our way down the riverbed, afraid someone will see or hear us.

"There is a militia base over there," Tahir says, gesturing to his left. "I don't trust them."

Neither do I. Earlier, Tahir had told me the Pakistani government tribal militia maintained a small checkpoint near the house. Turning ourselves in there would be a gamble. I still believe that our best chance is to surrender to a military officer on the main Pakistani military base in Miran Shah. I do not know where the base is, though. I am completely dependent on Tahir's knowledge of the town's layout.

"We have to go to the main base," I say.

"Impossible," Tahir says, continuing down the riverbed. "The guards said that Arabs and Chechens watch the main gate twenty-four hours a day."

I start to panic. We have made it over the wall but do not know where we are going. Despite his ankle, Tahir seems determined to hike fifteen miles to the Afghan border. As we walk, we argue over which way to go.

"We have to go to the Pakistani base," I tell Tahir.

Striding ahead, he doesn't respond. Dogs begin barking from one of the walled compounds to our right. "We can't make it to the border," I say. "We have to go to the base."

Tahir continues walking, but after a few minutes he complains about his ankle. "There is too much pain," he says.

We stop and I pull up his pant leg. His calf has not been cut. The dark stain on his pants is from the sewage ditch we both landed in outside our house. "There is another gate," Tahir says, changing his mind. "Come."

As we continue walking, I expect Taliban fighters to rush out of the darkness, but none do. Tahir tells me to put the scarf I am carrying over my head. "If anyone stops us, your name is Akbar and my name is Timor Shah," he says. "Act like a Muslim."

My sense of time is distorted, but it seems as though we have been walking in the darkness for five to ten minutes. I do not feel free. If anything, I am more frightened. I worry that a more brutal militant group will capture us.

We leave the riverbed and walk down an alleyway between two compounds for about fifty yards. We arrive at a two-lane paved street.

"This is the main road in Miran Shah," Tahir whispers. We turn right and begin walking down the street. To our left is a vacant stretch. To our right stands a gas station with four pumps and several shops. Dim lightbulbs outside the shops illuminate the area. As we walk down the street, I silently question why Tahir is leading us down the center of a paved road where we can be easily spotted. I have no idea if he knows where we are going.

Suddenly, shouts erupt to our left and I hear the sound of a Kalashnikov being loaded. Tahir raises his hands and says something in Pashto. A man shouts commands back in Pashto. I raise my hands as my heart sinks. The Taliban have recaptured us.

In the faint light, I see a figure with a rifle standing on the roof of a dilapidated one-story building. Beside the building is a mosque with freshly painted white walls. The building and mosque have concertina wire and earthen berms in front of them.

"If you move," Tahir says, "they will shoot us." Then he says words I can scarcely believe. "This is the base."

We have made it to the Pakistanis. Tahir has guided us brilliantly.

I hold my hands high in the air and dare not move an inch. With my long beard, scarf, and salwar kameez I look like an Uzbek suicide bomber, not an American journalist. Another voice comes from inside the building. It sounds as if the guard is waking up his comrades. One or two more figures appear on the roof and aim more gun barrels at us.

The Pakistani guard on the roof intermittently speaks in Pashto with Tahir. I hear Tahir say the words for "journalist," "Afghan," and "American." I struggle to slow my breathing. My arms begin to burn, I desperately try not to move my hands. "Tell them we will take off our shirts," I tell Tahir, thinking that will show we are not suicide bombers wearing explosive vests.

Tahir says something in Pashto, and the man responds.

"Lift up your shirt," Tahir says. I immediately oblige.

The guard speaks again. "He is asking if you are American," Tahir says.

"I am an American journalist," I say in English, surprised at the sound of my own voice in the open air. "Please help us. Please help us."

I keep speaking English, hoping they will recognize that I am a native speaker. "We were kidnapped by the Taliban seven months ago," I say, in the darkness. "We were kidnapped outside Kabul and brought here."

"Do you speak English?" I say, hoping one of the Pakistani guards on the roof understands. "Do you speak English?"

The guard says something to Tahir in Pashto. "They are radioing their commander," Tahir says. "They are asking for permission to bring us inside."

Tahir has asked the guards—who are also Pashtuns—to protect us under the tenet of Pashtunwali that requires a Pashtun to shelter a stranger in need, even at the cost of the host's fortune and life. He urges them to take us inside the base before the Taliban come looking for us. About two or three minutes pass. The Pakistani guards stand behind sandbags on the roof. Above us, stars glitter in a sparkling, crystal clear sky.

For the first time that night, it occurs to me that we might actually succeed. Escape—an ending I never conceived of—might be our salvation.

I hold my hands still and wait. Several more minutes pass, and Tahir and I grow nervous. "Please allow us in the mosque," Tahir says. "Please let us inside."

The Pakistani guard on the roof says they are waiting for a senior officer to arrive. Tahir asks what we should do if the Taliban drive down the road. The guard says that we should dive behind the dirt embankment, and that they will open fire on anyone who approaches. But they still will not let us inside. Tahir complains to me about the pain in his arms as he holds them in the air. His ankle hurts as well.

"Please wait, Tahir," I say, encouraging him. "Please wait. We're so close."

Tahir asks for permission to sit on the ground. The Pakistani guard grants it. Tahir groans and seems exhausted. I sense less nervousness from the guards. Soon after, the Pakistani guard says we can take a few steps toward the mosque. With our hands in the air, we walk over the surrounding earthen berm unsteadily. As the loose soil gives way, we both nearly lose our balance. I worry that we will be shot if we slip and fall.

"Lie down on the ground," Tahir says. "If you move, they will shoot us." I do so and stare at the stars above us.

Several minutes later, a Pakistani officer arrives, and Tahir tells me to stand up. The officer stands a few feet from us on the other side of the concertina wire. He speaks with Tahir in what sounds like a reassuring tone. "He is a very polite person," Tahir says. "We are under their protection. We are safe."

The frustration I have felt for months begins to fade. We are achingly close to going home. I thank the officer in Pashto, Urdu, and English, desperate to win his trust. Then in one moment, the humiliating narrative of our captivity reverses itself.

"How are you?" the senior officer says in English.

"How are you?" I reply loudly in English, trying again to demonstrate that I am a foreign journalist, not a suicide bomber.

At this point, Tahir and I have been standing outside the base for fifteen or twenty minutes. We still need to get inside. We again offer to take off our shirts, and the officer tells us to do so. Then we are officially instructed to come inside.

I watch Tahir step unsteadily over the concertina wire and into the base. "Come," Tahir says. "Come."

I follow Tahir inside, and the senior officer and several Pakistani guards shake my hand. "Thank you," I say to them in English, over and over. "Thank you."

The politeness of the Pakistani guards amazes me. I know we could still be handed over to the Taliban, but I savor the compassion we are receiving from strangers. For the first time in months, I do not feel hostility.

We are blindfolded and walked farther into the base. The officer politely apologizes and says this is temporary. He is following their standard protocol. A pickup truck arrives and they let us put our shirts on. We climb into the back of the truck and it drives us toward the center of the base. I stare at Tahir and slap him on the back. We are both in shock.

"Thank you," I say to Tahir. "Thank you."

I ask Tahir to tell the officer that I want to call Kristen. I need to somehow communicate to the outside world where we are—on a Pakistani base in North Waziristan. If we can get word to American officials, it will be extraordinarily difficult for the Pakistanis to hand us back to the Haqqanis. Tahir tells me to be patient and wait. I stop talking. Since we were kidnapped, Tahir has skillfully kept us alive and given me sound advice. He has never shown fear and navigated a cultural and religious labyrinth I do not understand. He has not abandoned me and remained true to his ideals, beliefs, and traditions. I know I will be eternally grateful to him for this night.

We arrive in the center of the base, and I get out of the back of the truck. A row of well-lighted, white one-story, colonial era offices sits fifty feet away on the other side of a neatly manicured lawn. It is the first green grass I have seen in seven months. I walk across it and relish the smell, sense of openness, and safety. The Pakistani officer brings us to a clean, modern office with a large desk and couches along the walls.

After several minutes, a young Pakistani captain who speaks perfect English introduces himself as Captain Nadeem, the duty officer. He looks as if he had just gotten out of bed. He says he had no idea that any American and Afghanistan hostages were being held in Miran Shah. No one had informed him of our case.

After explaining our kidnapping, I ask him if I can please call my wife. He hesitates at first and then says he will try to find a phone card to make a long distance call. As we wait, Tahir speaks in Pashto to the various militia members in the office. A doctor cleans and bandages cuts on Tahir's foot and on my hand. Tahir laughs and his face beams as he speaks. I have never seen him so happy. But after several minutes, his face darkens.

"David, I feel terrible about Asad," Tahir says of our driver. "What have we done?"

I look out the window in the direction of Miran Shah and wonder whether our former guards have awakened yet. When they do, they will be furious. "We had no choice," I say, trying to rationalize abandoning Asad. I know our escape could prompt our captors to kill him. I pray that they will spare him.

My stomach churns and I make small talk with Captain Nadeem. I remain eager to call Kristen. After what seems like an hour, a soldier arrives with a phone card, and I write my home number on a white slip of paper. The captain dials the phone on his desk and hands me the receiver. The phone in our apartment back in New York rings repeatedly. No one answers.

Finally, the answering machine picks up and I listen to Kristen's cheerful voice ask callers to leave us a message. Our escape still seems like a fantasy. The machine beeps, and I speak in an unsteady voice.

"Kristen, it's David," I say. "It's David. Please pick up."

I repeat the words several times. Fearing that the tape on the answering machine will run out, I finally blurt out, "We've escaped."

Moments later, someone picks up the receiver in New York.

"David," a woman's voice says. "It's Mary Jane."

My mother-in-law has answered.

"We've escaped and are on a Pakistani military base," I tell her.

I ask her to call the *Times* immediately and tell them to evacuate Tahir's and Asad's families from their homes in Kabul, as well as the people in the newspaper's bureau there. I remember Abu Tayyeb's threat in December that he could trigger a suicide attack on the bureau at any time.

I spend the next several minutes describing our exact location. I give my mother-in-law the names of the tribal area, town, base, and commanding officer. I tell her she needs to contact American officials and ask them to help evacuate us. I want Captain Nadeem to hear that the American government will soon know we are on his base. At the end of the conversation, I apologize to her for all the pain and worry I have caused.

"Just come home safe," she says.

ANSWERED PRAYERS

Kristen, June 19, 2009

I t's a warm summer Friday evening. I am sitting at an outdoor café along the Hudson River in Battery Park. I have tried to fill my spare time in the hopes that it will make waiting easier. I am catching up with an old friend from college who has been working abroad in Africa on a public health project. It's a calm, still evening, and the sun begins to set. There is the faint churning of river ferries and sailboat masts in the distance. Just as dinner arrives, my cell phone rings. It's my mother.

"Hello," I say. She is frantic.

"Kristen—come home right away. David called. He's with Tahir. They escaped. They need help getting out of there. Asad chose not to join them. He joined the Taliban.

"He asked me to call *The New York Times*," she adds breathlessly, "and tell them to evacuate the Kabul bureau and inform them that the families of Tahir and Asad should evacuate their homes. He's on the scout base in Miran Shah. But he needs help getting out of there."

My first reaction is one of terror. Then disbelief. It's one thing to escape captivity, quite another to get out of Miran Shah. I know they are in danger of being picked up by another militant group, shot by the Taliban, handed back to the Haqqanis, or detained by the Pakistani military for questioning. All these are harrowing options, and they're overshadowing the exciting fact of David's escape. I hurriedly say good-bye to my friend and head home. I glance at my cell phone. It is 7:15 P.M. The date is June 19. It must be early morning Saturday in Pakistan.

As I rush home I call David McCraw, our invaluable ally throughout. He will meet my mother and me at the apartment, along with the paper's foreign editor, Susan Chira, who has contacts in the region.

Part of me wonders if the escape is part of a deal—a planned release. Michael has been optimistic about a settlement of late. Yet when I call to alert him of David's status, he is shocked as well. He assures me that no money has changed hands.

I return to a sunny apartment with papers scattered everywhere. My mother has called *The New York Times*. They, in turn, relay information to the office in Kabul and on to the families of Tahir and Asad.

My mother looks frazzled but maintains her composure. She has written the details of her conversation with David on a Post-it pad. We sort through all the stickies. Miran Shah. Tochi Scouts base. Captain Nadeem. We spend the next hour calling government officials—our travels to Washington come in handy after all. David McCraw and Susan Chira arrive. Among the four of us, we are able to contact Richard Holbrooke, Hillary Clinton's office, and Ambassador Anne Patterson in Pakistan. This proves vital. The government officials alert their counterparts in Pakistan that we know David is on a scout base in Pakistan—and that we expect him and Tahir to be safely exited. Everyone is tense.

We fear the ISI will detain David for questioning. But Holbrooke's involvement serves as a safety net. He has repeatedly raised David's case with high-ranking officials in the ISI and pressured them to make the Haqqanis release him. As a result, the ISI insists on helping to facilitate David's transport out of Miran Shah.

I have waited months for this moment. I never thought it would end quite this way, but I am thrilled. I realize that David is not completely safe yet, but my prayers truly have been answered. John, our contact and negotiator on the ground, calls after hearing the news from Michael. He is overjoyed and amused at the outcome. "What can I say," John says. "Your husband saw an opportunity and he took it. He is a brave man." Michael tells me that he knows one of the officials on the scout base and calls to alert them that David is a decent fellow and to not let anything happen to him.

Agent Jim from the FBI stops by briefly. He is delighted. He has devoted the past seven months to our case and feels a huge sense of relief as well. He tells me he will be in touch with Lee and me regarding arrangements to travel to Dubai to meet David.

THE GLORIOUS ISLAM

David, June 20, 2009

A half hour passes, and Captain Nadeem again agrees to let me try to call my wife. With each minute, I begin to believe that we may finally return home. The phone rings. This time, Kristen picks up.

"David?" she says, breathlessly. "David?"

"Kristen," I say, savoring the chance to utter the words I have dreamed of saying to her for months.

"Kristen," I say, "please let me spend the rest of my life making this up to you."

"Yes," she says. "Yes."

My wife sounds exactly the same—calm, iron-willed, and utterly committed to me. I struggle to express all the regrets, thoughts, and emotion that have swirled through my mind and body for the past seven months. I also know that we are not completely safe and repeatedly ask her to help get us out of Miran Shah. I repeatedly praise Captain Nadeem and his men for allowing us on the base. I say we never could have escaped without their help. As he listens to my end of the conversation, I hope I am persuading him not to hand us back to the Taliban.

When I try to explain to Kristen what happened with Asad, I hear the confusion in her voice. I know part of me will never be proud of this night. Captain Nadeem urges me to finish the call and I tell Kristen good-bye. The conversation is rushed but blissful.

I ask the captain to let Tahir call his family. He reaches them and is ecstatic. Tahir—my sole friend and companion of seven months—looks as if he has been physically transformed. In captivity, a shroud seemed to hang over his features. His face now has a glow to it that I vaguely remember from our meeting at the Kabul Coffee House.

The captain's phone rings and he begins speaking with someone in English. "Yes," he says, "this is Captain Nadeem." Someone speaks on the other end of the line and the captain states that I am, indeed, on his base. The conversation continues for roughly thirty seconds and Captain Nadeem hands me the phone.

"David?" a man with an American accent asks. "Is this David Rohde?"

"Yes," I reply.

"This is Keith from the American Embassy," he says. "I'm a security person here."

He apologizes and says he must ask two questions to prove that I am, in fact, David Rohde. I name the university I attended and the town where Kristen and I married. As I speak with him, I feel my confidence rising. If the embassy knows we are here, the Pakistani military will have more difficulty turning us over to the Haqqanis. Covertly supporting the Taliban is one thing. Openly handing a kidnapped American back to a militant group, I hope, is another.

"Please do everything you can to get us out of here," I tell Keith. "Please, we need your help."

He says the embassy has contacted the Pakistani government and made it clear that our evacuation is vital. He promises to call back again with more details. I take down his phone numbers and say good-bye.

We move into Captain Nadeem's regular office. Outside, the sun is rising over Miran Shah. His office is identical to Pakistani military offices I have visited countless times for interviews. Heavy wooden furniture gives the office a British colonial feel. Plaques on the wall list the previous commanders of his unit, the Tochi Scouts. The first names on the plaque are British and date back to their founding in the late 1800s.

The young captain is a Pashtun himself but attended Pakistan's military academy—the equivalent of West Point. I will later learn that being posted in the area is extraordinarily dangerous for young officers. Pro-Taliban members of the tribal militia have killed or "fragged" young officers in the past.

With each passing hour, I am more impressed by his bravery and kindness. From the moment I met him, I have had the sense that Captain Nadeem will protect us. As we continue talking, I feel myself come back to life.

Keith calls back from the embassy and again asks if I feel safe in our current location. "Yes, yes, I do feel safe," I say, looking at Captain Nadeem and smiling. "Captain Nadeem and the brave men on this base have been wonderful to us." Privately, I hope that I'm adding to enormous pressure being placed on the Pakistani military. I repeat that we are eager to get out of Miran Shah. Keith says arrangements are being made to fly us out of the town. I thank him again for all his help and hang up.

More sandwiches and tea arrive. Giddy, I tell Captain Nadeem that he and his men, in fact, are the true Muslims, not our kidnappers. I tell him about reading the Koran and seeing the difference between the ideals the prophet preached and how our captors acted.

To my delight, Captain Nadeem agrees. He gives me a book entitled *The Glorious Islam* by a Pakistani writer. He says that the Islam followed by the Taliban is a distortion of his faith. As he speaks, my heart races in my chest. The world—and the Pakistan—I remember is still here.

I make him add an inscription in the book. In neat blue ink, he writes:

From Capt. Nadeem
To David Rohde
20th June 2009
Tochi Scouts Miran Shah
North Waziristan Agency

I will cherish this book for the rest of my life. He reminds me of all my other Pashtun friends—most of them fearless journalists who work on both sides of the border. Churchill was wrong. All Pashtuns are not inherently violent. They are deeply disenfranchised. The biggest difference between the Pashtuns who kidnapped me and the Pashtuns who saved my life is education.

Captain Nadeem tells us his men are reporting activity by the Taliban in Miran Shah. They are searching for us, but Captain Nadeem reassures Tahir and me that we are safe. Again I think of Asad. A Pakistani helicopter is on its way, Captain Nadeem says. We will be flown out of Waziristan in a few hours.

GRATITUDE

Kristen, June 19–20, 2009

I begin to feel that after seven months of working together as a team that my interests are suddenly at odds with those of the newspaper. Susan Chira, the foreign editor, is extremely helpful in assisting us to make calls to officials. Yet it becomes increasingly obvious that she is also under pressure to deliver a story about David's kidnapping and escape. Periodically she turns to me and says, "At some point, we need to start thinking about what we are going to write, what the story will say."

I tell her there is no need for a story now. In fact, I think it would put David in harm's way to write about his escape before he has safely left the region. She presses the point all night. I feel the wall I've built around myself over recent months begin to collapse with the realization that our struggle is nearing an end. Unfortunately, this wall does not crumble quietly. Frazzled, I finally tell her to stop mentioning the story and demand that she leave.

I just want to take this in and focus on getting David out of Miran Shah. The last thing I want is publicity. Lee and I are on the phone all night. He gets us two seats on a flight to Dubai for this evening—it's now early Saturday morning—from John F. Kennedy International Airport in New York. It was sorted out long ago that if David was freed, we would meet him in Dubai. I recall my conversation with Sean Langan, the British journalist and former Taliban hostage who contacted me several months ago. Sean urged me not to rush off to Kabul or Pakistan upon David's release. He suggested I give David a moment to collect himself. "He may need the time to make himself presentable and get his bearings.

"Meeting in Kabul would be tense," he cautioned me, adding, "most likely it would consist of the two of you in the backseat of an armored vehicle, covered or with a third party urging you to keep your heads down for security reasons."

Sean told me that his own debriefing was tiresome after the Taliban freed him, but it also made him feel like a journalist again, giving him a chance to tell his story and in the process resume his professional bearing. He advised me to keep the return as low key as possible. His own return was rather public and proved challenging when he was immediately confronted with cameras on the tarmac in London.

When David McCraw leaves the apartment, at 3 A.M, we are still awaiting confirmation that David and Tahir have been helicoptered out of the scout base in Miran Shah. My mother retires to the couch. I head to the bedroom to pack for tonight's journey. I am overjoyed at the thought of seeing David again, and slightly overwhelmed that this time tomorrow I will be on a flight to Dubai. It is impossible to sleep.

I've said countless prayers over the last seven months. They have taken various forms—from spontaneous pleas to personal rituals and traditional recitations. For me, prayer is a conversation of sorts. A give-and-take. A question seeks to be met with an answer or to elicit greater understanding. Occasionally the response is unexpected and unpredictable, yet makes complete sense at a deeper level.

I've always believed David would return—even though I could never pinpoint when. My internal clock never had a sense that it would be anytime soon. The conversation seemed to be lagging as I felt my questions were always met with an unsettling reply: *Wait*.

Tonight my lesson in patience is approaching an end. My prayers—and those of friends and family—have been met with a surprising response.

As I lie awake, I utter two simple words: *Thank you*.

INTELLIGENCE

David, June 20, 2009

At roughly 9 A.M., Captain Nadeem brings Tahir and me to his personal quarters. We have now been on his base for roughly five or six hours. A television plays a Pakistani news station. Captain Nadeem changes the station to CNN International and I stare at the television transfixed. The studio and stage lighting have changed slightly since the last time I saw it seven months ago. Images of protests in Iran flash across the screen. We are back in the universe I have inhabited all my life. I am amazed that I have been so physically close to civilization but felt so far removed from it.

Captain Nadeem lets me take a shower. When I return to his room, a Pakistani military officer is present. He welcomes us, takes photos of us, and asks us a few questions. All of them focus on Baitullah Mehsud, the leader of the Pakistani Taliban who is considered an enemy of the state by the Pakistani military. He shows little interest in hearing about the Haqqanis, Abu Tayyeb, or the Afghan Taliban. He leaves after half an hour.

Tahir and I are taken to an ornate bedroom for VIP guests. We are given more food. Sitting alone for the first time, we recount our escape. Tahir worries that something could still go wrong. I tell him what I have repeated for months: I'm confident my family is doing everything they can to help us.

There is a knock on the door, and two beardless Pakistani men with neatly trimmed mustaches, crisply ironed salwar kameezes, and sunglasses greet us. They announce that they are from the ISI, Pakistan's premier military intelligence agency said to still tacitly support the Haqqani and Afghan Taliban. This is the moment we have feared.

At first, they are friendly. "We have been looking for you," one of them says as he opens a thin green file. Inside is a white sheet of paper that looks like a news story about me. A photo printed out from the Internet is on top of it. I ask him why they were unable to find us, given that we were so close to the base. They insist again that they have been looking for us. As the conversation continues, it becomes clear they, too, are more interested in getting information about Baitullah Mehsud than about the Haqqanis.

One of them pulls out a video camera and begins filming us without asking. I don't trust them and demand that they stop. The ISI operative continues filming. I stop answering questions and demand to see Captain Nadeem. The two men disappear and Captain Nadeem arrives and apologizes. He insists that a helicopter is on its way to evacuate us. It should arrive in two hours.

Tahir and I remain alone in the room. Two hours pass. No helicopter arrives. Captain Nadeem says the flight has been delayed by the weather. The two ISI officials sit outside in the courtyard. I am concerned about what is happening. There is still a chance we could be handed back. I ask Captain Nadeem if I can call Islamabad or New York. He says he has no more phone cards left.

At around 1 p.m., we hear two helicopters land, and the head of the ISI office in Peshawar walks into our room ten minutes later. He is urbane, educated, and intelligent. He orders tea and in five minutes of polite conversation gets more information out of me than the low-level ISI officers. After roughly twenty minutes, we are driven to the helipad, where two Vietnam-era Huey helicopters await us.

We get into one of the helicopters with the ISI chief, and the military pilot informs us that we are in the wrong helicopter. This one is loaded down with cargo. He asks us if we can switch to the other helicopter.

The ISI chief stares icily at the pilot.

"Move the gear," he says, refusing to budge. I have long heard of the arrogance of some ISI officers. Now I see it.

While we wait, I ask the ISI chief to help other hostages in the area. He is polite but sounds disdainful of them. He explains that he has just spent several months bargaining with the Taliban to buy back the body of Piotr Stanczak, the executed Polish geologist. He is courteous but clearly sees me and other foreign hostages as reckless people who are a burden to him. I know that in some respects he is right.

The helicopter starts its engine and I try to grab Tahir's hand but can't reach it. Instead, I place my hand on his shoulder. For months, we have heard airplanes and helicopters take off from an airstrip somewhere in Miran Shah. We have stood in yards and watched Pakistani helicopters lumber across the sky. Now we are finally in one of them.

As we take off, I wait for a rocket to be fired at the helicopter. Instead, we levitate smoothly through the air. I look down at Miran Shah and see a sprawling, dusty town like so many I have visited across Afghanistan and Pakistan. I look for the house where we were held captive but have no idea of its precise location. I think of Asad and pray he is alive.

We gain altitude and fly toward a nearby mountain ridge. Once we pass over it, we will be out of Taliban rocket range. As we approach the crest, I stare intently at the hilltops and scour them for gunmen. They are deserted. I squeeze Tahir's shoulder as we clear the ridge.

We are free.

FEED THE BEAST

Kristen, June 20–21, 2009

At 6 A.M. New York time, David McCraw calls to confirm that a helicopter is en route to Islamabad, the capital of Pakistan. From there, David and Tahir will be escorted to a plane for transport to the American military base at Bagram and then on to Dubai.

It is now Saturday morning. I continue to prepare for my trip as I await further word from David that he is safe. Bill Keller phones to tell me matter-of-factly that the paper will run a short piece on David.

The *Times* has kept David's case quiet until now, but it is a news institution, and this is big news. They will need to report it. Calm and straightforward, he asks if I will give them a quote. I tell him I am grateful for all that he and the newspaper have done, but do not want to give any information until David is safely out of Pakistan and has left the region.

"I don't think I should talk to you now," I caution, knowing my emotions are a little raw. "You'll get a really sassy quote. Let's wait until David is safe." I do say that I am comfortable conveying my gratitude to government officials, the newspaper, and David's colleagues, but that is all I can provide at this time.

He understands, but says he wants to talk to David when I hear from him again. After keeping this story silent for so long, they'd like to "feed the beast."

While I respect Bill—and do not want to pick a fight with my husband's boss—I feel an intense need to hold my ground and protect David's privacy.

"Bill, I think David would ask that you starve the beast and let it die," I respond. (I'm going to be amazed if my husband still has a job when he returns home, given that I have spoken so bluntly. But I do not care.)

"Okay, but do you have any updates?" he asks casually.

"I don't know, Bill," I say exasperated. "They just walked over the wall of the compound."

The sass comes back to bite me. In a story about David's escape on the paper's Web site that afternoon, a quote appears from me: "They just walked over the wall of the compound."

Moments later, someone from a local news outlet shows up at the front desk of my apartment building. I alert the doorman to say that I am out. I also answer one or two calls on my home phone from reporters. I pretend to be a relative.

"Kristen? I'm sorry, she's out of town. Can I take a message or be of assistance? She does not plan to grant any personal interviews."

Being married to a reporter, I shouldn't be surprised at how aggressive and persistent television reporters are in their requests. Word has spread rapidly in the news community. A certain morning talk show calls the apartment three times, then moves on to contacting Lee, then my parents, David's mom, and even David's teenage nephew. The evening news has a story about David's escape. They use old photos because we have refused to provide current images of David, knowing that he would not want to be the story. It's somewhat comical to see him looking thirteen years younger, holding the four-year-old nephew who is now a young man.

Another quote from me in the *Times* is used as an innocuous sound bite on television news. "'We've been married nine months,' his wife said, 'and David's been in captivity for seven of them.'"

RETURN

David, June 20–21, 2009

At first, the sensation of hurtling through the air in a Pakistani military helicopter is delightful. I stare at the controls of this refurbished American-built Huey helicopter. For years, Pakistani military officials have seen this kind of secondhand matériel as a slight by the U.S. government. After my seven months in Waziristan, to me the helicopter is an astounding feat of engineering.

As the flight drags on, I find myself growing nervous for no logical reason. We are headed to the Pakistani capital of Islamabad, according to the ISI official, but the flight continues for more than thirty minutes. As I study the landscape outside, my thoughts are irrational. Part of me fears the helicopter will crash.

The terrain flattens beneath us and I realize we are moving from the mountains of northwestern Pakistan toward the plains of central Pakistan. The flight drags on for forty-five minutes. Finally, the four towering white minarets of the Faisal Mosque—an enormous house of worship funded by King Faisal of Saudi Arabia in the 1980s—emerge in the distance. It is one of Islamabad's landmarks. With a purported capacity of 100,000 worshipers, it was constructed in the 1980s when Saudi Arabia and the United States spread hard-line Wahhabi Islam to Pakistan. Today, it is a beacon of hope to me.

We fly over the city and approach Islamabad International Airport. As passenger jets land, I long for us to do the same. We circle for a few more minutes. Finally, our two helicopters fly low over the runway and touch down near the main passenger terminal. Our helicopter's landing gear gently touches the ground and relief washes over me. The surreal twelve-hour period that began when I first got up and crept to the bathroom as our guards slept is ending.

I step out of the helicopter, get down on my knees, and kiss the tarmac.

Brought inside a VIP lounge by the ISI officials, we are told to wait as the Pakistanis coordinate our handover to American officials. I speak with Tahir and urge him to remain in Islamabad and travel with me directly to the United States. If he returns to his house in Kabul, I believe Abu Tayyeb's men will kill him.

For months, Abu Tayyeb and the guards have repeatedly told Tahir and Asad that I would abandon them and leave them at the mercy of American, Afghan, or Pakistani intelligence officials when our captivity ended. As we wait, I am absolutely determined to protect Tahir and prove Abu Tayyeb wrong.

I ask the ISI station chief from Peshawar to allow Tahir to call his family, and he agrees. Tahir's father tells him to travel where he pleases. After fifteen more minutes, we are driven to the military side of the airfield by the ISI in brand-new sport utility vehicles. I have visited the area before. In 2005, I boarded helicopters here that ferried supplies to victims of a massive earthquake in northern Pakistan.

We enter the main terminal and several minutes later, the ISI walks us out onto the tarmac. I see a group of Americans staring at us. Anne Patterson, the American ambassador to Pakistan, steps forward and shakes my hand.

"I'm sorry for the problems I've caused you," I shout over the din of nearby aircraft engines.

"Welcome," she says.

Patterson is polite but icy. I realize that many people are probably furious with me for foolishly pursuing a Taliban interview. I turn and thank the ISI officials again for flying us to safety. I worry they will suddenly try to detain Tahir. Instead, they wave good-bye and quickly walk away.

Patterson motions for us to walk farther onto the tarmac and I grow confused. I assumed we would be driven to the U.S. Embassy, where I planned to profusely thank Keith, the security officer who had spoken with me by phone from the Pakistani base in Miran Shah.

Instead, we walk toward a C-130 military cargo plane with its engines running. As we approach the aircraft, I see that the plane's crewmen are Americans. After seven months in Waziristan, the clean-shaven Americans with their buglike flight helmets look like alien creatures. I shake Patterson's hand and she quickly says good-bye. Tahir and I follow an American woman onto the back of the plane. She tells me that we are flying to the U.S. military base in Bagram, Afghanistan, just north of Kabul. This flight, like the last, seems to drag on. Over the din of the engines, I shout to Tahir that he should not go to Kabul to see his family. He agrees that it is too dangerous. I make small talk with the woman escorting us but we can barely hear each other. I want the flight to end.

Our landing is flawless. I thank the crew and we step onto Bagram Air Base. In 2001, I visited the base when it was the front line between Taliban and Northern Alliance forces. Today, it hums with American attack helicopters, transport planes, and troops.

We are brought to the base hospital and examined by American military doctors. Band-Aids are placed on the cuts on my hands from the rope. An X-ray shows that Tahir's ankle is sprained but not broken. Still wearing a six-inch-long beard and my baggy local clothes, I notice that the soldiers are staring at me.

Karl Eikenberry, the American ambassador to Afghanistan, and his wife, Ching, greet me warmly. Three months before the kidnapping I spent a weekend at their home in Brussels interviewing Eikenberry for my book. They hug me excitedly and tell me they met Kristen before arriving in Afghanistan. They rave about her strength and composure. I feel enormous pride.

Tahir calls his family and they now demand to see him. Saying they don't believe he is free, his family tells him to come to Kabul immediately. The sun is beginning to set and there is no easy way to transport him there. I beg him to wait and at least spend the night on the base.

An embassy official tells me that Kristen is trying to reach me and hands me a mobile phone. I step outside the hospital and speak to her alone for the first time in seven months. I tell her I love her, apologize again, and begin saying things I have thought about for months. "Your god saved me," I say, and explain how praying each day helped me.

She laughs and says she hoped that I might find some type of spiritual connection during captivity. As she describes her efforts, I am more and more touched. She has been hurled into a chaotic morass and handled it skillfully. She urges me to fly out of Afghanistan immediately. The sun is setting and a flight the newspaper has arranged must depart during daylight under military rules.

Determined not to abandon Tahir as Abu Tayyeb predicted, I tell her that I want to spend the night in Bagram. I want to try to convince Tahir to leave with me for Dubai. Showing immense patience, she agrees.

I walk back into the hospital and I'm told that Richard Holbrooke wants to speak with me. A sense of shame washes over me as I dial his number. "I apologize" are the first words I say to him.

Holbrooke is gracious. "God, it is so good to hear your voice," he says. He too praises Kristen and tells me I am an extraordinarily lucky man. I agree wholeheartedly.

Tahir agrees to stay on the base that night and we are given adjoining bedrooms in a prefabricated living container. We turn on the desktop computer that is for guests and Tahir checks his e-mail. I check for a story about our escape that Kristen said is on the *Times* site. We have returned to the outside world with astonishing speed.

"Times Reporter Escapes Taliban After Seven Months" reads the headline. At first, I find it hard to believe that the story is referring to me, both in terms of the captivity and the escape. As I read the piece, I am alarmed to see it states that Asad is still in captivity. It also mistakenly says that Tahir and I climbed over the wall and ran into a Pakistani militia member who led us to the base. My exaggerated praise of Captain Nadeem and his men during my first phone calls to New York was misunderstood.

Fearing that too much publicity will endanger Asad, I e-mail the foreign editor, Susan Chira, and ask her to withhold his name. I also ask her to cut the incorrect reference to a militia member guiding us to the base. After welcoming me home, she happily agrees.

Tahir goes to sleep, and I venture outside to call members of my family. I tell my mother how sorry I am to have put her through this. She cries, tells me how elated she is to hear my voice, and says she is revoking my passport. My father is calm and tells me to look forward in life. I thank my stepparents, Andrea and George, for helping my parents survive this.

When I thank my brother Lee and his wife, Christie, for his seven months of effort, he says he knew I would do the same thing for him. My sister, Laura, and brother-in-law, Chris, had their children pray for me while I was in captivity. They say they are simply overjoyed that I am safe. My brother Erik says he missed our daily calls and friendship. He remains calm and supportive of me, as always.

I apologize in each conversation and promise that my days as a war correspondent are over. I describe how much I've missed them and tell them I want to spend more time with them. I try to explain how eager I am to come home. After the phone calls, I am astonished by everything Kristen, Lee, my family, my editors, and friends have done to help us. I am also deeply touched by what my parents, Laura, and Erik have endured. All of them stepped back and allowed Kristen and Lee to make major decisions. While I was in captivity, they had the strength to let go. In some ways, that is more arduous and courageous than insisting on being involved.

Exhausted after being awake for twenty-four hours, I try to go to sleep. The black duffel bag I left in the Kabul bureau on the day we left for the interview has been brought to Bagram for me. For the first time in seven months, I put on a T-shirt.

I climb into bed and I fear closing my eyes. I'm afraid I will wake up in Miran Shah and this all will have been a fantasy. As I try to go to sleep, an alarm sounds outside and a voice on a loudspeaker announces that all personnel should go to bomb shelters. A Taliban rocket attack is under way. I make my way outside but Tahir remains inside.

I crouch inside a concrete bomb shelter with a handful of American soldiers and embassy personnel. The soldiers wear reflective vests that are designed to prevent them from being hit by vehicles when they walk around the base at night. The shelter and vests seem odd to me. They embody a focus on safety—and preventing death—that did not exist in Waziristan.

The all-clear sounds over the loudspeaker. I return to my bed and lie down. Again I fear closing my eyes and waking up beside Timor Shah and our other guards. I awake early the next morning and feel euphoric. We have, in fact, escaped.

I plug in my BlackBerry and charge the battery. I turn on the phone and Kristen's face stares at me from the small screen. It is the first time I have seen her image in seven months. She is beautiful.

Three hours later, I say good-bye to Tahir. He insists on going to Kabul to see his family. They continue to not believe that he is actually free. Embassy officials have promised me he will not be detained. We hug good-bye, and for the first time in months, we are not in the same house together. I am delighted he will finally see his family, but miss him.

My plane takes off for Dubai and I stare out the window. For months, I looked up at the planes flying overhead as I paced back and forth in Waziristan and dreamed of being on one of them. As I fly over southern Afghanistan, I look down and wonder if "Little America" is somewhere in the desert below. I know I will probably never be able to return there.

I look to the east, think of Asad, and break into tears. He is dead or remains in captivity.

REUNION

Kristen, June 21, 2009

Around noon, I speak to my husband again briefly. The Pakistani military has flown David and Tahir to Islamabad, where they were picked up by an American military plane and taken to the sprawling base in Bagram, just north of Kabul. He refuses to leave Bagram until Tahir is safely reunited with his family. He does not want to leave Tahir in the lurch. He feels that the Haqqanis will target Tahir if he returns to his unguarded home in Kabul.

I am slightly hurt by his overwhelming desire to stay put until the situation is resolved, but I understand his concern. I know David will do everything possible to ensure that Tahir, who injured his foot during their escape, receives good care and is treated well. I also realize this is a confusing time and that perhaps David needs a moment to adjust.

The last few months have taught me to be patient. And I know no one suffered more from David's decision to go to the interview than David himself. If there is a reason to his surviving misfortune—lessons learned, wisdom gained—he has been given the chance to express it.

A few hours later, David calls back and says something unexpected. "Your God helped me through this experience," David says. I think it is somewhat funny that he would frame God in this way, as belonging to someone else—or anyone for that matter. But I assume he means that prayer and belief in a beneficent higher force has helped him survive this ordeal. I am relieved. My one wish was that David would find some sort of inner peace during captivity, a personal expression of faith. Clearly he has.

I tell him to take the time he needs—but not too long! I will be on the next flight to Dubai, which gives him about twenty-four hours to leave Bagram. Arrangements have been made to transport him to Dubai and he promises to be at the airport to greet me.

In the early evening, David McCraw stops by with a bottle of champagne. The label has an image of a windmill. "So you can stop chasing windmills," McCraw says, referring to Don Quixote. I save the bottle, vowing to share it with McCraw, Lee, and David when the four of us are together.

On the way to the airport, Lee and I listen to our voice mail, now overflowing with messages of relief and happiness from family, friends, and co-workers. Arthur Sulzberger Jr., the paper's publisher, left a message expressing the paper's joy at David's freedom. Throughout our ordeal, he's been kind and supportive—often inviting me into his office for coffee and pep talks during my frequent visits to the *Times* building. Christine Kay, David's editor, calls and says, "You made all the right decisions. He is alive. You kept him alive." Tearful, elated words pour in.

I also speak to David's sister, Laura, who is ecstatic about this unexpected turn of events. "I am so happy to think of him back home in your arms where he belongs," she says. She, too, has spoken with David and gotten more details of his escape, which she relays to me. From David and Tahir's bold, impromptu decision to flee and their physical discrepancies—David is thin, Tahir is stocky—we both agree that the whole thing is amazing and, at this safe distance, amusing—Butch Cassidy and the Sundance Kid meet Abbott and Costello.

The flight to Dubai is long—thirteen hours. Lee and I spend a good deal of it watching movies. I am too anxious to sleep. We are both rendered speechless by our long ordeal finally having reached a happy and unexpected ending.

Toward the end of the flight, I duck into the ladies room to change. This is my second trip to Dubai. The first was with David more than a year ago. I was careful to keep my neck and legs covered at all times, so as not to stand out as a foreigner. Despite its modern trappings, Dubai is still conservative. But this time around, I think it would be tragic to greet my husband after seven months of captivity wearing sweatpants and a baggy sweater. I change into a modest but flattering dress and heels.

As we descend into Dubai, I glance out the window. Dubai is eight hours ahead of New York. We have lost a day in transit, as if propelled forward in time chronologically and emotionally. The desert below begins to glow in the last vestiges of sunlight. I think about what I want to do when David and I are reunited. We traveled a lot throughout our courtship, and spent our honeymoon in France and India. Friends have assumed that we will now want to run off somewhere together. The truth is, the last thing I want to do now is jet to an exotic location. I simply want us to be at home together, enjoying the daily things—drinking coffee in the morning, grocery shopping, going to the dry cleaner, riding the subway—that give life continuity, consistency. I realize I have made many mistakes over the last few months. We probably both have. But, ultimately, we have each survived. David is alive. That is all that matters. We must have done something right.

The Dubai airport is massive and modern with touches of Middle Eastern detailing. Female customs agents greet us at passport control in full headscarves, their eyeliner exquisitely applied in a striking contrast to the modesty of their dress. Large, modern white columns flank the sides of the baggage terminal. I am slightly tipsy from exhaustion and apprehension as we proceed to the exit.

I spot David waiting with several men and carrying flowers. My first thought is that he looks unchanged. He is the David I remember, only slightly thinner and paler. His hair is well groomed, trimmed. His face is clean-shaven. He is wearing the same gray V-neck sweater and brown khakis he wore on our honeymoon and on the day he departed New York for Kabul in late October.

He runs toward me.

EPILOGUE

David

F ive weeks after our escape, Asad crossed from Pakistan into Afghanistan, called his family, and said he was free. Ten days later, I spoke with him by phone.

He said the guards had slept until predawn prayers on the night Tahir and I escaped. At first, they thought we were in the bathroom. Then they realized we were gone.

Asad said Timor Shah ordered the other guards to hunt for us. "If you find Tahir," he said, "shoot him." When Badruddin Haqqani learned we had escaped, he fainted.

The Haqqanis jailed all three of our guards and interrogated them about our escape, according to Asad. The guards called Abu Tayyeb for help but he said he would face problems in Miran Shah and declined to return. The man who had taunted us for months was too cowardly to return to the tribal areas to help his own men.

Asad said Taliban commanders accused him of knowing about our escape plan. They chained and held him underground for seventeen days. For three of those days, he was beaten. Removed from the underground jail, Asad was then used as a forced laborer on construction projects.

In mid-July, Asad's family, with the help of *The New York Times,* sent a tribal delegation to press the Haqqanis to release him. On July 27, the guard watching Asad build a wall said he was going to make some tea. Left alone, Asad fled, found a taxi, and took it to the Afghan border.

In our phone call, Asad denied cooperating with the guards during our captivity and said he had carried a gun because the Taliban had ordered him to do so. In the end, I believe that Asad played along with the Taliban to survive. I do not blame him for trying to stay alive.

After returning home, I learned of the wide array of people who had worked for our release. Chief among them was Richard Holbrooke. In December 2010, Holbrooke unexpectedly died from an aortic dissection, or small tear in his aorta. His death devastated me, Kristen, and our family. The American diplomat had helped save my life—twice.

After I returned home Holbrooke engaged me in a long series of conversations. Instead of chastising me for getting kidnapped, he tried to use my time with the Taliban as a means to better understand them.

"Who are they? Why are they fighting? What do they want?" Holbrooke asked, rapid-fire. Then a man who was stereotyped as an impatient egotist patiently listened to me for hours. He set up meetings with senior American officials that he thought should hear my story.

In the larger scale of events, Holbrooke's role in my case is trivial. The Dayton peace agreement that he wrought saved the lives of countless Bosnians. He engaged in extraordinary work to fight AIDS in Africa and reform and revitalize the UN. Always impatient with Washington's glacial pace, he prized being in the field and ferociously pursued pragmatic policies.

After his death, I was asked if Holbrooke's aggressive style caused him to struggle in Afghanistan and Pakistan. I do not believe it did. His experience reflects the ebb of American influence from the high of post–cold war 1995 to the low of the war on terror circa 2010. In the Balkans, Holbrooke used the threat of further American-led air strikes to persuade the Bosnian Serbs to make peace. In Pakistan, he labored to get military leaders to stop seeing the Taliban as friendly proxies they could use to thwart Indian influence in Afghanistan.

Holbrooke devoted his life to public service, a notion that is now derided in many quarters. Some say his death marks the end of a Kennedy-inspired generation—and an America—that believed it could be a virtuous force in the world. I fervently disagree. All of us have the chance to follow his example.

———

Many Afghans and Pakistanis also tried to gain our release. Most of them courageously volunteered. Some asked for money. Two of the Afghan men died in ambushes. A man carrying a message to our captors was killed in Pakistan in January, and an Afghan died in an ambush in Afghanistan in April.

Whether those attacks were definitively related to work on our case is not known. Determining the truth of events in the border areas of Afghanistan and Pakistan is notoriously difficult. I believe the only responsible thing to do is to assume the deaths were related to our case. I deeply mourn any loss of life. I accept responsibility for any deaths I may have unintentionally caused.

After our escape, false rumors surfaced that a ransom had been paid. Neither my family nor *The New York Times*, nor any contractors who worked on our case paid a ransom. American government officials maintained their long-standing policy of not negotiating with kidnappers, freeing no prisoners and paying no ransom. Pakistani and Afghan officials said they also released no captives and provided no money.

False reports that our guards had been bribed also circulated. Security consultants who worked on our case paid Afghan informants for information. The Afghans claimed they gave cash to Taliban members who were said to know our whereabouts. They also claimed to have somehow managed to identify and bribe our guards. But nearly all of the reports from the paid Afghan informants were false. The locations where they reported us being held were wrong during three of the four months when they purportedly tracked us. The names the Afghan informants gave for our guards were wrong as well. And no guards helped us before or during our escape.

Tahir and I do not believe our guards were bribed. We believe the Afghan informants hired by the private contractors did what people who inhabit the Afghanistan-Pakistan border area have done for centuries: When being paid for information, they told the foreigners what they wanted to hear.

Lastly, two of my colleagues at *The New York Times* discovered that two of the contractors who worked on our case participated in a secret Defense Department project. Nine months after our escape, my colleagues reported that a Pentagon program had hired private contractors to help track and kill militants. It is generally considered illegal for the military to hire contractors to act as covert spies.

Michael Taylor of AISC and Dewey Clarridge were subcontractors in the secret program, which was run by a Pentagon official named Michael D. Furlong. In the story, Taylor denied any wrongdoing and said they gathered information about possible threats to American forces but were not specifically hired to provide information to kill insurgents.

After the story appeared, I asked Taylor and Clarridge about their work for the Pentagon. They said they did not work on the program while I was in captivity. They said they began working for Furlong in November 2009, four months after our escape, and stopped working for him in May 2010. My family and newspaper had no contact with Furlong and were unaware of Taylor and Clarridge's work for him until my colleagues discovered it. Furlong played no role in our case.

My suspicions regarding the Pakistani military's relationship with the Haqqanis proved to be true. In December 2010, the *Nation* reported that the Haqqanis had turned two of our guards over to the ISI after our escape.

A bitter feud had erupted among our kidnappers according to the story. The Haqqanis accused Abu Tayyeb of secretly receiving a ransom and cheating them out of money. Abu Tayyeb, in turn, accused the Haqqanis of doing the same. Even the Quetta Shura got involved. They suspected that the Haqqanis were also not sharing ransom with them.

For weeks, the two guards, one of whom was Timor Shah, were brutally interrogated and tortured by the ISI according to the story. Pakistani intelligence officials demanded to know if a ransom was secretly paid or the guards had been bribed. They were intent on finding out the truth and preventing a rift from developing among Afghan Taliban groups.

Finally, the ISI concluded that we had escaped on our own and no bribes and no ransom had been paid. Then, instead of handing our guards over to American government officials, the ISI simply let them go. The fact that the ISI released our guards shows their true loyalties.

For years, Pakistani military officials have rebuffed repeated requests from American officials to launch a military offensive in North Waziristan, the stronghold of the Haqqanis. When this book went to press in August 2011, the Haqqanis continued to use North Waziristan to train suicide bombers and explosives makers who kill Afghan and American forces. At the same time, Pakistani Taliban are using North Waziristan to carry out attacks in Pakistan and the United States. Two young men who tried to carry out terrorist attacks in Times Square and on the New York City subway in 2009 and 2010 were trained in Waziristan.

The discovery—and killing—of Osama bin Laden in May 2011 in a military town close to Islamabad drove home the danger that the ISI's ongoing relationship with militants poses to the world. For five years, Bin Laden hid in the town that housed the Pakistan Military Academy, the country's equivalent of West Point. At the least, low-level ISI officials knew Bin Laden was hiding in the town. At worst, senior leaders of the Pakistani military did as well.

I believe the Pakistani military has played a double game. Since 2001, the Pakistani army has received over $10 billion in military aid from the United States. At the same time, they have sheltered Afghan Taliban leaders whose fighters killed 1,600 American soldiers. They may also have sheltered Bin Laden himself.

ISI and military hardliners who work with militants are a cancer on Pakistani society. Ultranationalists who believe they are Pakistan's true defenders, they use the threat of conflict with India to maintain their own hold on power. They suppress the development of democracy in the country. They kill journalists who expose their activities. And they mistakenly believe they can use militants as a tool to defend Pakistan. In truth, militancy is a Frankenstein's monster that the United States, Pakistan, and Saudi Arabia created together in the 1980s. They must now work together to eradicate it.

If the ISI and Pakistani military fail to sever their ties to militants—

or aggressively pursue a reasonable peace settlement in Afghanistan—the United States should threaten to slash military aid. Providing military aid to Pakistan without such conditions is no longer tenable.

At the same time, Americans should not blame all Pakistanis for the actions of the ISI. American aid should continue to flow to programs that strengthen civilian rule. Democratic rule, a thriving free market economy, and peace with India will eventually help stabilize Pakistan. The United States must ally itself with Pakistan's moderates, not its military, for the long term.

Unless hardliners in the ISI and the Pakistani military are confronted now, militants will steadily gain strength while the Pakistani military—and state—gradually weakens. Eventually, militants will threaten to take control of Pakistan itself. Some of the country's estimated one hundred nuclear weapons could fall into the hands of militants. A bold new policy approach by the United States and Pakistan's civilian leaders is the only way to prevent that catastrophe for Americans—and Pakistanis—from happening.

The Taliban continue to abduct journalists. Three months after our escape, they kidnapped a *New York Times* correspondent, Stephen Farrell, and the Afghan journalist working with him, Sultan Munadi. The two were reporting on a NATO bombing that had killed dozens of civilians in Kunduz Province in Northern Afghanistan. Four days later, a raid by British commandos freed Stephen, but Sultan was killed, along with a British soldier, an Afghan woman, and several dozen Taliban.

Sultan was the father of two and home on a break from studying public policy in Germany. After receiving his degree, he planned to return to Afghanistan and work to stabilize his country. He was also a wonderful colleague and friend.

British officials defended the military raid that killed Sultan. They said they had received intelligence that the Taliban planned to move Steve and Sultan to Pakistan's tribal areas. Afghan journalists dismissed the British claim and accused *The New York Times* of approving the raid instead of taking more time to negotiate. In truth, the British government carried out the raid without asking Farrell's family or *The New York Times* for permission. While the American military seeks family approval to carry out raids, the British military does not.

The discrepancy reflects the far broader problem of the lack of a coordinated international response to kidnapping by Islamic militants. The American and British governments refuse to pay ransoms, but the French, Italian, Dutch, and Korean governments do.

At the same time, Islamic militants are increasingly using kidnapping as a weapon of war. In Iraq, an estimated two hundred foreigners and thousands of Iraqis have been kidnapped since the American-led invasion of 2003. Islamic militants in Somalia, the Philippines, Yemen, and North Africa have adopted the tactic as well.

Three weeks before our escape, a North African military group that calls itself Al Qaeda in the Islamic Maghreb executed Edwin Dyer, a British tourist abducted in Mali. Dyer was killed after British officials refused to release Abu Qatada, a hard-line Islamic preacher with close ties to Al Qaeda. In July 2010, the group killed a seventy-eight-year-old French hostage, Michel Germaneau, after a rescue attempt by the French military failed. Other foreign hostages were released after their governments reportedly paid ransoms or freed prisoners.

Today, dozens of people remain captives in the tribal areas of Pakistan, most of them Pakistanis and Afghans. Tahir and I were extraordinarily fortunate to have escaped. Countless others in the tribal areas have not been—and will not be—so lucky.

American officials say a unified international approach will not stop Islamist militants from kidnapping, but could make it less lucrative and appealing over time. So far, attempts to broker an agreement among industrialized nations have failed. The lack of a coordinated approach to kidnapping makes it easier for families to be thrust into the murky world that we inhabited. Governments will say they are working closely with local officials to free hostages, but often be unable to do so. Contractors will continue to make promises that may be beyond their reach. And militants will continue to trade lives for ransom and executions for publicity.

Six years after I first journeyed to "Little America," southern Afghanistan briefly became the epicenter of what was called "Obama's war." In 2010 and 2011, over 20,000 American troops and 10,000 British soldiers battled the Taliban in Helmand. Helmand quickly became the deadliest province in Afghanistan. Twice as many American, British, and NATO troops have died there as in any other Afghan province.

As has occurred throughout the war, American troops drove the Taliban out of districts but Afghan government troops and police were often too weak to hold the areas on their own. In recent phone conversations, Fowzea and Andiwal—the two moderate Afghans I had followed in Helmand—called on the Obama administration to not hurriedly withdraw American soldiers from Afghanistan. With the arrival of more foreign troops, security in Lashkar Gah improved in 2010, according to Fowzea. She reopened the women's center she shuttered after the killing of her driver in 2006 and expanded programs for women. The amount of poppy produced in Helmand dropped by roughly one-third, fueled both by a flooded market and a crackdown on growers. And the Taliban withdrew from many districts they had controlled for years.

In June 2011, President Obama announced the end of the U.S. surge in Afghanistan. Over 10,000 U.S. troops began returning immediately and all 33,000 surge troops would return to the United States by mid-2012. A desire to limit American involvement, intense fiscal pressures, and low public support for the war drove the decision.

As it has been for a decade, the American approach in Helmand and Afghanistan remains erratic. A consistent, carefully calibrated strategy that builds up Afghan institutions, involves Pakistan and India in an Afghan peace settlement, and gradually reduces American troop levels is needed. Any Taliban willing to talk should be included in peace negotiations. Taliban hardliners with ties to Al Qaeda should be isolated.

If President Karzai fails to confront corruption, American aid to him and his relatives should be cut off. Wherever possible, funding should be shifted to Afghans trying to build effective national institutions. Skilled and committed Afghan moderates exist. They should not be blamed for the shortcomings of Karzai. Instead, they should be encouraged to challenge Karzai and his family politically. While success in Afghanistan may seem unlikely, this pragmatic, more modest approach should be pursued. Instead of spending $100 billion on a massive eighteen-month troop surge and quickly giving up, the United States should adopt a less ambitious, more consistent long-term approach that trains Afghan soldiers and civilians. Over 90 percent of the money the United States has spent in Afghanistan since 2001 has paid for American military operations. More time and effort should be spent on building Afghan capacity.

Simply walking away from Afghanistan and Pakistan and hoping for the best is not an option in an increasingly interconnected world. The attacks against the United States plotted in the tribal areas show that. A sweeping Taliban victory in Afghanistan would embolden hard-line militants across the Islamic world. Their belief that they can defeat Westerners who fear death and are unwilling to endure sacrifice will be reaffirmed. It will also send a signal to moderate Muslims that the United States will not stand by them. No simple, short-term answer has emerged to the question I posed in 2001: how can religious extremism be countered? But that does not mean the effort should be abandoned or the danger of what I saw in the tribal areas should be downplayed.

Militancy is not invincible. Public opinion polls in both Afghanistan and Pakistan show negative views of the United States but they also show that the vast majority of Afghans and Pakistanis disapprove of the Taliban. For years, Afghans and Pakistanis have told me they want a third way—an effective, stable, and noncorrupt government that is not dictated to them at gunpoint by Western secularists or Arab militants. Security remains the single most important issue to Afghans and Pakistanis, followed by corruption. A competition between hard-line Islamic law and democracy is playing out now across the Muslim world. The system that delivers stability, jobs, and an accountable government will triumph.

In the end, American success or failure will hinge on the Pashtuns. After thirty years of conflict, the Pashtuns are arguably more disenfranchised, fragmented, and religiously conservative than ever in their history. Pashtun tribal networks remain influential but any young Pashtun with weapons, cash, or a false claim of religious authority can seize control of a tribe from weakened traditional elders. Halting the Pakistani military's backing of radical Pashtuns in the tribal areas and Quetta, brokering political agreements with Pashtun insurgents where possible, and improving education in both countries will gradually strengthen Pashtun moderates. Pakistan must regain control of the tribal areas and enact long-promised reforms that introduce an independent court system, reduce the power of unelected political agents, and allow political parties to campaign there.

Pashtuns say they want stability, security, and an end to corruption, but on their own terms. Outsiders—whether they are American soldiers, Pakistani intelligence operatives, or foreign militants—will never be able to impose stability on the Pashtun belt. Only the Pashtuns can. I remain convinced that Tahir and Captain Nadeem are the true Pashtuns, not our Taliban captors. In an age of extremism, patiently engaging, empowering, and revitalizing moderates is the way forward.

I am still in touch with Captain Nadeem. When I spoke with him once by phone, I asked him why he was so kind to me that night. His answer was immediate.

"It's only natural," he said. "One man can see another man's suffering."

One of the most vivid memories I have of our time in captivity was seeing religion at its best and at its worst. On one level, religion was a nefarious force that gave our captors their rationale for abducting us, terrorizing our families, and trying to extort staggering amounts of money from them. I also saw religious faith as a positive force that gave Tahir the strength to survive and Captain Nadeem the compassion to see us as human beings. Personally, prayer proved invaluable in keeping me centered, hopeful, and rational. In the end, I let go of my focus on myself and my existence. By accepting death, I was rewarded with life.

In the wake of this experience, I do not believe that religion itself is inherently divisive or destructive. I believe that religion in moderation brings out our better angels. If I follow a faith at this point, it is the Unitarian Universalism that my father introduced me to as an adult. Its openness, acceptance, and tolerance appeals to me.

Religious dogmatism, on the other hand, is destructive. Any faith or creed that emphasizes that one group is "chosen" or reduces our empathy toward others is not a true faith to me. Religious zealotry plays upon what is perhaps our gravest flaws as humans: our ability to lose our compassion, to be dogmatic, to think our ideological beliefs are right and others' are wrong, to turn members of different groups into a dangerous other.

I have reported on or heard of members of every major faith committing tremendous acts of kindness as well as horrible atrocities. While covering religious conflicts, I found that people who did unspeakable things to their fellow man were not simply sadists who knew they were doing wrong and perversely enjoyed it. They were also people who believed they were acting in self-defense and saving their faith, group, and culture from attack. They believed they were acting righteously, just as our kidnappers did.

My feelings toward my captors are fluid. Most of the time, I rarely think of them. At times, I hate them again for what they did to our families and us. Abu Tayyeb, in particular, was cowardly, dishonest, and greedy. I, of course, am guilty of the sins of selfishness, recklessness, and ambition. Tahir and I spent hours in captivity talking about how we had wronged our families by going to the interview and been punished for it. During my flight back to the United States, I wrote down three things as Kristen sat next to me. "This world is fleeting," "I had my chance," and "Now everyone else first." Since I have returned home I try harder to live by those principles. Sometimes I succeed. Often, I do not.

For me, what I witnessed in Miran Shah is still vastly worse than the many mistakes of the American effort in Afghanistan and Pakistan since 2001. In the tribal areas, an unrelenting absolutism made nonbelievers subhuman. It brainwashed young men into carrying out depraved acts of brutality. It disparaged human life instead of cherishing it. I believe that no God would support such bigotry and hatred.

Many Afghans and Pakistanis agree with me. They say the bias, hypocrisy, and brutality that exists in the tribal areas must be challenged militarily, politically, economically, and religiously. I agree. Extremism in all its forms is something all of us must fight.

In the wake of this experience, I have an even deeper respect for people who are religious, but also believe that they have more in common with other faiths than they realize. I also believe that if you are skeptical of organized religion—as I remain—you can still have ideals. I believe that living a fiercely moral life is courageous, admirable, and right.

Professionally, my days as a war correspondent are over. I intend to make my calling the continued pursuit of truth through journalism, public service, and teaching.

Personally, I recommit myself to supporting my wife and family. My family, friends, and editors never gave up on me. Most of all, Kristen never gave up on me. Her faith in herself, in our future together, and in our love never wavered. She rose to—and surpassed—her mother's challenge to live up to our wedding vows. Her strength saved my life. For that, I owe her the world.

Kristen

During the weeks after David's return, we compared notes. Few of the reports we received and none of the rumors we heard from local sources matched his actual experience. David maintains that if he had not escaped, he would probably still be in Miran Shah. We may have made some mistakes on our end—trusting some reports, overlooking others, perhaps inadvertently raising David's value by reaching out to American and foreign officials. But neither David nor I felt the kidnappers were ready to negotiate. It's likely that their demands would have continued to shift and that they would hold David indefinitely. This is not to belittle the efforts of our security teams, government officials, and advisers. Many of the people who worked on our case devoted long hours and expertise, often with personal sacrifices, to help bring some semblance of clarity or conclusion to our case. We appreciate their efforts. And thank them for never giving up.

Over time I learned that kidnapping is a global phenomenon with entrepreneurs on all sides. Its aim is to terrorize people and to exploit suffering for profit. The effect is to make family members feel responsible and hopeless simultaneously. It is maddening to be singled out in this way. But it is also empowering to have survived the experience.

Our ordeal was an ongoing process of sifting through information and misinformation as well as dealing with a cast of ever-changing characters. I listened to all opinions, but trusted no one completely. At times the different agencies and consultants involved in trying to secure David's release were at odds with one another. Each held vehemently to their own beliefs based on their allegiances and experience. As a result, we often received conflicting advice. In the end, I realized I had no control over the situation. Despite our collective efforts back home, it seemed only the captors had the power to release my husband and his colleagues. We thought our fate was in their hands.

I am most grateful to former hostages and their family members who reached out to me, shared their experiences, and in the process demystified a strange emotional terrain. I will always appreciate their honesty and bravery in revisiting their memories in order to help me. They gave me hope and courage. And eased my sense of isolation.

Our family, friends, and colleagues provided support and sustenance. As a result, existing relationships were strengthened and many new friendships were forged. For this, I am grateful.

My mother used to joke that for a couple to live happily ever after, they'd have to both expire after saying their vows. I often thought about this during David's absence. I took our vows to heart, but never thought that "worse" would come so soon. This experience tested my own level of commitment and endurance. When the depth of my own sense of loyalty—an extreme interpretation of wedding vows—was challenged, I did not waver. This was not something I could have predicted in the early days after David disappeared, when I was overwhelmed with fear, anxiety, and loss.

For seven and a half months I felt my life was on hold. When I look back, I recall the kidnapping as its own season—one of endless waiting. Uncertainty. Fear. Confusion. Plagued by a series of unappealing options, impossible decisions, dubious characters, and an unforeseeable outcome. Nearly two years after our reunion, the only journey of which I am certain is the inner one. The spiritual insights that I held tightly during the kidnapping still resonate. This experience ultimately taught me how to let go without giving up, and to accept that sometimes there is strength and bravery in waiting. It underscored the fact that while things can go horribly wrong, they can also improve unexpectedly. Prayer centered and sustained me throughout and eased my anxieties when all other efforts and outreaches seemed to fail. I learned to listen patiently and to trust.

I always believed my husband would come home. I knew he would do everything he could to survive. I knew his patience, tenacity, intelligence, and reserve would serve us well. I remain so thankful that he had the courage to seize the opportunity to escape, and the patience and endurance to wait for the right moment to do it.

This book is dedicatled "to Faith": faith in a higher entity, religious faith, faith in each other, in family, and in the resiliency of the human spirit. We all have more than we realize.

NOTES

Wherever possible, we have consulted news stories, e-mails, and other sources to verify our recollections of what occurred and ensure the accuracy of the dates given in the book. The following notes are designed to give additional background and describe suggested readings on various topics.

A BLOOD MESSAGE TO OBAMA

6 **A European journalist:** The journalist asked not to be identified.

6 **An experienced journalist:** The journalist asked not to be identified.

10 **The driver punches the accelerator:** Rohde wrote a five-part series on his time in captivity for *The New York Times*. See David Rohde, "Held by the Taliban," *New York Times*, October 17–21, 2009. For the full series, videos, maps, graphics, and reader comments, see: www.nytimes.com/2009/10/18/world/asia/18hostage .html.

15 **wean Afghans from Soviet influence:** See Cynthia Clapp-Wincek, "The Helmand Valley Project in Afghanistan," United States Agency for International Development (1983), 1–3. The full report is a detailed history and assessment of the Helmand project.

15 **"Little America":** For elegant descriptions of Cold War Lashkar Gah see Arnold Toynbee, *Between Oxus and Jumma* (1961) and Nancy Dupree, *An Historical Guide to Afghanistan* (1977). For an exhaustive collection of the USAID-commissioned studies of the projects during the Cold War see Richard Scott, "Scott's Helmand Valley Archives" at www.scottshelmandvalleyarchives.org.

16 **a 5,000-year-old tribal code of honor:** See Louis Dupree, *Afghanistan* (1970), 104, 126–27.

16 **The grand American project:** Dupree is very critical of the project, particularly in its early phases. See Dupree, *Afghanistan*, 482–85, 497, 499–507, 634–35. Nick Cullather also criticizes the project; see Nick Cullather, "Damming Afghanistan: Modernization in a Buffer State," *Journal of American History* 89, September 2002, 2: 512–37. For USAID descriptions of the project see Lloyd Baron, "Sector Analysis: Helmand-Arghandab Valley Region" (1973), 2, 7–9, and

Mildred Caudill, *Helmand-Arghandab Valley, Yesterday, Today and Tomorrow* (1969), 31. Residents of Helmand and former USAID officials generally praised the project in interviews conducted in Afghanistan and the United States between 2004 and 2010.

17   **a cycle of Kabul-based, elite-backed:** One famous example is the 1929 uprising by conservatives that deposed King Amanulllah Khan. After he returned from a seven-month trip to Egypt, Italy, France, Germany, Britain, Russia, Turkey, and Iran in 1928, he convened a grand council and announced sweeping reforms. A new national parliament elected by male voters would be created. All young men would be conscripted for the army and all boys and girls would receive education. In the most shocking move, he declared that all visitors to Kabul should wear Western dress and all women should no longer wear veils. An uprising by conservative Afghans forced him from power the following year. See Willem Vogelsgang, *The Afghans,* Blackwell Publishing (2002), 281.

MILLIONS

32   **the Afghan government exchanged:** Figures stem from Sami Yusufzai, "For the Taliban, a Crime That Pays," *Newsweek,* September 6, 2008, and "Taliban Say S. Korea Paid over $20 Million Ransom," Reuters, September 1, 2008.

37   **Foreign armies:** Leon Poullada describes the phenomenon in his book. See Leon B. and Leila D. J. Poullada, *The Kingdom of Afghanistan and the United States: 1828–1973* (1995), 1. Poullada quotes from Arnold Fletcher, *Afghanistan: Highway of Conquest* (1965).

37   **Afghans deftly cultivated an image:** This argument comes primarily from Sarah Chayes, whose survey of Afghan history is incisive, exhaustive, and thoughtful. See Sarah Chayes, *The Punishment of Virtue: Inside Afghanistan After the Taliban* (2006), 68, 101, 202, 247.

38   **"a purely accidental geographic unit":** Cullather, 6. Cullather states that the Curzon quote is from Cuthbert Collin Davies, *The Problem of the North-West Frontier, 1890–1908,* Cambridge University Press (1932), 153.

39   **The division would rankle:** Poullada, *The Kingdom of Afghanistan and the United States*, 83.

39   **declined to recognize it:** Ibid., 37–40.

39   **the "Afghan blind-spot":** Ibid., 40–41.

39   **early American writing about Afghanistan:** Ibid., 9–17. Ben Macintyre, *The Man Who Would Be King: The First American in Afghanistan,* Farrar, Straus and Giroux (2004), xiv. Macintyre's book describes Harlan's many adventures and claims.

40   **Afghanistan's ruling family:** Poullada describes how the royal family began sending young Afghans to be educated in the United States and Europe in the 1930s. Several dozen young Afghan men studied at Cornell, Columbia, and other elite American universities. At the same time, Afghan officials invited young German, French, and American teachers to instruct in Afghanistan. See Poullada, *The Kingdom of Afghanistan and the United States*, 28.

41   **World War II finally ignited:** Ibid., 70.

46   **years of American and Afghan government missteps:** Much of the narrative describing the post-2001 American effort stems from interviews with senior Bush administration officials from 2006 to 2010 as well as David Rohde and David E. Sanger, "How a Good War Went Bad in Afghanistan," *New York Times,* August 12, 2007; www.nytimes.com/2007/08/12/world/asia/12afghan.html.

51   **he predicted that the cut:** Ronald E. Neumann, *The Other War: Winning and Losing in Afghanistan*, Potomac Books (2009), 50.

CRASH COURSE

61   **One of David's colleagues:** The reporter asked not to be identified.

62   **Jere Van Dyk:** Author of *Captive: My Time as a Prisoner of the Taliban* (2010) and *In Afghanistan: An American Odyssey* (1983).

63   **Michael Semple:** Semple is head of Talk for Peace International (TFPI). "TFPI is a network of concerned idealists who want to make a tangible contribution to achieving peace. We promote the use of dialogue and political engagement, backed up by practical interventions to improve people's lives, as a way of transforming conflict." For more information about this organization go to www .talkforpeace.org.

68   **American-style university:** We visited Lahore University of Management Sciences.

THE EMIRATE

72   **the Taliban and Al Qaeda have reestablished:** See Mark Mazzetti and David Rohde, "Amid U.S. Policy Disputes, Qaeda Grows in Pakistan," *New York Times,* June 30, 2008; www.nytimes.com/2008/06/30/washington/30tribal.html.

75   **"They kidnapped children":** See *Report on Waziristan and Its Tribes* (1901), 21.

77   **83 percent of the men and 97 percent of the women:** See Zulfiqar Ali, "Understanding Tribal Areas," *Dawn*, April 2, 2010; www.dawn.com/wps/wcm/connect/ dawn-content-library/dawn/the-newspaper/local/peshawar/understanding-tribal- areas-240.

78   **"Every man's hand is against the other":** Winston S. Churchill, *The Story of the Malakand Field Force: An Episode of Frontier War* (2005), 15–16. The book's first chapter, "The Theatre of War," is an extraordinarily vivid piece of writing, but deeply flawed and bigoted.

ALL THREE OF US

89   **"goodness personified":** Much of the Wilson narrative stems from George Crile, *Charlie Wilson's War,* Grove Press (2003), 470–74.

89   **The congressman half jokingly replied:** The prisoner anecdote is from a lecture Wilson delivered in Washington, D.C., in October 2008, one month before the author was kidnapped by Haqqani's sons.

90   **Born in the village of Srana:** In southeastern Afghanistan, his tribe—the Zadran—formed his main power base, in particular his subtribe, the Sultankhel.

90   **conservative Deobandi Islam:** This is the interpretation of Islam followed by many Taliban members. It emerged from the town of Deoband in northern India in response to British colonial rule in the late 1800s.

90   **He left Afghanistan:** Haqqani built the sprawling Manba Uloom madrassa in the 1980s just north of Miran Shah in the town of Danda Darpa Khel. The school's students served as his fighters in the 1980s and after 2001. The author was imprisoned in houses near the madrassa for most of his time in Miran Shah.

90   **garrisoned in the Afghan city of Khost:** The Soviets responded by building a sprawling airfield and flying in supplies. A massive 1988 Soviet offensive broke Haqqani's siege. It was the last Soviet victory of the war.

90   **Deft at cultivating support:** Throughout the 1980s, the ISI played Haqqani against Gulbuddin Hekmatyar, another mujahideen commander who competed with Haqqani for Pakistani and American support. For years, Haqqani would resent the ISI for not promoting him as the sole Pashtun leader of the Afghan resistance. See Ahmed Rashid, *Taliban: Militant Islam, Oil and Fundamentalism in Central Asia* (2000). During a fund-raising tour of Persian Gulf countries, Haqqani so impressed a young Egyptian journalist that the budding reporter traveled to Afghanistan and fought alongside Haqqani and his men. The writing of the journalist, who later became a senior member of Al Qaeda, turned Haqqani into a folk hero among the "Arab volunteers" who came to fight the Soviets. One of those volunteers was Osama bin Laden.

90   **The two men and a few dozen of their fighters:** The battle was in the village of Jaji in Paktia Province. Whether Haqqani was present is disputed by some researchers. Most describe him being there.

91   **"hero mujahed sheikh":** The descriptions of Haqqani's relationship with the CIA and Bin Laden stem from Steve Coll, *The Bin Ladens: An Arabian Family in the American Century* (2008), 294. For a detailed and insightful description of Haqqani's receipt of American funding, closeness to Bin Laden, and support for the Taliban see Steve Coll, *Ghost Wars: The Secret History of the CIA, Afghanistan, and Bin Laden, from the Soviet Invasion to September 10, 2001* (2004), 131, 157, 167, 202, 227, 231, 293, 521.

91   **When the victorious mujahideen:** The capital of Khost, the province Wilson toured, was the first major city to fall to the mujahideen. In April 1991, Haqqani and his men entered the city, but they continued to heavily rely on the support of the ISI. Pakistani army artillery and tanks reportedly fired shells from Pakistan to support Haqqani's assault. Khost was the first major city to fall to the mujahideen, but problems quickly emerged. After local mullahs told their followers that foreign aid workers were telling Afghan women to have free sex, an enraged mob burned a health clinic and threatened Afghan nurses and teachers. One was kidnapped and murdered. The American ambassador to Pakistan called for the CIA's covert support to the mujahideen to stop, and the administration of President George H. W. Bush requested no funding for fiscal year 1992. Yet Wilson continued to finance them, using his position on the House Intelligence Committee to maneuver $200 million in secret monies through Congress. Crile, *Charlie Wilson's War*, 515–19.

91   **He also commanded:** At the time, Haqqani funded the operations with donations from Arab countries and complained to journalists that the Taliban were unable to organize themselves.

92   **missiles struck the camp:** Crile, *Charlie Wilson's War*, 522.

92   **American bombs destroyed:** Haqqani became the third highest target on the

U.S. bombing list, ibid., 521. In a 2010 interview, a former American intelligence official confirmed the meetings with Haqqani in the fall of 2001.

92   **an acceptance of suicide bombing:** As many as 80 percent of suicide bombers dispatched to Afghanistan between 2001 and 2007 are believed to have passed through North Waziristan, according to a September 2007 United Nations study. For detailed accounts of the resurgence of the Haqqani network see Thomas Ruttig, "The Haqqani Network as an Autonomous Entity," in *Decoding the New Taliban: Insights from the Afghan Field* (2010), 57–88 and Anand Gopal, Mansur Khan Mahsud, and Brian Fishman, "Inside the Haqqani Network, The AfPak Channel, June 3, 2010, at afpak.foreignpolicy.com/posts/2010/06/03/inside_the_haqqani_network_0.

HUMAN RESOURCES

97   **The head of Clayton:** The subject has asked not to be identified.

100   **Samantha Power:** Senior director for Multilateral Affairs, National Security Council.

SPEAK GOOD WORDS TO AN ENEMY

112   **One of my colleagues:** The colleague asked not to be identified.

MULTITASKING

133   **They tell us:** We have not mentioned offer amounts to protect future captives. We do not want to set a precedent for future kidnappings.

THE TALIBAN TRUST THE RED CROSS

145   **I know from things I have previously read:** For a detailed description of Ghaffar Khan see Rajmohan Gandhi, *Ghaffar Khan: Nonviolent Badshah of the Pashtuns*, Viking (2004) and *Frontier Gandhi: Badshah Khan, a Torch for Peace*, a 2008 documentary written and produced by T. C. McLuhan.

WORDS AND PICTURES

162   **welcomed Arabs and Uzbeks:** Much of the background narrative in this section comes from Mazzetti and Rohde, "Amid U.S. Policy Disputes, Qaeda Grows in Pakistan." It was also supplemented with interviews in the United States and Pakistan from 2008 to 2010.

167   **tens of millions of dollars:** See David Rohde, Carlotta Gall, Eric Schmitt, and David E. Sanger, "U.S. Officials See Waste in Billions Sent to Pakistan," *New York Times*, December 24, 2007; http://www.nytimes.com/2007/12/24/world/asia/24military.html.

168   **The Pakistani military fought:** See Carlotta Gall and Mohammad Khan, "Pakistan's Push in Border Areas Is Said to Falter," *New York Times*, January 22, 2006. For a detailed history of missteps by Musharraf and American officials see Ahmed Rashid, *Descent into Chaos;* www.nytimes.com/2006/01/22/international/asia/22pakistan.html.

168   **killed or wounded:** See Associated Press, "Civilian Deaths Spike in Afghanistan, Pakistan," April 28, 2010; www.cbsnews.com/stories/2010/04/28/world/main6439690.shtml.

169   **a retired senior official from the ISI:** See Carlotta Gall and David Rohde, "Mil-

itants Escape Control of Pakistan, Officials Say," *New York Times*, January 15 2008; www.nytimes.com/2008/01/15/world/asia/15isi.html.

ARE YOU THERE?

179   **threaten to kill Solecki:** See Associated Press, "Kidnappers Threaten to Kill U.N. Worker," story on Solecki kidnapping, February 13, 2009; www.msnbc .msn.com/id/29183644/.

179   **Piotr Stanczak:** Pakistani journalists reported that Stanczak was killed because Pakistani Taliban commanders were fighting over him. See Mazhar Tufail, "TTP Infighting Led to Beheading of Polish Engineer," *The News*, February 12, 2009; www.thenews.com.pk/print1.asp?id=162048.

GOLDEN CHANCE

186   **The phone rings:** Parts of the conversation in which the authors discussed how much was offered at the time have not been included in the chapter. We are not disclosing the amount of the offer because we believe it could encourage or complicate future kidnappings.

GIFT FROM GOD

192   **weeps at a radio news broadcast:** It is not clear what civilian casualty report Abu Tayyeb heard that day. It may have been a UN report that said civilian casualties had increased in Afghanistan by 40 percent in 2008; www.nytimes.com/2009/02/18/world/asia/18afghan.html.

PEACE BE UPON YOU

195   **Afghan girl that appeared:** Photograph by Steve McCurry.

AN ALTERNATE UNIVERSE

205   **uses some type of weapon:** Akbar may have been referring to depleted uranium. American military officials say they have used no depleted uranium in Afghanistan, but some experts question their claim; www.news.bbc.co.uk/2/hi/science/nature/3050317.stm.

205   **they take turns attending bomb-making classes:** See David Rohde and C. J. Chivers, "Qaeda's Grocery Lists and Manuals of Killing," *New York Times*, March 17, 2002, http://www.nytimes.com/2002/03/17/world/a-nation-challenged-qaeda-s-grocery-lists-and-manuals-of-killing.html.

227   **my English-language Koran:** The English-language Koran I read was Marmaduke Pickthall, The Holy Quran with English and Urdu Translation, Kitab Bhavan (2001).

BIRTHDAY WISHES

220   **A shadow of the endeavor:** Much of the Helmand narrative stems from David Rohde, "An Afghan Symbol of Change, Then Failure," *New York Times*, September 5, 2006; www.nytimes.com/2006/09/05/world/asia/05afghan.html.

224   **"conveyor-belt courses":** The European official who derided the DynCorp police training was Michael Semple, who later advised Kristen on David's kidnapping.

225 **handed over the districts:** Tom Coghlan, "Weak Government Allows Taleban to Prosper in Afghanistan," *The Times* (of London), September 29, 2008; www .timesonline.co.uk/tol/news/world/asia/article4842499.ece.

225 **she feared that the Taliban:** While she expressed disappointment with the British, Fowzea reflected the shortcomings of the Afghan effort herself. Since 2001, Fowzea had not once traveled to Kabul to lobby for funds from the Ministry of Women's Affairs, even after USAID established direct, regular flights for Afghans. She could not tell me the size of her annual budget and appeared poorly organized.

226 **"Pakistani alley":** For an excellent piece on the company's deployment see Kristin Henderson, "A Change in Mission," *Washington Post*, June 12, 2009; www .washingtonpost.com/wp-dyn/content/article/2009/06/12/AR2009.

A STONE WILL NOT BECOME SOFT

244 **The videos are the latest example:** Rohde and *The New York Times* compiled a six-part video series that appeared on the newspaper's Web site with a five-part series he wrote on his captivity.

    To go to the beginning of the five videos: projects.nytimes.com/held-by-the-taliban/#intro.

    To go to the video that includes some of the films we watched: www./Proj ects.nytimes.com/held-by-the-taliban/#part-4.

LIES

270 **Vietnamese people are Muslims:** For more detail on the shooting in upstate New York see Robert D. McFadden, "Thirteen Shot Dead at Class on Citizenship," *New York Times*, April 4, 2009; www.nytimes.com/2009/04/04/nyregion/04hostage .html.

270 **an unprovoked war on Islam:** For additional information about Mullah Sangeen and his views see Bill Roggio, "An Interview with Mullah Sangeen," *Long War Journal*, September 17, 2009; www.longwarjournal.org/threat-matrix/ archives/2009/09/an_interview_with_mullah_sange.php.

270 **the Taliban's first group of suicide bombers:** For more information about Mullah Dadullah, who was killed by American Special Forces soldiers in May 2007, see his final two interviews at www.counterterrorismblog.org/2007/05/ video_the_last_words_of_mullah_1.php.

270 **black flags:** Various postings appear online discussing the prophecy, which supporters say is a Hadith. One example can be found at www.freerepublic.com/ focus/religion/771345/posts.

HOME MOVIES

277 **somatic experiencing (SE):** www.traumahealing.com.
277 **Peter Levine:** Author of *Waking the Tiger*.

PASHTUNWALI

287 **I lie awake in the darkness:** To see detailed graphics that show the layout of the house and how we escaped, see a video that *The New York Times* produced along

with the written series on our captivity in October 2009. The video can be seen at http://projects.nytimes.com/held-by-the-taliban/#part-5.

295   **to protect us under the tenet of Pashtunwali:** The specific element of Pashtunwali that Tahir requested asylum under is *nanawatai*.

THE GLORIOUS ISLAM

305   **He gives me a book:** A full description of the book is Muhammad Asghar Qureshi, *The Glorious Islam*, Lahore: Sajjad Asghar Qureshi (1997).

EPILOGUE

326   **secret program . . . to help track and kill insurgents:** See Dexter Filkins and Mark Mazzetti, "Contractors Tied to Effort to Track and Kill Militants," *New York Times*, March 14, 2010, http://www.nytimes.com/2010/03/15/world/asia/15contractors.html.

BIBLIOGRAPHY

Numerous books and studies are available for readers interested in learning more about Afghanistan, Pakistan, the Taliban, and kidnapping. The list below includes books we have read fully, read partially, or consulted. Numerous newspaper articles were consulted as well. Only the most central to our book are listed here.

ARTICLES

Ali, Zulfiqar, "Understanding Tribal Areas," *Dawn*, April 2, 2010, www.dawn.com /wps/wcm/connect/dawn-content-library/dawn/the-newspaper/local/peshawar /understanding-tribal-areas-240.

Associated Press, "Civilian Deaths Spike in Afghanistan, Pakistan," April 28, 2010, www.cbsnews.com/stories/2010/04/28/world/main6439690.shtml.

———, "Kidnappers Threaten to Kill U.N. Worker," February 13, 2009, www.msnbc .msn.com/id/29183644/.

Al Balagh Media Center, Interview with Sirajuddin Haqqani, April 10, 2010, http://www.globalterroralert.com/images/documents/pdf/0410/flashpoint _haqqani041210.pdf.s.

CBS News Investigative Unit, Interview with Taliban Commander Sirajuddin Haqqani, August 20, 2008, http://www.cbsnews.com/8301-502683_162-4366029 -502683.html.

Coghlan, Tom, "Weak Government Allows Taleban to Prosper in Afghanistan," *The Times* (of London), September 29, 2008, www.timesonline.co.uk/tol/news/world /asia/article4842499.ece.

Coll, Steve, "The Case for Humility in Afghanistan," *Foreign Policy*, October 16, 2009, http://www.foreignpolicy.com/articles/2009/10/16/the_case_for_humility_in _afghanistan?page=full.

———, "Letter from Afghanistan: War by Other Means," *The New Yorker*, May 24, 2010.

———, "Think Tank," *The New Yorker*, http://www.newyorker.com/online/blogs /stevecoll/.

Cullather, Nick, "Damming Afghanistan: Modernization in a Buffer State," *Journal of American History* 89, September 2002, 2: 512–37, http://www.indiana.edu/~hist web/faculty/Display.php?Faculty_ID=52.

Filkins, Dexter, "Afghan Civilian Deaths Rose 40 Percent in 2008," *The New York Times*, February 17, 2009, http://www.nytimes.com/2009/02/18/world/asia/18afghan.html.

————, and Mark Mazzetti, "Contractors Tied to Effort to Track and Kill Militants," *The New York Times*, March 14, 2010, http://www.nytimes.com/2010/03/15/world/asia/15contractors.html.

Gall, Carlotta, and David Rohde, "Militants Escape Control of Pakistan, Officials Say," *The New York Times*, January 15, 2008, www.nytimes.com/2008/01/15/world/asia/15isi.html.

————, and Mohammad Khan, "Pakistan's Push in Border Areas Is Said to Falter, *The New York Times*, January 22, 2006, www.nytimes.com/2006/01/22/international/asia/22pakistan.html.

Gopal, Anand, Mansur Khan Mahsud, and Brian Fishman, "Inside the Haqqani Network," The AfPak Channel, June 3, 2010, afpak.foreignpolicy.com/posts/2010/06/03/inside_the_haqqani_network_0.

Gregg, Tom, "Caught in the Crossfire: The Pashtun Tribes of Southeast Afghanistan" (policy brief), The Lowy Institute for International Policy, October 2009, http://www.lowyinstitute.org/Publication.asp?pid=1157.

Gul, Pazir, "Waziristan Accord Signed," *Dawn*, September 6, 2006, www.dawn.com/2006/09/06/top2.htm.

Haider, Zeeshan, "Pakistani Taliban Force Girls Schools to Close," Reuters, January 17, 2009, www.reuters.com/article/idUSISL282445.

Henderson, Kristin, "A Change in Mission," *The Washington Post*, June 12, 2009, http://www.washingtonpost.com/wp-dyn/content/article/2009/06/12/AR2009061202123.html.

Kirby, Alex, "Afghans' Uranium Levels Spark Alert," BBC News, May 22, 2003, http://news.bbc.co.uk/2/hi/science/nature/3050317.stm.

McFadden, Robert D., "Thirteen Shot Dead at Class on Citizenship," *The New York Times*, April 4, 2009, www.nytimes.com/2009/04/04/nyregion/04hostage.html.

Mazzetti, Mark, and David Rohde, "Amid U.S. Policy Disputes, Qaeda Grows in Pakistan, *The New York Times*, June 30, 2008, www.nytimes.com/2008/06/30/washington/30tribal.html.

————, and Eric Schmitt, "Afghan Strikes by Taliban Get Pakistan Help, U.S. Aides Say," *The New York Times*, March 25, 2009, http://www.nytimes.com/2009/03/26/world/asia/26tribal.html.

Moore, Jonathan, "Morality and Foreign Policy," speech given in Hanover, NH, The Dickey Center, 2007.

Rashid, Ahmed, "The Afghanistan Impasse," *The New York Review of Books*, October 8, 2009.

Reuters, "Taliban Say S. Korea Paid over $20 Million in Ransom," September 1, 2007, http://in.reuters.com/article/idlNIndia-29278920070901.

Roggio, Bill, "An Interview with Mullah Sangeen," *The Long War Journal*, September 17, 2009, www.longwarjournal.org/threat-matrix/archives/2009/09/an_interview_with_mullah_sange.php.

Rohde, David, "An Afghan Symbol for Change, Then Failure," *The New York Times*, September 5, 2006, www.nytimes.com/2006/09/05/world/asia/05afghan.html.

———, "Held by the Taliban," *The New York Times*, October 17–21, 2009, www.nytimes.com/2009/10/18/world/asia/18hostage.html.

———, "Army Enlists Anthropology in War Zones," *The New York Times*. October 5, 2007, http://www.nytimes.com/2007/10/05/world/asia/05afghan.html.

———, "GIs in Afghanistan on Hunt, but Now for Hearts and Minds," *The New York Times*. March 30, 2004, http://www.nytimes.com/2004/03/30/world/gi-s-in-afghanistan-on-hunt-but-now-for-hearts-and-minds.html.

———, "The Other Conflict Continues to Take a G.I. Toll," *The New York Times*, November 24, 2003, http://www.nytimes.com/2003/11/24/world/the-other-conflict-continues-to-take-a-gi-toll.html.

———, "Pakistan's Terrorist Factory: Fact or Figment," *The Christian Science Monitor*, April 14, 1995.

———, "Left Alone, Refugees Decry U.S. Indifference," *The Christian Science Monitor*, April 19, 1995.

———, and C. J. Chivers, "Qaeda's Grocery Lists and Manuals of Killing," *The New York Times*, March 17, 2002, http://www.nytimes.com/2002/03/17/world/a-nation-challenged-qaeda-s-grocery-lists-and-manuals-of-killing.html.

———, David E. Sanger, "How a Good War Went Bad in Afghanistan," *The New York Times,* August 12, 2007, www.nytimes.com/2007/08/12/world/asia/12afghan.html.

———, Carlotta Gall, Eric Schmitt, and David E. Sanger, "U.S. Officials See Waste in Billions Sent to Pakistan," *The New York Times*, December 24, 2007, http://www.nytimes.com/2007/12/24/world/asia/24military.html.

Ruttig, Thomas, "The Haqqani Network as an Autonomous Entity," in *Decoding the New Taliban: Insights from the Afghan Field* (New York: Columbia University Press, 2010), 57–88.

Shah, Pir Zubair, "U.S. Airstrike Kills 30 in Pakistan," *The New York Times*, February 14, 2009, www.nytimes.com/2009/02/15/world/asia/15pstan.html?_r=1.

Tufail, Mazhar, "TTP Infighting Led to Beheading of Polish Engineer," *The News International,* February 12, 2009, www.thenews.com.pk/print1.asp?id=162048.

Yusufzai, Sami, "For the Taliban, a Crime That Pays," *Newsweek*, September 6, 2008, http://www.newsweek.com/2008/09/05/for-the-taliban-a-crime-that-pays.html.

BOOKS

Adair, Liz, et al. *Lucy Shook's Letters from Afghanistan*. Ferndale, WA: GAL Editing & Publishing, 2002.

Alvi, Sohail Masood. *FATA: Beginning of a New Era*. Lahore, Pakistan: Printhouse, 2006.

Anderson, Terry. *Den of Lions: Memoirs of Seven Years*. New York: Crown, 1993.

Bissell, William Nanda. *Making India Work*. New Delhi: Penguin Viking, 2009.

Caroe, Olaf. *The Pathans 550 b.c.–a.d. 1957*. Oxford: Oxford University Press, 1958.

Carothers, Thomas. *Aiding Democracy Abroad: The Learning Curve*. Washington, D.C.: The Carnegie Endowment for International Peace, 1999.

Chatterjee, Pratap. *Iraq, Inc.: A Profitable Occupation*. New York: Seven Stories Press, 2004.

Chayes, Sarah. *The Punishment of Virtue: Inside Afghanistan After the Taliban*. New York: The Penguin Press, 2006.

Gul, Imtiaz. *The Most Dangerous Place: Pakistani's Lawless Frontier*. New York: Viking, 2010.

Churchill, Winston S. *The Story of the Malakand Field Force: An Episode of Frontier War*. Rockville, MD: Wildside Press, 1898, 2005.

Coll, Steve. *The Bin Ladens: An Arabian Family in the American Century*. New York: The Penguin Press, 2008.

————. *Ghost Wars: The Secret History of the CIA, Afghanistan and bin Laden from the Soviet Invasion to September 10, 2001*. New York: The Penguin Press, 2004.

Crile, George. *Charlie Wilson's War: The Extraordinary Story of How the Wildest Man in Congress and a Rogue CIA Agent Changed the History of Our Times*. New York: Grove Press, 2003.

Dupree, Louis. *Afghanistan*. Princeton, NJ: Princeton University Press, 1973.

Dupree, Nancy. *An Historical Guide to Afghanistan*. Kabul, Afghanistan: Afghan Tourist Organization, 1977.

Fergusson, James. *A Million Bullets: The Real Story of the British Army in Afghanistan*. London: Bantam Press, 2008.

Gandhi, Rajmohan. *Ghaffar Khan: Nonviolent Badshah of the Pakhtuns*. New Delhi: Penguin Viking, 2004.

Ghani, Ashraf, and Clare Lockhart. *Fixing Failed States: A Framework for Rebuilding a Fractured World*. Oxford: Oxford University Press, 2008.

Giustozzi, Antonio, ed. *Decoding the New Taliban: Insights from the Afghan Field*. New York: Columbia University Press, 2009.

Gul, Imtiaz. *The Most Dangerous Place: Pakistani's Lawless Frontier*. New York: Viking, 2010.

Jones, Owen Bennett. *Pakistan: Eye of the Storm*. New Haven, CT: Yale University Press, 2002.

Jones, Seth G. *In the Graveyard of Empires: America's War in Afghanistan*. New York: Norton, 2009.

Keenan, Brian. *An Evil Cradling*. London: Hutchinson, 1992.

Kiviat, Katherine, and Scott Heidler. *Women of Courage: Intimate Stories from Afghanistan*. Layton, UT: Gibbs Smith, Publisher, 2007.

Leeson, Frank. *Frontier Legion: With the Khassadars of North Waziristan*. West Sussex, England: The Leeson Archive, 2003.

Loyn, David. *Butcher & Bolt*. London: Hutchinson, 2008.

Macintyre, Ben. *The Man Who Would Be King: The First American in Afghanistan*. New York: Farrar, Straus & Giroux, 2004, xiii–xiv, 209–29.

Mohsin, Hamid. *The Reluctant Fundamentalist*. New York: Houghton Mifflin Harcourt, 2007.

Neumann, Ronald E. *The Other War: Winning and Losing in Afghanistan*. Washington, D.C.: Potomac Books, 2009.

Olivetti, Vincenzo. *Terror's Source: The Ideology of Wahhabi-Salafism and Its Consequences*. Birmingham, AL: Amadeus Books, 2001.

Pearl, Mariane, with Sarah Crichton. *A Mighty Heart: The Brave Life and Death of My Husband, Danny Pearl*. New York: Scribner, 2003.

Peters, Gretchen. *Seeds of Terror: How Heroin Is Bankrolling the Taliban and Al Qaeda.* New York: Thomas Dunne Books, 2009.

Pickthall, Marmaduke, trans. *The Holy Quran with English and Urdu Translation*, New Delhi: Kitab Bhavan, 2001.

Poullada, Leon B., and Leila D. J. Poullada. *The Kingdom of Afghanistan and the United States: 1828–1973.* Omaha and Lincoln, NB: The Center for Afghanistan Studies at the University of Nebraska at Omaha and Dageforde Publishing, 1995.

Punjab Government, *Report on Waziristan and Its Tribes,* Lahore, Pakistan: Sang-e-Meel Publications, 1901, 2005.

Rashid, Ahmed. *Taliban: Militant Islam, Oil and Fundamentalism in Central Asia.* New Haven, CT: Yale University Press, 2000.

———. *Descent into Chaos: The United States and the Failure of Nation Building in Pakistan, Afghanistan and Central Asia.* New York: Viking, 2008.

Rushdie, Salman. *Midnight's Children.* New York: Random House, 1995.

Sanger, David E. *The Inheritance: The World Obama Confronts and the Challenges to American Power.* New York: Crown, 2009.

Toynbee, Arnold. *Between Oxus and Jumma.* Oxford: Oxford University Press, 1961.

Van Dyk, Jere. *Captive: My Time as a Prisoner of the Taliban.* New York: Times Books, 2010.

———. *In Afghanistan: An American Odyssey.* New York: Coward-McCann, 1983.

Vogelsang, Willem. *The Afghans.* Oxford: Blackwell Publishers, 2002.

Woodward, Bob. *Bush at War.* New York: Simon & Schuster, 2002.

———. *Plan of Attack.* New York: Simon & Schuster, 2004.

———. *State of Denial. Bush at War, Part III.* New York: Simon & Schuster, 2006.

———. *The War Within, a Secret White House History 2006–2008.* New York: Simon & Schuster, 2008.

Zaeef, Abdul Zalam, with Alex Strick van Linschoten and Felix Kuehn, eds. *My Life with the Taliban.* London: Hurst & Company, 2010.

DOCUMENTS AND REPORTS

Aziz, Khalid. *Causes of Rebellion in Waziristan.* Peshawar, Pakistan: Regional Institute of Policy Research & Training, 2005.

Baron, Lloyd. *Sector Analysis: Helmand-Arghandab Valley Region,* Kabul, Afghanistan: Agency for International Development, 1973.

Caudill, Mildred. *Helmand-Arghandab Valley: Yesterday, Today and Tomorrow.* Lashkar Gah, Afghanistan: Agency for International Development, 1969.

Dobbins, James, et al. *America's Role in Nation-Building: From Germany to Iraq.* Santa Monica, CA: RAND, 2003.

International Crisis Group. *A Force in Fragments: Reconstituting the Afghan National Army.* Brussels, Belgium, 2010.

Jones, Seth G. *Counterinsurgency in Afghanistan.* Santa Monica, CA: RAND, 2008.

———, et al. *Establishing Law and Order After Conflict.* Santa Monica, CA: RAND, 2005.

Jordan, Leonard B. *Report on Development of Helmand Valley, Afghanistan.* Washington, D.C.: Tudor Engineering, 1956.

Neumann, Ronald. *Reconstruction Strategy in Post-Bonn Afghanistan—Setting Priorities to Galvanize International Donors, the Short Cable.* Washington, D.C.: U.S. State Department, October 18, 2005.

Singer, P.W. *Corporate Warriors: The Rise of the Privatized Military Industry.* Ithaca, NY: Cornell University Press, 2003.

Williams, Maurice. *Retrospective Review of U.S. Assistance to Afghanistan, 1950–1979.* Washington, D.C.: Bethesda, MD: Devres, Inc., 1988.

Wincek, Cynthia. *The Helmand Valley Project in Afghanistan.* Washington, D.C.: U.S. Agency for International Development, 1973.

RESOURCES FOR KIDNAP VICTIMS AND THEIR FAMILIES

Alvarez, James, "The Psychological Impact of Kidnap," in Elizabeth K. Carll, ed., *Trauma Psychology: Issues in Violence, Disaster, Health and Illness, Volume 1: Violence and Disaster,* Westport, CT: Praeger Perspectives, 2007.

Anderson, Terry. *Den of Lions: Memoirs of Seven Years.* New York: Crown, 1993.

Committee to Protect Journalists, 330 Seventh Avenue, 11th floor, New York, NY 10001, 212-465-1004, info@cpj. com, http://www.cpj.org/.

Johnston, Alan, "My Kidnap Ordeal," *From Our Own Correspondent,* BBC News, October 25, 2007, http://news.bbc.co.uk/2/hi/programmes/from_our_own_correspondent/7048652.stm.

Keenan, Brian. *An Evil Cradling.* London: Hutchinson, 1992.

Van Dyk, Jere. *Captive: My Time as a Prisoner of the Taliban.* New York: Times Books, 2010.

INDEX